UNADJUSTED MAN IN THE AGE OF OVERADJUSTMENT

July 04 to Alan Wolfe
am sure you won't time to
read this; but the concluding
Lindsay p.333 may have special interest
for you. (& maybe p.162 on red right, ff?
Peter Viereck

PROF. PETER VIERECK
12 Silver Street
So. Hadley, MA 01075-1616

Peter Viereck

UNADJUSTED MAN IN THE AGE OF OVERADJUSTMENT

Where History and Literature Intersect

Transaction Publishers
New Brunswick (U.S.A.) and London (U.K.)

Library of Congress Catalog Number: 2004046077
ISBN: 0-7658-0806-4
Printed in the United States of America

Library of Congress Cataloging-in-Publication Data

Viereck, Peter Robert Edwin, 1916-
    [Unadjusted man]
    Unadjusted man in the age of overadjustment : where history and literature intersect / Peter Viereck ; with a new introduction by the author.
        p. cm.
    "Originally published in 1956 by the Beacon Press"—T.p. verso.
    Includes bibliographical references and index.
    ISBN 0-7658-0806-4 (acid-free paper)
        1. United States—Politics and government—20th century. 2. United States—History—Philosophy. 3. Individualism—United States—History. I. Title.

E743.V5 2004
320.973'01—dc22   2004046077

The quotation from "Bryan, Bryan, Bryan, Bryan" by Vachel Lindsay is reprinted from *Collected Poems,* copyright 1948 by The Macmillan Company, and used with their permission.

The quotation from "The Rolling English Road" is reprinted from *The Collected Poems of* G. K. *Chesterton,* copyright @ 1911, 1932, by Dodd, Mead & Company, Inc., and used with their permission.

The quatrain by Roy Campbell is reprinted by permission of the Henry Regnery Company.

CONTENTS

Introduction to Transaction Edition   ix

"Autobiog"   xxiii

Foreword to the Original Edition   xxix

Part I. Beyond Conforming and Nonconforming

1. The Unadjusted Man: A New American Hero   3

2. The Overadjusted Man: Stereotypes Against Archetypes   11

3. In Praise of Mad Squires: The Feudal Origin of the Unadjusted Man   27

4. Distinctions: Conservatives and Two Sorts of Liberals   35

5. Which Kind of Equality?   42

6. Niebuhr in the Conformists' Den   48

7. Nietzsche as Challenge to the Overadjusted Man   53

8. The Mirror Images: Psychology of Anti-Americanism Abroad   64

Part II. The Burkean-Conservative Case Against the Republican Party

9. Social Change: Towards a New Legitimism   79

10. Socialists and Conservatives: Two Rival Protests Against Cash-Nexus   89

11. The Rootless Nostalgia for Roots: Defects in the New Conservatism   97

12. The Trend Behind Revisionism   109

13. The Suburbs Beat Us: Malcontents of Prosperity vs. Plushbottom Diabolized   113

14. Remolding the Republicans Into a Responsible Conservative Party   118

Part III. Direct Democracy:
From the Populist Left to the Nationalist Right

15. Defining Direct and Indirect Democracy   129

16. Two Current Triumphs Of Liberty Over "The People" 145

17. Reversal of Roles: Witch-Hunt Methods in Liberals   152
     and New Dealers

18. The New American Right: Radicals of   162
     "Anti-Radicalism"

19. Wisconsin Background: The La Follette Progressives   179

20. Smashing Plymouth Rock   193

21. Transtolerance: Monster Rally of the Status-Resenters 213

22. Modest Proposal: A Vice-Presidential Speech in a   223
     Surrealist Future

Part IV. The Importance of Adlai Stevenson

23. A Third View of the New Deal   231

24. Squires Incognito: The Advantage of Being   239
     Slandered as "Leftist" by Rightists

25. A Shared Framework for Liberals and Conservatives   246

26. Articulator, Not Yet Incarnator   255

27.   Restorer of the Intellectuals   258

28. The Impieties of Progress   262

Part V. The Free Imagination, Ethical and Lyrical

29. The Third Frontier   271

30. The Dignity of Ethics: Enough of Toughmindedness! 274

31. The Dignity of Lyricism: Form Yes, Formalism No.   279

32. Four Notes on Values   291
     I. WHY? HOW?   291
     II. COMMITMENT OF THE PERSONALITY   294
     III. THE INARTICULATE ROOTS OF FREE VALUES   297
     IV. INDEFENSIBLE AND UNINHABITABLE   302

33. Four Devaluations 306

    I. KINGS IN EXILE 306

    II. DRIVE-IN CHURCHES: THE SO-CALLED RETURN 310
        TO VALUES

    III. THE BURROW OF IRONIC CONFORMITY 314

    IV. SQUIRE CABOT BABBITT: NEW CONSERVATIVE 317

34. Four Notes on Imagination 322

    I. THE AMATEEUR HOUR 322

    II. HALF-PINT OF SOUL 324

    III. THE DREAM-NEXUS 325

    IV. SECRET AMERICA: THE LIBERATING GESTURE 328

Postscript 2004, Vachel Lindsay, 333
    Dante of the Fundamentalists:
    The Suicide of America's Faith in Technology

Selected Bibliography of Books by Peter Viereck 361

Index 363

ACKNOWLEDGMENTS

Grateful acknowledgment is made to the following periodicals, in which certain material in this book first appeared:

Antioch Review
Atlantic Monthly
Chicago Review
Christianity and Society
Christian Scholar
Commonweal
Current Issues in Higher Education
Hopkins Review
Inventario (Italy)
Journal of General Education
Mondo Occidentale (Italy)
New Leader
New Mexico Quarterly
New Republic
Pacific Spectator
Reporter
Saturday Review
Shenandoah
Southwest Quarterly
World Affairs Quarterly

Several chapters have been adapted from papers read at meetings of learned societies or as guest lectures at universities, including the following:

Poets' Conference, Harvard University, 1953
American Historical Association, New York, 1954
Higher Education Association of N.E.A., Chicago, 1954
Whittall Poetry Lectures of the Library of Congress, Washington, 1954
Elliston Poetry Lectures, University of Cincinnati, 1956

INTRODUCTION TO THE TRANSACTION EDITION: ADJUSTMENT REVISITED (2004)

The unrevised first part of this book appeared in 1956. In 2004, I have added to this book, as a new conclusion, my Vachel Lindsay essay to give a specific concrete example of the otherwise too generalized meaning of my "unadjusted" approach. This, plus my long 2004 introduction, make the book not just a reprint but a new book, changing some of my views in the unrevised 1956 edition.

I. Meta-Tech

I offer the following distinctions between seeming similarities, in each case favoring the first-named of the alternatives:—unadjusted versus overadjusted (robotized) and maladjusted (pathological); conserving versus conforming; deep versus obscure (two rival kinds of difficulty, especially in poetry); technology as useful servant (still a liberator for the third world) versus technology as America's tyrant today. For the tyrant, these pages coin the word meta-tech. We need to be freed from what freed us.

For brevity, I use the word meta-tech not only to include technics but also its consequence (and sometimes superseder), the service industry. Jointly, they overadjust us by being our tyrannical servants. I use the "man" of "unadjusted man" in the sense of mankind, female or male, and whatever the ethnic clan. Too bad English lacks a short word like the German "Mensch," meaning both genders. My concern, needless to say (or not needless?), is with our shared humanity.

I feel uneasy with the constant quotes and misquotes (preferably misquotes, less portentous) of Donne-via-Hemingway: "No man is an island . ... Never send to know for whom the bell tolls. It tolls for thee." Here two false alternatives are implied. Either you're totally insulated from society (Latin *insula*, island), or else

ix

you're a busybody "activist" whose public life leaves no room for the free inner self of imagination and love. By "unadjusted" I mean a third alternative: every complete man or woman is a half-island, an almost island, a peninsula (Latin *paene insula*). To preserve private creativity, whether against political dictators or against economic hucksters, advertisers, and TV, private lives must at times take public stands. The ivory tower is not bombproof.

Yet neither is the mechanizing conveyor belt of over-commitment. Fully an island means a cut-off egotist with a mirror, the snigger of the Narcissus. Fully non-island means to surrender ornery individualism to the flat mediocre mainland. The *l'art pour l'art* poet should remember that the word "word" is a social construct, expressing a socially invented language, just as is the word "individual." The collectivist should remember that the great social inventions, including the word "social," sprang from creative loners, as did the machinery—the car, the computer—he daily depends on.

The modifier "half" before "island" overlaps with what Whitman meant by both playing the game and laughing at it, in the game and out of it. Another overlap: with Eliot's "teach us to care and not to care" or Saint John's "in the world yet not of it."

A pluralism of allegiances is the way to avoid overadjustment. Not enough to belong to a variety of groups. I would uphold unadjustment not only against collectivism (the big isms) but even against your little subcollectivisms (province, clan, club). Up to a point the latter are needed roots, what Burke calls loyalty to your little platoon. But beyond this point your groups press on you their neat square grids. Life is biology, not geometry. Proteus, not Procrustes. A flexible improvisation like capitalism, not a rigid ideology like Marxism. Progress is by zigzag, not straight lines. A straight line is the longest distance between two points. And the bloodiest.

Nonconforming can be more show-off than liberating, depending on nonconforming against what: the age or the ages? Popular fads or Melville's "reverence for the Archetype"? In the past, students were asked to write essays about what values they admired. Now they are asked, in progressive schools, to write about themselves. This in the name of undisciplined "self-expression," "unchanneled spontaneity," "building self-esteem," all the social worker pieties. To what extent is the loner a self-indulgent crank, to what extent creative? Or both? The distinguished act is always to make distinctions.

And to clarify. Though protection from statism and nationalism is the right of humanist individualism, the latter can fall—but need not fall—into a trap. The trap is to deify man, leading to anti-moral self-deification. The trap is readily avoided as long as we keep recalling that man is not and never will be omnipotent, omniscient, or eternal. At best we're still frail, fallible clay. In body, in mind. As a brief flash in those 14 billion years, Earth for us is one of the uninhabitable planets. Man is not a self-sufficient godling nor a values-lacking earthling but the only animal reaching (overreaching?) beyond. Needed: a values-defending elitist without delusions of grandeur.

We have seen how sublime the beyond can be. And also how vile. Too bad there's been no better translation of the Nietzschean word than the comic book word "superman." "Beyond-man" would have been better. And when no longer rooted in the "human, all too human," then the would-be superman and the vilest sub-man are but opposite sides of the same counterfeit coin.

II. Sometimes for Elitism

From Tom Paine on (and he was jailed not by the French aristocrats but by the revolution he had supported), a common fallacy is to equate aristocrat with parasite or even, in a loose sense, with fascist. Often the equating is correct. But at best the aristocratic ideal differs sharply from oligarchy. Noblesse oblige: think Adlai Stevenson, think Chief Justice Hughes, think (who's afraid of sounding corny?) George Washington. It was a group of hereditary aristocrats with conscience, not only Stauffenberg and Moltke but many others, who gave up their lives resisting the resentful plebeian Hitler, the ally (1939-41) of the resentful plebeian Stalin, in contrast with the anti-fascist alliance of the Duke of Marlborough (Churchill), the Squire of Hyde Park (FDR), and the elitist General de Gaulle.

To call aristocrats and constitutional monarchs proto-fascists is unjust in precisely the same way as calling Social Democrats "Reds." The socialist mayor of Berlin, Reuter, and the socialist chancellor Brandt, did more to stop the communists and Nazis than did most German bourgeois.

The trouble with socialists, writ small or large, is not that they're "subversive" toward big money (refreshing) but that they cross what, in *Conservatism Revisited* (Transaction, 2004) I call "the statist line." This is the line beyond which the social gains are outweighed by the loss in private rights. The location of this line must be debated with civility, not with personal vilifications on either side. The line's location varies according to the given society's traditions. America rightly allows less statism than Russia, with its tradition of statist tsars. But even there the long Soviet interlude was a ghastly elephantiasis of Big Brother.

Even a benign state not only reforms but homogenizes. A homogenized state (hence the importance of independent courts) can be misused for ethnic cleansing of minorities, as seen recently in Serbia.

For years I had not re-read Ortega's *Revolt of the Masses*, dismissing it as carrying aristocracy too far. But on current re-reading I find it often reasonable and in no way soft on oligarchs or dictators.

Today is "aristocrat" in the good sense an exception or the rule? An exception. Noblesse oblige is what the plutocratic Republican Party and the big corporations are mostly lacking. My Part III, "Direct Democracy," argues against America's very popular populism of the west, whether left or right, Both are illustrated by the history of Wisconsin, from the idealistic Progressive Party to the cynical McCarthy. Usually associated with the left, populism in 2004 is being manipulated by plutocracy. The populists Reagan and Goldwater—and their present successors—are not so much right of center as west of center.

The bien-pensant liberals rightly see us threatened by dictators and censors. The unadjusted man agrees. But he also sees the threat (though less dangerous because voluntary) of being brainwashed by a mass democracy under meta-tech and its ads and

TV. The faults of Athenian democracy we all know: the subordination of women and of slaves. But why did a mere 100,000 Athenians—and 100,000 Florentines—create vastly more of cultural value (plays, poems, statues, philosophy) than 200 million free Americans with the highest living standard in history? Answer: most of the 100,000 were individuals; most of the 200 million are masses.

In the den of mass meta-tech there is littler room for either good or bad, either the creative loner or the criminal loner. Both are mostly leveled down to a bland average mediocrity. Yet both kinds of loner thrived under the poisoned daggers of the Borgias and Medicis. Is this another—nonmoral—reason for the greater creativity of the 100,000?

In America, the majority of the 200 million masses are bourgeois in outlook or aspiration. The word bourgeois contains conflicting connotations. The "respectable" bourgeois and the bohemian rebel are twin forms of bourgeois affectation. The bourgeois virtues, bless them, need not be either hypocritical or all too sincerely dowdy. But they often are. Thereby they provoke the responses of the immoralists, the *poètes maudits*, even the diabolists. All the would-be shockers.

Baudelaire and Marx were both of bourgeois origin. Contrast the aesthetic anti-bourgeois rage of Baudelaire and the economic anti-bourgeois rage of Marx. In his pre-1919 Marxist days Mussolini gloated, "There is no innocent bourgeois" after a radical's bomb murdered many innocent bystanders, including nonpolitical women and children. Mussolini's phrase "no innocent" had been coined 1892 by the French anarchist Ravachol. And a famous bourgeois surrealist said he longed to spray deadly bullets at random into a bourgeois café.

If the highest aim of one kind of "art" is to shock (be it the bourgeois or all mankind), then terrorist mass murder would be the highest art. Then Mussolini's son was an artist when he praised the beauty of blowing up an Ethiopian village from the air. Current example: the German avant-garde composer Stockhausen praised the 9/11 explosion of the World Trade Center as "the greatest form of art imaginable for the whole cosmos." Our counterattack: not censorship, not pompous respectability, not moralizing, but morals. Not self-righteous but righteous.

In America today, bourgeois respectability gets sublimated into "political correctness," usually referring to anti-bourgeois politics. And the most violent of the Weathermen revolutionaries were doted on by their rich parents who sent checks and gourmet caviar to their hideouts where their ineptness sometimes blew up themselves rather than capitalists. My 1952 book, *Shame and Glory of the Intellectuals* (repriny by Greenwood), coined the phrase radical chic for this elitist leftism. Practiced by Gayord Babbitt, the imagined son of Sinclair Lewis's Babbitt. The phrase has since been used elsewhere without acknowledgement and with tongue in chic.Was Alcibiades the first radical chicster?

What inspires anti-bourgeois outrage in bourgeois France is either aesthetics or economics. Among bourgeois Anglo-Saxons it is sexual outrage that triggers a moralizing crusade: Byron, Wilde, Clinton, obscene modern art. All these militant outrages share one emotion, self-righteousness. Righteousness, okay. But self-righteous crusades are always in the wrong. Especially when they're in the right.

III. The Value of Values

In calculating the precarious balance between private and public, our disagreements should be groping, not peremptory, as the balance keeps shifting through history. Today the pendulum has swung too far toward the public life. But not so during Roosevelt's preservation of capitalism by public reforms. Today it is not so much politics as meta-tech that crushes the private life. The best essay on the privacy debate is by Prof. Irving Louis Horowitz, "Networking America" (*ETC* magazine, Fall 1999).

Even more debatable: relative vs. absolute in values. This debate can be approached as abstract philosophy or just pragmatically, in terms of what works. Daily, we see around us the mischief of relativism: "anything goes," but we also see (for example, in Marxist or fascist societies) the absolutizing of the relative (race, state, or economics) and the relativizing of the absolute (personal freedom). Fascism is idealism diabolized. Marxism is materialism deified.

A further distinction: between a condition and a theory. Relativism and absolutism of values are both theories. But the human condition, call it unoriginal sin, makes us first do evil and only afterwards blame it on either relativism or absolutism, whichever better "justifies" evil-doing in a given culture. The condition precedes the two rival rationalizations. Thus I have heard the crimes of the Nazis blamed on their belief in absolutes and on their relativist ignoring of absolute standards. To prevent the moral chaos of "anything goes," is this the solution: to be relatively absolute? Behave as if the Christian-Judaic ethics are universal absolutes. Is not this what makes them so?

Here questions are being raised that cannot be answered but must be confronted. Take the demystifying of social norms known as eighteenth-century Enlightenment. Up to a point, clearly liberating. But at what point does the sabotage of standards ensure, in the next generation, standardless demagogues and dictators? To overcome the Wagnerian romanticism of the nineteenth century and its murderous nationalism, our eighteenth-century heritage of skeptical liberalism must be welcomed. But only up to a point. And what point? Does the point depend on the varying traditions of various societies, or is the point of sabotage universal? To dogmatize about such value-questions seems to jump to arbitrary conclusions. To evade them seems a cop-out.

Compared to the left-right totalitarians or to current terrorist zealots (Talleyrand: "Surtout pas de zèle") how slender are the differences between our conservatives, liberals, radicals, no matter how defined. Yet we must never be so smug about this fact that we overlook our own social wrongs by comparing them to the wrongs of "them." Again, balance. At times it is the zealots who get needed humane reforms done.

"Western civilization" is a supreme value and another ambiguity. It can mean colonial exploitation, America's Coca-Colonizing the globe, a hypocritical form of imperialism and exploitation. It can also mean all the values that German *Kultur* derided as "civilization," the values of free elections, free inquiry, and the rights of women, labor, and minorities. This positive meaning is what I mean by the West. During the two most dreadful wars in history, the choice was between Western civilization and German *Kultur*, as discussed at length after 1933 by Thomas Mann.

In my use, West is not limited to geography but is constantly including and learning from the geographic non-West. For example, so much science comes to us from China and from the medieval Arabs. Western civilizations stands for the same flexibility and self-reforming as the undogmatic kind of capitalism, the same salutary mess.

IV. Take Conservatism away from the "Conservatives"

What now is called Republican Party conservatism is a mix of old laissez-faire in economics (not in thought), jingoist nationalism (a contradiction of laissez-faire tolerance), and politicized piety. Clearly this is hardly what I described in the 1949 edition of *Conservatism Revisited*. And not what I admired and still admire in John Adams, Burke, Churchill, and the international peace-making in Metternich's Congress of Vienna. All these were quoted at length in my anthology (now out of print) *Conservatism from John Adams to Churchill* (New York, 1956), which made Adams the key figure for America long before the Adams revival of 2000 (reprinted by Greenwood Press, 1978).

When Willie Sutton was asked why he robbed banks, he replied, "Because that's where the money is." When right-wing Republicans rob the poor, it's because that's where the money isn't. Their state subsidies of goodies for the biggies is the socialism of the free enterprisers.

Regarding many Republican conservatives today, the word "touts" comes to mind, as used by Winston Churchill in 1903: "The old Conservative party with its religious convictions and constitutional principles will disappear, and a new party will arise like perhaps the Republican party of the USA .. rigid, materialist, and secular ... who will cause the lobbies to be crowded with the touts of protected industries." Well, the "religious convictions" remain, not as in Lincoln but as hypocritical homage to the fundamentalist media (Roberts, Falwell, Bob Jones University).

One must always ask what specifically a conservative is conserving. Are they conserving ethical or only materialist values? The Marxists were obsessed by economics. So are the "neo-conservatives" (economic obsession as scar left over from their abandoned youthful Marxist days). To many of them during, say, Pinochet's reign in Chile, what mattered most was whether the Chilean economy followed laissez-faire principles, and it did. But what mattered and matters to me is whether fingernails are being pulled out.

"Pragmatism" is now used in ways never intended by William James. For reasons different from those of Marxists and different from ex-Marxist neo-conservatives, many non-ideological Americans likewise explain an ethical issue "pragmatically," i.e., by economics. They simply can't take ideas seriously. Hitler was once seen as driven by big money, instead of by his Wagnerite and *ressentiment* demons. In 2002, jihad terrorists are often "explained" by poverty and illiteracy. Actually they often are well educated and well to do, especially the 9/11 terrorists and their sophisticated planners. "Pragmatism" is unpragmatic; it doesn't work.

Are all the isms now wasms? Would it were so. The problem not only with past isms (fascism, communism) but isms still around is that they are rigid and inflexible, hence Procrustean, hence gulag and concentration camp. American and Western capitalism mostly escapes this fate because it isn't an ism. It is a muddle and a mess in the good sense, not a rigid ideology that is spelled out and from which you can't deviate. Hence reformable.

I am not scared to use the words good and bad. Sometimes in history an issue can become a litmus-paper test, dividing the bad from the good. McCarthyism was such a test, and most self-styled conservatives failed it. Specific example: I had proposed a declaration, signed by conservatives of impeccable anti-communist credentials, denouncing the Wisconsin rabble-rouser as a liar and thought controller who attacked non-communists of the left as "communists" and who discredited anti-communism. No signers from most of the grand preachers of morality like Russell Kirk, summarized here by George Nash in *The Conservative Intellectual Movement in America*, (1996, Wilmington, Del.: Intercollegiate Studies Institute, p. 104):

Not surprisingly, Kirk's position [on McCarthy] failed to satisfy Peter Viereck. When Viereck attempted to organize conservative intellectuals to oppose McCarthy, Kirk refused—repelled, he later said by Viereck's overzealous "reverse McCarthyism." Several years later Viereck would accuse Kirk and his "group" of being "McCarthy-corrupted" and of failing to repudiate the "dangerous" Senator from Wisconsin.

The motive of general right-wing silence is not that they believed McCarthy's lies but cowardice and opportunism. My friend Max Eastman attacked me for criticizing McCarthy (except in "private") on grounds that the end of anti-communism justified the means. Yet the reason I had earlier admired colorful Max was that he had so eloquently renounced his youthful communism on the ground that noble ideals can't justify bad means. Incidentally, McCarthy never "caught" a single spy although there were plenty (Hiss, Coplon, Harry Dexter White, etc.)

It was an error of judgment (not of ethics) for so many intellectuals to get hysterical about hysteria, namely about the hysteria McCarthy fomented. He was no serious danger to America's existence, no kind of fascist movement. He had no organization, no organizers (only disorganizing buffoons like Cohn and Schine), no storm troopers, no such base. What he did endanger—and partly destroyed—was the honor, integrity, and credibility of many conservatives. And all over the globe he discredited the good cause of an honest non-mendacious anti-communism. My heterodox reinterpretation of the McCarthy phenomenon appears at length in my Part III.

On the John Birch Society, that *endimanché* McCarthyism of paranoid WASPs, Kirk was as evasive as on the populist McCarthy. Even Buckley's *National Review* condemned the Birchers when they called even Eisenhower a Commie. What do I mean by "evasive"? In *America* magazine (Feb. 17, 1962), Kirk dissociated himself from the utterly discredited Bircher, Robert Welch, but not from the thought-controlling Birch Society itself. And the reason for Kirk's "disassociating" from Welch was not the society's fascist-style politics but because Welch's occasional. "silliness" became "the kiss of death" for conservatives. A utilitarian, not ethical disassociation. That same month (Feb. 7, 1962, *New York Times*), James Reston quoted Kirk as calling Welch "a likable, honest, courageous, energetic man." Kirk's books respond to humane help with a prim, lace-curtain shudder: "Allowances for dependent children…make the rearing of bastards profitable."

Earlier, I'd applauded Kirk's excellent journalistic research into many important overlooked names. But such credentials made him the ideological respectability-giver for the crassest wing of the Republican Party, notably Goldwater, whom he haloed as "the new Disraeli." Kirk had become the house intellectual for the non-intellectual far right. Irving Kristol is too perceptive for them, too intelligent and independent an ally, therefore suspect. Kirk used long words and thought big: the kind of middlebrow whom lowbrows deem highbrow. His solemnly intoned "truths," though proclaimed as immortal, have—like immortalized Roman emperors—short lives. More convincing, because less pretentious, is the picturesque and frisky figure of William Buckley who, now mellowed, probably regrets his pro-McCarthy book.

Most current "conservatives" (including Kirk and Buckley) are omitting from their chief icons the key aspects that would attract liberals and mainstreamers. Omitting, for example, that Burke and John Adams fought against the slave trade. And omitting Burke's defense of colonials, as in India, against imperialist exploitation: his indictment of Warren Hastings.

Conservatism, above all, means roots. Yet these "conservatives" are conserving not roots but a rootless nostalgia for roots. Millions of small Churchills actually felt and lived roots. England resisted its fascists (Oswald Moseley) better than Weimar because Weimar lacked democratic roots.

In America, conservative idealism has degenerated into a an
Enron Disneyland. "Enron" is 2004 shorthand for robber barons
Veblenized into plebeian display (country club, gold bathtub,
Gucci wife), despised by patricians (Teddy Roosevelt, FDR).

Nor are the poor—why sanctify any group?—saints. As for the
stock market crash of 2000-2001, the blame is not merely on
what the two Roosevelts saw as "malefactors of great wealth" but
on the idiots of small wealth, the thousands of recklessly greedy
small investors.

The word "conservative" in general has, in current journalistic
use, become a false front of big ideas for an idea-less rightist self-
interest. And the confusing word "radical" can mean both rightist
and leftist extremism and more benignly, can mean getting at the
root of things. And "liberal," by whichever definition, is still tied
up with Rousseau's faith in the natural goodness of man and the
bankrupt faith in capitalized Progress, with a propensity for always blaming one's own country internationally. (Not to mention
a condescendingly "enlightened" fad for the pretentious kind of
foreign movies and for fake "organic" and "natural" fodder.) No
social creed is left us unless qualified by an adjective, such as the
terms "Burkean conservative" or "John Adams conservative."

And "socialism"? Sometimes social, sometimes virtually a religion, its world brotherhood has inspired some of the best minds
and hearts for centuries. To do it justice would take a very long
separate volume. Here suffice it to say: socialist parties in the
West, though now no longer really Marxist, are all still vulnerable
to collectivist utopian dreams.

America contains plenty of socialist revolutionary rhetoric. But
it gets lost completely between the bra and hair tonic ads. What
doesn't get lost completely is concrete socialist (and third party)
programs. Some of their reforms serve the useful role of later
being adopted by mainstream parties.

Socialist parties have always divided between those who work
within the legal and ethical framework (like the current German
Social Democrats) and those who (like Lenin) believe the end
justifies the means. "Justifies" has cost oceans of blood and tears
in the Soviet Union, China, Cambodia. Marx envisioned no safe-

guards against an almighty socialist state. Here, as Isaiah Berlin once emphasized to me, the socialist Herzen was more perceptive in foreseeing the horrors of the 1917 revolutionaries. Herzen: "The ancient dream of a perfect society.... But there is no such place, that's why it's called utopia. Until we stop killing our way towards it, we won't be grown up as human beings."

Philosophical socialists are correct in saying that an ideal socialism or communism (never yet achieved) is free of these horrors. What is incorrect: to compare ideal socialism with the flawed existing capitalism. You must either compare the ideal versions of both (no robber barons in the humane Adam Smith) or compare the existing versions of both (in the twentieth-century, Soviet Russia and America). What is impermissible: to compare the ideal of one with the reality of the other.

Almost all socialists share two pieties that just aren't so. First that many workers feel an international solidarity. They don't. Second, that the proletariat is the gutsy militant class. The lower middle class turns out to be the most militant, also the most aggressive in street fighting, often for nationalism. Two Marx superstitions have already been abandoned: that a socialist state will automatically wither away and that the poor are getting ever poorer. Revolution mostly leaves the poor still poorer. What has helped them are trade unions, reforms, and capitalist productivity. Obvious platitudes? Not yet obvious enough.

No changes have been made in my 1956 edition (except to add my concluding Lindsay monomgraph in 2004). In a reprint it would be dishonest to omit the false predictions in order to play the prophet. It would also violate the context. Better to admit the goofs. I goofed in not foreseeing our loss of the war against Viet-Stalinism. Also in overestimating Adlai Stevenson as a "great" statesman. To be great, you must not only articulate freedom, as he did, but incarnate it, as John Adams did, and even "Ike."

Do my present preface pages of 2004 ever contradict those of 1956? So much the better. Call it growing up. Do they ever repeat points made earlier? If so, call it senility. Certain references, clear in 1956, may have become obscure in 2004. For example, I ended

Part III with a "Modest Proposal." It may be less obvious today that I was inventing a surrealist speech by Richard Nixon.

A very personal conclusion: my 1949 book, *Conservatism Revisited*, is but a footnote to my *Metapolitics: From Wagner to Hitler* of 1941—and my 1956 *Unadjusted Man* a clarification of that footnote. My kind of conservatism comes directly from the experience of my *Metapolitics* research. There I learnt that the topsoil of Weimar democracy was too abstract, too thin to resist the totalitarian storm, being not deep-rooted by history but blueprinted from above by well-meaning intellectuals. It lacked the roots and time-tested traditions of British liberty.

My anticommunism? A second footnote to my *Metapolitics* research. How else could I react, seeing the very same Hitler crimes (police state, mass murder, Führer cult, anti-Semitism) under Stalin? And then hearing fellow-traveler intellectuals exculpate Stalin's fascist-style behavior while calling themselves anti-fascists. My book title, *Shame and Glory of the Intellectuals*? Well, was it not the glory of the intellectuals to lead against Hitler? And their shame to default on Stalin?

And so many never learn. If yesterday Stalin, then the next day Ho Chi Minh or Castro. Or, to quote a British intellectual of today, "Americans had it coming to them" after the tragedy of 9/11. I am highly gratified (as proof that I've not utterly lost my compass) that I was denounced the same day as a secret McCarthyite by a liberal editor and a secret pinko by a McCarthyite.

"Adjustment"? Yes to the *lacrimae rerum* of the human condition. No to the noble-browed banalities of cant.

Yeats's beast with poor posture (still slouching towards Bethlehem to be born) is no longer—in the U.S. and Western Europe—a compulsory dictatorship but voluntary, grinning overadjustment, the doom of creativity. Picture (as symbol-fantasy) a wee pile of the world's last four remaining books, Keats, Shakespeare, Dante, Sophocles, pleading, "Robots, let our yellowing pages live." Answer: a blaze of ignited machine oil.

As if only two alternatives, common sense interrupts me: "calm down, there's less ouch to losing your fancy cultural soul than feeling your fingernails pulled out by dictators."

Yes, but...

PETER VIERECK, MARCH 2004

AUTOBIOG

*by Peter Viereck**

(born N.Y.C., August 5, 1916)

I.

At four saw seagull. feathers
Trampled on Hudson piers.
Soldiering, saw others.
Naples. Algiers.

Born on Riverside Drive.
A weed no asphalt could kill.
First verses at five.
At it still.

They asked me at six what I'd do for a living
If I had a future to purchase.
They heard my reply with misgiving:
"I'll be a clown who builds churches."

I've moved far from that outburst,
But it is never far.
Crasser sweets have stoked my thirst,
But sweet they never were.

Church without clown?
Unleashes ayatollah.
A grin without icon?
Unleashes Coca Cola.

A reverence that smiles: I need that mantle
To hover without wish, and mild, and gentle.
But hubbub lashes out at me and rips
The feather of sereneness from my lips.

---

*Published April 2004 in *Boulevard* magazine, Washington University, St. Louis

So I take "stands" and brawl and vaunt.
It is—it isn't—what I really want.
I, ex-fetus: homesick to be in
Womb's sane asylum on earth's looney bin.

Everyman surfs some kind of perilous sea.
The inner kind feels sharkier to me.
Pratfalls? Not just by clowns. By Everyman.
Isn't that the point of *condition humaine*

Ban clowns, ban arts? They—soberly—lure to the brink.
Bartenders don't drink.
The poignant laughs that matter
Are—ouch—no laughing matter.

Your build-a-man kit. A good sport, well washed, noble browed.
Glue together these pieties. Gorgeous bunk.
He president, dictator, guru. Adored by crowd.
Till clowns laugh him apart into robot junk.

On my watch in the Thirties, in Russia, in Germany,
Secret loners had to metamorph,
Grabbing their own faces and peeling them off.
. . . That old gray nightmare, she ain't what she used to be.

New post-Orwell nightmare: first we're saved
From chore by gadget, then enslaved
By tech. "The road to hell is paved
With good inventions." In nuclear radiance bathed.

I warred for the American
"No" to the Mustache and Genghis Khan.
Ism-wars are a bust,
But these two were a must.

This brief free-mind "must":
More, more than futile pose.
Our tiny conscious dust
Outshining big blind cosmos.

                    II.

"Life," can I love you?—you (slow-action) poison clay ate.
Love earth?—one of the uninhabitable planets.
And a wrong-headed pa? And a wronging wronged mate?
I love you each, you memory nets.

How entice enticer?
With pasts my past is littered.
Love hasn't left me wiser,
Just more embittered.

Yet isn't it something to have been
Called "my beloved" now and then?
Catching—quick, quick—a hand to press
Just before my heart bypass.

My warmth is now charred air.
Am fading; dream me back soon.
Am unreal; dream at me harder.
Meanwhile I'll bay at the moon—

—discreetly. I've learnt to bay with proper
Herr Professor civility.
No lies. I've rarely bayed a whopper.
I tell truth slant like Emily.

My verse truthed forth a better planet's spore
And grew it next door.
Offbeat wildness, in strict form stashed.
Selling like cold cakes. I write for the past.

Or is it the future writes me forth? I'll be
Back when your grandchild jump-starts my poetry.
In times of cash and yawns, with art in tatters,
The resonance of lyric form still matters.

Not mechanized form, that net without the tennis,
Free verse? "The artlessness that conceals artlessness."
My prose books? Mostly remaindered.
I might as well be brain dead.

If write what rage requires,
Would riots make me stop?
No, stopped by bored non-buyers.
I might as well close shop.

But while demagogue woos and cult is quick booze,
Wordcraft's the durable muse.
When those idiots crown me, who foretells
If it's with laurels or bells?

Sure, I've delusions of grandeur.
So do you, *hypocrite lecteur.*

                    III.
Maybe on other worlds "living" re-happens.
Here we take turns at it. No choice; no weapons.
Birth battle, death rattle, refrain that deafens
Creed's defense.

We turn-takers eke healing song
From the pathos of this refrain.
But whatever it is that's feeling song
Can also feel pain.

Only old knows life. Too late to live it.
Knows when to change. But too stiff-kneed to pivot.

An exile from my own autobiog,
I leer at it through senior-citizen fog.

Like trusted hound, gone suddenly rabid
And hunting hunter instead of rabbit,
A mobile abyss from my trusted hearth
Is hounding my heart.

Whether 9-to–5 deals or soused at three A.M.,
Babbitt senior or junior both boast freedom:
"We're nonconformist individuals
Like everybody else."

Reversing such slick colors of my eon,
I am a rogue chameleon.
But when I've adjusted, boostered, blustered,
I got, like the General at Little Big Horn, Custered.

I've sought, since the Battle of Wounded Me,
Safety in shell: a turtle.
This traps me in walls I can't hurtle.
The jail of self: shell's entry fee.

When death's Custered pie hits face,
Let go with grace.

IV.

Go? My green hangs on unweakened
Till tailgated by fall.
Then shared mulch, fecund,
Connects us all.

My selves trans-selved: last leaf
Joins mulch. Relief.

August 5, 2003

FOREWORD TO THE
ORIGINAL EDITION

The fight is for the private life; abstract ideologies are
Saharas. The Overadjusted Man knows only the public life.
Three of the differing modes of creativity—religious, aesthetic,
intellectual—have this in common: they are what the individual does with his loneliness. In an impersonal machine-
age, the fight is to preserve the concrete, the intimate, the
inefficiently wayward; to preserve the inner life, whether as
the creatively alone or simply as the playfully private, the
unapologetic exhilaration of play. Hence, the Yeatsian insight:

> The Muse is mute when public men
> Applaud a modern throne:
> Those cheers that can be bought or sold,
> That office fools have run . . .
> For things like these what decent man
> Would keep his lover waiting? . . .

On the other hand, in certain moral crises the fight is not
only for the private life but also for the publicly-embattled
right to have a private life. All mechanized societies are overadjusted but not equally so; therefore, the right to the private
life has the corresponding duty partly to forgo itself, in its
own partly free society, in order better to preserve itself
against the total tyranny next door.

Yes. But first things first: the fight is for the private life.

PETER VIERECK

Part One   BEYOND CONFORMING

AND NONCONFORMING

"We are now in great haste to construct a magnetic telegraph from Maine to Texas; but Maine and Texas, it may be, have nothing important to communicate."—*Thoreau*

"New presbyter is but old priest writ large."—*A warning against the conforming of nonconformers, 1643*

Chapter One THE UNADJUSTED MAN

A New American Hero

"Only you must be honest with yourselves."—*General Epistle of James,*
I, 22 (Knox)

I

Without inner psychological liberty, outer civil liberties are
not quite enough. We can talk civil liberties, prosperity,
democracy with the tongues of men and angels, but it is merely
a case of "free from what?" and not "free for what?" if we use
this freedom for no other purpose than to commit television or
go lusting after supermarkets. In contrast with earlier eras, ever
more colleges (not to mention still more standardized communities) want to know: is the applicant well-adjusted, a good
mixer? No new trend and no bad trend would be involved if
social adjustment were means, not end; that would still allow
for ultimate spontaneity and personality. The depersonalization characterizing the present trend is the goal of adjustment
as an end in itself. Thereupon the goal of adjustment, defensi-
ble and indeed indispensable as a social lubricant, becomes far
more than that; it becomes a prime determiner of American
tastes, opinions, recreations, human relationships.

From being well-adjusted for its own sake, what a short step
to becoming overadjusted: the public-relations personality of
public smile, private blank. In effect, an ecstasy of universal
voluntary lobotomy.[1] Adjustment as the new art for art's sake
means far more than merely one more "age of conformity," that
undifferentiating understatement, or merely one more age
seeking shelter (from "the weight of too much liberty") in some

[1] Cf. "Modest Proposal," page 223.

3

supposed normalcy. It is a Procrustean and rather ga-ga normalcy, determined by a continuous secret plebiscite to which inner spontaneity is continually sacrificed. Thus we have moved qualitatively beyond the older, pre-industrial American conformity noted by Tocqueville.

An abnormal desire for normalcy, and that as end, not means, is the trend that countless social philosophers today—and, more important, your own concrete observations—are recording with helpless stupefaction. That helplessness of the recorder, in contrast with the heroism and free moral choice the situation calls for, sometimes conceals the same satisfaction of surrender that characterizes the trend recorded. Whether morally confronted or evaded, the American problem is not merely surrender of the personality but a complacent kind of surrender, a voluntary cultural thought-control more insidious than the coercive political kind.

This equation is still too new and too big to allow us to predict other than double-valued outcomes. Either the minus sign of the present: no Shakespeares, no Leonardos, no personal genius from such a world. Or the interchangeable plus sign of the possible future: what Shakespeares, what Leonardos, what redoubled counter-assertions of personal genius will be irritated forth from such an impersonal machine-world, which—inside each personal soul—makes what it does not break. The plus sign, then, need not be excluded; the all-too-convincing pessimism about the minus outcome may encourage, by replacing moral choice with historic determinism, an unheroic abdication of resistance—why vainly beat hands of vulnerable flesh against invulnerable machine-metal?—an abdication that only increases the mechanizing trend and indeed helped cause it. But the optimistic grain-of-sand-in-the-oyster explanation of beauty becomes cold consolation when the bourgeois-philistine grain of sand, goading forth a Joyce or Rimbaud, becomes not a grain but a dumped ton. At some point even oysters give up, leaving a well-adjusted, synthetic utopia to its mass-produced pearls of glass.

From this trend a new American idol emerges: the Overadjusted Man. Against it a new liberator emerges, a bad mixer and scandalously devoid of "education for citizenship": the Unadjusted Man. Unadjustedness seems the only personal heroism left in a machine-era of which William Faulkner said: "We all had better grieve for all people beneath a culture which holds any mechanical superior to any man."

Today the humanist, the artist, the scholar can no longer be the prophet and seer, the unriddler of the outer universe; modern science has deprived him of that function. His new heroism, unriddling the inner universe, is to be stubbornly unadjusted toward the mechanized, depersonalized bustle outside. The Unadjusted Man is the final, irreducible pebble that sabotages the omnipotence of even the smoothest-running machine. His refusal to adjust is a gesture beyond the need of colossal rhetoric; he is a hero partly because without heroic pose. Indeed he is no hero at all in the eyes of the majority but a laughable Quixote, too unadjusted to settle down with a steady, productive windmill. His values are not determined by a democratic plebiscite; he may even be arrogant enough to retort, "One man and God make a majority," when accused of being undemocratic for not joining the majority in filtering his reading through the roughage-removal machinery of the digest magazines.

By revering the infinite preciousness of each individual soul, Christianity builds up a deep, soul-felt, inner shield against the outer claims of overadjustment. This religious shield is often more effective against tyrants, in its underground way, than the brain-felt systematizings of liberty by the secular doctrinaires. Whether right or left in politics, whether capitalist or socialist in economics, the various secular and intellectual articulations of liberty are often weak shields against tyranny, even when strong in pure logic. They remain as irrefutable, independent, and irrelevant as the liberty of free Andorra in the Cold War.

The unadjusted should not be confused with the maladjusted, the psychiatric; nor with the never-adjusted, the merely crotchety; nor with the flaunted grandstand-nonconformity of

bohemia's "misunderstood genius" act. The alternative to these
mere caricatures of the Unadjusted Man is a viewpoint more
selective in its non-adjusting, a viewpoint whose coin has two
reciprocal sides: adjustment to the ages, non-adjustment to
the age. This distinction—between lasting roots and ephemeral
surfaces—the Unadjusted Man is committed to try to make,
even though gropingly, fallibly. A position gets defined in
part by its enemies: his selective unadjustedness gets ridiculed
by the overadjusted and the maladjusted alike. The overadjusted ridicule him as maladjusted (a Kafka-reading spoil-
sport at America's million-year picnic); the maladjusted ridicule
him as overadjusted (a renegade from their imagined vestal
purity of total alienation).

The easy conformity-baiting of adolescent radicalism refuses
to adjust even to deep and valid norms. The Unadjusted Man
rejects superficial norms not for rejection's sake but to serve
valid ones; his attempt to distinguish between such rival value-
claims is a dilemma of tragic soul-searching, not of easy
conditioned answers. Unadjusted, in the highest sense of tragic
freedom, were the dying words of Thomas More on the scaffold:
"I die the king's good servant but God's first." For "king's
servant," substitute today: "servant of the state" or "servant of
secularism." "Secular," used in no clerical sense, means keeping
up with the well-adjusted Joneses, the pushers and rushers,
the obscenely wholesome ones who never glimpse the abyss
behind whatever vanity they are go-getting.

An indiscriminate radicalism against authority says in effect:
"I die the king's bad servant; I refuse to serve the status quo
even in duties that must be rendered not unto God but unto
Caesar." More's revolt is essentially conservative because he
does remain voluntarily "the king's good servant" until driven
to some ultimate moral extreme.

"Good servant" distinguishes not only More's unadjustedness
from the radical's nonconformity; it also distinguishes western
man, deliberately committed to the guilt of action, from the
passive, otherworldly waiter for Nirvana. Western man, even
while rejecting the priority-claims of secular reality, knows he

must (in this life) live within it. He cannot misuse other-worldly morality as a pretext for evading the moral choices involved in facing the material problems of this earth. Without thoroughly material reforms, morality may become an empty phrase, equally condemning the rich and the starving for stealing bread. Even while rejecting the vanity of this world, western man remains not only its servant but its good servant—up to a point. That point occurs when society's demand for service encroaches on God or conscience.

Western man, with his not-to-be-despised material and organizational achievements, rejects being "the king's servant" only as the last resort, never the first. In our own time, the last resort did occur when the "king" was Hitler or Stalin. Let us make sure it will never occur in America. But if ever it does occur, during some ultimate hour of moral choice between principle and expedient survival, then the non-materialist, the Christian, the man with inner liberty, walks to his scaffold smiling and unhesitant, like Saint Thomas More, because he is "God's servant first" and not the servant of some healthy well-adjustedness.

II

An unadjusted value-conserver like Thomas More is rare in any age; the overadjusted and the maladjusted are more frequent and are often allied against him. Such has always been the case. What is new today is the more sophisticated ability of the Overadjusted Man to masquerade as his opposite: as the unadjusted conserver of humanistic, artistic, and religious values. On the more exquisite campuses and in the self-consciously advanced pages of the quarterlies, highbrow nonconformity has succumbed to its own kind of hacks as blithely as the lowbrow conformity of *Screen Romances* and *True Detective Stories*. This choice between lowbrow and highbrow overadjustedness allows humanistic values the choice of two modes of execution: starvation or bear-hugs.

So we must inspect closest the credentials of those writers who proclaim loudest their nonconformity, their anti-philistia, their sensitivity. Picture a conveyor-belt, endlessly unloading noble-browed educators, sonorously eloquent pillars of culture, and tweedy, pipe-smoking teachers of "creative-writing" courses, which—with "lovable" whimsy—they call "workshops." Genuine sensitivity, genuine humanity have nothing in common with this conveyor-belt of robots, each of whom intones dutifully: "I'm a real flesh-and-blood human being, wincing sensitively,—an independent, non-conforming individualist, just like everybody else."

Three alternatives: (1) the Unadjusted Man, cultivating his inner riches of independence and reverie; (2) the adjusted lowbrow-Rotarian, snug in his hellish heaven of plastics and hygiene-worship; (3) the adjusted highbrow-Rotarian. This third new alternative, like the first, affirms the humanities and spiritual values; but unlike the first, does so in a mechanical, uninspired way that only masks more subtly the crassness of alternative-two. Alternative-one has rightly taught us to return to the traditional humanistic and religious values of the spirit. But alternative-three is parloring God just as snobbishly as "parlor socialists" used to verbalize humanitarianism in the 1930's: in both cases, not out of inner conviction but out of adjustment to smart fads. To manicure our sacred humanistic and religious values into fads may kill them more surely than any invasion of open barbarians, torch in hand, burning our churches, our libraries, our universities.

When our graduate schools betray the humanities today, they no longer do so with the old-fashioned vulgarity of alternative-two but with the new elegance of alternative-three: by creating a generation of trained seals, leaping sleekly through the hoops of the criticism of the criticism of criticism— and, after each hoop of the newest New Criticism, gratefully swallowing some fishy "explication" in mid-air.

Educators are proudly "impressed" by the current growth of college courses in Great Classics, Great Issues and by the student shift from materialist radicalism to religion. More impressive is the fact that for these classics, these issues—now made gregarious, painless—their creators toiled in loneliness, faced the rack. And when anti-materialism gets publicized like toothpaste, when religion gets wrapped in cellophane, then commercial materialism wins its biggest triumph of all: a triumph in the name of anti-commercialism. In every city's "put Christ back into Christmas" campaign, the carols blare their anti-materialist reminder the loudest from the mechanical loudspeakers in the busy department stores. Is it accidental in our society or is it typical that precisely our most money-avid industry, the cinema, includes a firm whose motto is "Ars gratia artis"?

Synthetic food pills we already have. Why not synthetic culture pills, synthetic souls? This development is particularly exasperating for artists, writers, educators.[2] It forces us into a ceaseless lover's-quarrel with America. As James Baldwin says in his wise *Notes of a Native Son*, 1955: "I love America more than any other country in the world; and exactly for this reason, I insist on the right to criticize her perpetually."

In the novel and in the poem, the most corrupting development of all is the substitution of technique for art. What once resulted from the inspired audacity of a heartbreakingly lonely craftsman is now mass-produced in painless, safe, and uninspired capsules. This process is taking over every category of education and literature. The stream of consciousness for which James Joyce wrestled in loneliness with language, the ironic perspective toward society which Proust attained not as entertainment but as tragedy, the quick, slashing insights for which a Virginia Woolf or a Katherine Mansfield bled out her heart, all these intimate personal achievements are today the standard props of a hundred hack imitators, mechanically vending what is called "the *New Yorker*-type story." Don't underestimate that type of story; though an imitation job, it is imitation with all the magnificent technical skill of America's best-edited weekly. And think of the advantages: no pain any more, no risk any more, no more nonsense of inspiration. Most modern readers are not even bothered by the difference

---

[2] Many American novels have been written about this development, notably Alan Harrington's brilliant *Revelations of Dr. Modesto*, New York, 1955.

between such an efficient but bloodless machine job and the living product of individual heart's anguish.

What, then, is the test for telling the real inspiration from the almost-real, the just-as-good?

The test is pain. Not mere physical pain but the exultant, transcending pain of selfless sacrifice. The test is that holy pain, that brotherhood of sacrifice, that aristocracy of creative suffering of which Baudelaire wrote: *"Je sais que la douleur est l'unique noblesse."*

Chapter Two THE OVERADJUSTED

MAN: Stereotypes Against Archetypes

"Adjustment for the sake of adjustment . . . the whole subject is as yet scarcely noticed in all its complexity in Europe, and even keen European observers still seem worried mainly about the outward standardization in the United States, which is merely a tangible symbol of the process. Much European fear of America is due to an unconscious feeling of the subtle psychological adjustment that has been carried so much further in the United States. It is a process deserving of more illumination and more serious discussion."—*Elsa Gress, Copenhagen, Denmark, in a letter to* CONFLUENCE *magazine, April, 1955*

" 'Equality,' as a certain factual increase in similarity, which merely finds expression in the theory of 'equal rights,' is an essential feature of decline. . . . The plurality of types, the will to be oneself . . . the pathos of distance, that is characteristic of every strong age."—*Nietzsche, 1889*

I

Many liberals tend to assume, whether in Paris, Rome, or New York, that only the left in politics, only the avant-garde in literature are against conformity and philistia. Their bogeyman is a never-defined "conservative." Shuddering deliciously, they build him up into a kind of Abominable Strawman, forever devouring plump young nonconformists in some dank cave in darkest middlewest. Many liberal (and radical) writings use the word "nonconformist" with a special in-group tone that falls like music on Advanced Ears. Such ears twitch uncomfortably only at the more primitive grunts of conformity, whereas the Unadjusted Man rejects its more sophisticated

11

whinnies likewise. Conservatism should never be confused with
conformism; on the need for distinguishing between them,
the unadjusted position coincides with the sort of new conservatism (unfortunately not the only sort) represented by
Professor Thomas I. Cook of Johns Hopkins University:

"To the new conservative, not the least of the ills of our society is a
tendency, as we wholesomely consolidate against Communism and out-
moded Marxism, to become *smugly uncritical* and self-satisfied, content
with orthodoxy, conformity, and national power. Thereby we may lose
or suppress that fundamental ethical and philosophical radicalism so
vital to the purification of our traditions."[1]

Since the Republican victory of 1952, the primitive huckster
conformist has been enjoying a full-flowered Indian summer,
right alongside the sophisticated conformist (avant-garde,
progressive). In an era so conformist on both these levels, the
new conservative can only wish well, in the sense of the Cook
quotation, to the current liberal and radical efforts to transcend
what they rightly call "the age of conformity." But instead of
giving us real dissent, most of these liberal and radical efforts
result in platitudes just as stale and tame. They are not only
platitudinous but irrelevant when their protests merely repeat,
with the flourish of a new discovery, that intellectuals need to
"dissent from conformity." The relevant question is: which
standards merit dissent, which ones merit assent? In the
irrelevant duel between primitive and sophisticated overadjustment—the one defending, the other attacking all conformity—
both sides lack the standards for discriminating between what
is conform-worthy and what isn't. Beyond conforming and
nonconforming: the Unadjusted Man, just because he does
conform to the values he deems lastingly good, has a deeper
foundation than the rootless anti-traditionalist for resisting the
bad conformities, whether the coercive ones of dictator and
mob or the voluntary ones of the Overadjusted Man.

The currency of the actual word "nonconformist" has become
so debased since Emerson's golden use of it that one is no longer

[1] The *New Leader*, March 29, 1954.

surprised to read, in an Associated Press dispatch of October 3, 1955, this characterization of some typical movie star: "a nonconformist in the Marlon Brando tradition." Perhaps this abuse of the word "tradition" is as painful to serious traditionalists as this abuse of "nonconformist" is to Emerson's ghost. Another example: even such machines for overadjustment as the women's fashion magazines have put the imprimatur of chicté on "difficult" southern avant-garde novelists. "I'm the screwball type"—so a healthy, conventional, terrifyingly efficient steno was remarking the other day while reading one of these magazines—"just a li'l ole individualist."

Nor are those lowbrow examples any worse than an intellectual quarterly remarking: "We unfortunately miss in this book that rich surrealistic obscurity which our modern taste has been led to expect." In all those examples, the point is the change in what the burgher has been "led to expect." Aggressive nonconformity in Emerson's day and surrealist obscurity in Joyce's day were a justified heroic revolt against philistine stereotypes. They were weapons of liberation in those days because they gave their public what it did not expect. But the battleline reversed itself as soon as the public of the Big Magazines did expect "nonconformists in the Brando tradition" and as soon as the more rarified public of the Little Magazines did expect surrealist obscurity. Thereupon avant-garde became one more rearguard: the arthritic somersaults of aging *enfants terribles*.

The battleline reversed itself when the weapons (intellectual, artistic, political) of anti-philistine liberation were no longer denounced but adopted by the philistine enemy himself. They became, in subtly changed form, *his* weapons, now turned against the creative camp of their origin. Thereby *he* mass-produces these once-personal creations; "packages" them more "attractively" than before; commits adulteration. But many gallant old veterans of the creative camp, still nursing their honorable scars of the anti-burgher wars of the 1920's, fail to take that reversal into account. Hence, their sincere indignation when their own weapons, now mere stereotypes, are criticized (as being those of the enemy) by younger writers in their own anti-philistine camp. The old veterans retort in effect: "Traitors, you have abandoned liberalism in politics, avant-garde in literature. By criticizing the stereotyping of liberalism and avant-garde, you are guilty of that ultimate crime: playing into Wrong Hands." Heresy, loathsome enough to an open conformist, is ten times as loathsome to these nonconformists, except when it is one of their own official heresies.

The evidence for the reversed battleline is more obvious in literature than politics. In politics, revivals of the old anti-philistine battleline do admittedly become urgently necessary on certain occasions. Such an occasion was the hucksterdom that had its Indian summer after the Republican victory of 1952. But Indian summers don't stay; the future of American middlebrow tastes will not be with the real-estate salesmen but with their pretentious, chic-hungry sons, not with the George Babbitts but with what we have elsewhere called the Gaylord Babbitts. Those who begin by being ashamed to like the literature of Edgar Guest, will end up by being ashamed to like the Republican politics of the old inelegant hucksterdom. For "nature imitates art." And art imitates Protestant bourgeois self-haters who wish they could die young with open collars in Rome or at least sip an apéritif there.

The phrase "philistine enemy," when used so bluntly as in the preceding paragraphs, does admittedly lend itself to mis-uses, affectations. Nine out of ten who use the embarrassing word "philistine" are merely inventing a scapegoat for their frustrations or showing off their dandyism. And yet, and yet—there is one experience you can only discover empirically and, once discovered, can never forget: stick around for a while in any petty-bourgeois, two-dimensional surface-world (the surface of the stereotype without the depth of the archetype), and you will find soon enough that the philistine enemy does really exist. That enemy is a spirit simultaneously canny and mean, an overadjusted spirit irreconcilably inimical to the creative imagination.

The enemy is a spirit, not a class; concepts like "petty-bourgeois" and "philistine" are a matter of general attitude, not of any specialized economic group or regional group. The qualities noted in the philistine enemy (anti-imaginative, overadjusted, simultaneously canny and mean) may occur as well among the snob-preciosities of academe as among the heartier shop-talk of Main Street. Conversely, Main Street may as readily incubate the creative imagination as did the Greenwich Village of the old days. Owing to cities like Cincinnati, the midwest is no longer (if ever it was) the habitat only of Sinclair Lewis' caricatures but of a new creativity in music, art, letters. Owing to the standards set by catalysts like *Southwest Review, New Mexico Quarterly,* and regional writers like Thomas Hornsby Ferril, the far west and southwest, especially Texas, have a finer artistic appreciation than most of their ill-informed detractors. In real educational merit, though not yet in terms of the usual time-lag in prestige-status, our great midwestern and western universities, including those of Chicago and Berkeley, are overtaking the Ivy League ones of the eastern seaboard.

These various promising western and also southern gains are tunneling, all over our nation, ever new burrows for the creative, the unadjusted. The traditional flight, from west and south to New York, still was essential for the creativity of a Hart Crane in the 1920's. Today such a flight to the east seems outdated. So does the western status-resentment against the east, still found[2] among burghers and politicians but no longer among artists. Despite the outdated anti-western prejudice of Boston Brahmins, today philistia and anti-philistia are no longer regional (if ever they were) but evenly diffused over most of the continent, both of them too protean and intermingled for easy labeling.

Philistia being so protean, it goes without saying that the current return to orthodoxy, values, religion, tradition (best-selling novelists, uplift lecturers, peace-of-mind sermons) is 90% toadies and opportunists, forever finding pretexts to "reassure," a word usually meaning to sell out, lose nerve,

[2] Cf. the chapter "Smashing Plymouth Rock," page 193.

grovel, adjust. Still, you cannot blame the periodic returns to orthodoxy for containing more racketeers than Dostoyevskys unless you equally blame the periodic returns to rebellion for containing more racketeers than Shelleys. The remnant, in both cases equally small, saveth.

Every new philosophical, literary, or religious insight (emphatically including the new conservatism) soon finds itself adopted, adulterated by the Overadjusted Man. Often the adulteration takes the form of a metaphoric mimeographing, on the cultural mass-production market, of the style of one great writer. Thus the genuinely creative style of Ernest Hemingway gets mimeographed for the middlebrows in Robert Ruark's *Something of Value,* for the lowbrows in the books of Mickey Spillane. A similar cultural mimeographing took place in earlier centuries also. But today the process is faster, vaster than ever before, owing to a mechanization combining the highest technical competence with an incompetence in those realms of imaginativeness that lie beyond mere technique.

The philosophy of Reinhold Niebuhr is one example of this adulteration occurring against the intentions of the originator himself—and then getting partly rectified by his farsighted counter-measures.[3] A second example is the appropriation by middlebrows (college-veneered) of David Riesman's anti-middlebrow terminology. Today the lonely crowd rushes to buy an abridged pocketbook of *The Lonely Crowd* or, easier still, to read the still more abridged abridgment that appeared in a popular weekly. Purpose: to sound knowing. Consequence: exaggerated attacks against Riesman, himself a liberal, by the liberal avant-garde. Their attacks should more justly have been directed against those who jargonized and popularized him, against his own intentions, into a tool of the forces of smugness. Unless a man is to be held responsible for even his absurdest misinterpreters, it seems unjust to blame writers like Riesman for those who devaluated their coinage.

It seems equally unjust to blame the new conservatism for being devaluated by the forces of smugness into a weapon of

[3] Cf. the Niebuhr chapter, page 48.

Old Guard Republicanism and sometimes even into a weapon of such a shabby fraud as America's recent fit of thought-controlling nationalism. Properly employed, the new conservatism is a weapon of anti-smugness, challenging the shallow complacency of American optimism—liberal and Old Guard Republican alike—about man and material progress. Insofar as it is political at all, the new conservatism is closer to the anti-huckster conservatism of John Adams or even to the Tory socialism of Disraeli than to the plutocratic hucksterism of government by automobile dealers.

Though more persuasive than the arguments of his neo-radical detractors and though truly valuable in other contexts, nevertheless Riesman's contrast between "the autonomous man" and "other-directedness" is not helpfully relevant to the present point about creativity. Ultimately autonomy may mean rootlessness and lawlessness, in contrast with Goethe's truth that "law alone can give us liberty." Even short of that extreme, autonomy by itself is not necessarily either creativity or liberty, nor is other-directedness necessarily their opposite. All depends on what that "other" is; to conform to the Athens of Pericles is not the same as conforming to Middletown. It may be equally other-directed to conform with those who call two plus two four and those who call two plus two five, but the Unadjusted Man is delighted to commit the former kind of other-directedness and loses no liberty thereby. He is not self-analytically concerned about how autonomous his ego feels at any given moment. He is more concerned with what kind of roots, *beyond* the ego, his values and rival values are anchored in. The concepts "roots" and "archetypes" firmly distinguish the Unadjusted Man from the three otherwise extremely valuable classifications made by Riesman (other-directed, inner-directed, autonomous). The meaningful moral choice is not between conforming and nonconforming but between conforming to the ephemeral, stereotyped values of the moment and conforming to the ancient, lasting archetypal values shared by all creative cultures.

Archetypes have grown out of the soil of history: slowly,

painfully, organically. Stereotypes have been manufactured out of the mechanical processes of mass production: quickly, painlessly, artificially. They have been synthesized in the labs of the entertainment industries and in the blueprints of the social engineers. The philistine conformist and the ostentatious professional nonconformist are alike in being rooted in nothing deeper than the thin topsoil of stereotypes: the stereotypes of Babbitt Senior and Babbitt Junior respectively.

The traumatic uprooting of archetypes was the most important consequence of the world-wide industrial revolution. This moral wound, this cultural shock was even more important than the economic consequences of the industrial revolution. Liberty depends on a substratum of fixed archetypes, as opposed to the arbitrary shuffling about of laws and institutions. The distinction holds true whether the shuffling about be done by the a priori abstract rationalism of the eighteenth century or by the even more inhuman and metallic mass-production of the nineteenth century, producing new traumas and new uprootings every time some new mechanized stereotype replaces the preceding one. The contrast between institutions grown organically and those shuffled out of arbitrary rationalist liberalism was summed up by a British librarian on being asked for the French constitution: "Sorry, sir, but we don't keep periodicals."

II

Every overadjusted society swallows up the diversities of private bailiwicks, private eccentricities, private inner life, and the creativity inherent in concrete personal loyalties and in loving attachments to unique local roots and their rich historical accretions. Apropos the creative potential of local roots, let us recall not only Burke's words on the need for loyalty to one's own "little platoon" but also Synge's words, in the Ireland of 1907, on "the springtime of the local life," where the imagination of man is still "fiery and magnificent and tender." The creative imagination requires private elbow-room, free from the pressure of centralization and the pressure of adjustment to a mass average. This requirement holds true even when the centralization is benevolent and even when the mass average replaces sub-average diversities. Intolerable is the very concept of some busybody benevolence, whether economic, moral, or psychiatric, "curing" all diversity by making it average.

Admittedly certain kinds of diversity are perfectly dreadful; they threaten everything superior and desirable. But at some point the cure to these threats will endanger the superior and the desirable even more than do the threats themselves. The most vicious maladjustments, economic, moral, or psychiatric, will at some point become less dangerous to the free mind than the overadjustment needed to cure them. In both the preceding sentences, the qualifying phrase is: "at some point." It is a clear gain, up to a point, to replace the sub-average; but past that margin of diminishing returns, the mass-average cannot replace the sub-average without replacing the above-average also.

Some American educators assume it is to the interests of "the greatest good of the greatest number" to let them rise up to an average level of education *even* in cases when the price of that desirable rise is the disappearance of the above-average along with the sub-average. But to preserve the above-average is also to the interest of the average and sub-average—is, therefore, justified not only by aristocratic principles but by the democratic principle of "the greatest good of the greatest number." The existence of the average, the existence of society as a whole, is parasitic upon—is doomed without—the moral, scientific, intellectual, and economic contributions of the unadjusted, above-average minority.

In earlier centuries, illiterate did not mean uncultured. The average product of modern mass-education does admittedly know how to read (*what* he reads, not books certainly, is notorious by now). Does his overprized literacy bring him as much culture and meaning as the medieval illiterate derived from the concrete local rhythms of his life? It was a life too brutal for us to idealize retroactively yet meaningful with an elaborate pattern of churchbells, festivals, fairs, unwritten traditions, significant rituals. Since then, the quantitative gain in mass literacy and higher schooling has been enormous. Not so the qualitative gain:

Education for all . . . leads to education for none. . . . If school standards are geared to an almost invisibly low average there is not much real education available for anyone, even for the gifted. . . . There is no use in priding ourselves on the operation of the democratic principle if education loses much of its meaning in the process. . . . The great problem . . . will be the preservation of minority culture against the many and insidious pressures of mass civilization. . . . The rising flood of students is very much like the barbarian invasions of the early Middle Ages, and then the process of education took a thousand years.[4]

The solution is not a step backwards towards illiteracy; that would be reactionary in the wicked sense of the word. The solution is a step forward toward a sharper distinction between elementary and university education. Elementary education must continue democratically, unlimited for all. The university level should be limited to a far smaller élite than today by demanding far higher standards, standards not of money but of ability and effort, backed by far larger financial scholarships to keep access to the élite open to all.

Nothing can mechanically "produce" unadjustedness. But at least some studies—the "impractical" literary classics—provide it with more fertile soil than does "education for citizenship." The latter slogan has led to overadjustment in life, McCarthyism in education. The stress of many liberals on teaching ephemeral civic needs instead of permanent classics gave the anti-liberal demagogues their opening for trying to terrorize education into propagandizing for "Americanism." What "progressive education" forgot was this: its word "citizenship" would often be defined in practice not by some lofty John Dewey but by some thought-controlling politician, interested in garnering not wisdom but votes.

Yet all these seemingly irresistible pressures of overadjustment can be triumphantly resisted, after all, if the Unadjusted

4 Professor Douglas Bush, the *New York Times Magazine*, January 9, 1955.

Man makes full use of his many available burrows. The very vastness of America's machinery of depersonalization makes it easier in America than in "old cultured Europe" to safeguard undisturbed the burrows of the creative imagination. They often occur where least expected: in the drabbest, most bustling metropolis. So does the sure-footed sandpiper (to vary the metaphor) trace his free patterns unscathed between the crushing huge waves.

To rely on burrows does not mean to become isolated, deracinated. Such sane-asylums for individuality, spreading contagious health amid mechanized conformity, need never degenerate into the inhuman aloofness of the formalist, ivory-tower view of the artist. It is the strength of the Unadjusted Man, not his weakness, that a fraternal moral reaction binds him lovingly to the society he dodges even when most tempted towards isolation by a narrowly aesthetic reaction. A mere anarchic individualism, a mere bohemian nonconformity, means isolation *from* society; the conservative individualism of the Unadjusted Man means more elbow-room *within* a more organic belongingness. That distinction parallels the earlier one between maladjusted and unadjusted respectively.

When a mechanized society makes the individual part of the mass, it does not thereby increase his sense of organic belongingness but replaces it with two things: first, the mutually isolating cash-nexus; second, the synthetic, mechanical, inorganic belongingness of external stereotypes, mass-produced by the entertainment industry or by statist social engineers. It is a liberal oversimplification to see the contrast as the free individual versus the shackles of traditional unity. The real contrast is between an archetypal, organic unity of individuals and a stereotyped, mechanical unity of masses.

Our stress of the need for organic unity requires one cautionary qualification: even the coldest cash-nexus, the crassest commercialism is preferable by far to a hysterically exaggerated kind of organic unity, a kind which, instead of its proper function of fulfilling and sustaining the individual, swallows him up and relieves him of personal responsibility. Such an unbalanced organic unity is usually the hysterical counter-extreme to a preceding atomization of society: for example, the reaction of German romanticism against French rationalism. That reaction characterized the social philosophers of German romanticism: Adam Müller, Joseph Görres, Karl von Vogelsang, K. L. von Haller, partly Hegel. They made a cult of collectivity—"folk" in some cases, the state in others—as the only identity, the only responsibility. That cult had its familiar diabolistic consequences, reaching the vulgarized Nazi level from romanticism via Richard Wagner. To avoid such consequences, the basic unit must always remain the individual, his identity as a personality as well as his responsibility ethically. But in the American tradition there is no danger of that exaggerated organic unity. Instead, the two characteristic and alternating dangers in our particular context are an inorganic, state-contrived unity and an atomistic, deracinated individualism. Therefore, the cautionary qualification against making a de individualizing cult of the organic, while urgently relevant to continental Europe, is not relevant to the primarily American focus of the present study.

In contrast both with the anti-individual organicism of German romantics and the anti-organic individualism of Anglo-American hucksters, Coleridge best expressed that mutual fulfilment of organic unity and individuality which characterizes Burkean conservatives:

The difference between an inorganic and an organic body lies in this: in the first—a sheaf of corn—the whole is nothing more than a collection of the individual parts or phenomena. In the second—a man—the whole is everything and the parts are nothing. A State is an idea intermediate between the two, the whole being a result from, and not a mere total of, the parts,—and yet not so merging the constituent parts in the result, but that the individual exists integrally within it.[5]

The phrase "the individual exists integrally within it" is basic to the unexaggerated, Coleridgean-Burkean view of the organic. That view is compatible with Anglo-American individualist tra-

[5] Samuel Coleridge, *Table Talk*, London, 1835; item of December 18, 1831.

ditions; it reinforces our earlier point that the real choice ahead is not between indiscriminate conforming and nonconforming nor between unity and individualism but between an organic, spontaneous unity of individuals and a mechanical, state-coerced unity of massmen.

Unfortunately the European concept "massman" came to America not from its great originators, Burckhardt and Nietzsche, but via its popularizer, the brilliantly learned but over-simplifying Ortega y Gasset. "Massman" is a valid enough term for the American Overadjusted Man but only on condition that the middleclass nature of the American masses is first recognized and that "massman" is not made synonymous with workingman. Wealthy would-be conservatives, above all the prissy suburban "despisers of the mob," flatter themselves handsomely by assuming that "mass" means only manual worker and that they themselves are not massmen but rugged individualists. Hence the snobbish illusion that individualism is best protected from the mass by an anti-worker, narrowly commercialist politics and economics.

Self-flattery is self-deception; on the one-way traffic, ever upward, of America's ladder to heaven, each massman defines the masses as everybody below whatever rung he left one jump ago. Never is our new suburban more fully a creature of the masses he despises than when he is in the act of despising them. Like a human boomerang hurled into space by the fast tempo of American industrial life, the further he departs from the mass, the further he is really returning. In the American wonderland, the real massman is that fellow over there in the Buick who buys his mass-produced "popular edition" of Ortega's *Revolt of the Masses* because he feels so superior to the massman.

"Massman" is a valid term of reproach when used in its proper, classless meaning of rootless overadjustedness, stereotyped leveling, and direct, uncanalized mob pressure. To use "masses" as a verbal club against industrial workers only, instead of against bourgeois mobs also, had already long been a pretext for economic greed and rightist extremes in the big political arena. By failing to clarify, at least in the small intellectual arena, his overliteral use of "massman," Ortega did real harm; he inadvertently compounded that old confusion of the big arena on a more rarefied level that had hitherto been relatively immune from anti-worker snobbishness.

Nobody who has observed concretely the mobs of Long, Coughlin, or Peron will doubt that often "massman" does include millions of manual workers. But it is at least as likely to include petty-bourgeois businessmen on the make, above all in the case of the first and still basic unleashing of the massman in America: the Jacksonian revolution. This was a revolution of majority egalitarianism—but with middleclass, not worker psychology—against the aristocratic individualism and minority rights bequeathed by the two conservative foundations of American liberty: the Federalist heritage from New England, the Calhoun heritage from the south. The Jacksonian petty-middleclass massman, an intolerant conformist and keeper-up with the Joneses, still remains the basic type of American overadjustedness in the big political arena (just as the very different Gaylord Babbitt type does in the small intellectual arena). That political type remains remarkably the same, whether in his left-wing revolutionary role of the western Populist days or in his right-wing, would-be conservative role of the prosperous and anti-communist 1950's. He is merely a "would-be" conservative because in reality he radically uproots the basic cultural and ethical archetypes by the very act[6] of coercively conserving his latest stereotypes as if they were eternal truths. Conversely, the trade-union movement in the English-speaking world (see pages 84–87) often represents not the massman or Overadjusted Man but an anti-modern, unconsciously conservative protest against massman rootlessness and cash-nexus loneliness: a protest of an essentially medieval, organic spirit of community cooperation and its uncommercial human loyalties.

Psychological type cuts across economic class and seems the sounder basis of the two for classification. A white-collar

[6] Cf. the chapter "The New American Right," page 162.

burgher and a manual worker may both belong or neither belong to the overadjusted mass, depending on individual circumstance. Moreover, the burgher also "works," and the worker often also "burghers" or hopes his son will. As with "left" and "right," the partial discarding of such partly misleading phrases requires a rethinking that has only barely begun. For example, there needs to be a halt to an overinsistent contrast between capitalist materialism and Marxism. Although the former is by far the lesser evil of the two, they seem to warrant less contrast than comparison: two triumphs of mechanized quantity over personal quality, two triumphs against which Metternich's monarchic order had shielded Europe for half a century and against which the lingering spirit of the American Federalists had similarly shielded America during 1787–1828.

From the viewpoint of the cultural and psychological consequences of their quantitative, mass-production spirit, both European Marxism and American business materialism sometimes seem minor (though rival) variations of the same surrender to rootless stereotypes, to mass overadjustedness. Though the Unadjusted Man vastly prefers the American version of the two, he does so for an unflattering, negative reason: America's aforementioned burrows of creative individuality. These burrows will be increasingly rare in a Europe becoming more gadget-giddy, TV-avid, traffic-jammed, and "Americanized" than America ever was. These increasing crannies for unadjustedness in America refute the old-world cliché ("You Americans with your speed, speed, speed and Frigidaires!") about our supposed surrender to soulless materialism. America's cultural burrows are often left intact not out of appreciation but indifference; that fact does not reduce their value, their creativity.

The third alternative to the European-Marxist and American-bourgeois variations of the massman is the unadjusted yet traditional individualist, so radically independent of both Marxist and bourgeois overadjustment because so conservatively rooted. This third alternative has been better expressed in artistic symbols than in mere political ideologies; its American voices are Melville, Hawthorne, Henry Adams, Faulkner, Irving Babbitt, and sometimes Poe, Vachel Lindsay, Hart Crane; its European voices Coleridge, Goethe, Tocqueville, Burckhardt, Nietzsche, and sometimes Dostoyevsky and Donoso Cortés.

During 1848–1918 in Europe (after the crash of the Metternich system) and after the Jacksonian revolution of 1828 in America, well-meaning liberal egalitarians released Ortega y Gasset's massman from the traditional spiritual and hierarchical restraints of centuries. Today they cannot educate him up to their own valuable liberal ideal of tolerant individualism; to release is easier than to redeem. So they are among the first to be swallowed up by the intolerance, the coercive stereotypes of the genie they themselves have released from the bottle. Whether as radical left or nationalist right (distinctions increasingly secondary), the Overadjusted Man is rapping at the door. Stop him who can.

Chapter Three IN PRAISE OF MAD

SQUIRES: The Feudal Origin of the

Unadjusted Man

"The nobles have been essential parties in the preservation of liberty
. . . against kings and people. . . . The numbers of men in all ages have
preferred ease, slumber, and good cheer to liberty. . . . Blind, undis-
tinguishing reproaches against the aristocratical part of mankind, a
division which nature has made and we cannot abolish, are neither pious
nor benevolent. . . . It would not be true, but it would not be more
egregiously false, to say that the people have waged everlasting war
against the rights of men. . . . The multitude, therefore, as well as the
nobles, must have a check."—*John Adams, 1790*

I

The above quotation of America's first and wisest conservative and anti-egalitarian, John Adams, with its stress on the
aristocratic and feudal root of liberty, summed up the conservative nature and aim of America's Federalist founding fathers
and of the Constitution emerging from the great debate of
1787–88. The model for the Adams quotation and for the
anti-democracy of the Federalist party was the undemocratic
British parliament of the eighteenth century, as vindicated by
the mentor of the Federalists: Burke. Parliament in those days
was an exclusive gentlemen's club for Whig and Tory landed
noblemen and their protégés; they were elected by a limited
suffrage excluding the masses and even (until 1832) most
of the middle classes. Yet modern American democracy may

well envy the vigorous free speech and unlimited free debate of Burke's aristocratic parliament, a freedom unequaled by modern mass parliaments, dependent on mass elections and mass demagogy. Thus considered, feudal privilege and aristocratic individualism may be considered the true root of liberty; a leveling, democratic egalitarianism would then be liberty's true foe.

Parliamentary and civil liberties were created not by modern liberal democracy but by medieval feudalism, not by equality but by privilege. These free institutions—Magna Cartas, constitutions, Witens, Dumas, parliaments—were originally founded and bled for by medieval noblemen, fighting selfishly and magnificently for their historic rights against both kinds of tyranny, that of kings and that of the herd. Modern democracy merely inherited from feudalism that sacredness of individual liberty and then, so to speak, mass-produced it. Democracy changed liberty from an individual privilege to a general right, thereby gaining in moral sanction and gaining in quantity of freedom but losing in quality of freedom; that is, losing in the creative *intensity* of earlier aristocracies, such as Elizabethan England, the British Parliament before 1832, Renaissance Italy, or the brilliant French court that fostered Racine, Corneille, and Molière. The eighteenth-century "rotten boroughs," those much-denounced electoral seats controlled by a single noble family, sent into parliament great, freedom-defending statesmen like Pitt, Burke, Sheridan. Such men had intellectual standards too high to have assured their election with equal frequency to any democratic parliament.

But lost today is the self-confidence of the unadjusting aristocrat, secure in his sense of unchallenged personal privilege, unapologetic hereditary loot. That self-confidence produced in eighteenth-century England the wonderful Mad Squires, the attractive grand eccentrics whose battles against Roundhead middleclass morals continued even in the nineteenth and twentieth centuries, from the Byronic escapades of Lady Caroline Lamb (and the very peculiar ménages produced by the gusto for life of the great Whig landowners) to Lord

Bertrand Russell's outraging of burgher Puritans in City College of New York in the 1930's. Being out neither to fawn nor to shock, the unself-conscious squire-personality calls the basic patterns—copulation, dung, death, and a good juicy steak—by their right names. Not by the prissy, evasive euphemisms of burgher prudery. His vocabulary puts honest forthrightness above the social refinements of the climbers, the diction refinements of the insecure.

Diction "respectability" may reflect not only social insecurity but a comparable educational insecurity. Thus schoolma'am-personalities have a phobia of split infinitives and comic strips. As if their own woodenly correct infinitives and uncomic digest magazines of middlebrow uplift were more "cultured" than an ungrammatic lowbrow slang that is genuinely expressive or a comic strip whose roots are robustly organic. Better *L'il Abner* than Longfellow's *Excelsior* or Elbert Hubbard's *Message to Garcia*. The Mad Squire's robustness of tastes, robustness of diction need not crook a little finger at the vicar, the schoolmistress.

By striding their own way, without looking cautiously to right or left, Mad Squires avoid two overadjustments: surrender to the herd and an equally dependent (because herd-centered) defiance of the herd. This double independence requires more courage than any individual possesses by himself alone. Such courage requires, in turn, a sense of past generations bolstering it in unbroken historic continuity. Would Churchill, for example, have had the courage and independence to help England stick it out alone through the Battle of Britain, against fearful odds, had he not been bolstered by his constant awareness of his ancestor, the Duke of Marlborough and victor of Blenheim, sticking it out alone through very similar perils almost two and a half centuries earlier?

Where courage precedes and grabs, a socially-approved right to possess will often follow and confirm. Magna Carta in medieval England, the Duma in Kievan Russia, the parliament of nobles in Viking Iceland are merely three examples among many of "reactionary" feudal assertions of personal privilege being the narrow but indispensable starting-point of modern universal liberties. The *courage* to be a Mad Squire preceded historically and made possible the *right* to be unadjusted culturally, independent socially, civil-libertarian politically. Therefore, personal freedom, rightly cherished in politics by liberals and broadened into the unpolitical, cultural realm by the Unadjusted Man, originated neither in liberalism nor democracy but in medieval feudal aristocracy. Not merely the legal right of free speech but the social right of free outspokenness, the right to be eccentric without apology, is less likely, in terms of social psychology, to accompany either mass democracy or the burgher kind of respectability than to accompany feudal privilege. The spirit of feudal privilege conserves the right to not give a damn for the grubbing "seven deadly virtues" of either Calvinistic capitalists or uplift-saturated proletarians.

The feudal Mad Squire shares with the Thoreau-style anarchist several salutary bigotries, especially the prejudice against being "improved" by statist blueprints and pushed around by True Believers. The inner right to unadjustedness is forfeited by the egalitarian as the price for his outer democratic liberty, the bed-of-Procrustes "liberty" of joining the team. Democracy, though by now indispensable to our American pattern, is too outward and chummy to guarantee man's inner psychological and cultural liberties. Democracy may even threaten them more than does reactionary traditional monarchy. For democracy threatens them with what Walter Bagehot called "the tyranny of the commonplace":

> You may talk of the tyranny of Nero and Tiberius, but the real tyranny is the tyranny of your next-door neighbor. What espionage of despotism comes to your door so effectively as the eye of the man who lives at your door? Public opinion is a permeating influence. It requires us to think other men's thoughts, to speak other men's words, to follow other men's habits.

Until recently in America, the ethnic and religious minorities had the advantage once enjoyed by the eighteenth-century aristocrat, the advantage of being left inwardly alone. They were left un-Rotarian inwardly because they were so viciously discriminated against externally; like the aristocrat of yore, they were distrusted by burgher society. Hence, the disproportionately large cultural contribution from the minorities; Einsteins don't grow on every tree; here there was until recently the valuable equivalent of what once was the intellect-encouraging function of the aristocratic salon.

But now even that equivalent seems finished; the march of democratic progress in the last few years in America promises to efface both the inner gain and the outer loss suffered by minorities. The minorities can now gain more community acceptance and social equality than ever before in American history. They can gain it by the easy expedient of knowing the baseball scores, waving the flag, and grinning from ear to ear. The flag-waving serves to refute in advance the slanders of the bigots. The grin from ear to ear proves how affable and unmysterious any given minority really is—just folks and not in the least alien, not in the least Oriental or African or whatever else the particular minority and the slander of it happens to be. The democratic external equality achieved thereby is a clear gain, both for the minority and for society, the former becoming happier, the latter more decent. But what of the creative inner freedom lost by thus becoming like everybody else? What will it mean for society and for the now "equal" individual if he must in turn inhabit a culture of sterile uniformity, knowledge of baseball scores, flaunted flags, flaunted grins? In terms of liberty, what price equality? In terms of the Unadjusted Man, what price democracy?

Even in our own post-feudal era of democracy, one of the factors sustaining personal liberties continues to be aristocratic inequality; but today it must sublimate rather than flaunt its élitism. The least honorable of its sublimations are social snobbery and a show-off cultural chicté; the most honorable are not social but seriously cultural. Here "culture" is being used not in the easy culture-vulture sense of Helen Hokinson club-women but in the hard-earned humanist sense of Goethe,

Matthew Arnold, Irving Babbitt, Barrett Wendell, Paul Elmer More, meaning: value-conserving, ethics-enhancing. Thus defined, humanistic culture is the most honorable modern sublimation of feudal inequalities because it alone stands up against brute material force and says no. To reverse a much-quoted Nazi slogan: when I hear the word "revolver," I release the safety-catch of my culture.

II

The virtue of conservatives is to stress that liberty depends on traditional law; their vice is to overlook the frequent ethical discrediting of law by economic exploitation and its psychological and aesthetical discrediting by a literal-minded burgher woodenness, stultifying the free play of the imagination. This psychological discrediting may exasperate the anti-burgher aristocrat into radical lawlessness against the status quo, even or especially when the status quo benefits him economically and does not oppress him politically. The burgher "neighborhood tyranny" mentioned by Bagehot may exasperate the élitist individualist into striking a flamboyantly progressive posture politically, not for objective social motives nor to bring ethical amelioration in economics but for psychological and aesthetic reasons: *pour épater les bourgeois.*

This radicalism of aesthetic exasperation is an important psychological process, readily documented by concrete observations all round us. Yet it goes unanalyzed and even unlabeled because it does not fit, being illogical, into the logical analysis-schemes and label-schemes of our political science and also because aesthetic motives are mistakenly considered a characteristic of a few strange people called "artists," without political consequence, instead of a characteristic universally human, with constant political consequences, sometimes (as in Wagner, Céline, Pound) sinister ones. Let us label this world-wide process "the dandy-revolt": a subjective radicalism for the masses and against privilege that emerges from a situation objectively conservative and aristocratic and that aims not at responsible political, economic, or ethical gains but at an irresponsible, vaguely metapolitical nihilism against all established law and ethics. America, too, had its equivalent of the dandy-revolt: the ivied-college parlor radicalism (as opposed to objective, responsible radicalism) of the 1930's. Literary observers are more likely to record a process concretely present but theoretically unformulated than are political theorists. Thus Stendhal:

I had, and still have, the most aristocratic of tastes. I would do everything in my power to ensure the happiness of the masses. But I think I'd rather spend a fortnight of every month in prison than have to live with shopkeepers. . . . My family were the most aristocratic people in the town. This meant I became a fanatic republican on the spot.[1]

Thus also a more contemporary observer:

[Throughout Italian history] if the aristocracy was not liberal, many liberals were aristocrats. Ettore Carafa, the Duke of Andria and General of the Partenope Republic, was compelled to lay siege to his own fee, Andria, in order to abolish his own feudal rights, and he finally had to destroy the place because its inhabitants did not want to renounce feudalism and loyalty to him. . . . Count Luchino Visconti—descendant of the Lords of Milan—is one of the best Italian stage directors and a member of the Communist Party. Many young nobles have in the past joined the Communist Party, as a gesture of aristocratic revolt, against the vulgar and sordid bourgeois world.[2]

The more conservative the objective situation—that is, the more a man's anti-bourgeois self-confidence derives from the security of his lordly privileges—the more liberal or radical may be his resultant subjective politics. A conservative, even feudal situation is often the psychological prerequisite for an anti-conservative philosophy (whether good or harmful is a separate question, depending on the situation). Therefore, the fact of the feudal root of liberty is—in view of its anti-feudal consequences—cold comfort to the snobs, sentimentalists, and gigolos, the three categories who today sigh loudest

[1] *Vie de Henri Brulard.*
[2] Luigi Barzini, Jr. in *Encounter,* London, January 1956, pages 20, 21, 27.

for "aristocracy" (usually out of ostentatious—that is, anti-aristocratic—motives). This interpretation of liberty as aristocracy ought to embarrass liberal democrats and conservative aristocrats equally, the conservative *origins* of freedom embarrassing the liberal clichés, the liberal and radical *consequences* of freedom embarrassing the conservative clichés.

The social consequences of the squirearchic spirit may be plus or minus, depending on its self-discipline, Irving Babbitt's "inner check." To justify a greater independence from outer adjustments, the squire-personality is noblesse-obligated to be more greatly disciplined within. Otherwise, it degenerates into an orbitless comet: "a desolation and a curse, the menace of the universe," in the Luciferian diction of Lord Byron, who knew the occupational disease of his own lordly role.

Democratic equality became justified in proportion as aristocratic inequality was abused. This is no plea for *cultural* democracy, which leaves literary standards to the plebiscite of the best-seller lists. But *political* democracy does have one major advantage over its rivals: its faults, its extremes, its tensions tend to cancel out, neutralize each other's harm. This fact gives democracy (but only the indirect, constitutional kind defined on page 131) a unique capacity for self-correction, for stability. While romantic counter-revolutionaries try to resurrect a no-longer-rooted medievalism, the responsible sort of conservative today staunchly supports democracy (in the above sense) in politics. But in personal way of life, he supports a cultural, nonpolitical sublimation of aristocracy by his insistence on hierarchy: a hierarchy of ethical and aesthetic standards, defying the majority-rule of mass habits, mass tastes.

Cultural aristocracy and indirect constitutional democracy are not opposed, need each other, supplement each other, are both freedom-tending. Direct mass democracy and codeless, degenerated aristocracy likewise resemble each other, are both tyranny-tending. In the words of the greatest contemporary conservative, the most wisely-mad squire of them all, Winston Churchill: "Democracy is the worst form of government, except all those other forms that have been tried from time to time."

Chapter Four   DISTINCTIONS:

Conservatives and Two Sorts of Liberals

"Whoever would found a state must presume that all men are bad by nature."—*John Adams*

"I am not among those who fear the people."—*Jefferson*

"I never could understand the doctrine of the perfectability of the human mind."—*Letter from John Adams to Jefferson, 1814*

I

The non-theological term "perpetual evil" seems preferable to the theological term "original sin" when discussing only the political and social aspects of man and of history. To insist on the inherent residue of perpetual evil in man and history does not glumly deny the accompanying presence and effectiveness of good. What it does deny is that this good is "natural" or is achievable through reshuffling only external institutions or is ever securely established or historically inevitable. The liberal sees outer, removable institutions as the ultimate source of evil; sees man's social task as creating a world in which evil will disappear. His tools for this task are progress and enlightenment. The conservative sees the inner, unremovable nature of man as the ultimate source of evil; sees man's social task as coming to terms with a world in which evil is perpetual and in which justice and compassion will both be perpetually necessary. His tools for this task are the maintenance of ethical restraints inside the individual and the maintenance of unbroken, continuous social patterns inside the given culture as a whole. Hence, the conservative distrusts direct[1] democracy, unrestrained and unpatterned.

A second contrast: in temperament liberalism often is the articulate relating of abstraction to abstraction, conservatism the inarticulate relating of the concrete to the concrete. You can take the liberal position on this second contrast while taking the conservative position on the contrast about evil. Hence, the many crosscurrents; nobody is all conservative or all liberal. Still, the greatest Anglo-American conservatives did take the conservative position on both the above contrasts: John Adams, Calhoun, Irving Babbitt, Burke, Coleridge, Disraeli, Sir Henry Maine. The qualification "Anglo-American" distinguishes these seven concrete-minded conservatives from the abstract-minded Josephe de Maistre school within Latin conservatism. The Maistre school takes the same anti-liberal position as the Anglo-Americans on the contrast over evil. But, in the second contrast, the Maistre school in Latin countries is made inflexibly and hence self-destructively reactionary by doctrinaire *a priori* abstractions as rationalistic as those of the eighteenth-century liberals it detests.

Latin conservatism also contains a wing more concrete-minded in philosophy, more moderate and flexible in politics, represented by Alexis de Tocqueville and Hippolyte Taine. The latter differ from the Maistrean doctrinaires by taking the Anglo-American or Burkean position in also the second of the two contrasts.

Conservatism is commonly equated with traditionalism; rightly so within normal limits; thereafter, rigorous qualifications arise. We must never whitewash injustice, even when traditional, toward those that lack not the will but the living standards for Burke's "unbought grace of life." In contrast with romantics and reactionaries, balanced conservatives of the John Adams and Disraeli-Churchill heritage do not go to the extreme of accepting indiscriminately *all* past traditions (cultural relativism). They overcome what is unjust in the

[1] Part III of this book, page 127, defines at length direct and indirect democracy and the conservative case for the latter.

past by assimilating the past into a broader, juster framework, thereby really strengthening rather than disrupting historic continuity. The romanticizing reactionary swallows the past indiscriminately; the Adams-Disraeli-Churchill conservative assimilates it discriminately; the liberal rationalist of the French Enlightenment line of descent pretends the past does not exist at all or can be removed by abstract decree.

At first glance one would assume that liberalism is closer to the Unadjusted Man than conservatism; nobody else proclaims intellectual independence more insistently and more sincerely than the liberals. But those who proclaim and seek do not necessarily get; those who get and have may feel no need to proclaim.[2] The very unanimity of the liberal proclamations of intellectual independence may prevent their getting it. Intellectual independence is rare and fragile, endangered by any kind of unanimity, even one on behalf of intellectual independence. The so-frequent triumphs of liberal unanimity in American history have made liberalism fat and overadjusted when it should have been lean and imaginative.

America contains two advance-guards, both equally liberal by the above definitions yet so different that the only conformity they share is their pride in imagining themselves nonconformists. (Since Rasputin, Jack the Ripper, and Hitler were also nonconformists, the liberal pride in nonconformity seems more stance than sense; hence, our earlier distinction between the maladjusted and the unadjusted.) Let us reverently label the two rival versions of American progress the la-de-da liberals and the hip-hip-hooray liberals, representing eastern Ivy League and western prairies respectively. The first kind may be wearing a Brooks Brothers sports jacket (by now an overobvious caricature of smartness, *"presque cad"*) and would never say "howdy, folks" or admit he cannot understand an obscure poem. The second kind may be wearing a double-breasted suit and have a basement for fooling around

---

[2] Apropos the distinction between claiming and getting, Alexis de Tocqueville observed in his *Recollections* of the French Revolution of 1848: "The Republic . . . promised more but gave less liberty than the Constitutional Monarchy." Today substitute "liberalism" for "Republic," "conservatism" for "Monarchy."

with carpenter equipment, the do-it-yourself sort. The first fights bravely and justifiably to save libraries from thought-control. The second fights bravely and justifiably to save natural resources from plutocracy.

The hip-hip-hooray liberal was not deeply involved, either way, in the great debate over the Popular Front and Russia. He still cannot understand (as intra-liberal quarrels in current weeklies show) why New York liberals fuss so much about that debate. He is honestly bewildered by their feud as to who has the prestige of having been disillusioned by the Hitler-Stalin pact five minutes before some in-group rival was. In the cocktail parties of the 1930's, a hip-hip-hooray liberal, meeting a beautiful young girl alone on a balcony by moon-light, would have lectured her on the frantic need for the ever-normal granary. A la-de-da liberal would, instead, have used that same golden opportunity in order to ascertain what precisely was her stand on the Moscow trials. If he did ever mention agriculture, it would have been not the struggle of western Populist farmers against excessive freight rates but the borscht output of collective farms in the second Five-Year Plan.

The hip-hip-hooray liberal—a disciple, say, of the Wisconsin Progressive Party—had never heard of the Moscow trials or, if he did, did not like them. Hence, his public status today is stronger than that of the New York liberals. But his non-entanglement in that moral spider web of the 1930's was based less on morality and knowledge than on xenophobia and ignorance: "What can red-blooded American liberals of the west expect from all those loud, excitable foreigners with funny Slavic or Jewish last names?" A key defect of western hip-hip-hooray liberals is their nationalism, passing easily into isola-tionist anti-alien bigotry (Lemke, Wheeler, Nye). A key weakness of eastern la-de-da liberals, though not themselves Marxists, is their addiction to the Marxist categories and clichés of the European left, useful for interpreting nineteenth-century Europe and for misinterpreting twentieth-century America. Despite these weaknesses, both kinds of liberals are a helpful part of the American scene; they have introduced many reforms of social justice, often sound ones.

Liberals also have the great virtue of learning from their own past errors. Conservatives adhere more stubbornly to past errors; that is the high price they pay for the gain of adhering more stubbornly to past wisdom also. Liberals themselves are wisely reassessing the Popular Front errors of la-de-da, the Populist errors of hip-hip-hooray. A third area of liberal reassessment—let us venture a prediction—will be Andrew Jackson's movement for mass egalitarianism. In the scholarly world, some surprising discoveries (along the lines of rediscovering the anti-Semitic crusade in democratic Populism) may emerge from reassessing liberal pieties about Jacksonian democracy. The time is ripe for writing a conservative *Age of John Quincy Adams* to counterbalance,[3] from the viewpoint of the old aristocratic individualism of the Federalists, the brilliant but one-sided *Age of Jackson* by Arthur Schlesinger Jr.

Via the connecting link of the nineteenth-century Populist parties, not only the New Deal, which liberals admire, but the thought-control they dread, became possible only because the Jacksonian mass-equality of the new west partly replaced the Constitutionalist, individualist aristocracy of New England. That replacement was fortunately incomplete; much of our original squirearchy remains, though forced underground;[4] so does much of our original Constitutional safeguarding of liberty against equality. Even so, that Jacksonian turning-point was the historic starting-point of our overadjusted mass culture.

A serious scholarly critic of Jacksonian democratic equality need not play into plutocratic or rightist hands so long as he keeps a sense of balance. A sense of balance will discriminate between the shoddy, overadjusted half of our liberal democratic heritage and its indispensable freedom-enhancing half. If overzealous new converts to conservatism try to discard the

[3] Subsequent to going to press, the author has received an announcement of the forthcoming book, *John Quincy Adams and the Union,* a development auguring well for the above need for balance, as the book is to be another in the series by S. F. Bemis, who (like Mr. Schlesinger, Jr.) is, of course, one of the best qualified scholars in the field.
[4] Cf. the chapter "Squires Incognito," page 239.

whole liberal heritage indiscriminately, and this in America of all countries, then they will find themselves with surprisingly little left to conserve.

II

The spirit of an age is better plumbed by documents of artistic symbolism than by such surface-skimmers as political or economic manifestos. American professors in the social sciences do not always take this fact into account. They would teach their students more about the European conservative spirit during nascent industrialism by assigning them a half-dozen pages, indicting "enlightenment" and material advance, from the journals of Baudelaire or the novels of Balzac and Dostoyevsky than by assigning some big, still-born book by some forgotten apologist for the rich. Whether pro or con, teachers dealing with a controversial subject so important as conservatism have a responsibility to know what it is about, what it means culturally and not only politically, what its primary sources are, its great basic documents.

Conservative advocates of the aristocratic spirit in America today are called unrealistic unless they settle for a business-man aristocracy (actually not aristocracy but plutocracy); no other élite, so the argument runs, has the real political and economic power. But the American form of the aristocratic spirit (the qualitative, anti-quantitative spirit) is not political nor economic but cultural. Thus American conservatism, though certainly overlapping with politics, is primarily a cultural movement, serving not economic power but the ethical and aesthetic power of the creative imagination. In different countries conservatism takes different forms; its characteristic American form is the lonely soul-searching by which our unadjusted artists transcend the overadjustment that Melville called "the impieties of progress." In their anti-optimism, in their tormenting qualms about America's external advances, our greatest literary artists of the non-Emerson, non-Whitman wing have been cultural conservatives: Cooper, Hawthorne, Poe, Melville, Henry James, Henry Adams, William Faulkner.

The important book *Hawthorne,* 1955, by the new-conservative scholar Hyatt Waggoner, defines the real American cultural tradition as "a conservative tragic sense," affirming the perpetualness of evil and rejecting liberal illusions about progress and human nature. These liberal illusions, concludes Waggoner, "were useless for any artist who would not wilfully blind himself to the existence of tragedy. . . . The 'evolutionary optimism' of . . . nineteenth-century liberalism was affronted by anyone who concerned himself with the 'deeper psychology'." Accordingly, Melville's quatrain on "Greek Architecture" still remains the best expression of the ideal animating cultural conservatism in America today:

> Not magnitude, not lavishness,
> But Form—the site;
> Not innovating wilfulness,
> But reverence for the Archetype.

To reassess America's proudest material victories—to draw the often bitter balance-sheet in an age too prosperous to be bitter—is the function of cultural conservatism. The abacus for this calculation is not economic utility nor a statistical scientific positivism but the unadjusted imagination. Conservatism is spiritual arithmetic. It calculates the price paid for progress.

Chapter Five   WHICH KIND OF

EQUALITY?

"... No rich, no poor, no kings, no subjects—only brothers. ... In the words God and Religion I see only black darkness, chains and the knout. ... I am trying to love mankind *à la Marat* ... to destroy the rest by fire and sword. ... [by] the Robespierres and the St. Justs."
—*Belinsky (1810–1848)*

"Starting from unlimited freedom, I arrive at unlimited despotism."—
Shigalov in Dostoyevsky's THE POSSESSED, 1871

The two primary types of equality should not be confused, the first legal and objective, the second psychological and subjective.[1] In the definable, tangible, explicit sphere of legal rights, equality is possible in a country like America and also desirable; inequality in that sphere weakens liberty by making it seem hypocritical. But in the indefinable, intangible, implicit sphere of cultural and social status, equality is impossible; it involves too many insatiable, semiconscious cravings of pride. When these cravings are too narrowly egotistic and, so to speak, too visceral, they oscillate, with ever more uncontrollable violence, between prestige-feelings and inferiority-feelings. That oscillation is dangerous to liberty because it leads to the overadjusted leveling imposed by envious mass-mediocrity.

Though the second (psychological) equality is impossible to satiate fully, is it at least desirable to achieve as much of it as possible? Yes and no, depending on the context. Yes, when explosive tensions of status-resentment are thereby relieved.

[1] The other types of equality, notably the extremely important one of economics, are less often goals in themselves than material means for achieving these two primary (legal and psychological) goals.

42

No, when the gain in tension-relief is outweighed by the loss in diversity, creativity, and individuality, a loss resulting from a drab herd-equality. Two current trends in American education illustrate at its worst and at its best this second equality. At its worst: equally encouraging the qualified and unqualified to proceed to college and thereby to destroy the educational standards needed for survival. At its best: removing racial segregation in schools, thereby reducing psychological bruises that would otherwise discredit as hypocritical the first (legal) equality of the Fourteenth Amendment.

Devotees of liberty ought to defend a mellowed, history-rooted, and civil-libertarian aristocracy, despite its legal and psychological inequalities, whenever the only alternative is a brutal, rootless, and thought-controlling dictatorship, despite its equalities. Many eighteenth-century liberals refused to support the civil-libertarian aristocracy of England against the murderous new Jacobin egalitarians. The democratic egalitarian terminology of the Jacobins, like that of the communists in the 1930's, sometimes had a hypnotic attraction outweighing the despotic reality behind the terminology. Hence, Tom Paine, founder of American progressivism, ended by offering to guide the anti-civil-libertarian despot Napoleon against the relatively civil-libertarian aristocracy of parliamentary England. Paine succumbed to this moral trap because the egalitarian, plebiscitarian elements in a Napoleon (today substitute Mao or Lenin) can often make a man of democratic credo forgive a Napoleon his dictatorial methods. Paine's evolution was paralleled in our own century by that of the liberal reformer Lincoln Steffens; he moved from a liberal egalitarian democracy to an amoral, pragmatic pro-communism: "I have seen the future, and it works."

A liberal cliché in the 1930's was the notion that "economic democracy" was better than our political liberty because giving more "real" equality. The equality was "real" enough: an equal opportunity for doing slave-labor in Karaganda. Fortunately American liberalism proved wise and ethical enough to outgrow the "economic democracy" double-think. But it has still not outgrown the illusion that our liberty is based primarily on the will of the people, instead of on the potentially anti-people, anti-majoritarian principles of morality, tradition, Constitution.

Though American parties are fortunately unideological (no conservative, no liberal party), two rival emotional attitudes towards equality—never abstracted into intellectual ideologies —do run through American history. The first attitude prefers liberty to equality, the second vice versa, though in practice both try to combine both. The first can be traced through George Washington, John Adams, Hamilton, the *Federalist* papers, Gouverneur Morris, John Quincy Adams, the Federalist and Whig parties. Today that tradition of a libertarian social élite, educated in the Ivy League colleges of the eastern seaboard, leads into Wall Street and relatively right-wing attitudes when canalized into economics but into social reform and civil-libertarian[2] tolerance when canalized into intellectual politics. The finest fruit of this first American attitude, overlapping both its canalizations and found in both parties, is the aristocratic, selfless service-tradition of Charles Evans Hughes, Elihu Root, Stimson, Acheson, the Christian Herter and Cabot Lodge, Jr. kind of Republicans, the Roosevelt and Stevenson kind of Democrats.

The second American attitude, preferring democratic equality to élitist liberty, can be traced through Sam Adams, Patrick Henry, R. H. Lee, Freneau, and Paine in the American Revolution, through part but certainly not all of Jefferson, then

[2] As basic as it is unacknowledged is the connection in America between a traditional, undemocratic social-intellectual élite and the supposedly democratic cause of civil liberties. Thus Daniel Bell noted in a *New Leader* article of 1954: "A few years ago I encountered Robert Morris, then counsel for the Jenner Committee on Internal Subversion. He complained of the 'terrible press' his Committee was receiving. What press, he was asked? After all, the great Hearst and Scripps-Howard and Gannett chains, as well as the overwhelming number of newspaper dailies, had enthusiastically supported and reported the work of the Committee. I wasn't thinking of them, he replied: I was thinking of the *New York Times*, the *Washington Post*, the *St. Louis Post-Dispatch*. And, to some extent, he was right. These pages, few in number, are influential as shaping 'élite' opinion. And on civil liberties, they have been on the 'liberal' side. The paradoxical fact is that, on traditional economic issues, these 'liberal' papers are conservative."

through Andrew Jackson, later into the Populists, the Bryan kind of Democrats, the La Follette Progressives, the Rotarian businessmen of the west, as well as the western anti-business radicals, and today the Kefauver kind of Democrats.

Good men, good achievements are found among both American attitudes. Liberty and equality are both major virtues, liberty the more creative. But both groups are capable of degenerating into evil. The élitist libertarians may degenerate into the predatory economic class-privileges and the selfishness which (beneath grand talk about "stubborn integrity" and "Mister Republican") supported and exploited the late Senator Taft. The democratic egalitarians may degenerate into leftist (or else, would-be conservative) massman demagogy: the punch-the-élite-in-the-nose tradition of the Populists, the sit-down strikes of the 1930's, Father Coughlin, Huey Long, and the McCarthy-Jenner agitator-type of Republicans. American politics being non-ideological, the two degenerations or extremes need not (as abstract logic might dictate) fight each other. Instead, they often unite (today the Republican alliance of upper-class Old Guard and lower-class nationalist agitator) against the moderates of their own two groups. Thus the late Senator Taft, a clubby Yale man, an austere despiser of demagogic oratory, and hitherto in the anti-egalitarian group, joined hands temporarily with the western neo-Populist agitators in order to slander the motives and the loyalties of the General Marshalls and Achesons within his own Ivy League libertarian élite.

In the 1920's the liberal Democrat Bryan, veteran of the old western Populists, led his successful campaign to ban the teaching of evolution in Tennessee; his law remains unrepealed. Here is a clear example of academic freedom being thought-controlled not by the usual reactionary champion of privilege but by a champion of democratic equality. Those eager to exonerate democratic egalitarianism from its threat to liberty may retort: "Bryan's thought-control of schools in Tennessee (forbidding them to teach evolution) is merely the embittered old age of our democratic egalitarian hero and should not be read back from the 1920's into the saner Bryan and saner Populism of the 1890's." But already in the 1890's, the folksy religiosity of the Populists imposed a now-forgotten but important thought-control upon western rural areas. The surface motive was the old Bible-belt Fundamentalism. The deeper motive was the anti-urbanism and anti-intellectualism by which rural westerners expressed their status-insecurity in the presence of a city-slicker east.

These earlier thought-controllers of western colleges and libraries were not, as sometimes today, wealthy right-wing businessmen but folksy, pious egalitarians, battling radically against Wall Street's "cross of gold." In 1890 Thorstein Veblen was denied the right to teach at St. Olaf's College in Minnesota: not because capitalist reactionaries objected to his anti-capitalist democratic egalitarianism but because the democratic egalitarian Populist milieu insisted, on grounds of Fundamentalism, on thought-controlling his non-political, religious views. Thus does the craving for democratic equality often become the enemy of civil liberties when transferred from an attainable legal equality to an insatiable psychological and cultural equality.

The Populist assault upon the free and aristocratic colleges of the late nineteenth century drastically lowered their intellectual standards and academic freedom. Often the colleges seemed to provoke the assault by being a rich man's club: privileged, condescending, undemocratic. These admitted right-wing faults did not justify the left-wing attacks on academic freedom. Nor did the left-wing faults of the 1930's, including the execrable communist infiltrations of campuses, justify the recent right-wing attacks on academic freedom. Its consistent defenders must expect to get called aristocrat-coddlers by the left, commie-coddlers by the right. Since two wrongs don't cancel out, liberals cannot talk away the threat of equality to liberty by correctly noting that the Populist demagogy was often no worse than that of their enemies, the trusts, railways, and eastern finance. Nor can Republican nationalists talk away their threat to liberty by correctly noting the incomparably greater threat of world communism.

Out of the western Populist movement came such apostles of thought control and racist bigotry as Tom Watson, Cole Blease, Huey Long, Father Charles Coughlin and his presidential candidate William Lemke, and even the late Senator Pat McCarran. The demagogy of the Populists and La Follette Progressives was partly preferable to the present Republican nationalist demagogy because, unlike the latter, the former occasionally really did help the underprivileged it promised to help. But the fact that the Populists bled for widows and orphans does not exempt them from criticism for the harmful precedents they set for current thought-controllers. Let us hope one can be permitted to criticize those precedents without being accused by liberals of wanting to send widows and orphans back to sweatshops. The point is to distinguish between the valid social gains of America's various Jeffersonians, Jacksonians, and La Follettes and their invalid Rousseauist philosophy of human nature. Now that the social gains are safely rooted, is it not time to re-examine more rigorously the invalid philosophy? Cannot our aging New Deal liberals wake up to the fact that the child labor laws, the Wagner Act, and SEC have become victorious long ago and are no longer problem-number-one? The horse they ride is wood, the horse they flog is dead. Instead of trumpeting about the admitted need for those old, long-achieved battles, is it not time to ask why material social reforms have failed to do for man's spirit what they have done so ably for his body?

Chapter Six NIEBUHR IN THE

CONFORMISTS' DEN

"We live in a paradise of comfort and prosperity, but this paradise is suspended in a hell of global insecurity. This . . . is a parable of the entire human situation: Suffering from ultimate insecurity, whatever its immediate securities. . . ."—*Reinhold Niebuhr*

Two aspects of Reinhold Niebuhr are here relevant: first, his blend of religious conservatism with New Deal social reform; second, the way in which his independent-minded philosophy is threatened by the adulteration discussed on page 16. One of the best sources for his ideas are his two series of the Gifford lectures of 1939 at Edinburgh, later published together in 1951 in a convenient one-volume edition, *The Nature and Destiny of Man.* Also important are *The Children of Light and the Children of Darkness,* 1944; *Christian Realism and Political Problems,* 1953; *The Self and the Dramas of History,* 1955.

Compare two photographs: Charles Baudelaire and this angular, harsh-faced professor of the Union Theological Seminary, who for years was pastor of a congregation of automobile workers in Detroit. The eyes of both have the same intensity, the same bitter integrity. Like Kierkegaard,[1] Niebuhr is not merely "painfully sincere" but downright cadaverously sincere. The spiritual demands of his outspoken sermons indict not

[1] Not that the often-similar Kierkegaard can be actually equated, as is sometimes done, with Niebuhr theologically. It is true that Kierkegaard started out with "justification by faith alone." But it foreshortens the picture to ignore, as do many American philosophers, Kierkegaard's final six months of the "Attack on Christendom" and the feverish political action. For these points see Peter Drucker's article, "The Unfashionable Kierkegaard," in *Sewanee Review,* autumn, 1949.

only the dead rottenness behind a godless hedonism but also the self-deception behind a facile, overconfident idealism:

> The error of our tradition has been to forget that man is a creature as well as creator. . . . Virtue becomes vice through some defect in the virtue. . . . The ironic elements in American history can be overcome, in short, only if American idealism comes to terms with the limits of all human striving. . . . America's moral and spiritual success in relating itself creatively to a world community requires not so much a guard against the gross vices, about which the idealists warn us, as a reorienta-tion of the whole structure of our idealism.[2]

We may define the characteristic Niebuhr synthesis as an attempt to unite material social improvements with a return to a traditional dogmatic Protestantism. This same man, on the same day, can address a socially optimistic rally of "Americans for Democratic Action" and deliver a theologically pessimistic sermon on the innate depravity of all mortal "action," whether "American democratic" or otherwise. Consequently Niebuhrism has its left and right deviationists. At the point where both invite sarcasm by racing beyond their master's gospel, the former may be labeled the Extroverted Progressors, the latter the Introspective Brooders. Both neglect one or the other of Niebuhr's two wars: the inner war against evil, the outer one against social wrongs.

His *Irony of American History*, 1952, attempted, among other things, to bridge this left-right split. The book exhorted Americans to resist "both the enemy's demonry and our vanities"; that is, to "preserve our civilization" both from our Soviet foe and from our own "human frailties." For, "if we perish, the ruthlessness of the foe would be only the secondary cause. The primary cause would be . . . eyes too blind." Christian spiritual love is Niebuhr's solution for bridging social conscience and otherworldly conscience within ourselves. By loving God and neighbor simultaneously, a return to the original Christian spirit is to end the disassociation between the mystical and social parts of human nature.

[2] *The Irony of American History* (1952).

In politics and economics Niebuhr's viewpoint is more New Deal liberal than Adam Smith liberal. But really his viewpoint implies a third alternative, hard to label. Though supporting most of the economic program of the New Dealers, his motive for supporting their program is more religious, less economic than theirs. His motive is closer to a pre-Marxist Christian socialism than to the materialist pragmatism characterizing many (not all) New Dealers and ADA liberals.

Yet the term "Christian socialist" is likewise misleading for his elusive position. The term suggests a naive optimism about the capacity of mortal bureaucrats to implement Christian social ideals. He is more suspicious of statism than any socialist, Christian or otherwise. And he is more seriously concerned with Protestant theology and spiritual inwardness than was the external and shallow "muscular Christianity" of much of the nineteenth century. Because he carries his humane ideals neither to this-worldly statist socialism nor to an otherworldly escapist promise of pie in the sky, his pessimism avoids respectively the optimist materialism of the nineteenth century and that century's pseudo-religious, optimist sentimentality.

The gap between Niebuhr's religious, non-statist social democracy (writ small) and the usual materialist, statist Social Democracy (writ large) is the gap between Kierkegaard and Marx. Niebuhr reminds both socialists and businessmen that power is power and hence corrupts, whether labeled "welfare state" or "free enterprise." His synthesis of liberalism and conservatism, like that of Adlai Stevenson, distrusts equally a regimented public statism and what Niebuhr calls the "sometimes quite inordinate powers and privileges" of private wealth. By distrusting all kinds of power equally, these liberal-conservatives, Stevenson and Niebuhr, are in the tradition of the liberal Lord Acton, whose most-quoted remark needs no repetition here, and in the tradition of the conservative Federalist John Adams, who wrote: "Absolute power intoxicates alike despots, monarchs, aristocrats, and democrats."

Will Herberg, one of America's ablest exponents of Burke, writes in the *New Republic* (May 16, 1955): "Reinhold

Niebuhr, for all his involvement in liberal politics—or perhaps precisely *because* of his involvement—is to be counted among the 'neo-conservatives' of our time, who own kinship with Edmund Burke, rather than among the liberals, who draw their inspiration from Tom Paine and the French Enlightenment." The phrase "precisely *because*" gets at the heart of the Niebuhr synthesis. Many ADA liberals err in giving too little weight to his conservative philosophy. Many new conservatives err in giving too little weight to his cooperation with liberal politics (see page 104).

Philosophical conservatism is the awareness of what Niebuhr calls "the limits of all human striving, the fragmentariness of all human wisdom, the precariousness of all human configurations of power, the mixture of good and evil in all virtue." His most important achievement has been to re-establish this awareness, this "deep sadness of history," in terms of our own day. Thereby he is educating his liberal-intellectual readers and followers out of whatever faith in rationalist-progressive utopias may have survived in them from the illusions of the 1930's. Of his many books on this theme, *The Self and the Dramas of History,* 1955, gives one of his best brief definitions:

The universal inclination of the self to be more concerned with itself than to be embarrassed by its undue claims may be defined as "original sin." The universality of the inclination is something of a mystery. . . . This bondage of the will to the interests of the self is what is meant by "the bondage of the will" in Christian theory.

Three predictions. Before the end of the decade, Niebuhr will be our most influential social thinker. He will deserve this status because of his insight and integrity. Yet he will have this status thrust upon him not because of his deserts but in spite of them, and because of the accidental confluence of three fads.

The three fads are progressivism, artiness, and the religiosity of a mere fad-conservatism. All three fads overadjust Niebuhr into their respective images because he does unavoidably use their favorite magic words, activating their respective conditioned responses. The magic word "social reform" automatically titillates the progressivism of their political weeklies. The magic word "irony" (title of his book of 1952), not to mention "ambiguity," sets the artiness of their literary quarterlies purring. And when the third magic word, "original sin," flatters their Eliot-steeped sophistication, then snob-ecstasies swoon into a triple consummation: leftishly to eat their progress-cake; artily to have it too; and neo-conservatively to spice it with the tang of religious guilt.

Used rigorously and unglibly, "social reform," "irony," and "original sin" are valid terms for needed concepts. It is not Niebuhr's fault when, despite his partly effective counter-measures, these concepts become the pet toys of every intellectual playboy of the western world. The fifteenth century stopped its Niebuhr (Savonarola) by burning him. Today the forces of mere prestige—the Rotarianism of the highbrows—have a more effective method than the stake. They make their victim chic. They did it already to Baudelaire, they did it to Kierkegaard, they did it to Kafka: fashionableness is the ambush endangering the wise and good message of Reinhold Niebuhr.

Chapter Seven   NIETZSCHE AS

CHALLENGE TO THE OVER-

ADJUSTED MAN

"It is the age of the masses: they lie on their belly before everything that is massive. And so also in politics. A statesman who rears up for them a new Tower of Babel, some monstrosity of empire and power, they call "great"—what does it matter that we more prudent and conservative ones do not meanwhile give up the old belief that it is only the great thought that gives greatness to an action?"—*Nietzsche*, BEYOND GOOD AND EVIL, 1886

The necessary priority the Unadjusted Man places on creative inner reverie does not mean a self-centered egotism, ethically neutral or socially unengaged. The ethical and social role of the unadjusted was best defined by Friedrich Nietzsche: good writers as "the bad conscience of their age." "What," he added in 1888, "does a philosopher demand of himself, first and last? To overcome his time in himself. . . ." Other than Nietzsche, here are past examples of the Unadjusted Man in this role; incompatible with any party line, our examples range from democratic socialists to conservative monarchists: George Orwell ("conscience of his generation"), Simone Weil, Bernanos, Irving Babbitt in our own century; Tocqueville, Taine, Baudelaire, Thoreau, Hawthorne, Melville, Hoelderlin, Gentz, Kierkegaard, Burckhardt, Coleridge in the previous century. In any century, what counts is not the quantity but the intensity of its unadjusted ones. Characteristic is their capacity for being passionately committed to the problems of their age yet transcending them agelessly; socially responsible yet in some innermost core aloof; traditionally, conservatively rooted yet thereby strengthened, by those very roots, for speaking out—in creativity, in crisis—with a *personal* voice, unchainably unique.

Unadjusted-toward-stereotypes does not mean deracinated-from-archetypes. Here is Nietzsche on the coming "uprooting of culture" (*Thoughts Out of Season,* 1873–76):

The growing rush and the disappearance of contemplation and simplicity from modern life [are] the symptoms of a complete uprooting of culture. The waters of religion retreat and leave behind pools and bogs. The sciences . . . atomize old beliefs. The civilized classes and nations are swept away by the grand rush for contemptible wealth. Never was the world worldlier, never was it emptier of love and goodness. . . . Everything, modern art and science included, prepares us for the coming barbarism . . . the selfishness of grasping men and military dictators.

Every believer in American democracy rightly cherishes the way in which equality of rights has enhanced outer political liberty. The way in which it can diminish inner psychological liberty, by exalting the Overadjusted Man, is less welcome a field of discussion. Such a discussion, though culminating in the America of today, properly begins with the predictions of Nietzsche's *Beyond Good and Evil,* 1886:

. . . "Equality of rights" could all too easily be converted into an equality in violating rights. By that I mean, into a common war on all that is rare, strange, or privileged, on the higher man, the higher soul, the higher duty, the higher responsibility, and on the wealth of creative power and mastery. Today the concept of "greatness" entails being noble, wanting to be by oneself, being capable of being different, standing alone. . . .

In the same book, Nietzsche saw mass democracy and tyranny not as opposites but as related aspects of the same overadjustedness, both of them enemies of personal liberty, individualism, and aristocracy:

The democratic movement in Europe . . . will probably arrive at results on which its naïve propagators and panegyrists, the apostles of "modern ideas," would least care to reckon. The same new conditions under which on an average a leveling and mediocritizing of man will take place—a clever gregarious man—are in the highest degree suitable to give rise to exceptional men of the most dangerous and attractive qualities. For, while the capacity for adaptation, which is every day trying changing conditions, and begins a new work with every generation, almost with every decade, makes the powerfulness of the type impossible; while the collective impression of such future Europeans will probably be that of numerous, talkative, weak-willed, and very handy workmen who *require* a master, a commander, as they require their daily bread; while, therefore, the democratizing of Europe will tend to the production of a type prepared for *slavery* in the most subtle sense of the term; the strong man will necessarily in individual and exceptional cases become stronger and richer than he has perhaps ever been before—owing to the unprejudicedness of his schooling, owing to the immense variety of practice, art, and disguise. . . . The democratizing of Europe is at the same time an involuntary arrangement for the rearing of tyrants. . . .

A similar prediction of how egalitarian democracy would lead not to liberty but to totalitarianism was made by Nietzsche's contemporary and colleague at the Swiss University of Basel, the great historian Jakob Burckhardt (1818–97):

The people are being trained for mass meetings. It will end up with their howling whenever there are not at least a hundred of them in one place. . . . The big damage was done in the previous [eighteenth] century, especially by Rousseau with his preaching of the goodness of human nature. . . . As any child can see, this resulted in the complete dissolution of the concept of [legitimate] authority in the heads of mortals, whereupon they periodically had to be subjected to naked [illegitimate] force instead. The only imaginable solution would be if at last everybody, big and small, would get that crazy optimism [about progress] out of his head. . . . The world approaches two alternatives, either full democracy or an absolute lawless despotism. The latter will no longer be run by dynasties, for these are too soft-hearted, but by a military command disguised as republicanism. . . . A real power is building up which will make damned short work of suffrage, popular sovereignty, material welfare, industry, etc. . . .

I have a premonition which sounds like utter folly, and yet it will not leave me: the military state will become one single vast factory. Those hordes of men in the great industrial centers cannot be left indefinitely to their greed and want. What must logically come is a definite and supervised stint of misery, with promotions and uniforms, daily begun and ended to the sound of drums. . . . In the delightful twentieth century, authoritarianism will raise its head again, and a terrifying head it will be.[1]

In Nietzsche and Burckhardt the German language had its last great voices of the old Goethean individualism amid the triumphant Bismarck era of statism and mechanized material power. In their diagnoses of the threat of egalitarian conformity, Nietzsche and Burckhardt have been exceeded by none and equaled only by certain pages of Maistre, Cortés, Tocqueville. Nietzsche remains unequaled in anticipating our ever-increasing need today for the full, unmechanized personality. He represents no consistent ism whatever except that of honest gadfly, sometimes anarchist, sometimes conservative, always independent.

American writers assume that Freud originated the concept of unconscious sublimation of rejected impulses; Alfred Adler the concept of overcompensating the inferiority complex through aggression and status-claims; modern sociologists the concept of status-resentment as motive for nationalist mass-politics. Actually it was largely Nietzsche (his influence admitted by Freud and Adler) who originated all three concepts: sublimation, overcompensation, status-resentment.

Today in America these three Nietzschean concepts coalesce in explaining the motivation (part of it, not all) of one particular movement, the new right-wing nationalism. In that movement, an unconsciously *radical* resentment of status-humiliation (at the hands of a fancy-educated eastern-seaboard élite) gets sublimated and overcompensated into its seemingly

[1] Translated by P. Viereck from Burckhardt, *Briefe an seinen Freund Friedrich von Preen: 1864–1893*, Stuttgart, 1922. For translations of additional Burckhardt and Nietzsche documents on this theme and more details, cf. pages 81–83, 158–159, 168–170, 181–182, in P. Viereck, *Conservatism: From John Adams to Churchill*, New York and Princeton, Van Nostrand Company (Anvil pocketbook series), 1956.

"anti-radical" opposite. Namely into a self-deceiving élitist lingo of would-be "conservatism" and aggressive would-be "Americanism," often the lingo of those impatient to rise from immigrant manual-labor status into Republican suburban status.[2]

Earlier, in Nietzsche's own day, a lingo of nordic pseudo-élitism and anti-Semitic nationalism served to sublimate the status-resentment and inferiority-feelings of Germany's new petty-burgherdom. His analysis of this sublimation made Nietzsche the first man to foresee the coming world-menace of fascist nationalism. He who had declared himself "born posthumously," became Germany's first pre-natal anti-Nazi. Today his original texts have outlived the tamperings and annexations attempted by German militarists and nationalists, whose support he had repudiated in advance:

The Germans think that strength must reveal itself in hardness and cruelty; then they submit with fervor and admiration: they are suddenly rid of their pitiful weakness . . . they devoutly enjoy *terror*. That there is strength in mildness and stillness, they do not believe easily.[3]

The two leitmotifs of the present writer's *Metapolitics: From the Romantics to Hitler,* 1941, were the rival outlooks of Nietzsche, Wagner: Nietzsche as the voice warning Germany against nationalism, anti-Semitism, herd-collectivism; Wagner as the voice teaching Hitler his Aryan racism, anti-parliamentary leadership-cult, anti-aristocratic cult of the collective "folk." Though inacceptable at the time to those who preferred the then dominant economic explanations of history, that book's documented evidence for the decisive Wagner influence on Hitler has been newly confirmed by August Kubizek's *The Young Hitler I Knew* (New York, 1955). Nietzsche's was the only voice in the 1880's to say that Richard Wagner's

[2] Cf., within Part III of this book, the several chapters on America's right-wing Overadjusted Man. They were first published separately in magazine form in 1954 as a merely impressionistic, pioneering attempt to establish, by applying the Nietzschean tool of status-psychology, the close historical link between the direct democracy of our present right-wing nationalists and that of our old western Populists.

[3] *Gesammelte Werke*, XI, 112, tr. by W. Kaufmann.

folk-romanticism and anti-Semitism would make his German nationalist disciples "the destroyers of both German and European culture." In Nietzsche's own unheeded words:

The Germans . . . with their Wars of Liberation [of 1813] . . . are to blame for nationalism, this disease and madness most inimical to culture. . . . Abolish Wagner, Bismarck, and all anti-Semites . . . Fichte's lying but patriotic flatteries and exaggerations. . . . Sluggish, hesitating races would require half a century ere they could surmount such atavistic attacks of patriotism and soil-attachment and return once more to reason; that is to say, to "good Europeanism."[4]

Equally far-sighted was Nietzsche's analysis of how Wagner was habituating German youth to demagogic racist dictatorship:

German youth honors in Wagner a dictator . . . in the name of the "Chosen People," the Germans! Wagner belongs to the demagogues of art, knowing how to play upon the instincts of the masses and thereby knowing how to win over the instincts of such youths as crave power. . . . Wagner became now an oracle, a telephone from the other world. . . . I like not the agitators dressed up as heroes [like Siegfried] . . . the anti-Semites who excite the blockhead elements of the populace. The invariable success of intellectual charlatanism in present-day Germany [1887] hangs together with the desolation of the German mind, whose cause I look for in a too exclusive diet of papers, politics, beer, and *Wagnerian* music, not forgetting the condition precedent of this diet, the national vanity, "Germany, Germany above everything." . . . Richard Wagner [is] leading us to ruin.[5]

For present relevance, let us shift the application of Nietzsche from that German context to the American one. Thereupon he re-emerges as the man who said the words America most needs to hear today:

[4] E. Podach, *Nietzsches Zusammenbruch*, Heidelberg, 1930, pp. 75, 85; Nietzsche, *Beyond Good and Evil*, Modern Library, New York, n.d., pp. 171–172, 176.
[5] Nietzsche, *Die Unschuld des Werdens: Der Nachlass*, Leipzig, 1931, pp. 1, 160; *Genealogy of Morals*, Modern Library, New York, n.d., pp. 102, 172–178, 185.

One pays heavily for coming to power: power makes stupid. . . . It is the age of the masses: they lie on their belly before everything massive. . . . What does it matter that we more prudent and conservative ones do not meanwhile give up the old belief that it is only the great thought that gives greatness to an action? . . . The Germans think that strength must reveal itself in hardness. . . . That there is strength in mildness and stillness, they do not believe easily. . . . The man who would not belong in the mass needs only to cease being comfortable with himself; he should follow his conscience which shouts at him: "Be yourself! You are not really all that which you do, think, and desire now." . . . What does your conscience say? "You shall become who you are."

In Europe then as in America now, the stereotyping mold of the state threatened both the unadjusted individual and "the people." (In this particular passage, though not always elsewhere, "people" is used not in the sense of majority or mob but of traditional archetypal community.) Nietzsche on the state:

A state? What is that? . . . the coldest of all monsters. . . . "I, the state, am the people." It is a lie! Creators were they who created peoples, and hung a faith and a love over them: thus they served life. . . . Where there is still a people, there the state is not understood, but hated as the evil eye, and as sin against laws and customs. Many too many are born: for the superfluous ones was the state devised! . . . Just see these superfluous ones! Wealth they acquire and become poorer thereby. . . . There, where the state ceaseth—there only commenceth the man who is not superfluous. . . .[6]

To the good-mixer fetish in American education, Nietzsche's Zarathustra-loneliness has a relevance that today is redeemingly malicious. For example, his Zarathustra "Prologue" stated in sarcasm—"Everybody is the same: whoever feels different goes voluntarily into a madhouse"—the very same point that today gets stated in ghastly earnest on the recommendation blanks for Duke University, where each applicant must be classified under one of five adjustment ratings: "1. Very un-

[6] *Thus Spake Zarathustra* (1883–85) in *Works of Friedrich Nietzsche,* New York, Tudor, 1931 (five volumes in one); II, 64–65.

stable and poorly adjusted. 2. Occasionally demonstrates inadequacies of adjustment. 3. Satisfactory adjustment. 4. Good adjustment. 5. Exceptionally stable and well-adjusted." Such "confidential" classifications in many an American college may sometimes hound their unaware victims ever after, as inexorably as a confidential police dossier. Perhaps such chumminess-ratings even imply an unconscious police mentality, an FBI not of compulsory lawfulness but of compulsory fun. In any case these hygienic screens against unadjustedness should prevent any "unstable" Michelangelos or "bad mixer" Melvilles from sneaking into our sterilized utopia of academe.

Nietzsche was most incisive when least philosophical in the formal and academic sense of the word. He was most original not in his ponderous central arguments but in the quick, light casualness of his peripheral afterthoughts. He was the master of the parenthetical aside, saving many a trashy generalization by illogically adding to it an inspired *non sequitur*. For example, in only two casual sentences and while writing about something else, Nietzsche summed up the whole vast psychological distinction between a tradition-mellowed élite and a new one seizing power: "Whoever still wants to gain the consciousness of power, will use any means. . . . He, however, who has it, has become very choosy and noble in his tastes." Experience has taught the twentieth century to justify the value of these "choosy and noble" restraints, inherent in a traditional élite, by contrasting conservatively even the worst prison camps of monarchic times with the almost infinitely worse camps of the Nazi and Soviet parvenus.

Nietzsche speaks for himself, suffers when systematized by others, comes off best when quoted directly. Here is our own sample anthology of his quick aphorisms:[7]

1. One will rarely err if extreme actions be ascribed to vanity, ordinary actions to habit, and mean actions to fear.

[7] Order: chronological. Translations: from various editions (W. Kaufmann's the most discerning), selected according to fidelity to Nietzsche's spirit. Quotations 1–2, *Human, All Too Human*, 1878–79; 3, *The Wanderer and His Shadow*, 1880; 4–7, *Thus Spake Zarathustra*, 1883–85; 8–13, *Beyond Good and Evil*, 1886; 14–16, *Genealogy of Morals*, 1887; 17–21, *Twilight of the Idols*, 1889; 22–23, *Ecce Homo*, written 1888–89, published 1908.

2. Our destiny exercises its influence over us even when, as yet, we have not learned its nature; it is our future that lays down the law of our today.

3. The joyful kind of seriousness, the wisdom full of pranks that constitutes the best condition of man's soul.

4. No small art is it to sleep: it is necessary for that purpose to keep awake all day.

5. The sting of conscience teacheth one to sting.

6. Distrust all in whom the impulse to punish is powerful.

7. The greatest events are not our noisiest but our stillest hours. . . . Thoughts that come with doves' footsteps guide the world.

8. No one is such a liar as the indignant man.

9. It is not the strength but the duration of great sentiments that makes great men.

10. Woman learns how to hate in proportion as she forgets how to charm. . . . Where there is neither love nor hatred in the game, woman's play is mediocre.

11. Our vanity is most difficult to wound just when our pride has been wounded.

12. The thought of suicide is a great consolation; by means of it, one gets successfully through many a bad night.

13. There are few pains so grievous as to have seen, divined, or experienced how an exceptional man has missed his way and deteriorated.

14. The sick are the greatest danger for the healthy; it is not from the strongest that harm comes to the strong but from the weakest.

15. Christianity gave Eros poison to drink. Eros did not die of it, to be sure, but degenerated into Vice.

16. This . . . work of a soul which is willingly divided against itself, which makes itself suffer—this whole *activistic* "bad conscience" has . . . been the real womb of all ideal and imaginative events and has thus brought to light a fullness of new and strange beauty and affirmation—and perhaps altogether *beauty itself*. What would be "beautiful" . . . if contradiction had not first become self-conscious, if the ugly had not first said to itself: "I am ugly"?

17. Unconscious gratitude for a good digestion (sometimes called "brotherly love").
18. Architecture is a sort of oratory of power by means of forms.
19. Contentment preserves one even from catching cold. Has a woman who *knew* she was well dressed ever caught cold?—No, not even when she had scarcely a rag to her back.
20. If a man have a strong faith, he can indulge in the luxury of scepticism.
21. [In classical Greece] the *sexual* symbol was the venerable symbol par excellence. . . . Christianity . . . has made something unclean out of sexuality: it threw filth upon the origin, upon the presupposition of our life.
22. I know no more heart-rending reading than Shakespeare: what must a man have suffered to find it so very necessary to be a buffoon? . . . I do not want to be a saint, rather a buffoon. Perhaps I am a buffoon.
23. My time has not yet come; some men are born posthumously.

In contrast with such psychological insights, Nietzsche's official formal philosophy (for which he is unfortunately best known) again and again misfired. For example, it grossly oversimplified Christianity by unjustly equating it with a pale-faced, sentimental humanitarianism and "slave morality." Paul Elmer More and Irving Babbitt have more convincingly proved the opposite: the contrast between Christianity and the maudlin kind of humanitarianism. The Christian requires more heroism for his humility than any Nietzschean superman requires for his self-assertion.

But more important to contemporary America than Nietzsche's formal philosophy is his moral example. *There* was the man who never compromised with his age, with the majority, with the aesthetic and intellectual sacred cows of the moment, the opportunists and success worshippers. *There* was the man whose tragic laughter, like a ray of illuminating darkness, cut across all "enlightened" optimism about the fruits of democratic equality, mass education, material progress, mere external reforms.

Bolstered by the *esprit de corps* of the literary and educated world, it is relatively easy to resist the conformity of the bigoted majority. But to stand independent without that bolstering, to resist also the bolsterers, the nonconformists as being merely the literary, educated kind of conformists, is a lonelier task, more grueling, more needed. Nietzsche's uncompromised integrity remains the best model for that twofold task, beyond both kinds of overadjustment. Therefore, the Unadjusted Man today had better heed Nietzsche's words about needing energy and an artificially thick-skinned self-confidence: "the uncrushable energy with which they maintained faith in themselves when the hunting-pack of the whole 'cultured' world was whooping around them" (letter to Erwin Rohde, November 20, 1868).

Nietzsche is timely even in his weaknesses; they warn every future American Unadjusted Man against the consequences of losing touch with the small, concrete realities of humanity. Here are two occupational diseases of unadjustedness from Nietzsche through today: instead of suffering fools casually, being provoked into erratic counter-follies; not doing even more, by rigorous qualifications, to prevent unwanted readers from misusing valid conservative cultural distinctions in an invalid right-wing political sense and from misusing valid psychological insights as invalid social bigotries. For America, Nietzsche will always remain relevant as the first great writer to proclaim unadjustedness as the form heroism takes in a mechanized mass-society: "Today the concept of 'greatness' entails . . . wanting to be by oneself, being capable of being different. . . ."

Chapter Eight   THE MIRROR

IMAGES: Psychology of Anti-

Americanism Abroad[1]

"In interviewing one of India's highest ranking Cabinet Ministers, I found that the conversation led the familiar path to the subject of Negro lynching in America. Lynchings are invariably invoked when an Indian official wishes to illustrate America's 'reactionary tendencies.' I agreed that lynchings were a national disgrace but pointed out that race relations in America were being rapidly improved. . . . Then I asked the Cabinet Minister if, since India felt so strongly about lynchings, it was disturbed about the mass executions of hundreds of thousands of persons in China. 'Oh, we don't know anything about that,' the Indian Minister replied."—*Marguerite Higgins, dispatch from New Delhi, September 25, 1951*

To broaden the perspective, a book dealing with American overadjustedness had better also include one chapter on the reaction abroad against America's political overadjustedness (nationalism) and against her cultural overadjustedness (commercialism). The one conformity uniting the most diverse Europeans and Asians consists of reeling aghast at American conformity, often rightly aghast for wrong reasons. Criticism of America, the harsher the better, is more valuable to America than praise, as it may partly diminish her self-corroding

[1] This chapter reflects several years of firsthand experience in Europe, lecturing on American poetry at the University of Florence in Italy, at Oxford in England, at the Alpbach International Forum in Austria, as well as travel in France, Germany, Scandinavia. A shorter form of this essay, under the title "Sunrise in the West," was read into the *Congressional Record* in 1955 by Senator Fulbright

complacency about her prosperity and democracy. But today, in the abnormal context of the Soviet danger, anti-Americanism abroad, though still valuable to Americans themselves as a corrective to stuffiness, becomes a luxury suicidally expensive to Europeans and Asians, so long as Russian and Chinese armies stand poised to march the instant disunity in the free world goes too far.

America owes more to the old world—our Bible, our Dante, Goethe, Shakespeare, our Bill of Rights—than any merely material aid can ever repay. European literature, including Russia's, means so much to American writers that we may take Jefferson's saying: "Every man has two fatherlands, his own and France," and change it to read: "Every American writer has two fatherlands, his own and Europe." Yet Americans are constantly provoking anti-Americanism, and this not by their many real vices but by their best virtues. One clue to why this is so occurs in what schoolbooks call "history's greatest oration," a propaganda speech as irritating to the rest of the world in its own day as the American orations about our own democratic virtues today. The speech in question is that of 431 B.C. by Pericles, representing the part-slave, part-free empire of Athens against Sparta's totally slavish militarism:

We secure our friends not by accepting favors but by doing them. And so we are naturally more firm in our attachments; for we are anxious *as creditors* to cement by kind offices our relations towards friends. If they do not respond with the same warmness, it is because they feel that their services will not be given spontaneously but only as the repayment of a debt. We are *alone* among mankind in doing men benefits, not on calculations of self-interest but in the fearless confidence of freedom. [Italics added.]

This quotation of twenty-four hundred years ago, with its tone of self-righteous smugness, helps explain what ineffective propagandists Americans are and what ineffective propagandists the equally unpopular Athenians were. In both cases the self-satisfied Lady Bountiful tone struck allies as insufferable.

Surprisingly enough, American economic aid to Europe and Asia often turns out to be disinterested, idealistic, without strings. But these are mere facts, less important in politics than impressions. In terms of impressions, America would sound less offensive abroad if, instead of mentioning aloud the reality of her frequent disinterestedness (a reality unbelieved because uncomfortable), America pretended aloud that her aid is motivated solely by gain: the hope of making future profits by buttering up a potential market. If America would give economic aid with the pretense of mildly sordid motives, then the recipient would no longer feel obliged to invent really sordid motives to make America's aid believable. Mere financial blackmail would arouse less rage in the recipient, because not manipulating his conscience, than the moral blackmail of aid without a catch to it; America should not give aid without at least pretended strings. You may be able to persuade an illiterate peasant that, when the American housewife took time out from her daily lynchings and imperialist plots to send her usurious gold without strings to starving Armenians twenty years ago or to the starving Soviet Ukraine in 1945, her motive was an uncalculating impulse of compassion. But you will never persuade sophisticated Europeans or Hindus of so simple and obvious a truth.[2]

But this argument for concealing stringless good motives refers only to relief measures and economic relations, not to cultural and political relations, where candid good motives on both sides are the first need. Leaving out Europe's hard core of communists and fascists as relatively unconvertible, let us try to understand and thereby reduce the cultural and political causes of anti-Americanism among non-totalitarian western Europeans. The two main causes, above all among intellectuals, are their doubt of America's cultural creativity and their

[2] Nor will you ever persuade a Parisian café-intellectual that the Rockefeller and Ford fellowships are subsidizing useful scholarly research, usually non-political, rather than propaganda for the oil and motor industries. If you could introduce the Parisian intellectual, suspicious of Wall Street plots, to some American Congressman, suspicious of the same educational foundations as communist plots, the resultant conversation would have the wonderful talking-past-each-other quality of a play by Chekhov.

doubt of her fidelity to the anti-fascist sacrament uniting them and her in World War II. Let us take up the two causes in that order.

In Europe lack of cultural status can affect a nation's non-cultural influence, economic or military, more than America's narrow economic or military experts have the background to realize. In Europe, unlike America, it is not only culturally but politically essential to be respected by the intellectuals. Listen, for example, to the diary of Heinrich von Einsiedel, *I Joined the Russians,* describing the non-political, cultural motive behind his former anti-American, pro-Russian politics:

Is Americanism a future worth striving for? Haven't pursuit of the dollar, the conveyor belt, skyscrapers, crime thrillers, the jazz mania done more to demoralize the world and turn man into a mass creature than could a collectivist party dictatorship inspired by a socialist ideal? Where is the towering cultural achievement of America which would lend inner justification to the wealth of the ruling classes?

Our western alliance is hardly helped by such mistaken impressions that Hollywood and Mickey Spillane represent American culture. Let Europeans find out for themselves—not from American propaganda releases but from freer travel of men and ideas in both directions—that American culture is more truly represented by Thoreau, Emily Dickinson, Melville, Faulkner, none of them exactly huckster extroverts. Let America expand her Fulbright program of exchanging professors and students and her overseas libraries, now freed from McCarthy rampages; such a serious scholarly level, and not some nationalistic advertising campaign, seems the solution.

Not in order to exonerate our own hucksterdom, filmdom, and gadgetdom but in order to note that Europe's are just as prevalent, let it be recorded that nobody forces Europe to purchase so avidly not the best but the vulgarest Americana, which Europe's masses prefer to their own lofty heritage. By free choice Europe is becoming even more "Americanized" than our fortunately still pluralistic America. Europe's eloquent indignation against American materialism is so passionate

because it is self-disgust: disgust with Europe's own mechanized, uprooted postwar detachment from her own great past.
America is a more complicated creature, both better and
worse, than the stereotype created by America's self-satirizing
Babbitt-baiters. To that stereotype European and Asian intellectuals still cling. Instead of baiting us as uncultured George
Babbitts, let them bait us as overostentatiously "cultured"
Gaylord Babbitts; then at least they would be hitting moving
targets, not sitting ducks of thirty years ago. If America is to
be baited (and any country that has never been devastated by
bombs or real poverty, deserves to be devastated at least
by satires from those less lucky), then let it be a real bang-up
job, not the cracked old howitzers Europe has borrowed from
Sinclair Lewis.

In 1954 more symphony tickets were sold in America than
baseball tickets. Conversely a larger percentage of Frenchmen
than Americans voluntarily, without Wall Street twisting their
arm, read *Reader's Digest* and drink Coca Cola (to cite two
habits of the hasty modern tempo from which old-world culture
is supposedly immune). Italians, again voluntarily, prefer the
worst Hollywood movies to their own masterpieces like *The
Bicycle Thief;* they paid scant attention to the latter until after
it became a success on Broadway. In this writer's home state
in America, volunteer committees of citizens are successfully
preventing scenic highways and historic monuments from
being defaced by ads and commercialism. Abroad, he found
highways thicker with ads than at home. He found thousand-
year-old forums and colosseums turned into filling stations.
He found the traffic of Rome so jammed and noisy that he
longed for the pastoral peace and quiet of Times Square,
New York.

Old world disdainers of us soulless American vulgarians still
engage in heated debates about the rival aesthetics of the
"Cinquecento" and "Seicento." Those two Italian labels, however, no longer refer to Renaissance art but to Fiat automobiles.
Soon it may become necessary for left-bank sensitive-plants to

flee from modern, rootless, gadget-giddy Europe to ancient, medieval, traditionalist America.

Why do we American art-loathing materialists seem to monopolize Europe's art galleries? Partly because the Europeans are meanwhile crowding the TV sets in the coffee shops. Even in medieval Oxford, those who drop their H's raise them on their roofs; just look at all those antennae. When this writer tried to revisit one of the noblest views in Europe, the mountain view over the Arno from the restaurant at San Miniato, he was unable to do so. The restaurateur insisted on drawing the curtains because the clientèle of the city of Dante complained that the window-light spoilt their rapt concentration on television.

As for European comic books or drab modern utilitarian housing or—but little is gained in scoring against our European friends their own debating-points against us. The real point is that we are all in the same boat, the boat of technological mass-culture, except for unadjusted guerillas equally few in all our countries. Though America may have carried mechanized industrialism furthest, not America but Europe originated the industrial revolution in the first place. Why single out America alone as scapegoat?—the mechanization of the Overadjusted Man (which fortunately has its potential for eventually raising mass standards as well as presently lowering them) is a universal problem of all modern countries equally.

The second source of friction within the free world is the fact that Europeans find America forgetful of the fascist evil. The Nazi atrocities and the resultant residue of anti-Germanism are more important emotionally to a Hitler-ravaged Europe than to an unravaged America. Since 1815, France has never been invaded by Russia, its traditional ally against Germany, but has been occupied by Germany three times: 1870, 1914, 1940. But Americans for two years suffered death and torture from communists in Korea. Unless both Frenchmen and Americans keep in mind each other's historical scars, Americans will increasingly rage at Frenchmen for being "soft" towards communism, and Frenchmen will increasingly rage against

Americans for being "soft" towards fascist tendencies at home, towards German nationalism abroad. You will better arouse Frenchmen against communism by showing it is nothing but red fascism; you will better arouse Americans against thought-control by showing it is nothing but bolshevism of the right. When you stand in front of a mirror, every clenched left fist becomes a clenched right fist and vice versa. The mirror-image metaphor explains the reciprocal relationship between America's softness towards the right, western Europe's softness towards the left.

For example, every time our rightist Europe-baiters threatened to sink British boats for trading with Red China, Aneurin Bevan's leftist America-baiters gained more adherents. Every time Bevan made a speech for appeasing Red China, our isolationist nationalists gained more adherents. The great British liberal weekly, *The Economist*, called Bevan's slanders of America "a deliberate recipe for striking down the free world's shield." Exactly. And what else but this are the slanders of England by our nationalists? The political death of McCarthy was soon followed by the death of Bevan's bid for Labor party leadership. Had McCarthy remained a force in Anglo-American relations, then Bevan in 1955 would have won more votes away from the moderate, pro-American Laborite Gaitskell (and the *New Statesman* would have won more subscribers away from *The Economist*), thereby winning more votes for anti-British right-wing isolationists in America.

Here is a second example of mirror images. Europeans[3] tend to think that everyone accused of communism in America is being framed. They often deem such proved traitors as the Rosenbergs innocent and minimize the proved communist infiltration in that erstwhile sacred cow, the Institute of Pacific Relations. Conversely, many nationalist Americans tend to think that everyone accused of communism is guilty. They impute intentional pro-communism to a past Administration

[3] Here, as throughout this comparison, many American liberal intellectuals resemble in attitude the European side of the mirror; European neo-fascists and Poujadists resemble the more extreme fringe of the American-nationalist side.

that proved its effective anti-communism by the Truman Doctrine in Turkey and Greece. Here the American-nationalist mistake mirrors the European-liberal mistake, the former calling the innocent guilty, the latter calling the guilty innocent.

While left and right are still valid distinctions in certain special situations (especially in France), more often they need to be replaced in European-American relations by coining the adjectives "westernizing" and "separatist." These new adjectives would bring out the contrast that really matters today: suicidal aloofness versus that western collective security against aggression which could have prevented World War II and can still prevent World War III. This new terminology makes fellow-traveler tendencies in Europe and xenophobe thought-controlling tendencies in America forms of the same ism: separatism. Westernizing means mutual material and spiritual aid to defend against totalitarianism all nations, including non-western ones, who accept the western parliamentary, constitutional tradition (a tradition, as India has shown, not confined to the west in any literal geographical sense). Westernizing does not mean stultifying uniformity nor the end of vigorous disagreement and political pluralism within its ranks; that would be the very totalitarianism we combat. Westernizing means free individualism within a close but voluntary unity. With this western unity distrustful Asians will eventually find they can cooperate on free and equal terms; only thereby will they achieve their independence not merely from the diminished imperialism of Europe but from that far greater danger to Asia: the increasing imperialism of Red China and Russia.

Unlike left and right, this suggested new terminology puts together in the same camp, where they belong, all who opposed the Marshall Plan and the Atlantic Pact. For example, by the new terminology Senator McCarthy, who called the Marshall Plan "Operation Rat-Hole" and who voted against adequately financing our anti-communist armies in Europe, gets placed in the same separatist camp as Nenni; Kingsley Martin, Jean-Paul Sartre, Alvarez Del Vayo, the *New Statesman* enemies of the

Atlantic Pact in London, and its neutralist enemies in Paris and Rome. When European communists and American nationalists both booed in protest against giving the Nobel prize for peace to the founder of the Marshall Plan, they proved the validity of the mirror-image metaphor; both groups oppose western unity.

In October, 1952, the late Joseph Stalin made one of the most important speeches of the twentieth century. He made a prediction that may still come true: that world communism would triumph not merely because the west contained pro-communist tendencies but because the west was disunified by right-wing nationalist rivalries among its anti-communists. In the context of Stalin's speech, the American nationalist right (not merely McCarthyism but its successors) may be defined as that divider of the west which replaces a genuine, freedom-loving anti-communism with demagogic pseudo-anti-communism and which aids the real communist agents by falsely accusing of communism the leading anti-communist western-izers. Americans should blame anti-Americanism abroad not only on communist propaganda but on America's own xeno-phobes and anti-immigrationists. Our Europe-baiters and thought-controllers look more important from afar than they actually are at home. Abroad, they give wavering Europeans the impression, a false impression, that (in Sartre's phrase) "America has the rabies."

The more we tell western Europe about the all-too-true horrors of communism, the more will Europeans tell us about the all-too-true horrors of fascism, only recently overrunning their countries. Though never herself overrun, let America have the empathy to put herself in Europe's place in reliving the horrors of nazism. More Europeans would then have the empathy to relive the horrors suffered by American prisoners in Red China and Korea. This reciprocity is not logical—logically you make people anti-communist by talking against communism—but psychological. Psychologically our economic and military cooperation with western Europe, though indis-pensable for other reasons, will do less to inspire western

Europe against the Soviet aggressor than will a nationwide rekindling in America of our anti-fascist conscience. Conversely, by the law of mirror-images, more Frenchmen and Italians will have to vote against communism and for a closer military and economic cooperation with America in order to encourage more Americans to vote out of office our nationalist know-nothings.

During 1952–54, America's reputation abroad for liberty and reliability (today again rising) sank disastrously low for permitting communist victories abroad, McCarthy victories at home. Suppose, instead, that during 1952–54 Eisenhower had provided more leadership at home against the nationalist thought-controllers, more leadership abroad against the gains of communism in Indo-China, neutralism in Europe. What a thrill of renewed morale this twofold "suppose" would have sent through the free west; what panic and gnashing of teeth through the propagandists of communism! During 1952–54 our President, while never relaxing our alertness against communist spies, had the historic duty of leading a drive—not his platitudes about tolerance but naming names, hitting hard—against all legislative usurpers of the administrative and judicial functions, usurpers who were corrupting that necessary alertness into attacks on free institutions. Yet such anti-communist, anti-McCarthy leadership from the White House never did occur. In Asia communism is stronger than ever; in America the political death of McCarthy in late 1954 was an achievement (by a few courageous Senate traditionalists) that owed almost nothing to the White House, which merely supported them in a roundabout, furtive way, meanwhile cravenly throwing innocent public servants to the wolves.

As a result of that default of White House leadership, Europeans and Asians will use McCarthy as a neutralist argument for years after America has outgrown this almost forgotten figure. In the same way they still cite the alleged "yearly lynching" as a neutralist argument despite America's continuous gains against racial segregation. If European neutralists still use the lynching-and-McCarthy gambit, some Asians add the still older one of the 1929 depression; on being told what large concessions our supposed "capitalist dictators" have made to wage demands, a group of Iranian students recently replied: "But what about those eighteen million unemployed, today selling apples in your streets?" Why do America's never-to-be-minimized sins hurt her most after she has outgrown them? Partly because Europeans and Asians fail to credit her channels for parliamentary change and her humanitarianized capitalism with a saving grace often missing in European politics and capitalism, the grace of self-reform through self-criticism.

Asian and European readers of this book should not confuse genuine American anti-communism, a necessary shield for peace and freedom against communist aggression, with the pseudo-anti-communism of our nationalist demagogues, which is not anti-communism at all but a racket. Genuine American anti-communism is more sincerely and effectively mindful of civil liberties than realized abroad. Consider the American historical context: the disappointed hopes, the murderous provocations suffered by our unprepared public opinion in the five years between Yalta illusions and Korean casualty lists. In such a context the really impressive reality is not our nationalist thought-control racket, though admittedly important, but the more typical sobriety, the more widespread civil-libertarianism of America's genuine anti-communists (whether an Eisenhower, a Stevenson, or a Norman Thomas).

In turn, American readers ought not to conclude, "Europe is going neutralist or even anti-American," without defining which of several Europes is meant by that conclusion. We have discussed the special historical reasons, for which America and Europe are both to blame, why many *West* Europeans are indeed neutralists or anti-American. But Russians, Rumanians, Czechs, East Germans, are they not Europeans too? When thirty thousand men a month, not plutocrats but farmers, workers, and intellectuals, risk their lives to desert from east to west, are these typical Europeans behaving like neutralists or anti-Americans? In 1953 over a thousand refugees a day, sometimes even three thousand a day, fled westward from one city alone, East Berlin. Do these Europeans, knowing communism at first hand, act as if they consider anti-communism a "hysterical witch-hunt" and Western Europe enslaved by American capitalism?

The same false generalization arises when we are told: "most of Asia" hates America because it won't treat the Chinese Soviet as a "normal" law-abiding government. Yet in Korea most prisoners from the Red China army of communist volunteers voted to join this supposedly-hated American side. They freely chose not to return to the supposedly normal government imposed by Mao's policemen. These Chinese prisoners, not plutocrats but peasants, are at least as much "Asiatics" as the editors of the pro-communist Hindu periodical, *Blitz.* At least as much, and—in numbers—a lot more so. A lot less so, however, in intellectual and social status and in articulated world influence.

On the very same day, June 1, 1953, two mass riots occurred, in the east and in the west, that seemed each other's mirror images, but in this case with a difference. The eastern riot occurred among Czech munition workers in Pilsen, the western riot among Parisian workers. Both riots reached their climax by pulling down a flag. The Czech workers tore down the Soviet flag and, at the risk of their lives, raised an American one. The Parisians, directed by communists and without personal risk, tore down an American flag at the same moment the Czechs were raising one. Does this coincidence of June 1 merely prove that America's presence makes people pro-Russian and Russia's makes people pro-American? Not quite: the Czech rioters knew communism by personal experience, but the Parisian rioters did not know much about America; their communist union-bosses of the CGT did not allow them to. In a poll of 1953, Frenchmen who lived in the same community with American soldiers and Frenchmen who had never met Americans were asked what they thought of America. The first group responded favorably, the second unfavorably. These responses suggest that the eastern riot of June 1 was based on familiarity, the western riot on ignorance. So here, too, American policy should facilitate more contact and travel between America and Europe to dispel the communist and American-nationalist falsehoods dividing the west.

The reciprocity between European left and American right sustains our thesis of an earlier book (*Shame and Glory of the Intellectuals*): "The *Nation* magazine mentality and the McCarthy mentality need each other, feed each other, and are both wrong." Since then, both these related mentalities have declined together inside America. Therefore, our earlier thesis must now be restated in more global terms: American nationalism and European neutralism need, feed each other; so do American internationalism and European anti-communism. Let Europe deepen her knowledge of American cultural achievements and her alliance with America against aggression; let America deepen her world-mindedness and her anti-fascist passion for civil liberties. The resultant unity between Europe and America would make freedom globally secure at last. Only yesterday this voluntary unity saved Europe and America from Hitler. If today it saves us both from world conquest by Chinese and Russian communism, then for a second time in one century, and by a reversal of astronomy, the sun will rise in the west.

Part Two THE BURKEAN-

CONSERVATIVE CASE AGAINST

THE REPUBLICAN PARTY[1]

"A state without the means of some change is without the means of its conservation."—*Edmund Burke, 1790*

"No festering wound stinketh more unbearably in the nostrils of God than the dung of covetousness."—*Saint Peter Damian*

---

[1] Main emphasis here: on the Burkean-conservative case not against Eisenhower Republicans (still too unresolved for assessment) but against the Old Guard cash-nexus Republicans. For the conservative case against their temporary allies, the nationalist-agitator Republicans, see the chapter "The New American Right," page 162. For appreciation of the positive side of the Republican party, namely the possibly valuable future of the unresolved Eisenhower Republicans, see the chapter "Remolding," page 118.

Chapter Nine SOCIAL CHANGE:

Towards a New Legitimism

> "Liar: no goddess was your mother,
> No Dardanus the founder of your tribe!"—*Virgil*, AENEID

When you cannot find a single living philosopher to bless you, why not dig up a dead one unable to repudiate you? Intellectual apologists of Old Guard Republicanism are trying to invoke Burke as the god-like founder of their tribe. Yet their inflexible attitude toward change is irreconcilable with Burke's most basic warning: "A state without the means of some change is without the means of its conservation" (1790).

To see what distinguishes Burkean conservatism from both right and left in America, let us first distinguish between the different attitudes men may take toward social change. Change may be revolutionary, counter-revolutionary, or evolutionary, outside or inside the established traditional framework. Radicals wish revolutionary change outside it; reactionaries wish counter-revolutionary change outside it ("back to 1932") or else, like King Canute, no change at all. The Burkean conservative and the rationalist liberal both wish evolutionary change; how then do they differ from each other? The rationalist liberal, descended from the eighteenth-century Enlightenment, plans change from abstract *a priori* generalizations; the conservative—in Metternich's phrase *"tout à terre, tout historique"*—sees change as disruptive to the traditional framework unless, instead, it grows organically out of the concrete historical context. The Tory Prime Minister Disraeli summarized this distinction: "In a progressive country change is constant; and the great question is, not whether you should

79

resist change which is inevitable, but whether that change should be carried out in deference to the manners, the customs, the laws, the traditions of the people, or in deference to abstract principles and arbitrary and general doctrines."

Conservatism puts the burden of proof on the innovator, liberalism on the anti-innovator; but both are willing to let the proof persuade them in either direction. Thereby both are less doctrinaire than the novelty-intoxicated radical on the left, the stand-pat Old Guard reactionary on the right. Burkean conservatives—consider Churchill's record of opposing both Nazi Germany and Soviet Russia—oppose leftist and rightist doctrinaires simultaneously. Burke simultaneously opposed the abstract *a priori* liberals of England and America, the radical revolutionists of France, and the doctrinaire royal reactionaries of England and France.

When *Shame and Glory of the Intellectuals* defined Old Guard Republicans as Jacobins *endimanchés* (and found trade-unions more conservative than they), the term "Jacobin *endimanché*" was objected to universally, by Republican and New Deal reviewers alike, on the ground that supposedly Republicans are conservative, Jacobins radical. But the resemblance between both is this: Old Guard doctrinaires of Adam Smith apriorism, though dressed up in their Sunday best (like any Jacobin gone smug and successful), are applying the same arbitrary, violent wrench, the same discontinuity with the living past, the same spirit of rootless abstractions that characterized the French Revolution.

In 1790, when the French Revolution was still relatively peaceful and beneficial, Burke virtually founded modern conservatism by warning that a coming despotism and terror were innate in every utopian apriorist break with the past. That innateness was denied by the anti-Burkean Anglo-American liberals. They hoped, like Paine, that well-meaning, rootless abstractions could violate rooted traditions with impunity. Here the notable point about Burke's conservatism was his defense of historic liberties on not one but three fronts: against French Jacobinism; against the optimistic Anglo-American liberalism that looked to France in 1790 (to Russia in 1917); against the right-wing tyranny of George III that threatened historic British and American liberties. Burke helped George Washington restore these old British liberties in the American Conservation of 1776.

Historic liberties are legitimate because evolved from concrete, lived experience, in contrast with liberalism's abstract, unlived Rights of Man. The wise concept of legitimism was adopted as their first principle by the great Burkean conservatives of the Congress of Vienna. Legitimism has the same capacity for assimilating new social changes that Burke—in contrast with static reactionaries—defined as "the means of conservation." In its ultimate sense of history-engendered lawfulness, the legitimism of Metternich, Talleyrand, and Castlereagh need not be confined (as theirs too often was) to hereditary rights of kings. The historic rights of all citizens, not only kings and aristocrats, are also inherent tacitly in this Burkean-Metternichian concept. Legitimism may be redefined, in order to assimilate social change today, not merely as legitimate succession in monarchy—merely one metaphor of legitimacy—but as something broader: the prescriptive right of unbroken institutional continuity, the unspoken community sense of what is lawful. Thus defined, the legitimism of our own era is the parliamentary, constitutional method of change plus the community feeling, not expressible in precise economic abstractions of either capitalism or socialism, that humane reform take precedence over *laissez faire*.[2]

The wonderful quality of an Old Guard Republican like the late Senator Taft was his loyalty to the first half of that

[2] This twofold legitimism can take place under an elective ruler, as in America, or under a hereditary constitutional king. Preferably a king in the case of Europe: outside Switzerland, the grapevine of parliamentary government has never grown well unless supported on the traditional monarchic trellis. The lack of that unifying trellis in France, where wrong-headed monarchists did even more than radicals to discredit monarchy, is a major cause of the failure of the Third and Fourth Republics to gain national respect. Respect depends on an aura of legitimacy and on historic continuities transcending the partisanships of the moment. But past monarchies, once uprooted, can rarely be restored; the magic of continuity is dispelled. And though it would have been far preferable to have kept such a lost past, the first concern of the future must be with a rooted, not uprooted legitimism.

combination: constitutional procedures, which he defended against the short-cuts of New Dealers-in-a-hurry. The wonderful quality about the New Dealers was their loyalty to the second half of that combination: social humaneness, which they defended against Republicans like Taft. The social inhumaneness of the McKinley era no longer has many living American roots; social conscience, instead, is now almost as deep-rooted as Europe's legitimate monarchies of the old days. A new legitimism will combine lawful, constitutional procedures (protecting the individual against statism and collectivism) with the now deeply traditionalized social conscience. That combination, no monopoly of either party, is found alike in Stevenson Democrats and in certain Eisenhower Republicans like Christian Herter and Clifford Case.

To be lasting, humane reforms must be achieved not in a Gallic, apriorist, revolutionary way, which creates a pendulum-swing to counter-revolutionary reaction, but in that gradual, piecemeal way which makes British trade-unions such a force for conservatism (with a small "c") inside the Labor party. A doctrinaire progressivism seeks social betterment by over-all formulas and general solutions (but general solutions are impossible, because the human dilemma is, like most interesting problems, unsolvable). A new legitimism seeks social betterment by moving, via channels and precedents, from the concrete to the concrete.

The gap between the new legitimism and the old is sometimes smaller than realized. A case can be made for defending much of the Metternich-Disraeli monarchism against Manchester liberals on grounds of social humaneness. Monarchy, aristocracy, and what remained of medieval feudalism in the Central Europe of Metternich were a freedom-enhancing, countervailing force against middleclass attempts to set up, in the name of liberal democracy, a mechanizing dictatorship of urban capitalism over peasants and workers. The nonrepressive half of the Metternich era and the Congress of Vienna era, 1815–1848, can be historically justified against liberals because it slowed up into a sane and gradual industrial evolution what in England had been a mad and hectic industrial revolution. And evolution is ever preferable to revolution because less disruptive psychologically.

Consider only the cultural shallowness and moral callousness caused by England's overhasty industrial *revolution*. A non-evolutionary industrial revolution, triumphing too overwhelmingly, brought with it the materialist schools of philosophy, whether a soulless, Benthamite utilitarianism or a heartless Manchester liberalism, the former hostile to art and religion, the latter hostile to a decent compassion for child-labor and slum conditions. From 1800 right through the Tory reform laws of Lord Shaftesbury and the battle of Disraeli's "Tory socialism" versus Gladstone's Manchester liberalism, decent compassion was more often felt by aristocratic conservatives and by democratic socialists than by nineteenth-century "economic" liberals. Likewise the old legitimism of Metternich, who in 1847 called himself "a conservative socialist," showed more social humaneness (the new legitimism) than did the *laissez faire* liberals. He was closer than they to the New Deal spirit, according to the following summary of Austrian monarchist economics by a leading scholar in the field:[3]

By 1817, it was estimated that the funds which the Austrian government had given for its public works program in Italy had enriched the poorer classes by Fr. 5,000,000. The Austrian policy of taking care of the destitute masses in the Italian provinces by giving food and money to those incapable of employment and providing a public works program for others, is in its general outlines *surprisingly similar* to the public works and emergency relief programs initiated in our own country by the *Roosevelt administration*. . . . The actions of Francis I, meager as they were in comparison with the billion-dollar spending of our own times, did actually save many persons from intense suffering. . . . The financial condition of the Austrian government was so precarious that actual bankruptcy was feared. In spite of numerous difficulties, however, the Hapsburg monarch did earnestly endeavor to *improve the lot* of his Italian subjects, the hapless victims of a great depression.

[3] R. J. Rath, "The Hapsburgs and the Great Depression in Lombardy-Venetia, 1814–1818," *Journal of Modern History*, September 1941 (italics added).

In Central Europe, the feudal and aristocratic remnants were a valuable brake, slowing up the industrial revolution into evolution. In England, unable to slow it up, they valuably undid much of its harm afterwards: by allying with the factory workers against industrial inhumaneness, so long as there was a seventh Earl of Shaftesbury and later a Disraeli with sufficient vision to conceive that alliance. After Disraeli's death in 1881, the alliance gradually faded, so that by the turn of the century the majority of workers naturally turned either to the Liberal party or the newly-founded Labor party. But even in the 1950's, owing to the Disraeli heritage, one third of British workers still vote for the Conservative party; the remainder keep their Labor party, against the wishes of Labor intellectuals, the most conservative, gradualist worker-party in the world. Disraeli, personal friend and avowed disciple of Metternich, preached the Tory alliance of worker and nobleman in his novels of the 1840's, *Sybil* and *Coningsby*. He also preached it in his speeches of the 1860's, defending workers' suffrage as a balance against the 1832 thraldom of a middle-class-dominated suffrage:

Instead of falling under . . . the thraldom of capital—under those who, while they boast of their intelligence, are more proud of their wealth— if we must find a new force to maintain the ancient throne and monarchy of England, I, for one, hope that we may find that novel power in the invigorating energies of an educated and enfranchised people.

Many a demagogue makes promises to the workingman. But Disraeli actually put that preaching into practice during his second ministry. In the 1870's the Conservative party enacted his "charter of trade-union liberties," helping to legalize strikes and pickets and for the first time solidly protecting the rights of trade-unions. In turn, in England today nothing has done more to block communist fellow-travelers and Bevanites than the traditionalist anti-extremism of the Laborite trade-union, the anti-cash-nexus institution *par excellence*. In America today, in contrast with the social inhumaneness and the atomistic cash-nexus of Old Guard Republicans, the trade-union serves as conservative a function as monarchy did in Metternich's day, even though doing so as inarticulately as any really effective conservatism. Thus does history grow blindly, in ways no less decisive for being unplanned. Contradicting the conscious, intentional formulations of American trade-unions, Frank Tannenbaum describes their hidden conservative function (*A Philosophy of Labor*, New York, Knopf, 1952):

Trade-unionism is the conservative movement of our time. It is the counterrevolution. Unwittingly, it has turned its back upon most of the political and economic ideas that have nourished western Europe and the United States during the last two centuries. In practice, though not in words, it denies the heritage that stems from the French Revolution and from English liberalism. It is also a complete repudiation of Marxism. This profound challenge to our time has gone largely unnoticed because the trade-union's preoccupation with the detailed frictions that flow from the worker's relation to his job seemed to involve no broad program. In tinkering with the little things—hours, wages, shop conditions, and security in the job—the trade-union is, however, rebuilding our industrial society upon a different basis from that envisioned by the philosophers, economists, and social revolutionaries of the eighteenth and nineteenth centuries.

The importance of trade-unionism has been obscured until recently by the claims upon public attention of movements of lesser historical significance. The Communist, Fascist, and Nazi eruptions are secondary outcroppings of the same social rift that has brought trade-unionism into being. . . . Their dependence upon dogma reveals their inner debility, and their weakness is attested by their readiness to use force to impose upon society the design their ideology calls for. This assumes an ability to model and freeze man within some preconceived mold, which is contrary to experience. . . .

In contrast with these self-conscious and messianic political movements, the trade-union has involved a clustering of men about their work. This fusion has been going on for a long time. It has been largely unplanned, responsive to immediate needs, irrepressible, and inarticulate of its own ends because, on the whole, it had no general purposes. A sparsity of general ideas and a lack of any "ideology" kept the trade-union movement from being obtrusively vocal and permitted mesmeric political groups to look upon it as something of no great importance. But its very lack of ideas made it strong and enabled it to concentrate upon immediate ends without wasting its energies in a futile pursuit of Utopia. The trade-union movement could go on for generation after generation despite many failures, gradually accommodating itself to a changing industrial environment. It could do that without challenging the political or moral ideas current at the time, all the while slowly shaping new institutions, habits, and loyalties. It has gathered power within the community until it has suddenly dawned upon men that a new force—not an idea, but a new force—has come into being. This force is changing the structure of our economy and redistributing power in our society. . . . The trade-union is the real alternative to the authoritarian state. The trade-union is our modern "society," the only true society that industrialism has fostered. As a true society it is concerned with the whole man, and embodies the possibilities of both the freedom and the security essential to human dignity.

Although that quotation comes closer than any cash-nexus Republican in its feeling for the conservative spirit, yet one exceedingly strong reservation must be recorded against the otherwise very stimulating Tannenbaum thesis. The effectiveness of the conservative spirit depends on its diffusion among all classes, even if in varying proportions; therefore, his singling out labor as the almost messianic bearer of conservative values seems as one-sided as the Republican idealizing of businessmen. American labor, moreover, feels no sense of separatist class-destiny; feels often as middleclass as business does. Still, perhaps that fact need not prevent labor from also performing in part and on the side—history as sleep-walking, so to speak—the anti-middleclass, conservative function attributed to labor by Mr. Tannenbaum. A parallel would be the "fit of absent-mindedness" with which, in part, the British Empire was founded. The real question, then, is one of our learning to reassess more sensitively the gap in America between chosen explicit credo and lived implicit credo.

The Disraeli-Roosevelt build-up of worker movements (Tory democracy or even Tory socialism) is a wise counter-balance against the social irresponsibility of daemonic millionaire shopkeepers[4]—but can lead to the sentimental fallacy of worshipping the manual worker as Noble Savage. All such romanticizing (in this case an insulting because patronizing worship) results from underfamiliarity with the concrete object, overfamiliarity with preconceived generalizations about it. The antidote against systematized delusions, deifying or diabolizing any particular class, profession, or nationality, is to revere whatever lives as individual, ever growing and unclassifiable, and not to dehumanize it into a walking category. So long as this proviso is kept in mind, generalized categories can and should be used: as changeable conveniences, not as static rigidities of logic-chopping.

Whoever sincerely conserves religious, aesthetic, and historical values should resist those who exploit such values for material greed. In every generation the sincere conservative learns anew, to his sorrow, how little he has in common with the pseudo-conservative rightist movements that are merely ideologized greed. Half a century ago, in a speech of 1903, none other than Winston Churchill distinguished sharply between British conservatism, with its non-materialistic, non-secular values, and the American Republican "touts of protected industries":

The new fiscal policy [of commercialism and high tariffs] means a change not only in the historic English Parties, but in the conditions of our public life. The old Conservative Party with its religious convictions and constitutional principles will disappear and a new party will arise—like perhaps the Republican Party in the United States of America —rigid, materialist, and secular, whose opinions will turn on tariffs and who will cause the lobbies to be crowded with the touts of protected industries.

Industrialism is still a young force, a post-1789 force, a force still unpatterned and experimental. If its strutting, success-

[4] Those Republicans who call themselves "new conservatives" have usually no more read the gospel they cite than a parlor-Marxist reads Marx. If they ever do read their texts, amusing consternation may result when they discover that their preceptors Coleridge and Metternich deemed the capitalist class radical, subversive, anti-conservative.

intoxicated children will subordinate the raw material energies
of that new force to the old, legitimizing pattern of the
Christian-Judaic ethic, then American democratic capitalism
will increasingly evolve a non-huckster, non-philistine business-
man, just as America has already amazed continental Europe
by evolving a non-Marxist workingman. Then the new legitimism of a more deeply-rooted, ethic-centered west can transcend
the false choice between plutocratic and Marxist materialism.
Such transcendence can still save America from a warning of
Emerson that ought especially to haunt an atomic age: "Things
are in the saddle and ride mankind."

Chapter Ten SOCIALISTS AND

CONSERVATIVES: Two Rival

Protests Against Cash-Nexus

"There is no antithesis between Conservatism and Socialism. . . . The point which principally distinguishes their attitude . . . is a rigorous adherence to justice. It is in insisting that injustice [statist tyranny] shall not stain national help to the afflicted that Conservatism finds in respect to social reform its peculiar and distinctive task. . . . The State is a clumsy, rigid instrument, difficult to handle and operating heavily and unexpectedly. It might easily have happened that workmen would have found themselves [under socialism] in a position unpleasantly approximating to State slavery, governed at every turn by bureaucratic regulations and, worst of all, enervated by having all the conditions of their industry ordered for them and nothing left to their own initiative and resolution."—*Lord Hugh Cecil,* CONSERVATISM, *1912*

"The left has always believed in three things: the possibility of a complete systematic solution to economic problems; the perfectability of man; and the proposition that thorough education for all will produce a rational, and therefore a good, society. The Tory rejects all these propositions."—*Angus Maude, Conservative M.P.,* THE LISTENER, *January 15, 1953*

The conservative philosophy developed partly as an ethical reaction against the value-dissolving huckster-materialism accompanying the industrial revolution in the early 1800's. Though founded earlier by Burke as an answer to the French Revolution, the conservative philosophy gained its depth-psychology only under the agony of industrialism. The main impact of industrialism on western man was not economic but psychological: the trauma it inflicted on the traditional value-heritage. The post-Burkean depth-psychology of conservatism derived not from politicians but from sensitive creative artists like Coleridge, Matthew Arnold, Cardinal Newman in England; Baudelaire, Dostoyevsky, Nietzsche, Burckhardt on the continent; Melville, Hawthorne, Poe, Henry Adams, Faulkner in America. Melville was the one to state the most succinctly the attitude they all shared:

> The spider in the laurel spins,
> The weed exiles the flower;
> And, flung to kiln, Apollo's bust
> Makes lime for Mammon's tower.

Such literary or religious value-conservers could not endure the dissolving of society's aesthetic, ethical, and religious ties by the arid cash-nexus. Its dissolution of these traditional ties was opposed, long before Marx, by Tory spirits like Donoso Cortés, Metternich, Disraeli. Therefore, most (not all) new conservatives have actively opposed that last Indian summer of hucksterdom which flowered in America after the Republican victory of 1952.

But unlike socialists, with their class-determinism, new conservatives do not indiscriminately equate most businessmen with a huckster-mentality. It is a kind of Aryan racism of economics to brand classes instead of individuals. A mentality characterizing more individual businessmen in the McKinley context of yesteryear may, under a new context, characterize more individual trade-unionists, rustics, grand dukes, or professors. Such a mentality should no more be attributed permanently to a party than to a class. The cash-nexus Old Guard is not the whole Republican party, did not represent it in Lincoln's day, need not represent it tomorrow.

It is mere romanticism to ignore the reality of industrialism and flee into some never-existent idealization of the Middle Ages. What is deadly is not the industrial gadgetry itself nor the material prosperity itself but the overadjusted smugness, self-sufficiency, and betrayal of spiritual traditions that accompany this gadgetry, this prosperity unless these become servants, not tyrants of man. In their different ways, the starting point 150 years ago of both aristocratic conservatism and democratic socialism was their shared fear that the middleclass *laissez faire* liberalism was allowing industrial mechanization to become not the servant but the tyrant of man. In their historical and European origins, conservatism and socialism are both psychological reactions against the intolerable cash-nexus mentality of the nineteenth-century burgher.

In twentieth-century America, that same capitalism has achieved (in contrast with the high-priced, low-production capitalism of Europe) miraculous economic benefits for all, benefits which its socialist-proletarian and conservative-aristocratic opponents never dreamed of in Europe and in the nineteenth century. The diffusion of these benefits among workers has rendered out of date most of the socialist attacks on capitalism, insofar as these attacks were mainly economic and material. But these admittedly attractive benefits have not rendered out of date the traditional conservative attacks on middleclass capitalism, attacks which were not economic but spiritual (Coleridge, Carlyle, Newman, Ruskin, Arnold, Melville). Nor have these material benefits of modern American capitalism rendered out of date that minority within socialist thinkers which represents not materialism but Christian ethics.

The benefits of American capitalism, its admirable flexibility, its ability to reform its own weaknesses via free parliamentary channels, its wide diffusion of private property (which Henry Maine in *Popular Government,* 1885, showed to be indispensable to full personal liberty), and the greatest material well-being in history—all these benefits, while refuting and outdating the Marxist predictions of ever greater poverty and inequality under capitalism, have neither outdated nor solved the problem of the Overadjusted Man. That is, the problem of mass-mechanization leading to an economically delicious but stereotyping prosperity. There is, therefore, no need to abandon smugly those attacks on the cash-nexus which characterized almost all the greatest religious, philosophical, and literary figures of America's past. Today and tomorrow those attacks must continue on cultural, ethical, or religious levels—the three proper levels of conservatism in contemporary America— even though those attacks on capitalism have been outdated on the economic level, the proper level of socialist materialists.

In Europe socialism and conservatism both had a social base, a party, a class: proletariat or landed aristocracy. In America, where the whole country is diffused with middle-class psychology, the two anti-middleclass movements cannot play a role in terms of political parties or economic classes. This obvious lack of a class base for either socialism or con-servatism in America has led to their being scorned as having no role to play in America. What their scorners forget is that attitudes can work through diffusion as well as through a move-ment. Both conservatism and socialism work in America as a whole, equally in all parties and classes, as an unlabeled and unconscious diffusion, not as a movement. When they become a movement, they become small, comical splinter-groups. They become cranks who imagine nostalgically a non-existent class of feudal southern landowners or class-conscious proletarians, as the case may be. To make this statement is not to minimize the important role of conservative and socialist thought. Diffusion can be more influential than any localized movement or party. But that important intellectual influence will be jeopardized if New Conservatives should make the mistake of trying to localize their essentially cultural and ethical thought into one particular political party or into apologetics for one particular American class, whether that class be the no-longer-existent agrarian nobles of the Middle Ages and the feudal south or the all-too-existent urban hucksters.

In the case of Europe, conservatism and socialism differ in their class base, their economic base, and their general historical base. In the case of America, neither has inherited any class base from history, and neither is identified with any political party (except for irrelevant splinter-groups, our parties are

neither aristocratic nor proletarian but middleclass). Therefore, in the case of America, conservatism and socialism are
not only weaker than in Europe (except for diffusion under
other labels) but differ far less from each other than they do in
Europe. What unites them in America is their distrust of the
commercialism prevailing ever since the defeat in the Civil
War of the agrarian south as well as the subsequent defeat of
the Lincolnian non-commercial idealists inside the north.

In America, ever since the death of the truly conservative
Federalist party, we must speak (except for rootless, doctrinaire
fringes) not of socialist or conservative ideologies, parties,
movements but of diffused and unlabeled conservative or
socialist attitudes, at their most effective when least labeled and
at their least effective when articulate and conscious. Despite
their close kinship in America as fellow anti-commercialists,
there is one important area where conservative and socialist
attitudes do differ from each other, even in America, with an
unbridgeable gap. That area is their view of human nature.
Socialism shares with Jeffersonian liberals a faith in human
nature, the masses, the natural goodness of man; sometimes it
also shares with Progressives and Populists of the Paine heritage
a faith in direct democracy (as defined on pages 130–131).
In contrast, the conservative view of human nature takes into
account its complexity, its tragic tensions between incompatible
impulses, and therefore its inability to plan the long-range
rational blueprints desired by socialists. Historically the conservative view of human nature is a secularization of the
Christian doctrine of original sin. At the same time the
conservative view of human nature is close to the discoveries
of the Freudians about the subconscious and about stifled
impulses, discoveries that Coleridge and Nietzsche so uncannily
anticipated.

Liberals, *laissez faire* capitalists, and conservatives all agree,
for their own various reasons, that socialism would give too
much power over society for any one party, bureaucracy, or
administration to manage without abuse. Even at their worst,
capitalists can be checked with countervailing forces, can be

played off against each other, are fortunately devoid of the conspiratorial sense of class solidarity attributed to them by economic determinists and witch-hunters from the left. What socialist thought still has not provided for is the powerful private groups needed as a balance against even the best of governments. Even the so-called "absolute" monarchies were in practice limited by such private groups as an independent clergy, nobility, bourgeois Third Estate, guilds of workers, and those real but unwritten limits imposed by ancient traditions. Where will be the independent private bailiwicks of the future to counterbalance the modern mass state? The weakness of socialism is its failure to answer this question of the traditionalists. The question concerns all forms of the modern mass state; it concerns—not equally but almost equally—our non-socialist societies also. Liberty is allergic to too much concentrated central power, whether socialist or plutocratic.

The usual capitalist defense of private property against socialists sounds appalling, especially in the ears of idealistic artists and scholars, because of its grubby materialist basis. If the issue is debated on that basis alone, then trade-unions of Europe and the majority of the intellectuals of Asia and Europe are justified in strongly sympathizing with the socialists, who at least have a generous breadth of vision. Yet it is the socialists who are wrong, the American kind of capitalists who are right about the need for a widely-diffused possession of unmolested private property. The capitalists are right, not in sloganizing about a maximum *laissez faire* (which they themselves fail to practice whenever they can get tariffs and state subsidies) but in insisting upon some minimum level of property beyond which not even the kindliest state may intervene. However, the proper argument for their excellent case is not their profit-motive but the fact that capitalist private property has also a non-material, moral function. It educates its possessor in the moral qualities of sturdy independence, sense of responsibility, and the training of judgement and character brought whenever free choice is exercised in any field, including the economic field. It is these moral qualities, not the gluttonous material ones that have historically associated the rise of personal liberty with the rise of personal property. To recognize this concrete historic fact about property and liberty is not, be it added, the same as abstracting that fact into a vast, rigid ideology of Manchester liberalism or into an imagination-stifling cash-nexus.

Most socialists are anti-communists. The horrible example of Soviet terrorist dictatorship, which socialists like George Orwell and Norman Thomas opposed more effectively than most capitalists, has forced most socialists to reconsider their frequent earlier minimizing of the danger of statism to their own lofty ideals. The best socialist thought today, independent and non-sectarian, is ably engaged in trying to work out a formula preserving personal choice in all non-economic spheres at the same time as having centralized economic planning. To a distruster of the abstract, the flaw in even the best of these socialist theorists lies not in their sincerity, intellect, and good will (often superior in those three qualities to their detractors). Their flaw lies in their assumption that society can be understood or perfected by over-all formulas in the first place. Thomas I. Cook has defined the new conservatism as the rediscovery that liberty depends on concrete traditions and is menaced by "excessive reliance on human reason, functioning deductively and *a priori* on a foundation of abstract principle."

The proper corollary to the able socialist indictments of Soviet Russia is not to contrive some new and shinier formula to replace the discredited old one but to stop seeing salvation in any brand of over-all formula. The proper corollary is to begin seeing history as the darkly growing relationship of concrete to concrete. No kind of socialist over-all explanation and chart, no pedantic, top-of-the-brain ideology (whether it calls itself socialist, liberal, or conservative), can ever systematize or control the rich, helter-skelter plenitude of man.

The latest thought of certain socialists and of certain *laissez faire* capitalists is producing insights no conservative can neglect without being the loser. A number of those writers are far removed from being the usual grubby caricatures of materialism. And yet, even when one leans over backward to consider their writings without prejudice, how many others turn out to be just that. And how much such big-business materialists and socialist materialists resemble each other! They differ on the non-essentials: on economic theory, on the boring wrangle about whether the fat swine or the lean swine of materialism should hog a bit more of the economic trough. But they agree on certain essentials: a mechanistic view of life, utilitarianism, the unpleasant duty of dutiful pleasure-seeking, faith in bigger and better progress, in sterile efficiency, in doctrinaire apriorism. To these goals both sacrifice what the conservative cherishes: all that is warm, concrete, human in human nature, everything precarious, diversified, unpredictable, unorganized, unadjusted.

Chapter Eleven   THE ROOTLESS

NOSTALGIA FOR ROOTS: Defects

in the New Conservatism

"It is not remarkable that the new conservatives should take *particular* care to disassociate themselves from what often goes by the name of conservatism, but which for them is a dangerous perversion or misrepresentation of an honorable faith: blind resistance to change; a tyrannical élite; ignorance of the social process; negativism which leads to the stifling of dissent. . . . The new conservatives regard the nineteenth-century Spencerians and their modern equivalents as false conservatives, anarchic if not reactionary. . . . But contemporary conservatism will do no better if it ignores its own reformers and constructive thinkers and permits a noisy riff-raff to speak for it."—*Daniel Aaron, "Conservatism, Old and New," a paper for the Mississippi Valley Historical Society, May 8, 1953*

I

In the 1930's, when the present author, still a student, was writing an article for the *Atlantic Monthly* urging "a Burkean new conservatism in America," and to some extent even as late as his *Conservatism Revisited* of 1949, "conservatism" was an unpopular epithet. In retrospect it becomes almost attractively amusing (like contemplating a dated period piece) to recall how violently one was denounced[1] in those days for

[1] For example, the author's above *Atlantic* article, written in pre-war student days, was denounced more because the word used was so heretical ("conservative") than because of any effort by the Popular Frontist denouncers to read what was actually said. It was the first-written and worst-written appeal ever

97

suggesting that Burke and Tocqueville were not fascist beasts and that our conservative Constitution was not really a plot-in-advance, by Wall Street lackeys like George Washington, against the coming American *Front Populaire* of "broadminded sympathizers with the Soviet experiment and other progressives." As the liberal Robert Bendiner then put it: "Out of some 140,000,000 people in the United States, at least 139,500,000 are liberals, to hear them tell it. . . . Rare is the citizen who can bring himself to say, 'Sure I'm a conservative'. . . . Any American would sooner drop dead than proclaim himself a reactionary." In July, 1950, a newspaper was listing the charges against a prisoner accused of creating a public disturbance; one witness charged: "He was using abusive and obscene language, calling people Conservatives and all that."

When conservatism was still a dirty word, it seemed gallantly unadjusted to defend it against the big, smug liberal majority among one's fellow writers and professors. In those days, therefore, the present author deemed it more helpful to stress the virtues of conservatives than their faults. In the new mood that followed, blunt speaking about conservatism's important defects no longer runs the danger of obscuring its still more important virtues (virtues defined in the chapter "Distinctions," page 35).

The main defect of the new conservatism, threatening to make it a transient fad irrelevant to real needs, is its rootless nostalgia for roots. Conservatives of living roots were Washington and the Federalists in the America of their day, Burke and Coleridge in their particular England, Metternich in his special Austria, Donoso Cortés in his Spain, Calhoun in his ante-bellum south, Adenauer and Churchill today. American conservative writings of living roots were the *Federalist* of Hamilton, Madison, Jay, 1787–88; the *Defense of the Consti-*

published in America for what it called a "new" conservatism (non-Republican, non-commercialist). This it viewed, rather incoherently and ineffectively, as synthesizing in some future day the ethical New Deal social reforms with the more pessimistic, anti-mass insights of our Burkean founders. Such a synthesis, argued the article, would help make the valuable anti-fascist movement among literary intellectuals simultaneously anti-communist also, leaving behind the Popular Frontist 1930's.

tutions of John Adams, 1787–88; the *Letters of Publicola* of John Quincy Adams, 1791; Calhoun's *Disquisition* and *Discourse*, posthumously published in 1850; Irving Babbitt's *Democracy and Leadership*, 1924. In contrast, today's conservatism of yearning is based on roots either never existent or no longer existent. Such a conservatism of nostalgia can still be of high literary value. It is also valuable as an unusually detached perspective toward current social foibles. But it does real harm when it leaves literature and enters short-run politics, conjuring up mirages to conceal sordid realities or to distract from them.

In America, southern agrarianism has long been the most gifted literary form of the conservatism of yearning. Its most important intellectual manifesto was the southern symposium *I'll Take My Stand*, 1930, contrasting the cultivated human values of a lost aristocratic agrarianism with northern commercialism and liberal materialism. At their best, these and more recent examples of the conservatism of yearning are needed warnings against shallow practicality. The fact that such warnings often come from the losing side of our Civil War is in itself a merit; thereby they caution a nation of success-worshippers against the price of success. But at their worst, such books of the 1930's, and again of the 1950's, lack the living roots of genuine conservatism and have only lifeless ones. The lifeless ones are really a synthetic substitute for roots, contrived by nostalgia.

Such romanticizing conservatives refuse to face up to the old and solid historical roots of much American liberalism. What is really rootless and abstract is not the increasingly conservatized New Deal liberalism but their own utopian dream of an aristocratic agrarian restoration. Their unhistorical appeal to history, their traditionless worship of tradition characterize the new conservatism of many younger writers and educators today. In contrast, a genuinely rooted, history-minded conservative conserves the roots that are *really there,* exactly as Burke did when he conserved not only the monarchist-conservative aspects of William the Third's bloodless revolution of 1688 but also its constitutional-liberal aspects. The latter aspects, formulated by the British philosopher John Locke, have been summarized in England and America ever since by the word "Lockean."

Via the Constitutional Convention of 1787, this liberal-conservative heritage of 1688 became rooted in America as a blend of Locke's very moderate liberalism, Burke's very moderate conservatism. From the rival Federalists and Jeffersonians through today, all our major rival parties have continued this blend, though with varied proportion and stress. American history is based on the resemblance between moderate liberalism, moderate conservatism; the history of continental Europe is based on the difference between extreme liberalism, extreme conservatism. Therefore, the Anglo-American and the continental versions of conservatism serve their contrasting histories best by contrasting attitudes toward the sort of liberalism they find at hand, assimilating it in the former case, rejecting it in the latter. But some American new conservatives import a conservatism that totally rejects even our moderate native liberalism. Thereby they are bookishly importing a plant suited to continental Europe (where liberalism is more extreme, more Jacobin, less Lockean) but not suited to American soil.

An esoteric frond, an orchidaceous petal are always welcome when presented as such. But instead of presenting their continental conservatism to America as a rootless blossom of decorative charm, such romanticizing new conservatives present it as viably rooted and functionally American. Their claim of "Americanism" (a word also claimed by rightists of a less sincerely intellectual, more demagogic level) does not square with American history. In the name of free speech and intellectual gadflyism, they are justified in expounding the indiscriminate anti-liberalism of hot-house Bourbons and tsarist serf-floggers. But they are not justified in calling themselves American traditionalists or in claiming any except exotic roots for their position in America. Let them present their case frankly as anti-traditional, rootless revolutionaries of Europe's authoritarian right-wing, attacking the deep-rooted American tradition of liberal-conservative synthesis. Conservative authority, yes; right-wing authoritarianism, no. Authority means a necessary reverence for tradition, law, legitimism; authoritarianism means statist coercion based only on force, not moral roots, and suppressing individual liberties in the continental fashion of tsardom, Junkerdom, Maistrean ultra-royalism.

Our argument is not against importing European insights when applicable; that would be Know Nothing chauvinism. The more foreign imports the better when capable of being assimilated: for example, the techniques of French symbolism in American poetry, the status-resentment theory of Nietzsche in our social psychology. But when the European view or institution is neither applicable to the American reality nor capable of being assimilated therein, as is the case with the sweeping Maistre-style anti-liberalism and tyrannic authoritarianism of many new conservatives, then objections do become valid: not on grounds of bigoted American chauvinism but on grounds of distinguishing between what can, what cannot be transplanted viably and freedom-enhancingly.

The Burkean builds on the concrete existing historical base, not on a vacuum of abstract wishful thinking. When, as in America, that concrete base includes British liberalism of the 1680's and New Deal reforms of the 1930's, then the real American conserver assimilates into conservatism whatever he finds lasting and good in liberalism and in the New Deal. Thereby he is closer to the Tory Cardinal Newman than many of Newman's American reactionary admirers. The latter overlook Newman's realization of the need to "inherit and make the best of" liberalism in certain contexts:

If I might presume to contrast Lacordaire and myself, I should say that we had been both of us inconsistent;—he, a Catholic, in calling himself a Liberal; I, a Protestant, in being an Anti-liberal; and moreover, that the cause of this inconsistency had been in both cases one and the same. That is, we were both of us such good conservatives as to take up with what we happened to find established in our respective countries, at the time when we came into active life. Toryism was the creed of Oxford; *he* inherited, and made the best of, the French Revolution.[2]

II

The present nationalist demagogy would never have become such a nuisance if liberal intellectuals and New Dealers had earlier made themselves the controlling spearhead of American anti-communism with exactly the same fervor they had showed when spearheading anti-fascism. Only because they defaulted that duty of equal leadership against both kinds of tyranny, only because of the vacuum of leadership created by that default, were the bullies and charlatans enabled partly to fill the vacuum and partly to exploit the cause of anti-communism. Today, however, it is no longer to the interest of liberals and conservatives to go on forever with recriminations over the 1930's. What is to their interest is to make sure that both are not replaced in the 1960's by the "rejoicing third": nationalist demagogy. Conservatives have no more excuse to refuse to cooperate with liberals and New Dealers against right-wing nationalist threats to our shared liberties than to refuse to cooperate against comparable left-wing threats.

Fortunately many Burkean new conservatives—Raymond English, Chad Walsh, Thomas Cook, Clinton Rossiter, J. A. Lukacs, August Heckscher, Will Herberg, Reinhold Niebuhr, and other distinguished names—are active and effective foes of the thought-control nationalists. Every one of these names achieved a record of all-out, explicit anti-McCarthyism in the days when that demagogue still seemed a danger and when it still took courage, not opportunism to attack him. The new conservative Russell Kirk, though naturally anti-McCarthy, has failed to share their clear-cut stand against American and European right-wing authoritarians and against the misuse of the conservative label by the midwest Republican nationalists and old America Firsters. The balanced Clinton Rossiter concludes in *Conservatism in America:* "Unfortunately for the cause of

[2] From appendix of second edition (London, 1865) of Newman's *Apologia Pro Vita Sua.*

conservatism, Kirk has now begun to sound like a man born one hundred and fifty years too late and in the wrong country." On the other hand, in fields outside politics, Kirk has made two contributions so attractively valuable that it seems preferable to dwell on them instead of on his Old Guard Republican pronouncements. These contributions are: first, his sensitive rendering (non-political, almost aesthetic) of rich old religious traditions and décors; second, his recalling to the attention of modern readers how much they can still learn from Irving Babbitt.

Even the best variety of conservatism in America will be subject to sources of corruption. It may help to anticipate these sources well in advance.

One source of corruption is to claim as traditional those shells of the past that no longer have a living content. Another is to devitalize even the genuinely living traditions by making them a rigid, mechanical cult instead of continually re-experiencing them in fresh ways. A third corruption is to let what is good in value-conserving be used merely to rationalize the unjust, inhumane, or authoritarian aspects of the status quo. A fourth is to goad into revolutionary extremes a moderate and lawful opposition to the status quo by lumping it together, as the tsars did, with a violent and lawless opposition. A fifth is the emotional deep-freeze today making young people ashamed of generous social impulses. New conservatives point out correctly that in the 1930's many intellectuals wasted generous emotions on unworthy causes, on totalitarianism masked as liberalism. True enough—indeed, a point many of us, as "premature" anti-communists, were making already in those days. But it does not follow, from recognizing the wrong generosities of the past, that we should today have no generous emotions at all, not even for the many obviously worthy causes all around us.

Having learnt how often such corruptions have invalidated conservatism and validated nihilism in the past, those new conservatives who are genuinely Burkean are now trying their limited best to avoid these corruptions at all cost. That cost includes being misrepresented in two opposite ways: as being really liberals at heart, hypocritically pretending to be conservatives; as being authoritarian reactionaries at heart, hypocritically pretending to be devoted to civil liberties. So far as the first misrepresentation goes: devotion to civil liberties is not a monopoly of liberals. It is found in liberals and Burkean conservatives alike, as shown in the exchange of letters between the liberal Thomas Jefferson and his good friend, the conservative John Adams. So far as the second misrepresentation goes: the test of whether a new conservative is sincere about civil liberties or merely a rightist authoritarian is the same as the test of whether any given liberal of the 1930's was sincere about civil liberties or merely a leftist authoritarian. That test is twofold, involving one question about practice, one question about theory. In practice, does the given conservative or liberal show his devotion to civil liberties in deeds as well as words? In theory, does he show awareness of a law we may define as the law of compensatory balance? The law of compensatory balance makes the exposure of communist fellow-traveling the particular duty of liberals, the exposure of right-wing thought-controllers the particular duty of conservatives.

Here are some further implications of the law of compensatory balance. A traditional monarchy is freest, as in Scandinavia, when anticipating social democracy in humane reforms; an untraditional, centralized mass-democracy is freest when encouraging, even to the point of tolerating eccentricity and arrogance, the remnants it possesses of aristocracy, family and regional pride, and decentralized provincial divergencies, traditions, privileges. A conservative is most valuable when serving in the more liberal party, a liberal when serving in the more conservative party. Thus the conservative Burke belonged not to the Tory but the Whig party. Similarly Madison, whose tenth *Federalist* paper helped found and formulate our conservative Constitutionalist tradition of distrusting direct democracy and majority dictatorship, joined the liberal Jeffersonian party, not the Federalist party. Reinhold Niebuhr, conservative in his view of history and anti-

modernist, anti-liberal in theology, is not a Republican but a
New Dealer in political party activities.

While the law of compensatory balance often places the
best conservatives within the more reformist or liberal party
(Burke, Madison, Niebuhr), these yet retain their basic
conservatism—and this with doubled effectiveness—by alerting
their liberal colleagues to the dangers of revolution and subversion: Jacobin in Burke's day, communist in Niebuhr's. In
both cases this alerting takes personal courage because one
runs the danger of being stigmatized as a "hysterical witch-
hunter" and maliciously classified with bad company (the
real witch-hunters, those who expose not real Soviet dangers
but slander innocent liberals). Burke's exposure of the real
terrorism of the French Revolution disgraced him as "hysterical" among liberal intellectuals still clinging to their illusions;
so did similar exposure of Soviet terrorism during the 1930's
and 1940's.

In this connection, Niebuhr, by his dramatic act of publicly
resigning from the *Nation* magazine to protest against its
attitude towards Soviet Russia, set off a valuably clarifying
controversy about the fellow-traveler role in the world of
literary intellectuals. Doubtless only a tempest in a small,
unnoticed teapot. But if that teapot is the world that we as
writers and teachers live in, then we have an ethical duty to
take it seriously, even while retaining enough sense of proportion to realize that the bigger internal danger today is not the
ever-fewer fellow-travelers but the coercive conformity of
right-wing nationalists.

Today the fight has been more than half won for the soul
of "the liberals who haven't learned"; it would be ungenerous
to belabor them disproportionately so long as every radio blares
forth the voices of coercive Republican nationalists, who not
only have never learned but never will learn. But had that
fight for the souls of the liberal intellectuals not been fought
and won from 1945 to 1953 (a fight for which George Orwell
deserved much of the credit), had we as writers and teachers
not learnt during that struggle to face up to Popular Frontists

and to Yalta myths and ethically to set our own house in order, then our whole world of anti-fascist literary intellectuals would surely have succumbed to the McCarrans, Jenners, McCarthys, Dirksens. Our world would in that case have succumbed because it would not then have been able with a clear conscience to deny their Red-baiting slanders against intellectuals and anti-fascists.

Instead, we were able to rally the successful counter-attack of our literary media against McCarthyism because the intellectual has been partly rehabilitated as a leader against both kinds of totalitarianism, not merely against the right-wing kind alone. What rehabilitated him was his facing-up ethically, with self-criticism, to the dishonesty of anti-anti-communism. That facing-up involved not only a teapot tempest over the *Nation*, and over its unjust libel suit against the *New Leader*, but the exposure in 1948 by "Americans for Democratic Action" of Communist control of the Wallace Progressive party. By that act of "premature" anti-communism, long before more headlined demagogues took any interest in the Soviet danger, ADA has earned a place of honor among all defenders of liberty.

That special honor of these effectively anti-communist liberals can never be tarnished, even if ADA itself has subsequently declined into an increasingly deracinated organization. Its membership includes several of America's sanest, bravest champions of civil liberties. But, even more, it includes too many zombie Gaylord Babbitts, the dead who walk, aging ambitious professors with a frustrated will to power, still mumbling dead liberal clichés from a long-since conservatized New Deal. They seem to be eternally waiting (as if for the Second Coming of FDR) for a big economic depression to call them back to Washington, just as in their nostalgic 1930's:

> They liked their dictaphones a lot;
> They met some big wheels and will not
> Let you forget it.[3]

Our main stress in this chapter is on rightist threats, a stress reflecting both the objective situation and the law of compen-

[3] W. H. Auden, "Under Which Lyre."

satory balance, making rightist threats the particular concern of conservatives, leftist of liberals. On the other hand, a solid case (given the silent treatment shockingly often) does exist concerning unfair academic discrimination against rightist Republicans by New Deal liberals in the colleges of the 1930's and 1940's. Unfortunately that solid case gets exaggerated— self-pitying exaggeration is another defect of many new conservatives—when applied even to the present decade by the bleeding-hearts of the right. The latter even have their own humorless little sectarian magazines springing up now, three in New York alone, each claiming to be still more right-wing and still more bleeding than its rivals for the true nationalist gospel. Self-evident is the parallel between them and the magazines of the rival leftist splinter-groups of the 1930's. Each magazine in either group, besides knowing it is the one true, persecuted voice of the people, has been wonderfully nimble at detecting subtle heresies in its own camp. So far, the new right-wing magazines are not at all the menace to civil liberties that the menace-avid American liberal imagines them to be. The only thing they are menacing with real success is the good word "conservatism," to which they give the same bad name that their mirror-images of the 1930's gave to the good word "liberalism."

Owing to the Socrates-hemlock identification that so fascinates intellectuals (an identification both flattering and masochistic), liberal professors and right-wing professors equally need to feel witch-hunted; instead of boasting how strong they are, each group boasts how crucified it is. America being big and pluralistic, both can dig up atrocity-stories that often turn out to be really true. And we are certainly all guilty every time we fail to defend boldly the free speech of right and left alike, especially when we disagree with it. But perhaps we may be permitted a wee bit of impatience with lack of sense of proportion when either version of Socrates acts as if his American campus hemlock were comparable to the persecutions suffered under a Stalin or Hitler. At that point anyone who witnessed with compassion the dignity with which anti-Nazi or anti-Stalinist refugees bore their persecution, may feel like retorting with feigned callousness: "Throw him out, he's breaking my heart!"

The need for new conservatives to maintain continuity also with rooted liberal traditions does not mean conservatism and liberalism are the same. Basic contrasts, symbolized by their contrasting spokesmen in our history, will always remain. George Washington, John Adams, and the Federalists are not the same as a priorist egalitarians like Paine or believers in natural goodness like Jefferson. John Calhoun is not the same as Andrew Jackson. Barrett Wendell, Irving Babbitt, Paul Elmer More are not the same as the spokesmen of our liberal weeklies or of the *New York Post*. Charles Evans Hughes is not the same as La Follette or even as Woodrow Wilson. No, the need for conservative continuity with America's liberal past does not mean identity with liberalism, least of all with optimism about human nature, utilitarian overemphasis on material progress, or trust in the direct democracy of the masses. Instead, conservative continuity with our liberal past simply means that you cannot escape from history; history has provided America with a shared liberal-conservative base more liberal than European continental conservatives, more conservative than European continental liberals.

All this is but another way of saying that true conservatism may be defined as the organic relationship of concrete to concrete in history, rather than the mechanical relationship of abstraction piled on abstraction (whether of Adam Smith, Rousseau, Paine, Marx). So let new conservatives stop becoming what they accuse liberals of being: rootless doctrinaires.

In the same way that many new conservatives underestimate how deep-rooted is America's tradition of Lockean liberalism and of Jeffersonian liberalism, many liberals underestimate how deep-rooted is America's tradition of Burkean and Federalist conservatism (the Conservation of 1776). Both liberals and conservatives, whenever minimizing each other's American roots, weaken the shared opportunity for the creative richness of the American past to serve America's future.

Chapter Twelve **THE TREND**

BEHIND REVISIONISM

Birds of ill omen are the flock of revisionist books and articles trying to exonerate German war guilt for World War II. They blame Hitler's war not on Hitler but on America's love of liberty; that is to say, on those anti-Nazi interventions which were and ought to be a matter of course for any unservile republic. The trend behind the symptom of revisionism—not a personal intention but an impersonal trend—is to make our present struggle against communism seem a struggle *only* against communism, instead of a struggle against all forms of totalitarianism.

Instead of feebly answering the revisionists by bleating defensively: "We did not really intervene so terribly much before Pearl Harbor," our historians should retort belligerently: "Yes, we did intervene but, to our shame, not enough."

Had the free world intervened[1] with full effort against the Brown murderers in 1933 and against the Red murderers in November, 1918, and strangled these world-arsonists in their cradles, as the conservative prophet Churchill tried to do in both cases, then there would have been no World War Two in Europe, no World War Two and a Half in Korea. Moral evil is moral evil; diabolism is diabolism; it is not merely a misunderstanding, nor a neurotic childhood, nor a lack of slum clearance. Evil being evil, it ultimately leads not to a self-

---

[1] "Intervened" need not at all mean the morally-confused doctrine of preventive war. On the contrary, in the *early* stages, means short of military action would still have sufficed a more united free world to topple the totalitarian oppressor, before he had time to consolidate his police state and to build up his armaments. What ends peace, brings war is not intervention, not so-called war-mongering, but an aggression-encouraging vacillation between ineffectual peace-mongering and ineffectual intervention: that is, between head-in-the-sand optimism and what Churchill called "too little and too late."

deceptive "co-existence" at Yalta, nor to a self-deceptive "peace in our time" at Munich, but to Dachau, slave labor, Korea.

The revisionist school in America is indignant, in several cases rightly so, at being called "pro-Nazi." (For example, an exception should be made for a sincere anti-totalitarian scholar like W. H. Chamberlin.) In one regard, however, the American revisionist school is even more pro-Nazi than any candid Nazi. At least Hitler (in his war-plotting staff conferences, of which we have stenographic records) and Goebbels (in his captured diary) did not disassociate themselves from starting World War II. They honestly boasted of that supreme achievement; Hitler's only fear, as he told his generals in a recorded speech, was that it would start too late, when he would be too old to savor it fully. What a pitiful spectacle when today Americans out-Hitler even Hitler in blaming World War II on our bipartisan Roosevelt-Willkie policy. Such Americans are rushing to exonerate Hitler of a war he admitted starting and for which, if victorious, he would have demanded the credit.

The truth is: the man whom the revisionists revile, intervened not too much but too slowly; 1935–36 was the ideal time for stopping Nazism peacefully, by lawful world intervention against its two pyromaniac treaty-violations (conscription, the Rhineland). But as second best, American lives would have been saved most effectively not by isolationism, nor by pacifism, but by a pledge in early 1939 to declare war if Hitler crossed any more frontiers. By blaming Roosevelt for the war, the revisionists offer a pro-Nazi argument so fantastic that not even the Nazi criminals used it in their defense at Nuremberg.

The twin of the *Chicago Tribune* view of 1939 that American democracy was to blame for Nazi aggression, was a 1951 article in the *Nation* by I. F. Stone. This article implied that American or South Korean aggression was to blame for the Red aggression in Korea and that the latter was a civil war on behalf of North Korean "social reform." Exactly the same kind of moral insanity inspired both views.

In the 1940's, the west fought for its very existence against

Hitler and Mussolini. In the 1950's, indignation against fascism seems to be becoming a monopoly of the left. For conservatives and moderate liberals, for our whole non-leftist capitalist democracy, this fact is still another kind of "intellectual shame." We know the false but superficially plausible conclusions against capitalism that any economic determinist would deduce from the increasingly leftist nature of anti-fascist idealism, and we know into whose Marxist hands such deductions would play.

Yet it was conservatives and moderates like Churchill and Anthony Eden who denounced the Nazi danger from the start. They denounced it when pacifistic Labor party leaders like Lansbury and MacDonald urged even more disarmament and appeasement than Neville Chamberlain. They continued to denounce and fight it when the leftist fellow-travelers supported the Hitler-Stalin Pact. No radical tribune of the people, "unmasking" Wall Street, but that middleroad Republican newspaper, the *New York Herald Tribune,* was the first to expose the Nazi sympathies of the Coughlinites and of the vermin press in the 1930's. Such forgotten facts show that anti-fascism can again be made to animate all supporters of freedom, whether conservative, liberal, or radical, whether democratic capitalist or democratic socialist.

In World War II, rightly eager to defeat the Nazi version of totalitarianism, America was careless about the democratic credentials of one of our allies and about our vast concessions to him: the old religious problem of bad means to good ends. As a result, public opinion dozed too long; not freedom but communist totalitarianism replaced the Nazis after World War II in half of Europe and Asia. When the same danger looms in reverse, the same lesson will apply. Increasingly the right-wing totalitarians will offer themselves as intimate political allies "against communism."

Perhaps they will triumph in a post-Adenauer Germany, by no means neo-Nazi yet cynically playing off east and west against each other, as at Rapallo in the 1920's and at Munich in 1939. Or perhaps these forces will triumph not in Germany at all but in a Know-Nothing American chauvinism at home. Whether in Germany or in America and under whatever respectable disguise, these forces will betray themselves in advance by an uncontrollable psychological need to "revise" the history of World War II in an unscholarly and anti-anti-fascist direction and to discredit anti-fascism.

In the current climate, America needs a nation-wide revival of our anti-fascist moral heritage of World War II. Simultaneously, of course, we must prevent this heritage from being exploited by apologists for Soviet Russia. By scrutinizing the past writings of such apologists, especially by the key test of whether they switched their line in August, 1939, to isolationism, you can easily distinguish between sincere anti-fascists and those anti-anti-communists who cry "wolf" over fascism merely in order to distract you from crying "bear" over Russia. While guarding against the insincere distractionists, we must equally guard against those who slander as "Red" the absolutely indispensable voice of our sincere anti-fascists (whether radical, liberal, or conservative).

Ever a pendulum between left and right, history will inevitably confront us again with a major right-wing threat, at home and abroad. When that times comes, will we make the same mistake as in World War II? Will we again win a war, lose a peace by concentrating solely against one of the several forms of the totalitarian threat? Unless we learn this lesson of the Hitler war, our national epitaph (to misquote Hegel) will be: "the only thing America has learnt from history, is that it failed to learn from history."

Chapter Thirteen   THE SUBURBS

BEAT US: Malcontents of Prosperity

vs. Plushbottom Diabolized

"Will any man pretend that the name of Andros and that of Winthrop are heard with the same sensations in any village of New England?" —*John Adams,* DEFENSE OF THE CONSTITUTIONS, *1787–88*

"The suburbs beat us." With these four much-quoted words, Jake Arvey, Democratic boss of Chicago, supposedly characterized the election of 1952. But he did not go on to answer the real question: what made them *want* to "beat us" in the first place? In confronting that question here, let us avoid the many vague meanings of so broad a term as "suburban" and confine ourselves to merely two specific ones: (1) the Republican old-suburban, who was born in the suburbs, has always voted Old Guard Republican, and will continue to do so; (2) the nationalist new-suburban, who has just moved in from urban slums, who was brought up to be a Democrat, and whose Republican vote of 1952 will not necessarily be repeated in the future, unless accompanied by neighborly social acceptance from the old-suburbans.

Both groups were voting Republican in 1952 (in local elections sometimes earlier, sometimes later than 1952). But their motives for doing so were different. Only the old-suburbans had the genuine Old Guard Republican motives: protection of business, a frozen Manchester liberalism in economics, a demure, understated, unviolent kind of nationalist intolerance. The new-suburbans voted Republican, sometimes for the first time, because of a qualitatively different kind of nationalist intolerance: passionate, overstated, and with a nervous energy that Goetheans would call *daemonisch*.

Let us examine the psychological connection between this second kind of nationalism and the fact that the new-suburbans are, for the first time in their lives, less worried about their economic earnings than about their standing in the community. That standing is ambiguous. Their parents were manual laborers, voting Democratic and New Deal. Their sons have left the parental immigrant proletarianism far behind and wear white collars as a matter of course. That rise in the world the sons owe to that same New Deal to which they show ironic ingratitude every time they cheer a Nixon or a Dirksen. Here is a case not of "twenty years of treason" but of twenty years of rags-to-riches. Perhaps the reason these unthankful sons are so eager to associate the New Deal with Alger Hiss is because they don't want to admit the association it really suggests to their mind: Horatio Alger.

By switching their votes to the Republican column in 1952 and sometimes thereafter, they were switching their surface-ideology, not their deeper impulses, from genuine radicalism to the imagined respectability of Republican nationalism. Such a switch bolstered the self-esteem of these sons of Democratic urban day-laborers who rose too suddenly into stuffy Republican suburbia. Why too suddenly? Because a rise in social standing cannot keep pace with too rapid a rise in income. Here for once is a radicalism expressing not the platitude of unbearable poverty but the paradox of unbearable prosperity. Their rebellion is not class war, that external war between poor and rich, but inner war, the war between self-hatred and self-esteem.

Insecure about their non-suburban or even foreign origins, and eager for acceptance among their new neighbors, the radicals of prosperity over-assimilate; they become not 100% but 200% patriots—that is to say, ersatz middleclass Anglo-Saxons. Like ham-actors of Americanism, they become more aggressively "anti-communist," nationalist, and so on than any old-stock neighbor of theirs. The less sure they are of their own Americanism, the more intolerantly they support the various investigating committees against "un-American activities," committees often led by fellow-immigrants who delight in pinning the "un-American Red" label on Mayflower-ish Anglo-Saxons from Yale, Harvard, or the Episcopal clergy.[1] Thus the prosperous new-suburban patrioteers pass from a left radicalism to a right radicalism without any intervening phase of moderation (that is, of a balanced liberal-conservatism) and without changing the real target of their resentment.

Republican businessmen used to moan: New Deal Democrats will stay in office forever because "You don't shoot Santa" and because Harry Hopkins would "spend and spend" to win elections. Wrong twice. Shooting Santa, that is exactly what the prissy Republican sons and daughters of Democrats did in 1952. Their motive was not economic insecurity (a motive much overrated for Americans except in depressions) but insecurity about social status.

Consider, apropos status-insecurity, the wise comic strip about Jiggs and Maggie ("Bringing Up Father"). The lovable Jiggs and the equally Irish, equally lovable Dinty Moore would quite likely vote Democrat if they ever bothered to vote at all; in any case, we could safely trust them with our civil liberties. The trouble starts with Jiggs's wife Maggie, a snob and a climber. She goes suburban, lace-curtain; forces Jiggs to desert his earthy friends of shanty days like the wonderful Dinty Moore. Maggie gets satirized for her resentment at never quite crashing the drawing room of a comic, monocled character named Duc de Bilgewater. (Borrowed from Mark Twain, the name symbolizes the healthy irreverence of comic strips towards snobbishness—in this case towards the pretentious Anglo-Norman French origins claimed by humorless titled Britons.) Maggie in 1956 will vote for 200% patriot xenophobes, and we would no sooner entrust our civil liberties to her than to Eva Peron.

[1] Dubious labels like "Anglo-Saxon" and "immigrant" are here intended in the sense that seems to matter most: symbolically, not literally; in terms of tacit pecking-order, not of imaginary "race."

The treatment of "Lord Plushbottom," in the even wittier comic strip "Moon Mullins," reflects a mixed attitude—half friendly kidding, half envious malice—towards Anglo-Saxon fancy folks and the eastern-seaboard élite. Monocled and walrus-mustached, poor Plushbottom potters about futilely, trying in vain to assert his dignity and getting ridiculed for his educated-sounding diction. Occasionally the fun becomes barbed: when Plushbottom uses his overrefined poses to welch on his debts. For example, while he hides under the bed from his creditor, his wife deceives the creditor by saying: "Lord Plushbottom is out of the city. . . . You know how them aristocrats are about speaking to people they don't know and don't want to know—the snobs!"[2]

Despite these barbs, Lord Plushbottom is intended as a likeable comic character, not a villain. But let us see what happens when you tilt the emphasis ever so slightly from the comic to the villainous. In a kind of surrealist nightmare-vision, Plushbottom diabolized turns out to be the image that right-wing nationalists ultimately hate the most. In a fanciful photomontage of the associations linked in the nationalist mind, imagine a diabolized Plushbottom plotting at the Boston Harvard Club with General Marshall, Acheson, Eleanor Roosevelt, and the ghosts of George III and Benedict Arnold: in order to lend American money to the monocled and walrus-mustached British Empire, to appoint 257 or whatever-the-number communists to the State Department, and to introduce nude bathing, modernist art, and the United Nations in our Sunday schools.

But how explain the fact that so many genuinely bourgeois and unexotic old-suburbans have also been supporting the promulgation of this kind of surrealist nightmare? How explain their willingness to accept such *outré* allies as the new-suburban thought-controllers? What on earth were the DAR and the Colonel Blimp-ish veteran-groups doing— and until late 1954 all kinds of high Republican stuffed

[2] Quoted from the instalment of *Moon Mullins* appearing in the *American Daily*, Rome, February 23, 1955.

shirts—as backers of such outlandish figures as McCarthy? The conformity of Babbitt Senior was the dull and quiet kind, not the present noisy and violent kind. Then why are his Old Guard followers susceptible, for the first time, to the appeal of the daemonic? First, because a crowd out of power long enough will back almost anybody; even the late Senator Taft, so solid, so undaemonic, did praise and hope to "use" the agitator McCarthy. Second, because Old Guard Republicans have been trying to revive a symbol not merely sick but dead: the late George Babbitt and the Coolidge era. So doing, they forgot a sinister fact about all exhumations: no Lazarus, returning from his grave, returns the same man he was before. In this case the grave was the burying and national discrediting of Babbitt Senior by the economic crash of 1929.

When buried loves return from the grave, they return as demons.

Chapter Fourteen   REMOLDING THE REPUBLICANS INTO A RESPONSIBLE CONSERVATIVE PARTY

"The principal instrument of America is freedom, of Russia slavery."
—*Alexis de Tocqueville, 1835*

"The more we condemn unadulterated Marxian socialism, the stouter should be our insistence on thorough-going reforms."—*Theodore Roosevelt*

In interpreting from conservative standards the agitator-era introduced by the Republican party during 1952–54, let us ask: what specific qualities can a genuinely conservative government be expected to bring? It can reasonably be expected to bring a return to established ways; an end to agitation and soap-boxing; reverence for the Constitution and for every single one of its time-hallowed amendments; a calm confidence in our public servants; orderly gradualism; protection in particular of the executive branch (including the army and foreign service) from outside mob pressure. The conservative kind of government would bring an increased respect— even to the point of pompous stuffiness—for time-honored authority and for venerable dignitaries. That would mean (but failed to mean) an increased respect for such authority or for such dignitaries as the Chief Justice of the Supreme Court, any ancient famous general decorated with medals for heroism or with a Nobel Prize for statesmanship,[1] the presidents

---

[1] See page 174 on general-baiting.

of such venerable institutions as America's oldest university, the spokesmen of some of our most deep-rooted churches,[2] the preceding Presidents of the United States (Truman, Roosevelt) because of the impersonal dignity of that office and because of the conservative's reverence for historical continuity, and the full Constitutional prerogatives of the present President and his top appointments, especially in such preserves of old-fogey traditionalism as the foreign service.

The above-listed venerations, often stodgy, are not always a good thing. The list merely intends to say: these qualities happen to be the conservative way of governing, and the Republican party (aside from the detached personal moderation of Eisenhower) has not brought us a single one of them. Despite its vaunted anti-radicalism, the Republican party produced more radical-style soap-boxing in two years (1952–54) than all the Roosevelt speeches of the whole "twenty years of treason" put together. The Constitution and Supreme Court, the two most venerable and conservative institutions of all, fared ill during those two Republican years (and this entirely aside from the over-obvious example of McCarthy). Never before in our history during so short a period were so many motions introduced—by Bricker and other right-wing Republican Senators—to amend the Constitution. (These attempts failed; so did those to revise away clauses of the Bill of Rights; their failure suggests that America's free heritage is sturdier than dreamt of by our worried European allies.) Justice Warren's confirmation to the Supreme Court was delayed unprecedentedly long in order to let him be baited as subversive, without a scrap of evidence, in front of a Senate investigating committee. Harlan, another Supreme Court Justice, suffered similar delay and wild charges.

Such traditional dignitaries should not in the least be exempt from Congressional investigation and newspaper criticism, two watchdogs of free government. But once charges are clearly disproved, to continue shouting them in Congress and the press is not serious criticism and investigation but the

2 See page 214 on investigating-committee slanders against Bishop Oxnam.

publicity stunt of baiting the élite and subverting a time-hallowed institution. The Republican slanders of General Marshall, Ambassador Bohlen, and the permanent Foreign Service hardly made for the conservative virtues of calm, dignity, historical continuity. Nor did the allegation—by a high Republican cabinet official—that President Eisenhower's former chief and friend, the anti-communist President Truman, "knowingly" promoted a communist spy.

As for our most traditional universities: both President Conant of Harvard and his successor, President Pusey, were attacked by Republican hunters of un-Americanism on grounds of aiding communists. Both presidents were anti-communists long before the present nationalists and can hardly be blamed for those shocking moral confusions of the 1930's that made communism so attractive to many intellectuals, including Harvard ones. The real ground for attacking presidents of Harvard, and of other venerable eastern universities, was not anti-communism but anti-élitism, anti-conservatism, anti-traditionalism. One of the most intelligent and influential columnists of right-wing Republicanism charged in 1955: "Apparently the current president of Harvard seeks to establish an élite, an intellectual élite whose qualifications would make them warders of our civic virtue." A service-élite dedicated to intellectual standards may or may not be a crime (Washington and John Adams believed democracy depended on "natural aristocracy"); in either case, it is not the same crime as communist treason. It is revealing that many right-wing Republicans pretend to attack the communist crime in their victims when they are only attacking the élitist one.

To identify the Republican party with the calm middle road of Eisenhower was entirely too optimistic. To identify the Republican party with the McCarthy movement was unjustly pessimistic. The party lies somewhere in-between these two opposite identifications that were so frequently made during 1952–54. Later the active participation of both these figures was sharply curtailed: Eisenhower's by physical illness, McCarthy's by political illness. Those changes left the party an unresolved battleground between new forces: on the one hand, the younger Eisenhower Republicans now emerging; on the other hand, the temporary alliance of the new, post-McCarthy nationalist demagogues with the Old Guard commercialists. In the decade ahead, the task of the young Eisenhower Republicans is to remold their party in the pattern begun by Eisenhower himself, a pattern of increased sense of responsibility, a generous world vision, and a repudiation of the McCarthy methods.

The McCarthy methods are living on under other names and in more reputable Republican circles, even though the McCarthy movement itself is certainly dead. These methods have set a dangerous precedent for the far future by introducing a new concept of guilt. The new concept has three aspects: retroactive substitution of bad intentions for bad consequences; the paranoid and often rather brilliant logic of sophistical amalgams known as "objective guilt"; the subversion, by amalgam-slogans like "Fifth Amendment Communist," of the Constitutional (traditional, conservative) restraints that protect the individual from the state.

This new concept of guilt is a two-edged sword. Once the Republicans accept its logic, they become as vulnerable to it as were the Democrats. To call the Republicans traitors for losing Indo-China abroad and for sabotaging scientific atomic research at home, would be a slander so far as Republican intentions go. They did not intend to lose Indo-China; they did not intend to sabotage our scientific defense-effort when they handicapped research with over-zealous security errors, over-rigid restrictions on travel, publication, exchange of knowledge. But neither did Truman intend to lose China or intend sabotage by his initial security laxness. Once America adopts the Republican-sponsored concept of objective guilt, Eisenhower's subjective intentions are no more of a defense against guilt than were Truman's.

Though false, the treason charge against the Republicans would perhaps be no more false than Attorney-General Brownell's original wording of his charge against Truman's "knowing" promotion of spies and certainly no more false than McCarthy's charges of "twenty years of treason." These charges were backed during the 1952 and 1954 campaigns by the Republican National Committee, which in those days still officially sponsored McCarthy's appearances. The Democratic party has plenty of dirty fighters and reverse-McCarthys also (as proved in the days when they slandered Wall Street businessmen indiscriminately as fascists and merchants of death). With a bit of ironic speculation, one can already picture future headlines indicting right-wing Republicans for "FOUR YEARS OF TREASON": four years of aiding the Kremlin by letting McCarthy disrupt Fort Monmouth and the Voice of America and by losing Indo-China and depriving America of the use of valuable scientists like Oppenheimer.

The belated Republican repudiation of McCarthy has not prevented official Republican spokesmen, including their Vice-President, from continuing to substitute objective guilt for Constitutional criteria of guilt. Unless this trend is reversed more emphatically, the Republican party may become the most anti-Constitutionalist major party in our history, partly abandoning the traditional Bill of Rights framework. Since Americans in time of prosperity are middle-roaders, avoiding radicals of right or left, this development would leave the Republican party as extinct as the old Know Nothing party. Upholders of parliamentary government, even if voting anti-Republican, should fear this development. They should work for the survival of the Republicans as a major party (by encouraging the abler of the Eisenhower Republicans to remold it drastically). Our balanced, Anglo-American kind of freedom depends on keeping both our parties alive.

The late Senator Wherry, one of the most typical Old Guard Republicans, protested strongly against being labeled "conservative." The protest was more justified than he himself knew. In contrast, the Republican Senator from New Jersey, Clifford Case, a man of scholarly learning in political philosophy as well as a practical statesman, has explicitly called himself a conservative in the tradition of John Adams, Burke, Disraeli, and the *Federalist* papers. His enemies in the party reveal the bankruptcy of their vision and of their terminology when they denounce as "too leftist" his balanced liberal-conservatism and that of Senator Flanders. What they really mean is that Case and Flanders show too much moral courage for their party; back in the days of McCarthyism, they were too bravely, too outspokenly for civil liberties. In the *New Leader*, February 7, 1955, William Bohn summarizes: "Clifford P. Case . . . is a moral, decent, intelligent progressive conservative. We need good conservatives. The sort of reactionaries who cut so much of a figure in the Republican party have brought conservatism into ill repute." To end that ill repute and to preserve the two-party system by preserving the Republican party, the national interest requires the strengthening of the abler Eisenhower Republicans: Justice Warren, Governor Christian Herter, Irving Ives, Cabot Lodge, Jr., Margaret Chase Smith, John Sherman Cooper, Aiken, Flanders, and Clifford Case among others.

First of all, the Eisenhower Republicans must re-assert the lawful Constitutional prerogatives of the Presidency against the direct democracy (government by counting telegrams) of demagogic nationalism. Second, as a matter of general attitude and not only of specific laws, they must educate their party further into canalizing the material forces of commerce within the bounds of the Christian ethics. Both these tasks are in the normal groove of the original American tradition, except for the relatively recent interlude of the commercialist Gilded Age that followed the Civil War. Both tasks require no innovating rash plunge into the unknown but a return to the true and tried ethical tradition of the *Federalist* papers and to the era before Grant, as opposed to the newfangled hucksterism of the Gilded Age.

Among older party members, the Eisenhower Republicans would tend to be those who supported Thomas Dewey and Wendell Willkie against Old Guard figures like the late Senators Taft and Wherry. The Eisenhower, Warren, Dewey, and Willkie Republicans, though sometimes differing from each other, are the party's "liberal" wing, in the sense that popular journalism uses that term. In contrast, those who continue in the footsteps of Taft and Wherry represent that combination of Manchester liberalism in economics and Social Darwinism in philosophy which journalese would call the "conservative" wing. The most influential American spokesman of the latter wing was W. G. Sumner.

Sumner imported from England the economic liberalism of Adam Smith and the Social Darwinism of Herbert Spencer as an after-the-event rationalization of our post-1865 industrial plutocracy, an untraditional, "un-American" plutocracy that temporarily filled the vacuum in genuine aristocracy created by the military defeat of our southern states. An even more important cause for that vacuum was the gradual osmosis from politics into literature of the New England Brahmin tradition and Federalist party tradition in the north. The most revealing example of this osmosis of Yankee conservatism and genuine aristocracy from politics into literature, thereby abandoning politics to the plutocrats of the Grant era, was the literary and scholarly career of Henry Adams, grandson and greatgrandson of two Presidents who had been political conservatives in the Federalist tradition.

In 1952 the national interest required Eisenhower to defeat Taft for the Republican nomination in order to enable Eisenhower to remold the party in the older values defended in 1912 against another Taft by Theodore Roosevelt. Once mistakenly denounced as a radical[3] for wanting to lead the Republicans back to America's precommercial ethical traditions, Theodore Roosevelt is now being increasingly called a

[3] It is important to distinguish between conservative and radical use of the pre-1914 Progressive movement in its overlapping with the Republican party. La Follette's purpose was radical (see the La Follette chapter, page 179), hostile to the conservative spirit of the American Constitution. TR's purpose, even when often backing the same economic reforms as La Follette, was conservative: to deprive radicalism of its appeal, to preserve the old, Constitutional heritage, to redeem the Republican party from the hucksterism of Presidents McKinley and Taft, to lead the party back to its old Lincoln ideal of ethics before commerce. TR's neglected warning to Old Guard Republicans remains permanently valid: "The more we condemn unadulterated Marxian socialism, the stouter should be our insistence on thorough-going reforms."

"conservative" by important scholarly biographies like Professor John Blum's. Will the genuinely conservative remolding of the party, which Theodore Roosevelt was unable to achieve, be achieved some day by the Eisenhower Republicans or their successors? If so, the Republican party will deserve to win back in the 1960 elections those independent voters whom it had attracted in 1952 and whose support it no longer deserved (but too often received) in 1956.

Already prior to his illness and indeed during many long stretches within 1952–56, President Eisenhower seemed either unwilling or unable to give the Eisenhower Republicans the aggressive backing needed to remold the party and to overcome their intra-party opponents. Several times both Eisenhower and Dulles failed to protect their own internationalist kind of Republicans when these were attacked by nationalists like McCarthy while the latter Senator was still powerful. Did this lack of protection merely express the legitimate need of keeping the Presidency above the battle? Then how explain Eisenhower's willingness to enter the battle and protect Richard Nixon from attack during 1952–56? Yet Nixon's political position (personal ties aside) was usually not with the Eisenhower Republicans but with their Old Guard enemies.

History gave a decent, popular President the prestige-power to remold the Republican party into responsible conservatives meriting re-election. Thereupon he partly squandered the historic opportunity for the sake of an imaginary party unity. That Christian Herter, John Sherman Cooper, Clifford Case, Flanders, Cabot Lodge, Jr., and Margaret Chase Smith are Eisenhower Republicans we know well enough. But is Eisenhower an Eisenhower Republican?

So far, we have noted merely the familiar differences— merely the political and economic differences—between the above-named Eisenhower Republicans and the nationalist right. But the deeper, more irreconcilable difference, the difference least discussed in speeches, campaigns, newspapers, is not a matter of this or that political or economic doctrine. It is a matter of appealing to an ethical, educated individualist élite in the first case; to a blind, diversity-crushing, overadjusted mob in the second case.

Even when President Eisenhower's ambiguous and intermittent leadership was at its height, the problem of Republicanism was this: could a party and a current Cabinet that was both rich and plebeian (that is, a traditionless product of post-Civil War commercialism) be trusted to conserve our free traditions in such perilous times? Will such a party ever recapture the *noblesse oblige* it once possessed so magnificently in leaders like Charles Evans Hughes, Elihu Root, and Stimson, but today better personified in the Democrats Harriman and Stevenson?

Here is a characteristic example—taken from the complex Oppenheimer case—of that problem of millionaire plebeianism. What is the tacit hierarchy of values, what is the *tone* of an entire Administration that lets a tradesman, unrebuked, compare a loyal scientist and national benefactor to an absconding bank-teller? May we not define the intangible tone of such an Administration as respect for quantity, disrespect for quality? Nobody was expecting, in 1954, a Cabinet of philosopher-kings; but surely Cabinet status need not stoop to the almost boorish callousness of comparing scientists to crooks and the unemployed to lazy dogs. In more mature civilizations, an auto dealer may or may not approach a great scientist cap-in-hand, but in no case with condescension. Will such well-meaning business minds, who are understandably tax-weary, really be able to improvise inexpensive substitutes for scientific armaments against Russia? Hardly by losing the use of some of our ablest and most anti-communist scientists. Even less by letting (until recently) a clown throw custard-pies at Fort Monmouth, the Voice of America, the free press, the churches, the universities, the Statue of Liberty itself.

To replace expensive but effective anti-communism by underrating intellect, burning books in U.S.I.A., demoralizing Fort Monmouth, and then being coached by professional actors on how to sound re-assuring on TV was not only heartbreaking when our very lives are at stake. It was also frivolous.

Part Three   DIRECT DEMOCRACY:

From the Populist Left to the

Nationalist Right

" 'Equality of rights' could all too easily be converted into an equality in violating rights. By that I mean, into a common war on all that is rare, strange, or privileged, on the higher man, the higher soul, the higher duty, the higher responsibility, and on the wealth of creative power and mastery."—*Nietzsche, 1886*

"Society cannot exist unless a controlling power upon will and appetite be placed somewhere; and the less of it there is within, the more of it there must be without."—*Edmund Burke*

Chapter Fifteen   DEFINING DIRECT

AND INDIRECT DEMOCRACY

". . . The Communist party has now extended its tentacles to the United States Senate. . . . I will no longer be in a position to conduct a formal committee investigation of communism. Therefore, I shall proceed as I proceeded before. . . . I shall *take to the people* what evidence I have. . . ."—*Joseph McCarthy, November 9, 1954 (italics added)*

"The big damage was done in the previous century, especially by Rousseau with his preaching of the goodness of human nature. . . . This resulted in the complete dissolution of the concept of [legitimate] authority in the heads of mortals, whereupon they periodically had to be subjected to naked [illegitimate] force instead . . . the *terribles simplificateurs*. . . ."—*Jakob Burckhardt (1818–97)*

"By a wise constitution, democracy may be made nearly as calm as water in a great artificial reservoir; but if there is a weak point anywhere in the structure, the mighty force which it controls will burst through and spread destruction. . . . American experience has, I think, shown that by wise constitutional provisions, democracy can be made tolerable."
—*Sir Henry Maine, 1885*

Vox populi, warned the Tory Coleridge in 1832, may turn out to be not *vox dei* but *vox diaboli*. *Vox populi* speaks through universal suffrage, but does universal suffrage speak for liberty? "In France," wrote the harmfully reactionary but sometimes perceptive tsarist Pobiedonostsev in 1898, "universal suffrage was suppressed with the end of the Terror, and was re-established twice merely to affirm the autocracy of the two

Napoleons." Lovers of democracy imagined they were cheering for individual liberty when they cheered for universal suffrage under Andrew Jackson in America, under the French Revolution in Europe. Did they realize they were also cheering themselves into the slavery of universal conscription, militarism, and the statist leveling away of individual diversities? The great conservative historian Hippolyte Taine, anti-Jacobin, anti-centralizer, and a defender of traditional local diversities, foresaw unerringly how universal suffrage—through its twin, conscription—would subject all citizens to the tyrannic militarist state:

From war to war this institution [compulsory universal military service] has grown, like an infectious disease. . . . At present it has got hold of all continental Europe, and it rules there together with the natural companion which always precedes or follows it, its twin brother, universal suffrage . . . , both blind and formidable leaders and regulators of future history, the one of them placing into the hands of every adult a ballot, the other placing on the back of every adult a knapsack.

In the exceptional historical context of America, universal suffrage is too deep-rooted to permit even a hint of a discussion of less quantitative, more qualitative alternatives (even though it was no reactionary but John Stuart Mill, himself a democratic liberal, who demanded a double vote for the educationally qualified). Without sharing the positive faith in universal suffrage that animates those whose religion is "the century of the common man," an American new conservative in the John Adams tradition can still find a negative reason for rejoicing in the indiscriminate counting of noses. It is at least a salutary check against the insolence of office, the tyranny of entrenched bureaucracy. But that check performs its function only when safely canalized within the stern Constitutional limits of indirect democracy. Let us start off by defining direct and indirect democracy very briefly, then proceeding to a lengthier consideration of the concrete problems raised by that distinction.

In Europe, direct democracy derives from Rousseau, indirect

democracy from Burke. In America, direct democracy derives from Paine, sometimes from Jefferson, still more often from Jackson, and from a tacit assumption—in the Populist and Progressive parties—that original sin stops west of the Alleghenies. In America, indirect democracy derives from John Adams, Madison, the *Federalist* Papers, Calhoun, our majority-checking, non-recallable judges, and our Constitution's insistence on round-about government "through channels." Direct democracy is government by direct, unfiltered mass pressure, government by referendum, mass petition, and popular recall of judges, government by Gallup poll and by the intimidating conformity of the lowest common denominator of public opinion. Indirect democracy likewise fulfils the will of the people but by first filtering it through the people's representatives, through the parliamentary, judicial, and constitutional sieve, and through the ethical restraints of religion and tradition. Direct democracy is immediate and hot-headed, indirect democracy calmed and canalized. Ultimately both are majority rule and, in the American context, *ought* to be. But direct democracy facilitates revolution, an unrestrained dictatorship by demagogues, and Robespierrean or Huey Longian thought-control; indirect democracy facilitates evolution, a self-restrained leadership of *noblesse oblige,* and the judicial safeguarding of civil liberties.

Freedom is attacked from the right by compulsory inequality, enforced by caste lines and despotism from above. It is attacked from the left by compulsory equality, enforced by guillotines and despotism from below. Yet freedom, inner and outer, equally menaced by left and right, is the indispensable prerequisite to fruitful creativity. That fact makes it more important to the longrun interest of society than either equality or inequality—either left or right, either direct democracy or caste tyranny. The ideal context, though not the only context, for freedom and for the creativity of the Unadjusted Man is a liberal-conservative indirect democracy.

Plebiscitarian direct-democracy, as a base for intolerance and tyranny, was represented for ancients by the democratic demagogue Cleon of Athens and the other mob-supported tyrants of the Greek agora and the Roman forum. Until the eighteenth century, these movements lacked elaborate conscious justification; mob instinct was its own excuse for being. Its greatest conscious justification by ideology was Rousseau's *Social Contract*, 1762. Among other things, this history-making book emphasized the superiority of the mystic General Will (*volonté générale*), incarnating the people as a collective whole, over the parliamentary Will of All (*volonté du tout*).

The practice of Cleon and the theory of Rousseau were combined for moderns by the Jacobins of the French Revolution under Robespierre and by Napoleon's plebiscite-based "democratic dictatorship." Contrast Napoleon's dictatorship, based on universal suffrage, with the traditional Bourbon monarchy, which ruled not by popular referendum but by historical prescriptive right. Neither side of that contrast was even remotely desirable from freedom's viewpoint; but the monarchical alternative was at least the less absolute and less statist of the two, since concrete traditions do more to check a bad Bourbon king than abstract Rights of Man and universal suffrage do to check a bad Bonapartist dictator.

Officially or unofficially, all government, without exceptions, is by élites. The distinction is: what kind of élites? Direct democracy means not an end to élites but the replacement of a tradition-checked or constitution-checked élite by one totally unchecked by anything at all so long as it can split the ears of the groundlings. Direct democracy does not end aristocracy but replaces a relatively mellowed one by what Byron called "democracy as an aristocracy of blackguards."

The original theory of direct democracy was formulated, especially in France, by thinkers of the left. Its subsequent left-wing descendants have included the Jacobin terror, the June days of 1848, the Paris commune of 1871, and the dictatorship of Lenin. But in actual practice, in contrast with theory, direct democracy has as readily been used by partly right-wing demagogues: Napoleon III, Mussolini, Hitler, Poujade. Thus the right (and its usual vast quota of rich, would-be-conservative dupes) is as guilty as the left in practice, though not guilty of the initiating theory. Frequently both extremes merge; in such cases direct democracy appears in a "patriotic" mob combination of right and left appeals. Major examples of that combination are Napoleon I, Boulanger, Peron. Minor examples are Huey Long, Coughlin, McCarthy.

To move from theory to practice, here is a recent example of an unsuccessful attempt to establish direct democracy in America. In December, 1954, the McCarthyite Senator, Herman Welker, tried to substitute an illegal, unconstitutional, and democratic dictatorship-by-referendum for the legal, Constitutional, and aristocratic right of ninety-six senators to judge one of their peers. Senator Welker's exact words were: "In this political trial . . . the ninety-six [Senators] were not the judges. The 150,000,000 Americans were the judges of the trial of McCarthy." When Senator Watkins was asked whether he thought McCarthy's innocence was established by his getting several million signatures from the grass-roots, the conservative Watkins illustrated indirect democracy by replying: he would determine his vote by the objective evidence about McCarthy and not by the fact that the pro-McCarthy petitions from the masses did win a numeric majority over the anti-McCarthy petitions.

Since right-wing nationalists cling so tightly to their feigned conservatism, it is amusing when their direct-democracy traps them into openly praising mass revolution. In November, 1954, Hugh Gregg became the state chairman for New Hampshire of the organization "Ten Million Americans for McCarthy." At a meeting of an economic organization called the New England Council, Gregg was quoted by the Claremont *Daily Eagle* as saying: "If you want to start a successful revolution, New England is the place. . . . The very idea of revolt is inherent in New England tradition. . . . The people may, and of right ought, to reform the old."

Most proposals for direct democracy in America today come from the nationalist right. Far from being traditionalist, conservative, pro-status-quo, this group sponsors such fantastic proposals for anti-élitist mob rule as trying to override our independent judiciary in civil-liberties cases, offering more newfangled Congressional amendments to the Constitution than ever before in one session, and uprooting ancient university traditions of academic freedom. The tradition of academic self-government by an élite of the qualified scholars themselves goes back eight hundred years to the free universities of the Middle Ages. Yet one best-selling book of the American far right, calling itself traditionalist and conservative, has proposed turning over academic freedom, teaching policy, and new schemes for value-indoctrination to the majority vote of a direct democracy of alumni, marching on New Haven or wherever like McCarthyite Jacobins storming democratically the ancient, privileged château of some Ivy League Louis XVI.

Reactionaries may distort our arguments against direct democracy into arguments against all democracy, even indirect democracy. To forestall that distortion, let us emphasize the following distinction: unlike the Europe of the age of Metternich, which still had organic and salutary roots in the feudal Middle Ages, America has no organic roots in hereditary class privilege but has very real roots in democracy. Not democracy, not ultimate majority rule, but only the direct kind of democracy is the enemy for a responsible, history-recognizing conservative in America.

Democracy is housebroken, is tolerant, humane, civil-libertarian, only after being filtered, traditionalized, constitutionalized through indirect representation. Suppose America had retained the indirect election of Senators (originally provided for by her Federalist party founders and abolished by the pressure of the La Follette movement in 1913). In that case, our Senate would today contain more pompous asses and more stealers of graft but fewer thought-control demagogues, fewer stealers of our civil liberties. That gain would have been worth the price; a country so over-rich as ours can afford waste and graft. What it cannot afford is demagogues mauling our liberties and muddying our foreign policy.

Inefficiency and corruption are two of the hopes of saving

the American individualist from the stereotyped massman. Inefficiency—the joy of putting grit in the well-adjusted machine —is the weapon against mass mechanization. Corruption— the mellow, warmly human sort of old Boss Tweed—is the weapon against the ruthless righteousness of mass crusades, the ruthless righteousness of what Robespierre called "the Republic of Virtue." In those instances when the choice is between two bad candidates, vote for the less efficient one. When both achieve heights of inefficiency equally sublime, so that you again cannot decide, then vote for the one who is more corrupt.

Non-corruption is preferable to corruption solely when the former reflects that *summum bonum,* an unruthless mellow kind of righteousness. But an inefficient, mellow corruption in government is preferable to the efficient, ruthless righteousness of the incorruptible Robespierres, Calvins, Lenins. In part, the ruthless righteousness of the Robespierres, Lenins, and other personally incorruptible purgers is a secularization of Calvinist Protestantism. This seemingly spiritual idealism is really an "unspiritual determination to wash the world white and clean, adopt it, and set it up for a respectable person. The world is not respectable; it is mortal, tormented, confused, deluded for ever; but it is shot through with beauty, with love, with glints of courage and laughter; and in these the spirit blooms timidly, and struggles to the light among thorns."[1]

Partly for sound, liberty-loving reasons and partly for sentimental, Rousseauistic reasons, liberal democrats detest the very notion of legitimate monarchy, hereditary rule, the formula "throne and altar." Therefore, some liberals have overlooked the menace to civil liberties of direct democracy, especially when of the leftist and not rightist variety, because direct democracy does liberals the service of destroying monarchy and aristocracy. But before liberals rejoice at Jacobin direct democracy for ridding them of the admittedly reactionary kind of legitimacy, let them note what happens soon afterwards. Soon afterwards, direct democracy rids them of all

[1] George Santayana, *Platonism and the Spiritual Life.*

other kinds of legitimacy likewise, including all legal and ethical checks on what mass conformity can do to the individual. Whether the masses then use their flood of direct, uncanalized power to create anarchy or to elect a tyrant, in either instance freedom perishes, and with it the democracy-installing liberals themselves.

Reliable opinion polls (cited in S. A. Stouffer's *Communism, Conformity, and Civil Liberties,* New York, 1955) reveal the American masses as overwhelmingly more hostile to civil liberties than their supposed exploiters and corrupters, the powers-that-be. What saves civil liberties from the intolerant majority is not universal suffrage, not equality, not universal rational Rights of Man, but an educated, self-restrained élite, the Constitution, the Supreme Court, and an organic, historical continuity of the unwritten, concrete habits of free men ("prescriptive right"). Reinhold Niebuhr sums up this conservative view in *The Self and the Dramas of History,* 1955:

> George Santayana pays eloquent tribute to the British genius for establishing liberty within the framework of stability. . . . The wisdom which combines the two approaches runs from Ireton through Edmund Burke to Winston Churchill. Ireton preferred the "rights of Englishmen" to the "rights of man." That phrase incorporates an awareness that rationally conceived "rights" are not very secure, even if defined as "inalienable," if they have not been acknowledged in the living community; and that the inordinacy of the ambitions of fellow men, which imperils our rights, are checked with more effect by historical habit than by appeals to reason. For each party is so intransigeant in its claims precisely because it regards them as "rational."

Hitler and Peron were the products of the very democracy they destroyed. Both were elected to power legally by majority votes. The true opposite of despotism is not democracy (which often elects fascists) but restraint on power. No fascist or communist ever defined his ism as "restraint on power"; many defined it as "democratic." The communists call their dictatorships "people's democracies." Hitler called himself an "arch-democrat" (*Voelkischer Beobachter,* November 10, 1938), defined National Socialism as the "truest democracy" (*Ibid.*, January 31, 1937), and in *Mein Kampf* praised "the truly Germanic democracy with the free election of the Leader." Mussolini: "Fascism may write itself down as 'an organized, centralized, and authoritative democracy'." Mussolini's son Vittorio (in *Tempo,* Milan, December 8, 1955): "My father was asked [by the King of Italy] whether he liked the title of prince for himself and his descendants, but he firmly said, 'No.' Of all titles, my father most appreciated that of 'Knight of Labor.'" Lenin: the Soviets are "a higher form of democracy."

Bertram Wolfe, perhaps America's foremost authority on communism and how to combat it: "Stalin announced that his 'Constitution' was 'the most *democratic* constitution in the world,' even as he was killing 14 out of 34 of its authors in the blood purges [and] insisting on the worship of his person like the cult of a living god." Erik von Kuehnelt-Leddihn, author of the insufficiently read *Liberty or Equality:*

[In 1933] certain German "conservatives" (I am thinking of Herr von Papen, and his ilk) betrayed liberty by disestablishing their unpopular dictatorship and by yielding to the largest party in the German Parliament. They should have kicked "democracy" in its teeth and let the *Volonté Générale* be damned. As long as the great majority of Germans voted the totalitarian (Nazi and Bolshi) ticket, they were morally obliged to continue at the helm of the State—to rule against the "dear people" with the help of the Army and the Police. But the ruling clique was too much *infected by democratic notions* to gather the courage to govern permanently *against* the "people" and *for* liberty, intellectual freedom, and generosity in racial matters. . . .[2]

The "bourgeois liberal" wants to feel himself simultaneously progressive and respectable. Therefore, he is more susceptible than either the Marxist or the conservative to a rhetoric that sounds respectably democratic but conceals despotism. More liberals than either conservatives or Marxists were fooled by the direct democracy and plebiscitarian despotism of Napoleon

[2] *Confluence* magazine, July, 1955.

III. In his important essay on this French dictator-by-referendum, Marx attacked the Bonapartist brand of direct democracy as acutely as the conservative attacks made on it by Madison, Calhoun, Henry Maine, Irving Babbitt.

One qualification: in practice the distinction between direct and indirect democracy is often less clear-cut, more shaded than the preceding definitions may have brought out. Few Americans consciously take either a direct-democracy line or an indirect-democracy line. Many great American statesmen were in the middle area; they could on occasion practice direct democracy without harm, because using it merely as a safety-valve—not a replacement—for the more basic indirect democracy of our Federalist Constitution. Thus John Quincy Adams argued strongly against Calhoun, though both were conservatives, for the right of direct popular petition in the context of the slavery controversy. The new-conservative stress on the value of indirect democracy is not meant as an abolition of such rights as petition and mass meeting; what causes concern is not the existence of these rights but pushing them disproportionately to a majoritarian dictatorship that threatens personal liberty. What is being criticized here is not the legality of direct-democratic appeals but the abuses of that legality in ways never intended by J. Q. Adams and his special New England tradition of petitions and town meetings.

If there has always been some direct democracy in the American practice (and if it sometimes is a useful safety-valve supplementing our more basic indirect democracy), then why is it a serious threat to liberty today? Because the hundredfold increase in the mechanized media for mass communications has put salesmanship, whether of soap or of politics, on the lowest common denominator, at the cost of everything individual, exceptional, and nobly aloof. Direct democracy now has an audience larger and more responsive to hysteria than ever before in history. Although demagogues like Hitler, Peron, Huey Long destroy democracy and equality, they are only possible in a background of democracy and equality, not of aristocratic individualism.

Those who rightly praise the direct democracy of the New England town hall, should not confuse a small village square, where participants know each other and are well-informed about shared local problems, with a radio address to millions of strangers all over the country. John Quincy Adams, and other conservatives of that very special New England tradition, did defend in Congress the right of popular petition. But their legitimate, sober, local tradition is not analogous to the emotional mass-impact of the nationwide agitation now made possible by radio and television. Such distinctions must be stressed against the attempt of Arthur Schlesinger, Jr. to justify direct democracy by making this analogy (in his attack in the *Reporter*, February 10, 1955, on the present writer's hypothesis). The reader will find the issue of direct versus indirect democracy, as originally posed by Paine versus Burke, still very much alive between liberals and conservatives if he consults the fiery debate over the issue in the 1955 letter columns of the *Reporter* (February 10 and March 24, pages 6–7). There the defence of direct democracy by many able liberals proves that Richard Rovere was too optimistic when remarking that they had outgrown that defence.

By combining mass equality and direct democracy, the new techniques for mobilizing the masses emotionally are threatening not only civil liberties but civil reasonableness. For example, in 1952 Richard Nixon was able to distract from a complex and debatable ethical problem by the mass-success of his sentimental Scottie-dog talk on TV. Gerald Sykes's novel, *The Children of Light*, 1955, unravels fascinatingly in fiction form the implications of the fact that Mr. Nixon's speech *succeeded*. The implications cut across party lines; equally ominous evasions of our Constitutional indirect channels were FDR's summonings of direct mass pressure by radio "fireside chats." But these at least had his usual patrician dignity. Now that entire Cabinet meetings of the Eisenhower Administration are staged for TV, rouged up as slickly as a soap opera, where will this trend finally lead us? It is a trend no politician can afford to halt once his rival has adopted it. The situation was well summarized by an Associated Press dispatch from Washington, October 17, 1955:

> The truth is that presidential candidates—and candidates for Congress, too—must have "television appeal" in the new scheme of things. This means developing a knack for acting before a camera. . . . It's got to *look* spontaneous and, in the *merchandising language*, sincere. . . . The agency which represented the Republicans in 1952 was Batten, Barton, Durstine, and Osborn of New York. The Democrats depended on the Joseph Katz Agency of Baltimore. Both parties again will have *merchandising experts* behind the scenes in the next campaign. It appears they have come to the political platform to stay. . . . Some wags are suggesting that the 1956 campaign should be reported by the drama critics rather than political reporters. [Italics added.]

When "a knack of acting before a camera" determines elections and complex national issues, what effect will that have on the wisdom of policy decisions? In order to serve the public best, policy decisions must often be unpopular, not coddling their audience but demanding of it effort and sacrifice. When heads of state, warned Burke, become "bidders at an auction of popularity," they become mere "flatterers instead of legislators."

Five of the best American statements for indirect against direct democracy are John Adams' *Defense of the Constitutions,* 1787–88; Madison's tenth *Federalist* paper, 1787; John Quincy Adams' *Letters of Publicola,* 1791; Calhoun's *Disquisition* (published posthumously, 1850) on "concurrent" majority versus mere numerical majority; Irving Babbitt's *Democracy and Leadership,* 1924. Here let brief excerpts from three of these classics speak for themselves in their contemporary relevance. (For John Adams, see our citations on pages 27, 148, 186.)

Madison, 1787:

> [In] a pure democracy . . . [in] a common passion . . . felt by a majority of the whole . . . there is nothing to check the inducements to sacrifice the weaker party or an obnoxious individual. . . . Theoretic

politicians who have patronized [pure democracy], have erroneously supposed that by reducing mankind to a perfect equality in their political rights, they would at the same time be perfectly equalized and assimilated in their possessions, their opinions, and their passions. . . . The first difference [between direct democracy and indirect democracy] is . . . to refine and enlarge the public views, by passing them through the medium of a chosen body of citizens. . . . Under such a regulation, it may well happen that the public voice, pronounced by the representatives of the people, will be more consonant to the public good than if pronounced by the people themselves, convened for the purpose.

John Quincy Adams, 1791:

Does he [Thomas Jefferson, who sponsored its publication] consider this pamphlet of Mr. Paine's as the canonical book of political scripture? . . . [Paine] scruples not to say, "that which a whole nation chooses to do, it has a right to do." This proposition is a part of what Mr. Paine calls a system of principles in opposition to those of Mr. Burke. . . . This principle, that a whole nation has a right to do whatever it pleases, cannot in any sense whatever be admitted as true. The eternal and immutable laws of justice and of morality are paramount to all human legislation. The violation of those laws is certainly within the power, but it is not among the rights of nations. . . . It is of infinite consequence that the distinction between *power* and *right* should be fully acknowledged, and admitted as one of the fundamental principles of legislators. . . . If a majority . . . are bound by no law human or divine, and have no other rule but their sovereign will and pleasure to direct them, what possible security can any citizen of the nation have for the protection of his unalienable rights? The principles of liberty must still be the sport of arbitrary power, and the hideous form of despotism must lay aside the diadem and the scepter, only to assume the party-colored garments of democracy.

Finally Irving Babbitt, 1924:

The opposition between traditional standards and an equalitarian democracy based on the supposed rights of man has played an important part in our own political history, and has meant practically the opposition between two types of leadership. . . . America stood from the start for two different views of government that have their origin in different views of liberty and ultimately of human nature. The view that is set forth in the Declaration of Independence assumes that man has certain abstract rights; it has, therefore, important points of contact with the French revolutionary "idealism." The view that inspired our Constitution, on the other hand, has much in common with that of Burke. If the first of these political philosophies is properly associated with Jefferson, the second has its most distinguished representative in Washington. The Jeffersonian liberal has faith in the goodness of the natural man, and so tends to overlook the need of a veto power . . . embodied in institutions that should set bounds to its ordinary self as expressed by the popular will at any particular moment. The contrast that I am establishing is, of course, that between a constitutional and a direct democracy. There is an opposition of first principles between those who maintain that the popular will should prevail, but only after it has been purified of what is merely impulsive and ephemeral, and those who maintain that this will should prevail immediately and unrestrictedly. The American experiment in democracy has, therefore, from the outset been ambiguous, and will remain so until the irrepressible conflict between a Washingtonian and a Jeffersonian liberty has been fought to a conclusion.

Since many American liberal democrats sincerely believe in both liberty and unrestricted popular sovereignty, their easiest evasion of a painful choice is to point out that often plebiscites (direct democracy) do admittedly vote for liberty. But often is not enough; an easy evasion today may prove more costly tomorrow than the courage of meeting a painful choice head-on. The contradiction between direct democracy and liberty is not merely theoretical nor confined to a dead past (Hitler, Peron) but about to burst upon an unprepared west in a practical problem of the near future: what if, as seems likely, the majority of Indo-China, in a fair election, votes for installing a communist reign of terror? What stand will western liberal democrats take on the right of a voting majority, perhaps 51%, to enslave, torture, jail a minority, perhaps 49%?

The Geneva plan for Indo-China pledges the west to prevent

the non-communists, if they lose the forthcoming plebiscite, from defending their liberty with arms against the armed majority. That pledge has been signed by some free western powers; its moral claim on them is undeniable. But so is the moral claim of perhaps 49% of a population against being enslaved, tortured, jailed. Between two such strong claims on the honor of the west, one of them also involving its humanity, have all of us thought through in advance the problem of which claim has priority?

Not only in the Indo-China agreement, too late to change, but in future situations that can still be changed, the objectionable principle is not democracy itself, not the west's agreement to elections and majority rule, but its failure to place them in a moral and legal framework (indirect democracy) protecting minorities. By definition communist or Nazi totalitarianism, whatever it may pledge, is incompatible with any such moral and legal framework. The various constitutions and judiciaries of the free western nations all agree in denying their majorities the privilege of slaughtering their minorities. Therefore, what right has the west (particularly France and England in this instance but the principle applies to us all for the future) to grant some foreign majority a tyrannical privilege we deny our own majorities? Is the west really bound, legally or morally, to tell the possible 51% of Indo-China in effect: "Go ahead and slaughter your non-communist 49% while we obligingly hold them down for you in the name of a Geneva agreement about which they were never consulted."[3]

If, as good Tom Paine majoritarians, western democrats do agree with Paine's dictum: "That which a whole nation chooses to do, it has a right to do," then why stop merely at its right to enslave, torture, jail all non-communists or non-Nazis? Why not, in the name of direct democracy, give the

[3] In practice not more than a fraction of the post-election non-communists would be able to escape from the country or get adequate refuge from the west. The fact that the possible communist majority may be vastly higher than our merely symbolic figure 51%—Hitler's, Peron's plebiscites were also vastly higher—does not change the moral issue of what happens to the rights of the minority.

majorities in all our countries also the right to institute can-
nibalism and to require all lampshades to be made of human
skin? If majorities do indeed have "the right" to vote for
communist mass-murder and Nazi genocide, then they certainly
also have the right to make soap from the fat of anybody
who believes in some old-fashioned aristocratic prejudice like
civil liberties, or like disagreement with the tastes of mass
culture. This is where America's post-1828 Jacksonian slogans
of popular rule would lead (just as Adams, Madison, Calhoun
feared they would) if she really meant them.

Of course, America does not really mean those slogans.
Nearly every explicit American enthusiast for popular rule and
moral relativism knows in his heart that popular rule must be
within an implicit moral framework to avoid self-destruction.
Some day in the future he will have to choose between what
he knows in his implicit, concrete heart and his explicit,
theoretical majoritarianism. The purpose of this chapter is
to make that choice less easy to evade. Unless liberal democrats think through that choice right now, the future will
take them by surprise with still another Indo-China abroad,
still another and next time more dangerous Long or McCarthy
at home.

Conservatives, in the American Federalist, British Burkean,
or French Tocquevillean tradition, know already where they
stand on the moral dilemma of some future Indo-China, some
future election of totalitarians at home or abroad. The conservative stand of indirect democracy was thought through
already in 1791 by John Quincy Adams (see above): "That a
whole nation has a right to do whatever it pleases, cannot
. . . be admitted. . . . justice and morality are paramount to
all human legislation. . . . If a majority . . . are bound by no
law human or divine . . . what possible security can any
citizen of the nation have for the protection of his unalienable
rights?"

Chapter Sixteen TWO CURRENT

TRIUMPHS OF LIBERTY OVER

"THE PEOPLE"

"Popular representations, resting on the comfortable fiction that the parliaments are 'us, ourselves,' control the private lives of 'citizens' to a far *greater* extent than the *monarchs* of the past would ever have dared to regulate the doings of their 'subjects.' Even a Louis XIV, autocratic centralist and breaker of many of the best traditions as he was, would hardly have ventured to exercise three prerogatives which 'progressive democracies' have claimed and do claim without batting an eye: prohibition of alcoholic beverages, conscription, and an income tax involving annual economic 'confession' to the State . . . not to mention 'nationalization' which is a special form of theft."—*Erik von Kuehnelt-Leddihn*, LIBERTY OR EQUALITY (*Caldwell, Idaho: Caxton Printers, 1952*)

"The judicial power ought to be distinct from both the legislative and executive, and independent upon both. . . . The people [are] as tyrannic as any king."—*John Adams*

Direct democracy is not the enemy only of liberty. It is also the enemy of humaneness. Most triumphs of humaneness were achieved by unpopular, highhanded, aristocratic actions, carried out against the democratic will of mass majorities. Only thus did nineteenth-century England get rid of its legal and academic disabilities against Jews and Catholics. In the words of Chuter Ede, former British Home Secretary: "I doubt if at any time during the last hundred years a plebiscite would have carried any of the great penal reforms which have been introduced. There are occasions when this House has to say that a certain thing is right, even if public opinion may not at the moment be of the same opinion" (February 10, 1955). A current American news item implies the same point:

The state supreme court declared today that racial segregation is unconstitutional in Florida public schools. It was the second state high tribunal in the South to take a stand on the side of the U. S. Supreme Court, which ruled May 17, 1954, that Negroes may not be kept out of heretofore white schools for racial reasons. The Texas supreme court ruled last week that state segregation laws were unconstitutional and that state money could be used to finance integrated schools.[1]

Would Florida and Texas judges have been able to perform such freedom-conserving rulings on behalf of the Constitution if direct democracy had succeeded in introducing into those southern states its goal of electoral "recall of judges" or if majority votes in those states had decided the issue?

After the McCarthy subcommittee had recommended sentencing a Harvard research assistant for contempt of Congress, Federal Judge Bailey Aldrich—not "the people" but one unelected member of an élite—acquitted him and sustained his contention that Senator McCarthy never had the Constitutional authority to investigate universities in the first place. What if the issue had instead been decided by two principles of direct democracy: plebiscite and popular recall of judges? In any referendum, "the people" of Massachusetts would have voted to sustain the un-Constitutional investigating committee, to throw the Harvard instructor in jail, to throw the law-abiding judge out of office, to replace him with some all too servile "servant of the people."

The year 1954 witnessed two magnificent defeats of "the people": the Senate censure of McCarthy, the Supreme Court ban on Negro segregation in schools. Neither triumph of liberty would have been won in a direct democracy, a government settling issues only by majority vote. Senator Watkins frankly admitted that the count of telegrams ran against censuring

[1] United Press dispatch, October 20, 1955.

McCarthy but declared his censure Committee would instead be guided by ethics and the Constitution.

By twice placing ethics and law above majority bigotry in 1954, the Senate and Supreme Court justified the insistence of Madison, Adams, Hamilton, Jay during 1787 on two undemocratic institutions to preserve liberty: the Supreme Court, the Senate. The Supreme Court is neither elective nor subject to popular recall. The Senate until 1913 was elected only indirectly through State legislatures; even today, not being based on population statistics, it remains less democratic than the House. In contrast, many Jeffersonian liberals of 1787 had preferred (fortunately foiled by the Federalists) a more direct democracy, no aristocratic veto power for the judiciary, and only one House of Congress, elected directly and democratically—no Senate.

The refutation of McCarthy's slanders by the rational logic of liberals had failed to dent the popularity of this now almost forgotten demagogue. What, then, did eliminate most of his following? America still retained enough respect for the aristocratic, Constitutional traditions, established during 1787–1800 by Washington, Adams, and the Federalist party, to drop McCarthy permanently after a committee of nonliberal Senate traditionalists censured him. When the Senate appointed the Watkins committee in 1954, liberal magazines and the author's liberal friends predicted unanimously that it would "whitewash McCarthy" because its members were "outdated fuddy-duddies, too conservative and élite-minded." Just because they were "too conservative," too steeped in the "outdated" undemocratic concept of the Senate as a clubby élite, the fuddy-duddies rose up and stopped McCarthy, at a time when the egalitarian masses were still supporting him overwhelmingly in the plebiscite of telegrams.

Let us place in historical perspective that censure-vote by the "gentlemen's club" of the Senate (a "club" never intended by our founders to be elected by popular vote). Symbolically that censure was the victory of the privileged, propertied, and aristocratic Federalists of 1787–1800 over Tom Paine and his Rousseauistic direct democracy. To formulate the issue in such candid alternatives has a comically enraging effect upon thought-controllers and liberals alike. The formulation seems anti-Watkins-committee and pro-McCarthy only if you are a doctrinaire Tom Paine democrat who deems the privileged and aristocratic always wrong. Alexander Hamilton, deeming them always right, was equally doctrinaire. They are wrong when privilege frustrates liberty, right when it fuses with liberty; our Constitution was designed to facilitate the fusing, not the frustrating.

Hence, the contrast between the two rival founders of the Federalist party, Hamilton and John Adams. Not Hamilton, the adventurous centralizer and *a priori* blueprinter, but our second President, John Adams, was America's truest Burkean conservative, our most balanced apostle of indirect democracy. Balanced: because half aristocratic, half democrat, distrusting power-concentrations in either half, whereas Hamilton distrusted only mass-power, not élite-power. "Despotism, or unlimited sovereignty, or absolute power," wrote Adams to Jefferson in 1814, "is the same in a majority of a popular assembly, an aristocratical council, an oligarchical junto, and a single emperor. Equally arbitrary, cruel, bloody, and in every respect diabolical. . . ." Other conservative aphorisms of Adams with new relevance today:

The multitude, therefore, as well as the nobles must have a check. . . . Paine's wrath was excited because my plan of government was essentially different from the silly projects that he had published in his *Common Sense.* By this means I became suspected and unpopular with the leading demagogues. . . . From a malignant heart [Paine] wrote virulent declamations, which the enthusiastic fury of the times intimidated all men, even Mr. Burke, from answering as he ought. . . . Mr. Jefferson [and I] . . . differed in opinion about the French Revolution. He thought it wise and good, and that it would end in the establishment of a free republic. I saw through it, to the end of it, before it broke out, and was sure it could end only in a restoration of the Bourbons, or a military despotism, after deluging France and Europe in blood. . . .

There will always be giants as well as pygmies . . . the former will be aristocrats, the latter democrats, if not Jacobins. . . . I never could understand the doctrine of the perfectibility of the human mind. . . . I am not of Rousseau's opinion. His notions of the purity of morals in savage nations and the earliest ages of civilized nations are mere chimeras. . . . Helvetius and Rousseau preached to the French nation *liberty*, till they made them the most mechanical slaves; *equality* till they destroyed all equity; *humanity* till they became weasels and African panthers; and *fraternity* till they cut one another's throats like Roman gladiators.[2]

History repeats not only the same infamies but the same alibis. During the censure debate, McCarthy's supporters called his opponents wily aristocrats and minimized his excesses as due to hurried zeal. Note the exact words used in 1793 by the left-wing terrorist Bertrand Barère, an apostle of direct democracy, in defending fellow Jacobins against a local French motion of censure: "These charges . . . have been suggested by wily aristocrats. . . . Terror must be the order of the day. . . . The man who crushes the enemies of the people, though he may be hurried by his zeal into some excesses, can never be a proper object of censure."

Liberty's second triumph of 1954, the ban on segregation by a non-elective, non-democratic Supreme Court, was likewise a triumph of the Federalist tradition of John Adams and of his son, John Quincy Adams. The influential anti-slavery speeches of John Quincy Adams in Congress were as characteristic of his conservatism as his anti-radical speeches. Less familiar is the fact that already his father, John Adams, had demanded in 1819 "the eventual total extirpation of slavery. . . . the turpitude, the inhumanity, cruelty, and the infamy of the African commerce in slaves. . . ." Long before liberal democrats like Garrison and Harriet Beecher Stowe, these two undemocratic New England aristocrats (the Adamses) took

[2] For source and date of each Adams aphorism, plus longer selections from Adams, Madison, Hamilton, Calhoun, Irving Babbitt, Tocqueville, Cortés, Coleridge, Disraeli, Dostoyevsky, Burckhardt, and Churchill, see the document-anthology section of P. Viereck *Conservatism*, 1956, an Anvil Book published by Van Nostrand, New York.

the lead in denouncing the anti-Christian infamy of Negro slavery in America. Their motive was not liberal rationalism nor democratic equality but the Christian moral law. Theirs was the fitting conservative position on slavery. In the exceptional case of the south, the same tragic historical context that warped conservatives on this issue, warped liberals almost equally. Moreover, the most rabid lynchers and Negro-baiters come not from the conservative aristocrats of the south but from its poor white trash, the same element—radical egalitarians on everything but the race issue—that followed the southern Populist demagogues against "the rich and well-born."

In 1788 Burke supported a motion for investigating the slave trade; he urged the total abolition of slavery. There is a harmonious pattern in the fact that the founder of conservatism should on moral grounds defend Negro liberty against slavery in 1788, just one year before attacking the professed liberty and actual slavery of the French Revolution. Burke's pro-American stand of 1776 and his pro-Negro stand of 1788 did not contradict his anti-revolutionary stand of 1789. In contrast with the 1688-rooted liberties demanded by George Washington and the Christianity-rooted liberties to which the Negro slave was entitled, the rootless "liberté" and a priori Rights of Man of the French Revolution were based neither on concrete traditions nor on Christian moral law but on Rousseauistic abstractions of democratic "General Will" and natural goodness of man.

Now for a non-Anglo-American example: the Dreyfus case in France could end happily only because (among other important factors) a tiny, unelected handful of civilian judges were sufficiently "the Unadjusted Man" to defeat the people's short-run will. The brave civilian judges of the Court of Cassation, when declaring Dreyfus innocent in June, 1899, knew that any French plebiscite of that date would have voted him guilty. Their condemnation of the anti-Semitic frame-up of Dreyfus by the nationally-popular army, like the American Senate condemnation of the then-popular McCarthy and like the Supreme Court condemnation of racial segregation, was a defeat of direct democracy by rooted moral law. In the words of the best brief summary of the Dreyfus case, his acquittal "was a triumph not of public opinion but of institutions that could withstand the public. Juries, the most democratic of our legal institutions, were against the man. Dreyfus was freed by a small group of professional judges, an independent judiciary."[3]

The frequent tyrannic intolerance of direct majorities may mislead reactionary counter-doctrinaires to call the masses "always wrong." Not "always" but "frequently" is the more accurate adverb, also the more damning one; to call them "always" wrong credits them with more character than they are capable of. The opinions of the Overadjusted Man are, by definition, a putty stereotyped by the external pressures of mass acceptability; he is no more motivated by an inner moral choice of evil than of good. Therefore, mass majorities, far from having even the Luciferian dignity of "always" choosing evil, *are* sometimes on freedom's side—by accident.

[3] James Grossman in *Commentary* magazine, New York, January, 1956, page 31.

Chapter Seventeen REVERSAL OF

ROLES: Witch-Hunt Methods in

Liberals and New Dealers

"Whenever a Congressional committee inspects the so-called private papers of a corporation official, the cry goes up that this is an outrageous invasion of the *rights of private citizens.* There are always plenty of newspaper apologists to join in the indignant protest. . . . In the munitions investigation something new was tried. A munitions manufacturer said its correspondence in many cases referred to government munitions business and that this was confidential to the government. It produced its papers under *compulsion,* but all over every document was 'confidential by order of the *War Department.*' Needless to say, the committee *paid no attention* to this stamp."—*Article in* HARPER'S *magazine, February 1936, by Hugo Black, then a New Deal Senator, chairman of the lobby investigating committee (italics added)*

History has its boomerangs; not always is the moral law violated with impunity. The epigraph for this chapter is the above quotation of 1936 from the New Deal Senator, Hugo Black, defending the invasion of individual rights by Senate investigating committees. The quotation must be read several times in order to savor how many different nuances of the present situation were anticipated by liberal inquisitional procedures. One of the few New Deal liberals to admit how much McCarthy learnt from the liberal precedent is Murray Kempton, writing in the *New York Post* in December 1954:

Conservatism reveres an institution. . . . The case against McCarthy enunciated by Ervin and Watkins was a case for the old-fashioned virtues.

152

Its essence was that ends do not justify means, and that gentlemen must rise up against muckers. Its core was manners and procedure. Ervin and Watkins stood at the end of the truth that there are codes of personal conduct which transcend the passions of a moment. . . . That sort of conservatism is back, and its renaissance is the most heartening thing in the McCarthy debate. When William F. Buckley said that Joe McCarthy had learned the language of controversy from liberals, he was only exaggerating a sound point.

Our aim is not to exculpate the Republican nationalists by falsely equating them with the obviously preferable liberals of the New Deal but to suggest a third alternative: a new conservatism that respects Constitutional procedures more than did either of these.

The New Deal's precedent-setting use of direct democracy (agitating mass-pressure against Congressional and Supreme Court independence) facilitated the McCarthy-style direct democracy of twenty years later. But even before the New Deal, liberals in the 1920's set grave precedents against what is now their pet mascot, the Bill of Rights. The liberal *New Republic* of the 1920's (not under today's editorship) openly admitted that the Senate committees investigating business were sometimes guilty of smearing the innocent and of guilt by association but justified the means by the end:

The investigators . . . occasionally turn the limelight on innocent persons, and are not wholly unconscious of the political effects of their activities. [But] the newspapers which bend every effort to belittle and deride the Senators who are surveying the condition of our Augean stables, lay themselves open to the grave suspicion that what they want is no investigation at all, but the sealing up of the whole malodorous mess. . . . There are several aspects of the Senate investigations which we regret. But after all, the choice is between such investigations as we are now having and none at all.

This *New Republic* statement went on to attack demands for improved investigating procedures (despite its admitting the need for improvements) on the ground that those demands might give the public the impression that Senate investigations were "hysterical." How familiar this round-about defense of hysteria sounds again today! Today the nationalist right uses the several witch-hunt sophistries of the above quotation, having been educated to use them by the liberals. Unfair investigations of liberals and Democrats are defended today by the same immoral argument then used by the Democratic Senator Reed to defend unfair liberal investigations of business-men. Reed: "The only man who fears investigations is the man who has done something he does not want the country to know about."

The parallels of these pages are objective; they cut both ways. For example, while liberals in those days used McCarthy arguments, capitalists in those days used the arguments used today by communists invoking the Fifth Amendment. When the left-wing Wheeler Committee investigated Harry Daugh-erty and tried to force his reluctant testimony, his lawyers accused it of transforming its investigating function into an unconstitutional judicial function: "To pillory Harry M. Daugherty before the American people, [the Wheeler Com-mittee] has assumed all the functions of a prosecutor, judge, and jury, with apparently none of the customary rules governing evidence and procedure."

That pattern of investigation speeded up after 1933 with the New Deal in power. When the Nye Committee of 1934 accused gun manufacturers of a conspiracy verging on treason, a conspiracy to cause war with Germany for gun profits, did the liberal press say: suspend judgment on so serious an accusation till the accused can state his side also? No, the *New Republic* began its article on the Nye Committee by assuming the truth of this serious, never-proved charge and by gloating melodramatically over the accused: "Here they sit, in the flesh, the merchants of death."

Senator Wheeler of Montana, then still a liberal hero, tried to violate the Constitutional rights of the Wall Street house of Morgan in order to make it surrender private documents. Thereupon, Professor Charles Beard, also still a liberal hero then, argued in the liberal press: Wheeler's investigation of Morgan must not be hampered by qualms about Constitutional rights and about wounding "the susceptibilities of perfectly honorable men." Instead, added Beard, we must view the battle not in terms of the civil liberties involved but simply as a power struggle: "new public right against old private right."

When the Hearst press appealed to the courts for its Constitutional rights against the inquisitors of the Black Committee, the liberal *Nation* sneered: "Under the pressure of a vigorous legislative attack, the bourbons always turn to the courts for extreme unction." Surely the disreputable right (Hearst yellow press) was as much entitled to Constitutional rights as is the disreputable left, whose court appeals the liberals defend today: both or none! Yet the *Nation* editorial then dismissed right-wing and business appeals to the Bill of Rights as issues of economics, not of objective law: "As usual in business appeals to the Bill of Rights, liberty is being invoked in order to protect entrenched privileges." John T. Flynn, then the business-baiting assistant of the Nye Committee, at least has the virtue of consistency. He supported the McCarthy investigations in the 1950's with the exact same argument he used against the rights of capitalists in his Nye Committee days:

John T. Flynn, while willing to concede that the courts were there to protect invasions of rights by Senate committees, nevertheless argued that *even if* the courts found that the committee had exceeded a just limit, such an *"infraction or two* of citizens' rights, however much to be condemned, ought not to be permitted to damn a whole investigation."[1]

Here again it is a Constitution-revering, procedural conservatism, not New Dealism, not liberalism, that emerges as the true opposite of the unethical investigating methods, right or left, of the Nyes, Blacks, Wheelers, McCarthys. As so often with chain reactions, the last on the chain is the worst. But the worst (McCarthy) might never have occurred if the milder (liberal) evil had not precipitated the chain:

[1] Albert A. Mavrinac, "Congressional Investigations" in *Confluence,* December, 1954. Italics added. The author is gratefully indebted to the entire article.

Say anything else you will about the Senate liberals' bill [of 1954] to
outlaw the Communist party. It is in character. . . . Its *disregard for
the Constitutional proprieties* takes me back to the old days of the
Thirties. . . . The thing that counted in the [New Deal] was to get
something politically useful on the books within a minimum of time.[2]

One of the crucial years was 1934. In addition to the Nye
Committee, that year witnessed two tremendously influential
best-sellers, the book *Merchants of Death* (by H. C. Engelbrecht and others) and the *Fortune* magazine issue of *Arms
and the Man* (March, 1934). These shot-gun accusations
against Wall Street, without sufficient evidence blaming it for
treasonably plotting war, have exactly the same paranoiac,
conspiratorial tone as the later hysterical accusations against
all New Deal intellectuals. "The Senate Munitions Investigating Committee of the mid-thirties, which gave great vogue to
the argument that the United States was pushed into
World War I by greedy businessmen, was largely a liberal
performance."[3] That Senate committee for investigating subversive capitalists even had its equivalent of Roy Cohn
(meaning merely: Senator Nye's bright young assistant behind
the scenes), namely a bright young law-school graduate called
Alger Hiss.

Earlier, Nye had campaigned for La Follette on the Progressive ticket. Wheeler had been La Follette's vice-presidential
running-mate on the Progressive ticket of 1924. Though
Gerald P. Nye and Burton K. Wheeler ended up in the
Republican and Democratic parties respectively, they are
best defined as Progressives in the tradition of western Populist
liberalism. So, in part, is their intellectual supporter, the great
historian Charles Beard, ending like them in the Hitler-
appeasing camp of America First.

Despite their common fight against Wall Street Republicans
during 1933–36 and their similar economic programs, it is
entirely unfair to equate the maturer New Dealers with the

[2] *Baltimore Sun,* editorial, August 17, 1954. Italics added.
[3] Eric Goldman in his ably pro-liberal *Rendezvous With Destiny,* New York,
1952.

Populists. To their credit, many New Dealers were unhappy about the Nye Committee. To their discredit, what made them unhappy was not Nye's witch-hunt against Constitutional rights of businessmen but merely the isolationist foreign policy which Nye, Wheeler, Beard deduced from that witch-hunt by reasoning: if all wars are conspiracies of Wall Street munition-makers, then so is the interventionist propaganda for collective security against Hitler. This ambivalence of New Dealers toward the Nye Committee in the 1930's reflected the gap between eastern internationalist business-baiters, western isolationist business-baiters. (Cf. the distinction made on page 37 between la-de-da and hip-hip-hooray liberals.)

Back in 1924, liberals had applauded the following callous defense by Felix Frankfurter of the Congressional investigations that already then were usurping judicial authority:

The question is not whether people's feelings here and there may be hurt or names "dragged through the mud," as it is called. . . . Critics, who have nothing to say for the astonishing corruption and corrupting soil which have been brought to light, seek to divert attention and shackle the future by suggesting restrictions in the procedure of future Congressional investigations.[4]

No wonder, after their own past callousness about "names dragged in the mud," the liberals did not evoke much public response when they tried in vain to rally the country against McCarthy. Instead, the country turned to Constitutionalist conservatives like the Watkins Committee, Senator Flanders, and ex-Senator Harry Cain for the brave and effective leadership that finally broke McCarthy's power. Senators Watkins, Ervin, Flanders, Cain, and Clifford Case, as well as Walter Lippmann, have a consistent record of opposing the earlier anti-capitalist hysteria as staunchly as the later anti-liberal hysteria.

In contrast with these Constitution-conserving traditionalists, note the inconsistency toward the Constitution of both right

[4] *New Republic*, May 21, 1924. In those days Justice Frankfurter was still a "crusading liberal." But today, increasingly conservative, this great jurist is rightly known for his Constitutionalist, pro-judicial role.

and left direct democracy. Businessmen who dismiss the Fifth Amendment as a Communist invention should be reminded that in January, 1892, the Supreme Court protected from the wrath of Populist witch-hunters a grain capitalist who, as they then put it, "hid behind the Fifth Amendment." Conversely, those who defended the McCarthyism of Vishinsky against the innocent Bukharin at the Moscow trials (many of them today on the Emergency Civil Liberties Committee) have no right to feel morally superior to any right-wing thought-controller today. *Their* attempt to justify Russia's bad means by an admitted Nazi menace was morally no sounder than McCarthy's attempt to justify his own bad means by the admitted Russian menace.

Even those many liberal New Dealers who have a flawless anti-communist record were often silent when the victim was not one of their own pet professors or pet Foreign Service aristocrats but the thousands of innocent, penniless Japanese-Americans interned during World War II or the helpless Minneapolis Trotskyites jailed in 1940 under the Smith Act, in both cases under Roosevelt and by New Deal officials. In short, civil liberties, claimed by businessmen twenty years ago and liberals today, are too often a matter of whose pet ox is gored when they ought to be defended for all. Embarrassing for contemporary Republicans and New Dealers alike is the following key accusation in the Republican campaign platform of 1936: "The New Deal Administration . . . has intimidated witnesses and . . . promoted investigations to harass and intimidate American citizens. . . ." Evidently both Republicans and New Dealers wax virtuous about "intimidations" and "investigations" only when they are on the receiving end.

Left or right, the rabble-rousers of direct democracy hate the Constitution for protecting minority rights against Congressional usurpers of judicial functions and against the mass majority. Does American liberty depend on majority rule? Not according to Supreme Court Justice Robert Jackson: "Liberty . . . is not a spontaneous product of majority rule, it is not achieved merely by lifting underprivileged classes to power. . . . It is achieved only by a rule of law." Behind that statement, new conservatives and chastened liberals can both unite today.

The fact that the liberals of yore were willing to believe that all wars were plotted in dark corners by munition-merchants and yet recognized the same nonsense as paranoiac when "Jews" or "Free Masons" were substituted for "munition-merchants," is an indictment of the liberal double-standard of the 1930's, which seemed to say: leftist bunk, yes; rightist bunk, no. This indictment of double-standards should not be dismissed—so often it is—as "McCarthyite baiting of intellectuals" but accepted in the same sincere good faith in which it is here stated: in terms of one anti-fascist, anti-McCarthy "intellectual" speaking to another, in a shared search not for debating-point victories but for truthful understanding.

The point is not to deny the need for investigating rotten conditions, a need too dogmatically denied by anti-anti-communists today, by anti-anti-businessmen in the 1930's. The point is to educate not only the public but the educators to the distinction between legitimate procedures, based on the Constitution, and inquisitions based on a paranoiac-conspiratorial approach to history. The legitimate procedures uncover the real Hisses and meanwhile preserve the Constitutional rights of all citizens, including the guilty. The paranoiac-conspiratorial approach of the Nyes, Wheelers, McCarthys, Jenners produces procedures slandering the innocent and subverting the Constitutional rights of innocent and guilty alike.

Since the more extreme liberals of the 1930's favored packing the Supreme Court or discredited it as "nine old men," since they minimized civil liberties as less important than economic democracy (parroting: "America may have political democracy, but Russia has economic democracy"), since they often derided free speech as a luxury for the rich to distract the workingman from progress, since they let Congressional investigators of business usurp judicial functions illegally, since they tried to deny the nonpartisan shield of the Constitution to Fifth

Amendment reactionaries—since so many of them are on record for doing the above things, how could they expect the country to follow them against the McCarthyite assault on those decent limits which the Constitution sets on Congress? Two points in their favor: their inquisition was often milder than that of the Republican right, and they meanwhile were achieving valid social reforms. Both points are partly offset by the fact that one has a right to expect more from them. When an educated liberal idealist commits daintily an offense against liberty that the Neanderthaler commits grossly, then one is tempted to comment: "Well, I still prefer you, the civilized idealist, to the Neanderthaler when it comes to personal conversation on a long train ride. But ethically you are the worse of the two because you are the better: the one who *knows* better."

Appealing for more "new conservatives," Will Herberg defines their freedom-conserving function as resistance to both kinds of "government by rabble-rousing":

Suspicion of "direct democracy" implies no distrust of the *individual* American citizen. A mob is something very different from the individuals who compose it . . . . a rabble, passionate, reckless, irresponsible. The wisdom of the Founding Fathers was directed primarily toward preventing the people, in whose hands ultimate power in some sense had to be lodged, from becoming a mob or a rabble. This wisdom is voided by the regime of government by rabble-rousing. . . . What is needed today is a good, sound, responsible conservatism. (Let us recognize that the new situation requires a new semantics.) We need a *new conservatism* dedicated to the conservation of the American constitutional tradition of freedom and order and unalterably opposed to government by rabble-rousing from whatever direction it may come. There are signs of a genuine realignment in American political thinking that cuts across and renders obsolete the old distinctions.[5]

Today liberals are still furtive, almost shame-faced about the Constitutionalism, the traditionalism, the conservatism into which they have been forced by the anti-Constitutionalism of the right-wing radicals. Outgrowing their obsolete anti-

[5] The *New Leader*, January 18, 1954.

Constitutional alignments of the 1920's and 1930's, let liberals have the intellectual courage to espouse openly the conservatism history is forcing on them in any case. A truly conservative defence of liberty would be less confused, less feeble than a unilateral defence by New Deal Democrats against McCarthy committees or a unilateral defence by *laissez faire* Republicans against Nye committees. Conservatism sees the root of liberty not in the abstract economic formulas of either of these groups, nor in the natural goodness of either the common man or the businessman, nor in the majority dictatorship of unconstitutional direct democracy, but in the combination between a universal and a particular: the universal of the Christian-Judaic moral law, the particular of the Anglo-American reverence for constitutional precedent. Both halves of the combination unite to cry out today that personal liberty is holy, holy, holy.

Chapter Eighteen   THE NEW

AMERICAN RIGHT:[1] Radicals

of "Anti-Radicalism"

"A human being needs only one thing: to *reach* his satisfaction with himself. . . . Whoever feels a dissatisfaction with himself is always ready to revenge himself for it: the rest of us will be his victims. . . ." —*Nietzsche,* THE JOYFUL WISDOM, *1882*

"Americans are so enamored of equality that they would rather be equal in slavery than unequal in freedom. . . . The subjection of individuals will increase amongst democratic nations, not only in the same proportion as their equality, but in the same proportion as their ignorance." —*Alexis de Tocqueville,* DEMOCRACY IN AMERICA, *1835–40*

"La haine du despotisme et l'amour de la liberté ont toujours été proclamées chez des peuples supportant fort bien le despotisme et très mal la liberté."—*Gustave LeBon,* APHORISMES DU TEMPS MODERNE

The more sophisticated members of the American right will soon be claiming that it is an unjust "guilt by association" to associate them with McCarthy. If anything can create a justified human sympathy for him, it is the effort of the nationalist right to make him a sacrificial animal, whom they

[1] When our status-resentment thesis about the new American right appeared in 1955 in the same symposium book (*The New American Right,* New York, Criterion) with Richard Hofstadter's partly similar thesis, there were third parties, not the authors themselves, who raised the question of priority and influence. Both authors had published their conclusions on the same date and reached them independently, as pointed out by Daniel Bell's preface to *The New American Right.* Based on Nietzsche, the present author's thesis (here

162

now piously repudiate after placing on his shoulders alone the thought-control sins they all share alike. Wolf packs devour their wounded member, then charge on; McCarthy was repudiated by his allies not for attempting thought-control but for being wounded in the attempt.

It would be going much too far to call the bulk of these right-wing nationalists "fascists." (That sort of name-calling can be left to them and to the *Daily Worker*.) Though definitely not fascist, they are often anti-anti-fascist, in the same way that some liberals are not communist but anti-anti-communist. The new right, among other things, is an attempt of discredited anti-anti-fascists (isolationists, America Firsters) to regain, via their pseudo-anti-communism, the status and influence they quite properly lost as appeasers of Hitler. A still smaller group, the Gerald L. K. Smiths and unrepentant Coughlinites, are indeed close to actual European fascism—but for that very reason are a relatively small fringe of the new American right. If only the new American right were fascist, it would be less dangerous; it would then be merely an alien importation of an unsuccessful European adventure, lacking American grass-roots. The bulk of the nationalist right is

Chapters 15, 18, 20, and 21) appeared in print December 30, 1954, in the *Reporter* ("The New American Radicalism: Mob Rule From The Jacobins to McCarthy"); January 24 and 31, 1955, in the *New Leader* (essays entitled "Old Slums Plus New Rich: The Alliance Against the Elite"; "Behind the Mask of 'Anti-Communism,' a New Nationalist Amalgam Does Battle With the Old Ruling Class"); December, 1954, in a mimeograph by the American Historical Association (the author's lecture on McCarthyism and conformity at the AHA meeting in New York). Mr. Hofstadter's partly similar and better-written thesis appeared in the winter 1954–55 number of *American Scholar* (aptly entitled *The Pseudo-Conservative Revolt*). This simultaneous consensus of separate research projects was equally exemplified in particularly valuable articles by Leslie Fiedler, Andrew Glazer, S. M. Lipset, Talcott Parsons, David Riesman. It bolsters one's morale to have one's merely impressionistic reactions to Americana partly sustained by more scientific researchers.

Somewhat earlier, my partly related thesis—namely, to trace McCarthyism to the left-wing Populist-Progressive movements—was presented on June 26, 1954, on *Town Meeting of the Air* in a public radio debate with Senator Wayne Morse about the La Follette era of reform and its direct democracy. Parts of that debate were printed as a pamphlet in June, 1954, by *Town Meeting of the Air* and recur in the Populist-Progressive sections of the present book. A still earlier analysis of McCarthyism as direct democracy remains the best: Will Herberg's "Government by Rabble-Rousing," the *New Leader*, January 18, 1954.

sincerely against fascism; that is, sincerely against failure and for success. But the bulk of the nationalist right was never sincerely against McCarthy and his methods; it differed merely quantitatively, not qualitatively from that particular failure. Therefore, our post-mortem on McCarthy is also a pre-mortem on the still-living and dangerous nationalist right in general— and, as such, even more relevant to the future than to the past.

The new American right claims that its mass base, its moral justification derive from the very real faults of the liberals. Its claim is accurate about mass base: mass disillusionment with the deservedly-discredited symbols Yalta and Hiss. Its claim is inaccurate about moral justification: mass anger, undiscriminating, strikes the innocent, misses the guilty, fights a cellar-blaze by burning the house.

The belief that ends do not justify means is axiomatic, at least in lip-service, to all societies based on the Christian-Judaic ethic. But in the case of the new American right the question does not even arise of whether its bad means (direct democracy, anti-liberty) are justified by its claimed anti-communist ends. For it has not furthered these ends (whether by bad means or good) but impeded them. Who, for example, can name a single notable anti-communist end achieved by Joseph McCarthy? It would have been better for America's moral education if he had achieved such ends; in that case, America would have had the opportunity of learning through experience that his achievements *even then* failed to justify his means. But he never did catch a single Red saboteur; never did substantiate his spy hoaxes at Fort Monmouth or at the *Voice of America;* never did prove the existence of those "eighty-one card-holding Communists" in the State Department. Herbert Philbrick, FBI infiltrator into highest communist circles, testified that the communists secretly loved McCarthy for giving anti-communism a bad name and for distracting us from really effective measures against communism.

It is only fair to concede that the nationalist right does have its more moderate spokesmen, its more plausible columnists. They claim that the McCarthy movement, even though led by its red-blooded zeal into "excesses" they sincerely condemn, never went so far as to be guilty of thought control. For it was supposedly trying to control subversive deeds, not thoughts. Yet McCarthy himself defined his aim as purging what he called "communistic *thinkers*" (emphasis added). "*Thought*-control" remains, therefore, the *mot juste.*

You can, if you wish, argue for the blessings of nationalist thought-controllers; that is your privilege. Or instead, if you wish, you can be an anti-communist. But one thing you cannot be is an anti-communist and a nationalist thought-controller at the same time. For anti-communism's first article of faith is love of the free mind.

The average liberal is correctly aware that the thought-control nationalists have an obvious reactionary root: Old Guard Republicanism. He is usually unaware that they also have a left-wing root, older, less obvious: the western radicalism of the former Populist and Progressive parties. To halt a foe, you must understand his real roots and fight him accordingly, instead of fighting only partial or only imaginary roots. Hence, liberals will never exorcise our nationalist overadjustedness by mumbling in their sleep the old incantations against "conservatism" or against "Wall Street," still sounding like yellowed pages from *PM* editorials of the 1930's.

At the risk of giving a surface-impression of deliberate paradox and of having one's motivating earnestness discounted accordingly, it is our maturely-considered thesis that the new right is the most anti-conservative uprising in native Americana since the Whiskey Rebellion of 1794. The new right is the form taken in America today by direct democracy. The new right is the form American overadjustment takes when it becomes coercive, instead of the voluntary or seductive form it takes in the entertainment industries. The chapters of this section will try to demonstrate that our right-wing nationalists are motivated unofficially and with perverse sincerity by that radical egalitarianism which the Soviets profess officially and with insincerity.

The leitmotif of our conservative case against this right-wing direct democracy is the Nietzsche epigraph on page 127: "Equality of rights" ending up as "equal violation of rights." Correct for Central Europe, perhaps that Nietzsche prophecy need not prove correct for countries with a pre-1789 Bill of Rights tradition. But America's Bill of Rights tradition will not be effectively defended by liberals if they misinterpret its strongest internal enemy—the spirit of Coughlin, Long, McCarthy—as a product of either capitalism or conservatism; it is a product of Rousseauistic mass democracy.

Eastern liberals and radicals today often forget how much anti-intellectualism (prelude to thought control) and Anglophobia (prelude to isolationist or pro-fascist foreign policies) were present in western liberals and radicals: the pre-1914 Populist and Progressive parties. Not always but often, these earlier orators distrusted eastern intellectuals and "perfessors" as alien, un-American city-slickers, whether as the "Harvard plutocrats" hated by the Populist farmer or the "Harvard Reds" hated by his Republican grandson today. In either case, behind that hate is the same instinct, whether verbalized in Populist radicalism or in Republican anti-communism.

Untroubled by subtle moral dilemmas of means versus ends, the old western frontier-instinct trusts the rough-and-ready means of a plebeian "Indian Charlie," not the finicky, legalistic means of non-earthy cosmopolitans with an educated ("alien British") accent. Hence, the disproportionate intensity of the hate for Dean Acheson and all who resemble him in Yale-Harvard mannerism and in educational and social status. Acheson's initial complacency and initial negligence toward the monstrous Red menace in China do not suffice to explain the intensity of the movement against him and why it picked him out as a single scapegoat for a negligence and a complacency so widely diffused among leaders of both parties. And he did at least help stop communism in western Europe; this is more than Republican isolationists, with their hate of the Marshall Plan, would have done. The real Acheson is a fairly conservative Wall Street financier, a symbol of civilized privilege and undemocratic reserve. He would have been denounced with equal intemperance as an "eastern banker" and "international capitalist reactionary" instead of as an "international Red," had this been the day of the Populist-Progressives.

It is a statistical fact[2] that the Ivy League representation (Yale, Harvard, Princeton) in the State Department is proportionately twice as high as in any other branch of the whole American civil service. Similarly the attacks of the old La Follette Progressives and new Republican rightists have been at least twice as vehement against the State Department (those tea-sipping "boys in striped pants") as against any other branch of government. The opening gun of the now defunct but once powerful McCarthy movement was the Senator's 1950 speech at Wheeling, West Virginia, "exposing" eighty-one or whatever the number Reds in the State Department. Rescrutinized from our present post-mortem perspective, his speech now emerges in its true light: an attack not on communism but on that traditionalist Ivy League aristocracy which centers statistically in the State Department branch of our civil service. In McCarthy's own words at Wheeling, 1950:

It is not the less fortunate, or members of minority groups, who have been selling this nation out, but rather those who have had all the benefits . . . the finest homes, the finest college educations, and the finest jobs in the government that we can give. This is glaringly true in the State Department. There the bright young men who are born with silver spoons in their mouth are the ones who have been worst.

America's post-McCarthy nationalism today continues to smolder against these "silver-spoon" scions in the State Department and the academic world. It charges them with three specific political vices (not to mention the more personal ones of godlessness, homosexuality, and chichi cocktail-swigging): first, smoothie internationalism in general; second, showering American dollars upon the lordly slicksters of British plutocracy in particular; third (linked[3] with the second), deliberately

[2] R. Bendix, *Higher Civil Servants in American Society,* Boulder, Colorado, 1949; pp. 92 ff.
[3] For example, columnists of the tabloid-rightist press are using captions like "Links British Nobility With Reds" to feature the book *Around the World Confidential* by their star reporter, Mr. Lee Mortimer.

betraying China to communism. In a parodying pile-up of clubby veneers, not one but three or four Brahmin schoolings have sleeked several of the State Department officials most associated with these political vices in the tabloid-fed popular mind. Thus ex-Secretary of State Acheson was schooled successively in Groton, Yale, Harvard Law, Wall Street—a quadruple provocation to the out-group majority! Equally provocative, and more frequent in the State Department and academic world, is the gamut of at least two or three such veneers. That gamut cannot help but condition the mannerisms and diction-patterns of its graduates; thereby it unintentionally goads beyond endurance, at some deep half-aware level, the egalitarian direct democracy of old Populists and new rightists.

But the above musical-comedy farce changed to potential tragedy when it became the unconscious "depth psychology" behind attacks in the early 1950's on academic freedom at Yale and Harvard and ultimately on the Constitutional liberties of all Americans of whatever status. Subsequently most of these attacks on academic freedom and civil liberties have failed or declined. Their failure or decline, though not justifying a complacent relaxation of vigilance, is the most reassuring aspect of American life today. Their failure or decline reflects forces still deeper and stronger than the above "depth psychology" of direct democracy, namely the underground forces of America's tacit Federalist-party heritage, America's permanent traditionalism beneath our overpublicized innovating flux, in short America's unlabeled, unaware conservatism.

Yet even the decline of the rightist out-group still leaves the public with a downright morbid overawareness of ivied schooling in government service. Whether a toadying pro or a sour-grapes con, any such emotion-charged overawareness distracts from the obvious duty of judging the government servant on his individual merits.

The new American right expresses the status-resentments of the left but with an emotional compulsion—here is the new twist—to clothe them in the lingo of the right. In those cases where it was not economic but psychological, the open radicalism, open aristocrat-baiting of the original Populists and Wisconsin Progressives was an inner shield for a yokel sense of being patronized and humiliated. Today the right-wing lingo of those same resentments (Anglophobia, isolationism, anti-intellectualism) is a shield against a shield. It is the second inner shield enabling those resentments to conceal from themselves their earlier inner shield—unendurable in the new American context—of Populist radicalism. That inward-facing mask, a mask against a mask, consists of waving too ostentatiously the flag of patriotic anti-radicalism. Patriotism, to misquote Dr. Johnson, becomes the last refuge of the ex-radical.

For example, in late 1955 the western Senator Goldwater, a former McCarthy enthusiast and now chairman of the Republican Senate Campaign Committee, made the fantastically sweeping charge that America's labor leaders were plotting "a conspiracy of national proportions." Evidently the American right, though abandoning McCarthy personally, cannot abandon its psychological origin in the western Populist *idée fixe* (similar to *Vulgarmarxismus*) that all disasters come from a monstrous anti-labor conspiracy by the educated upper class. Of course, that *idée fixe* today usually operates, as in Goldwater, with this anti-labor reverse-twist, a reversal reflecting the fact that Populism has now gone rich and suburban in a context of a cold war both angry and prosperous.

Though the McCarthy fad itself proved ephemeral, it was merely a fraction of a continuing radical egalitarianism, in revolt against the concept of the gentleman (a concept having its pompous idiocies as well as its ethical disciplines). That revolt is revealingly vindictive against three gentlemanly concepts: honor, *noblesse oblige,* mutual trust. Nobody's word is to be believed any more, nobody's reputation to be respected. Hence, the equally revealing obsession to subject everybody, from Ambassador Bohlen to Generals and Senators, to the lie-detector machine. Being a machine, it is an egalitarian leveler, not overawed by traditional honor and rank, nor duped by the big words of the educated, nor taken in by any well-earned lifetime reputation for public trust and public service. Thus the leveling radicalism of the new American right is merely the same old resentment of the Overadjusted Man, from the Jacksonian revolt against quality through today.

The entire status-resentment thesis of the present interpretation is frankly borrowed—elaborated—from Nietzsche (see page 56). He defined a sublimated *"ressentiment"* (he preferred the French term) as the basic, half-unconscious motivation of mass politics. Thereby he was the foremost of those making possible for America today that whole new branch of social psychology. Other early authorities who also helped make it possible, by their explorations of status-resentment, include Tocqueville (*Ancien Régime and the Revolution*), Henri de Man (*Psychology of Socialism*), Vilfredo Pareto (doctrine of circulating élites).

Nietzsche in *Genealogy of Morals,* 1887: "That most dangerous explosive, *ressentiment.* . . . The slave-insurrection in morals begins when *ressentiment* itself becomes a creator of values. . . . Slave morality says 'no' to everything outside [the conformist mass], everything different. . . ." In other words, the resentment of the quantity-minded Overadjusted Man is forever trying to crush, beneath the weight of mass mediocrity, everything private, unadjusted, quality-minded, whether as "too aristocratic" (in the traditional terminology of resentment) or as "too leftist" (in the inaccurate terminology—a drugstore "conservatism"—of the new American right).

Resentment, to be sure, takes varying forms. Owing to the physical priority of bread over culture, the form is often economic during depressions (also during all other times in the case of the cash-nexus commercialism analyzed in Part II). But in prosperous contemporary America, the rebel plebeian impulse behind the would-be anti-radicalism of the new right is not the usual, familiar resentment against economic exploitation but a resentment against social, educational, and sectional aristocracy. This resentment is a part of the Overadjusted Man's preference for new stereotypes over traditional archetypes, for conforming over conserving. The Old Guard huckster-type of Republican differs from his merely expedient and temporary ally, the nationalist-agitator type, in motivation; the former's motivation is economic and complacent, the latter's psychological and resentful.

Not only economics but also ethnic and religious rivalries have become less important a base for status-resentment, and hence for thought-controlling nationalism, than social, educational, and sectional rivalries. The same American prosperity that has relaxed ethnic and religious resentments has intensified the competition for social and educational status. Knowland, Bricker, Dirksen, the whole coalition of Asia First and Europe Last, are stoking their emotional nationalism with the social, educational, and sectional status-resentment of the west against a "fancy" and condescending east.

In the west, that resentment has been sufficiently emotional to unite a poor, business-baiting wing with a rich, big-business wing. That is, to unite the down-with-everybody left of the Populists (barn-burners from way back and distrusters of Anglicized city highbrows) with the pro-industrialist right of the *Chicago Tribune* nationalists. Both these western groups are mainly Protestant, not Catholic. Both resent the east as internationalist, overeducated, highfalutin'.

The east likewise has its status-resenters. Their characteristic emotion is the resentment felt by lower-middleclass Celtic South Boston against institutions like Harvard and Yale, alleged symbols simultaneously of communism and plutocracy. Each resentment, western and eastern, was relatively powerless when by itself. It was only when an unrich Catholic South Boston became allied, via the new American right, with newly-rich Protestant Texans (excluded from the *chicté* of Wall Street) and with flag-waving Chicago isolationists that the old American seaboard aristocracy was seriously threatened in its domination of both governmental and intellectual opinion and in its special old-school-tie preserve, the Foreign Service. Against the Foreign Service, the old Populist weapon of "you internationalist Anglophile snob" was replaced by the deadlier weapon of "you egghead security-risk"—meaning either atheist, subversive, or homosexual, allegations made for centuries in any society by "wholesome" peasants against "effete" noblemen.

That the radical nationalist right normally accuses only non-communists of communism is one of the rules of the game. Why? Because its quarry is not communists in the first place but the old Constitutional traditionalists. The reason for mis-labeling its quarry is the unadmitted revolutionary aim of this seemingly anti-revolutionary movement: to replace an old ruling class by a new one from below. "Ruling class" is here being used not in the Marxist economic sense but to mean the psychological determiners of culture-patterns, taste-patterns, value-patterns (within a special American context of class vagueness, class fluidity). The ultimate reality is always the individual, never the class; the term "class" is used merely as a convenient static snapshot—an approximation at best but an illuminating one—of the ever-fluctuating realities.

America's old ruling class includes eastern, educated, mellowed wealth, internationalist and at least superficially liberalized, like the Harrimans and Achesons of Wall Street or the Paul Hoffmans of the easternized fraction of Detroit industrialism. The new, would-be rulers include unmellowed, plebeian western wealth (Chicago, Texas, much of Detroit) and their big, gullible mass-base of the aforementioned alliance between western sticks and eastern slums. Nationalism—not synonym but antonym of national self-interest—is merely the means-to-power of the would-be rulers. Despite speeches by this out-group right about invading Red China (speak loudly and carry a small stick), our European allies need not fear that America would ever start a preventive war. The struggle to be the new American ruling class is a strictly domestic struggle, in which foreign policy and Our Boys in China have merely furnished heartless demagogic pretexts to embarrass the older ruling class.

From the viewpoint of McCarthyism, it was almost too good to be true that Hiss looked so superciliously civilized, that he dressed[4] in what caddish tailors for eastern colleges call

[4] The symbolic importance of clothing status-resentments in the old left and the new right would require a book by itself. Such a book would range from

"the Ivy League look," that like Roosevelt he had gone to
Harvard Law School, that he had been a personal friend of
someone so haughtily reserved and distinguished-looking as
Acheson, and that he was at the same time rich and intellectual.
In total defiance of ethics, McCarthy was even able to exploit
in a radio speech the coincidental resemblance between the
sounds of the first names of Alger Hiss and Adlai Stevenson.
Appeals to status-resentment are hard to prove because tacit
and often unconscious; they are the invisible writing in the
white spaces between the lines of American politics. Yet it
seems reasonably certain that the real appeal to status-resenters
behind McCarthy's unethical pun on "Alger" and "Adlai" was
the fact that both names have a Little Lord Fauntleroy sound.
Anyone familiar with gent-baiting comic strips like "Moon
Mullins" and "Bringing Up Father" will recognize that similar
British-sounding first names are used to characterize untrustworthy foreign idlers or over-educated young snobs just back
from Oxford.

Irrelevancies like the above served to inflate the public
indignation against Alger Hiss. That indignation was justified
but only on a different and more moral ground: the fact that
he was proved guilty. While deserving of attack, Hiss was not
sufficiently attacked for the right motives. The Dead End
kids of politics attacked him for the wrong motives, gloating
over any pretext to avenge their twenty years not of treason
but of status-humiliation. At the same time he was defended
for the wrong reasons by many liberal intellectuals; some had
their own unexpressed reasons for identifying with Hiss their
past fellow-traveler illusions of the 1930's and their bad
conscience about those illusions.

Even when, as so often, they had anti-communist records, the
liberal intellectuals of the old in-group were publicly compromised by Hiss: first, because he symbolized the social and
educational élite; second, because they were, with some notable

the "sans-culottes" of Jacobin France to the "shirtless ones" of Perón's Argen-
tine, from the nickname of the most famous Kansas Populist leader, "Sockless"
Jerry Simpson, to a pro-McCarthy gossip columnist's triumphant revelation of
March 6, 1956: "Alger Hiss shopping in Brooks Bros."

exceptions, much slower than the non-intellectuals in seeing and saying that Hiss was lying. Thus, the in-group liberals and New Deal intellectuals were partly to blame for adding fuel to the thought-control menace. Their blame should be stressed but not overstressed. More important than their blame was the fact that not they alone but all supporters of civil liberties and of middleroad decencies, the entire educated in-group, became more vulnerable than before to attacks by the right-wing coercive conformists. But their vulnerability and that of civil liberties will not prove fatal; through Senators Flanders, Clifford Case, and Margaret Chase Smith, the old New England civil-libertarian in-group has fought back hard and successfully.

Besides the older sport of baiting Harvard presidents and Eleanor Roosevelt, the newer national thought-controllers derive a particular emotional excitement from baiting generals. Especially generals spangled with medals and honorary degrees by the patrician in-group for projects of international cooperation (Marshall) or for helping the envied élite-symbol of England defend liberty against Nazi Germany (Eisenhower, Zwicker, Telford Taylor). Though later McCarthy's opportunism allied him with MacArthur backers, nobody has delivered a more malicious personal attack on MacArthur than McCarthy did in 1948 in "exposing" that general's marital difficulties. After Ike replaced Mac as our most prestige-exuding general, McCarthy's attacks on Eisenhower soon exceeded those made by any Democrat. This underdog resentment of bemedaled images of authority has been a clue to the leftist instincts concealed beneath the anti-leftist rationalizations of the new nationalism. Hence, McCarthy's wild swings at Generals Marshall, Clay, Zwicker, Telford Taylor, the whole Pentagon and CIC, and those various, mysterious generals who were guilty of coddling Major Peress or uncoddling Private Schine.[5]

[5] Some may interpret McCarthy's general-baiting in his favor: a sign of being for the little man against bigshots. But since freedom is not the same as the smashing of traffic-lights, a blind impulse to smash generals indiscriminately need not make a radical a champion of the little man; it may make him merely a would-be bigshot, the top tyrant of them all. Hitler took particular personal

All these generals were charged with non-existent left-wing sympathies; in other words, the radical instinct that baited symbols of authority had to be rationalized as anti-radical. According to the able Rorty-Decter book on McCarthy, a few real pro-communist infiltrators were still left in some of the government organizations McCarthy attacked; but these infiltrators McCarthy significantly did not bother investigating. For it is not the guilty but the innocent, whenever of old-family in-group status, who are the targets of the American nationalist movement. Only thereby can that movement achieve its purpose of enabling its immigrant following to feel and talk more old-American than the old-Americans themselves.

In addition, the far right always has a few generals, admirals, and Mayflower scions conspicuously on display. Does this fact contradict our Nietzsche hypothesis of status-resentment? Not if it be noted that these prestige-names are fallen angels, their wings frayed by some public status-humiliation. In the case of the generals and admirals (sometimes genuine war-heroes), the humiliation consists of being ousted by the status quo for trumpeting intemperate policies, unsustained accusations. In the case of the wilted mayflowers, the humiliation consists of feeling submerged and unrecognized under an alien flood of alleged inferiors. This reaction occurs not in the Anglo-Saxon who feels himself respected, and hence can afford to be a tolerant internationalist, but in the Anglo-Saxon who imagines himself a failure owing to non-Anglo-Saxon immigrants "ruining the country."[6] This kind of right-wing nationalist seems the nearest American equivalent of a British remittance man or a French general's *carrière manquée*.

The aristocrat-gone-cad, daintily brutal, is a leitmotif throughout the authoritarian nationalist conspiracies of history. Not major figures but major-minor, these dandified desperados

---

pleasure, after the revolt of aristocratic army officers in 1944, in hanging his generals by slow strangulation, several of them from the oldest patrician families in Germany; the proceeding, made as sadistically painful as possible for the generals, was recorded on movie film for the little corporal's delectation.
[6] For this symbolic use of "Anglo-Saxon" and "immigrant," cf. the footnotes on pages 115 and 211.

amble across the stage of all the bungled but dangerous
adventures of the far right: the anti-Dreyfus fraud, Boulangism,
the Guy Fawkes *putsch,* the Kapp *putsch,* the 1814 Hartford
Convention of epigone Federalists gone sour. All these
shadowy figures, forever "abusing the patience" of every
constitutionalist Cicero, seem psychologically descended from
the same protoype: Catiline.

In America, the Catiline from above, with his petulant
anti-democracy, remains the weaker partner within the
nationalist right. His dominant partner, the burly status-
resenter climbing up from below as if over the side of a ship,
uses as his characteristic cutlass not aristocracy but unconstitutional direct democracy. Both partners have their very
different reasons for an emotional investment in xenophobe
nationalism. Cleon plus Catiline: right-wing thought-control
is what happens when the immigrant successes team up with
the anti-immigrant Anglo-Saxon failures. The first are the
radicals of prosperity, the second the reactionaries of poverty.
The first rule the reality of the American right, the second its
letterheads. Too rapid a rise, too rapid a sinking: in either case
the human nervous system, being attuned to gradualism, gets
jangled into aggressive, intolerant discords. The alternative
to over-rapid change is not the reactionary's static defence of
some shabby social injustice but gradual change-within-
framework.

Too many commentators assume that the discredited
McCarthy will be replaced by a smoother operator, by a more
reliably Republican type like Richard Nixon. To be sure, an
Arrow-Collar Anglo-Saxon Protestant, clean-shaven and grinning boyishly while assessing the precise spot for the stiletto,
is socially more acceptable in the station-wagons of all kinds
of Junior Executives on the make. However, even though the
tamer, cleaner McCarthyism[7] of this able and intelligent

---

[7] Nixon: "Adlai the appeaser . . . Ph.D. graduate of Dean Acheson's cowardly
college of communist containment. . . . And isn't it wonderful, folks, to have
a Secretary of State who will stand up to the Russians." Such talk is common
enough among the petty politicians of both parties, definitely above the glee-
fully libelous level of McCarthy, but shoddy goods for a potential President.
No mere quibble about diction but a psychological difference between status-

Vice-President would make the Republican party more acceptable in the sticks, the gain would be offset by the loss of votes in the slums. The latter would thereupon revert to the Democratic party, from which they can be lured not by a bourgeois, Rotarian Nixon but only by a proletarian, non-Protestant McCarthy, himself originally a Democrat (significantly the very similar McCarran remained one to the end). Therefore, solely a future McCarthy-type (not the present discredited one from Wisconsin but no Nixon either) can combine these incompatibles of eastern Catholic slums and western Protestant sticks into a single Republican nationalist movement. In terms of demagogic technique, the flaw that destroyed McCarthy (not necessarily future ones) was the time-lag between his low organizing ability and his high publicizing ability; the censure motion hit him precisely during one of those lags.

A second cause of his destruction was more basic, will operate overwhelmingly against future McCarthys also: the fact that the two rival wings of the old ruling class—New Deal social reformers, Wall Street big business—can today team up (partly, temporarily) to protect their common in-group status quo. It was one thing for New Deal and Wall Street to battle in the 1930's, when their imagined interests seemed irreconcilable. But during World War II their common Anglophilia of the internationalist, educated eastern seaboard united them on the interventionist, anti-Nazi side (fortunately for the cause of liberty, though their motives were less pure than that). By today, the Roosevelt reforms have become so rooted in the status quo that the new plebeian money from the west can no longer count on a split between social chic (deodorized eastern money in New Canaan and Long Island), progressive chic (liberal clichés of "forward"-looking uplift), and commercial chic (State Street, Wall Street). Whether under eastern Dewey-Eisenhower-Chase Bank Republicans or millionaire-

---

levels lies in the fact that, where the middle-group Nixon twanged the word "folks" in the above quotation, McCarthy would have rasped "fellers" and Roosevelt would have genially drawled "my friends."

industrialist New Deal Democrats like Harriman, there will be no such split.

Unless there is a lost war in China (the out-group's best bet), this partial and only partial unity between the financial and the social-reformist wings of the American aristocracy will smash the plebeian insurrection of right-wing direct democracy.

Chapter Nineteen WISCONSIN BACK-

GROUND: The La Follette Progressives

"The common, average judgment of the community is always wise, rational, and trustworthy. . . . Over and above constitutions and statutes, and greater than all, is the supreme sovereignty of the people! . . . The Constitution, which has ever been the retreat of privilege, must be changed."—*La Follette editorials, 1910–14*

". . . Unlimited sovereignty, or absolute power, is the same in a majority of a popular assembly . . . and a single emperor. Equally arbitrary, cruel, bloody, and in every respect diabolical."—*John Adams to Jefferson, November 13, 1815*

> "Nobody's for McCarthy but the PEE-PUL,
> And we just love our Joe."
> —*Chorus sung at a Wisconsin mass meeting, 1954*

Senator Robert Marion La Follette, Sr., leader of the Progressive party and an honest idealist, was the dominant personality in Wisconsin during the first quarter of the twentieth century (Governor 1900-05, Senator 1906-25). In 1952, Wisconsin shocked the nation by re-electing the then still dangerous Senator McCarthy. When one special local area behaves in a special way, it seems only normal to examine whether any special local movement of the past helps explain that area's present behavior. Only normal; yet so far (written 1954)[1] almost no historical research has appeared even raising tenta-

[1] This chapter is the expanded text of the author's public radio debate with Senator Wayne Morse about the La Follette reform-era and direct democracy. The debate was held over the *Town Meeting of the Air* in June, 1954, on the historical occasion of opening the La Follette papers in Madison, Wisconsin.

tively the question of the possible connection between the only two major movements originating in Wisconsin. Is that partly because most liberal historians feel attracted by the first of these movements and regard it as the opposite of the second? It is easier to be blind to what one does not want to see than to surrender one's assumptions that egalitarian democracy is a bulwark of liberty and to concede that the local state roots of the McCarthy movement were less conservative than Progressive.

In turn, the roots of the Progressive party go back to the older Populists preceding it in the west (Populist party, Greenback party) and, still earlier, to the Jacksonian revolution. The subject of the psychological link between the Populists in general and the Republican nationalist right in general is resumed in the chapter after this one. The present chapter is more concerned with one specific Populist party, namely the Progressives, and one specific Republican nationalist, namely McCarthy.

The two Wisconsin movements shared six important and potentially dangerous characteristics: direct democracy, conspiracy-hunting, Anglophobia, Germanophilia, nationalistic isolationism, anti-élitist status-resentment. The first Wisconsin movement accompanied these characteristics with an unselfish devotion to the masses, the second with a cynical manipulation of the masses. Yet the first helped make the second possible by habituating the midwest to these six explosive characteristics.

Here is an ironic crosscurrent to these parallels: in 1946 McCarthy won his first Senate seat partly because communists supported him in his close race against none other than La Follette's son, Robert, Jr., whom the communists hated. The son, a level-headed statesman, had abandoned his father's isolationism while retaining his father's anti-communism. McCarthy defeated the son by drawing simultaneously upon two groups: the isolationist vote and the small (but electorally decisive) pro-communist vote, the former a heritage of the Progressive party, the latter of Yalta illusions. By the time of his 1952 campaign for re-election, McCarthy had become a belated convert to anti-communism. But though he made "anti-communism" his chief slogan, his peculiar use of the term was less anti-Soviet than Anglophobe, isolationist, anti-élitist.

The little-known facts about McCarthy's original party-affiliations may also be worth recording. He began his career as a supporter of the La Follette Progressives. Next he became a registered Democrat, attracting local attention as a New Deal campaigner against Herbert Hoover. His later shift to the Republican Party typified the shift of an entire generation of prospering sons of poor immigrants. Yet such shifts are often only on the surface; when McCarthy was espousing 100% farm parity in 1954–55, he was just as much in the Wisconsin Progressive tradition of garnering the rebellious farm vote as when he was denouncing Hoover as the Wall Street candidate in the 1930's.

The faith of La Follette Progressives in direct popular action, outside traditional and constitutional channels, was a faith in the natural goodness of the masses. Those modern Rousseaus and Paines, the Wisconsin Progressives of the early 1900's, expected utopia from such panaceas of direct democracy as the following: referendum; direct primaries; direct election of Senators; recall of judges by popular vote; overruling the Supreme Court by such quick and easy devices as a two-thirds Congressional majority; exposing the Constitution as a reactionary restraint on the mass will.

La Follette's drive was against Fifth Amendment plutocrats. He viewed them as hiding behind Constitution and Supreme Court in order to escape Senatorial exposure of their more than twenty years of treason against the man with the hoe. Two of La Follette's leading disciples, Senators Nye and Wheeler, with their earlier-analysed investigating committees, renewed in the 1930's that same La Follette Progressive witch-hunt against capitalist "conspirators," "hiding" behind the Bill of Rights. To discover where today's vocabulary of free-wheeling "treason" and "conspiracy" charges arose, leaf through the speeches of the Progressives and through the writings of the anti-capitalist muck-rakers before 1914. Typical is this outburst of the very western radical and socialist, Jack London: "Our statesmen sell themselves and their country for gold. Our municipal servants and state legislators commit countless treasons. . . . The world of betrayal!"

When McCarthy, Jenner, and Welker made a big point about defending Congressional investigators against hamperings by the President and by the courts, they were successfully appealing (no matter how opportunistically and insincerely) to a basic tenet of the Progressive heritage in the west, the grass-roots anti-patrician tenet of Congressional rights versus the executive and judicial branches. La Follette had campaigned in Wisconsin, long before McCarthy, for a law to forbid the executive branch from withholding information from Congressional committees. In fact, during the McCarthy-Army hearings of June, 1954, an old La Follette law was quoted by McCarthy in order to defend his violation of the executive order against getting executive secrets direct from the Civil Service. The La Follette law was a federal statute, introduced by the earlier Wisconsin Senator before World War I, about the rights of the Civil Service to communicate directly to the people. What is that but the direct democracy theme again?

In November, 1954, in defending McCarthy against censure, Senator Welker in two separate instances cited none other than La Follette as precedent for McCarthy in regard to the tactics of agitational radical democracy. First instance: Welker quoted La Follette's attacks on fellow Senators in the same violently strong language; tribunes of the people do not mince words like effete easterners. Second instance: Welker cited the precedent of La Follette's refusal to accept a subpoena from a Senate Committee he regarded as handmaidens of the upper class's international plutocratic conspiracy.

Liberals and progressives tend to regard a nation's institutions as loose pieces of furniture which the people can roll about arbitrarily in the room to please any abstract blueprint of the moment. Conservatives regard constitutions and institutions as created not by conscious abstract blueprints nor by the whims of momentary majorities (called "the people") but by the special concrete context and deep, half-conscious past of each society. Therefore, the liberal innovator's arbitrary shifting about of institutions created by history is really not a case of moving furniture; it is a case of forcibly uprooting deep-rooted trees, with the French and Russian revolutions as warning examples. In the light of this contrast between liberal and conservative views of institutions and constitutions, let us examine some representative passages of La Follette's speeches and writings[2] and see how they unintentionally prepared Wisconsin and America for McCarthyism.

On October 17, 1914, La Follette wrote in *La Follette's Magazine:* "Constitutions and statutes and all the complex details of government are but instruments *created by the citizen* for the orderly execution of his will." No (retorts the new conservatism): created not by any deliberate social contract of the citizens but by history, growing organically from centuries of the concrete experience of the past, whose roots are a country's strength and freedom.

La Follette in the same issue of his magazine: "Over and above constitutions and statutes, and greater than all, is the supreme sovereignty of the people!" The new conservatism retorts: Again no! Over and above popular sovereignty, and restraining it from lynching minority rights, stand the majesty of the moral law and the great oak of the Constitution. Despite history's lessons of how the mass referendum leads to Bonapartist dictatorship, La Follette could write these two dangerously incorrect statements: "The common, average judgment of the community is *always* wise, rational and trustworthy. I would see them clothed with the largest power to say the *final* word as to the laws under which they are to live and the government they maintain."[3] "The initiative and referendum will place in the hands of the people the power to protect themselves against the mistakes or indifference of their representatives in the legislature. Then it will always be possible for the

[2] *The Political Philosophy of Robert M. La Follette,* Madison, Wisconsin, 1920, pp. 174–178. Italics added throughout.
[3] *Letter to Wisconsin Voters,* November 3, 1910.

people to demand a *direct* vote and to repeal a bad law which the legislature has enacted."[4]

In rebuttal to a similar but earlier direct democracy, George Washington warned Jefferson: "We pour legislation in the Senatorial saucer to cool it." Those few words refute the entire case for direct democracy. They sum up why Washington and our Federalist founders "cooled" off democracy with countless saucers. The saucers included not only the then indirectly-elected Senate but a non-elective, unrecallable judiciary, an electoral college for the Presidency, and a Constitution deliberately made difficult to amend and making referenda difficult.

La Follette's drive against the cooling saucers succeeded in 1913 in the case of direct election of Senators. But he failed in his campaigns—they would have smashed our threefold Constitutional balance—to exalt the Congressional over the executive and judicial branches. He failed to make a declaration of war depend on a prior nationwide advisory referendum (this La Follette law might have left America helpless to defend itself after any Pearl Harbor). He failed in his important plan for allowing Congress to override Supreme Court decisions by a two-thirds vote. Finally, he failed to enable voters to recall judges for being allegedly plutocratic. Let us hope right-wing Republicans fail equally in their pressures to recall or intimidate judges for being allegedly communistic. Was the Republican attack of 1954 on Judge Youngdahl (when an Administration prosecuting attorney tried to make him remove himself from a case involving the Constitutional prerogatives of leftists) partly a La Follettism of the right?

The shoe may shift back and forth between the left foot and the right, but the battle between direct democracy and justice remains the same. Justice, not subject to elections, continues to protect the rights of all unpopular minorities, including the genuinely conspiratorial and wicked one that threatens America's existence today. Not the least part of that wicked communist threat to our existence is its threat to provoke us into lowering our high standards of constitutional

[4] *La Follette's Magazine,* October 17, 1914.

government-by-law to our enemy's low standards of a lawless, unconstitutional police-state. The following news item concretely illustrates how direct democracy, and the old Progressive platform of recall of judges by majority-demand, has served McCarthyism:

Sheridan, Arkansas. About 300 patrons of the Sheridan School District voted last night at a meeting to retain racial segregation in their schools. J. H. Duncan, a candidate for State Representative from Grant County, told the meeting that "I am wondering if the Supreme Court Justices are not Communist-infiltrated and if maybe Senator Joseph R. McCarthy shouldn't investigate the Supreme Court."[5]

On May 24, 1913, *La Follette's Magazine* thundered: ". . . The Constitution, which has ever been the retreat of privilege, must be changed." Conservative rebuttal: Of course, the Constitution is the "retreat" of privileged minorities; so it ought to be. Equally it ought to be the retreat of non-privileged minorities, now that it is the reactionaries who deride the Constitution as much as liberals used to deride it in the days of La Follette and Charles Beard. La Follette correctly saw that the Constitution and the nine old men protected conservative rights and Wall Street rights. What he failed to foresee was that these old men and their scrap of paper would likewise protect liberal rights from thought-control, Negro rights from segregation.

In 1910, La Follette called the average judgment of the people *"always* wise, rational, and trustworthy." Let the scandal out, let it be said aloud that by itself the voice of the people is never wise, never rational, never trustworthy. What, then, does deserve these three adjectives? The people, replies the new conservative, is "wise" only when acting within the framework of history, as incarnated in our living institutions and Constitution; only the moral laws of God are infallibly "trustworthy"; a society is only "rational" when it puts those historic roots and those moral laws higher than mere majorities.

As Rousseau's trust in the unlimited sovereignty of the

[5] The *New York Times*, June 3, 1954.

Volonté Générale of the people set the precedent for the French Revolution, so La Follette set the precedent for McCarthyism. Such liberals are sincerely fighting for the free and humane values that we anti-fascist and anti-McCarthy new conservatives also believe in; but they pave the way for their and our tyrannical enemies. The liberals do so because they tacitly assume evil as innate only in institutions, not in man himself. Consequently they entrust liberty to something untrustworthy: the sovereignty of the people. Against that misplaced trust by their liberal friends, the new conservatives quote the words used by John Adams in 1815 to refute a similar trust in mass sovereignty by his liberal friend Jefferson: ". . . Unlimited sovereignty . . . is the same in a majority of a popular assembly . . . and a single emperor. Equally arbitrary, cruel, bloody, and in every respect diabolical." We may characterize Adams and the rest of our freedom-conserving Federalists as a whole with the sentence used by H. L. Mencken (in "Pater Patriae," 1918) to characterize George Washington: "He had no belief in the infallible wisdom of the common people but regarded them as inflammatory dolts, and tried to save the Republic from them."

At this point the conventional liberal kind of anti-McCarthyite may interrupt: "Stop, stop!—*admit* there was never any hint, among La Follette Progressives, of McCarthy-style witch-hunts against innocent textbooks by professors. Does not that fact refute your malicious and paradoxical analogies between two movements having nothing in common?" Unfortunately the La Follette movement did lead a witch-hunt against perfectly innocent textbooks (as the scholarly Robert Guttman has pointed out) and did want to purge our schools of imaginary infiltrations by international conspiracies. In 1922 Charles G. Miller wrote articles for *La Follette's Magazine* denouncing a number of highschool textbooks of American history written since World War I—that is, since England became our ally in the defense of freedom against autocracy. Among them were texts by A. B. Hart and A. C. McClaughlin. The books were subjected to a recklessly unfair inquisition for refusing to bait the British or to repeat the exploded anti-British fables of early American nationalism.

This more objective approach of these textbooks—tied in with the English-Speaking Union and Rhodes scholarships by the proto-McCarthy technique of guilt-by-association—was unmasked by the Progressive Mr. Miller as a conspiracy of international British finance. Poor Yanks at Oxford!—the first Wisconsin movement unmasked them as agents of international capitalism, the second as agents of international communism. In both cases their pure Yankee souls were corrupted by being draped in Oxford sports-jackets and being plied with seductive tea, depraved crumpets. Thus, in Wisconsin rural lore, do red-blooded Americans from Main Street suffer a trans-Atlantic sea-change into sleek Alger Hisses.

In early 1955 the Senate Judiciary Committee subjected the distinguished jurist John M. Harlan to an unusually long delay before approving him for the Supreme Court. He stood accused, among several other things, of a crime called "one-worldism" (how many worlds, then, are there, short of space travel?). G. R. Jordan appeared before the Senate committee to accuse Judge Harlan of unfitness for office. Why? Partly on grounds of Harlan's having once received a Rhodes scholarship! In 1954 the same Mr. Jordan, leading a drive of plebiscitarian direct democracy, tried hard to collect ten million signatures for a petition supporting McCarthy against Senate censure.

The Miller articles of 1922 were not signed by La Follette. But *La Follette's Magazine* only printed articles reflecting its viewpoint. Furthermore, in this particular case an approving editorial explicitly endorsed the articles for exposing: "a vicious system of British propaganda which has been foisted upon the American people and which is now being forced through our school system." Let us not exaggerate; Progressivism is here not being equated with insolences like recent book-burnings. Yet any fairminded anti-McCarthy liberal of today, reading the textbook exposés in the pro-liberal *La Follette's Magazine*, will squirm with embarrassment at their really quite irresponsible insinuations. Their atmosphere exudes what James

Wechsler, in the title of his book on McCarthyism, rightly called an "age of suspicion."

Two generalizations follow. First, typical incidents like these do certainly demonstrate the *implicit* tendency (today rarely mentioned) of the Progressives to see issues in paranoiac terms of treasonable conspiracies; this tendency prepared Wisconsin psychology to temporarily accept McCarthy. Second, on all *explicit* questions of civil liberties, La Follette personally was on the side of the angels. The implicit (proto-McCarthy) trend in the Progressive movement overtook the explicit (liberal) trend when America confronted the Hitler menace; Senator Wheeler, La Follette's running-mate on the Progressive ticket in the 1924 election, and Senator Nye, another major western veteran of the La Follette movement, moved openly into the camp of Hitler-appeasers and intolerant America First nationalists.

La Follette denounced the New York internationalists as capitalistic, reactionary, and pro-British; McCarthy denounced them just as strongly but as Red, liberal, and pro-British. Both Senators wooed Wisconsin's German vote by their pro-German and isolationist foreign policy. In contrast with McCarthy, La Follette defended a Germany only partly authoritarian; it would be hard to picture a man of his high personal ethics ever stomaching the Nazi war criminals of Malmedy, whom McCarthy tried to exculpate on the Senate floor. Even so, La Follette went much further than normal liberal tolerance of "the other side" in his concessions to the aggressive foreign policy of the semi-authoritarian Germany of 1917. One of America's most balanced liberals, Eric Goldman, concludes: "The pro-German, anti-English tone of much of progressivism's 1917 program emerged with La Follette's attack on Britain."[6] Denouncing England during the height of the world war, La Follette called the Germans a nationality "of honesty and high ideals second to no people who inhabited this earth since the dawn of history."[7] He imprinted on Wisconsin and much

[6] *Rendezvous With Destiny*, New York, 1952; p. 240.
[7] *Congressional Record*, 65th Congress Spec. Sess. LV, Pt. 1, pp. 234 ff.

of rural America his favoritism towards Germany and Ireland, his intense dislike of England, his isolationism. In the Senate he played a leading role in keeping America out of the League of Nations; that imperfect organization might yet have prevented German and Russian aggression and World War II if America had joined.

This Progressive heritage in foreign policy, plus the slander of our necessary re-armers as "merchants of death" by La Follette disciples and some New Dealers in the mid-thirties, resulted in the Neutrality Act, that monument of suicidal isolationism. Thereby Hitler, the killer of liberals, almost won World War II, thanks in part to the well-meaning liberals of the Progressive movement.[8]

McCarthy called General Marshall's honest misunderstanding of China a "conspiracy of infamy so black that" etcetera, etcetera; that is exactly how La Follette saw the capitalist "business conspiracies" against the farmer. At first glance, the conspiracy-hunting of the two Wisconsin Senators may seem inconsistent with their cult of direct democracy. But actually the combination of these two absurdities was necessary for face-saving; in no other way could the Progressives explain to themselves why they lost all nationwide elections. They could not blame the mass voter; that would be heresy, for they deemed him full of "natural goodness" (Rousseau's noble savage). Therefore, they had to blame their electoral defeats not on the infallible will of the people but on some malignant conspiracy of eastern bankers and war-mongers, cheating their hero of his rightful place in the White House. That was precisely how La Follette himself explained his defeat after running for President in 1924. The people intended to vote for him, he reasoned, but the big interests would not let them; through some unproved mysterious plot, the big interests kept the toilers from the polling booths.

[8] Thanks in part, but only in part: the larger part of the blame for fascism continued to lie with the would-be conservatism of right-wing nationalists; they must not be allowed to get off the hook merely because it here becomes necessary, on grounds of scholarly honesty, to criticize the disasters caused by well-meaning liberals. Fools cause disasters; unlike fascists, they still are fools, not knaves.

These two errors of the Progressive movement combined with a third: economic determinism. The complex causalities of all history, whether our Constitution or our war with Germany, were oversimplified into mere capitalist profiteering. For example, La Follette's disciple, the great historian Charles Beard, derived from economic determinism his two most unfortunate obsessions: his debunking the Constitution, his "America First" opposition to FDR's anti-Nazi intervention. In the tradition of La Follette, Nye, and Wheeler, Beard "explained" American resistance to aggressive German militarism as economic plots by bankers and munition-makers. If one prefers liberty to totalitarianism, one can only comment on his allegations: thank God for the plots of bankers and munition-makers against Hitler; would that there had been bigger and better plots sooner against Hitler and Lenin alike.

In the Progressive style of Beard and La Follette, today right-wing Republicans are oversimplifying history into economic profiteering when they accuse our British allies of "blood-money in China." An old tune: La Follette had been preaching the same combination of Anglophobe isolationism and economic determinism already in 1916. That year he made his famous accusation and oversimplification that "financial imperialism . . . was back of all modern war."

La Follette's most admired virtues were his incorruptibility and his righteous indignation. These two virtues did more than his defects to prepare Wisconsin for McCarthyism. For they diffused a self-righteous attitude treating opponents not as merely mistaken but as conspirators, traitors. Like his epigones Senators Nye, Wheeler, Black (famous for their ruthless investigating committees against "conspiracies"), La Follette had the ruthless righteousness of the crusading inquisitor. Robespierre, too, had been nicknamed "the incorruptible." In *Nelson W. Aldrich*,[9] Nathaniel Stephenson called La Follette a man "forever brooding on his wrongs," suffering from a persecution complex on behalf of everybody west of the treacherous, internationalist east: "[La Follette] charged

9 New York, 1930; pp. 341–57.

the air with hysteria. . . . in a cloud of recrimination, charges, denials, counter-charges, screaming and fulmination. . . . With this went a lack of intellectual realism. He exaggerated conditions, he twisted evidence, he had little sense of the value of temperance." As if nature were imitating art, every word of Stephenson's description of almost three decades ago applies even more to the recently-ended McCarthy era.

What Wisconsin and America need today are not these self-righteous qualities of La Follette but the really attractive aspects of his nature: his humaneness; his instinct for making free enterprise work better by protecting it from both communism and monopoly capitalism; his respect for cultural attainment, shown when he built up the University of Wisconsin so admirably. He and the democratic socialist Eugene Debs were the knightliest, most nobly compassionate personalities in America's unfashionable, anti-bourgeois protest movements. They have little in common with the fashionable, bourgeois Stalinoids of the fellow-traveling "liberal" weeklies of the Popular Front era. Contrast, for example, the attitudes toward communism of the La Follette Progressive party of the 1920's and the Wallace Progressive party of 1948. Asked if his kind of Progressive party would work closely with admitted communists, Wallace replied in 1947: "If they want to help us out on some of these problems, why God bless them, let them come along."[10] In 1920, when communists tried to capture the earlier Progressive party, La Follette repudiated them as a bloody tyranny; when their familiar infiltrations captured several delegations to a Progressive convention, he threw them out as a fifth column. Would that the same had been done by more Popular Front liberals in the 1930's. Meanwhile his record on issues of civic courage, unlike that of many later anti-communists, was impeccable.

The old distinction between heart and head best explains why La Follette was both so good and so bad a force in history. When he used his head, philosophizing about isms and direct democracy, he was wrong with the deep, hopeless

[10] Quoted in the *New York Post,* December 11, 1947.

wrongness that can only be achieved by an abstract doctrinaire of the highest intellect. But he was right when he used his warm undoctrinaire heart, dealing with the concrete problems of real human beings: the insulted and injured, the farmers exploited by railroads, the sailors exploited by profiteering, the small businessmen exploited by big monopolies. Hence his famous Seamen's Act and his trust-busting.

In the arena of history, the massman is alternately the martyr and the lion. In La Follette's day the massman was the martyr, shockingly exploited by railroads and trusts; hence La Follette quite rightly tried to help him, partly with wise social reforms, partly with the unwise direct democracy of by-passing the Constitution and judiciary. Today the massman is no longer the martyr but the raging lion: the Overadjusted Man of anti-civil liberties, of anti-individual-diversity, of a unity not arche-typal but stereotyped—a modern and mechanized lion. The Unadjusted Man faces him in the arena.

Chapter Twenty SMASHING

PLYMOUTH ROCK

"An American . . . is afraid of ranking himself too high; still more is he afraid of being ranked too low."—*Alexis de Tocqueville, 1840*

"Defeat of western silver.
Defeat of the wheat.
Victory of letterfiles
And plutocrats in miles
With dollar signs upon their coats
And spats on their feet.
Victory of custodians,
Plymouth Rock,
And all that inbred landlord stock.
Victory of the neat. . . .
Defeat of the Pacific and the long Mississippi. . . .
And all these in their helpless days
By the dour East oppressed, . . .
Crucifying half the West,
Till the whole Atlantic coast
Seemed a giant spiders' nest. . . .
And all the way to frightened Maine the old East heard them call,
Prairie avenger, mountain lion,
Bryan, Bryan, Bryan, Bryan,
Smashing Plymouth Rock with his boulders from the West."[1]

---

[1] From Vachel Lindsay's "higher vaudeville" imitation of how a sixteen-year-old Bryanite Populist radical in 1896 would have viewed the revolt of western mass egalitarianism against Atlantic coast traditionalism and aristocracy. Note the stress on revenge ("avenger, mountain lion") for having been humiliated and patronized intellectually or socially by "that inbred landlord stock" of Plymouth Rock; this emotion of revenge for humiliation has often been shared by recent immigrants in Boston and the east as well as by the Populist older stock in Wisconsin and the west.

I

The emotional desire of nineteenth-century Populist movements in America was to "smash Plymouth Rock" with the
Grand Canyon of the West, to quote the frank metaphor of
Vachel Lindsay's poem about William Jennings Bryan. The
metaphor and the entire poem illuminate the non-economic
emotion concealed beneath the top-of-the-brain economic
slogans of "free silver." Thus legitimate economic grievances
against railroads and bankers intermeshed with psychological
grievances against the social and intellectual taste-determiners
and prestige-determiners of the eastern seaboard élite. The
third-parties of 1880–1900, including the Populist party, the
Greenback party, and other Free Silverites, were out to smash
the egalitarian west down upon old New England and Wall
Street. The new American right of the 1950's is out to smash
the *Tribune* tower of Chicago, the Texas oil fields, and South
Boston down upon that same patrician Plymouth Rock.

When calling the Populists "anti-capitalist," the term is used
as psychology, not economics. The target of their revolt was
not, of course, their own small-town capitalism but Wall Street.
In economics, the revolt of Populist petty-middleclass farmers
against eastern railroads, like the battle between the Jacksonians and the Biddle Bank, was not "proletarians" versus
capitalists but small capitalists versus big capitalists, the impatient versus the entrenched. Still, since our discussion is psychological, not economic, "anti-capitalist" describes correctly
America's periodic Jacksonian-Populist-Progressive revolts;
that is how they often felt and talked, regardless of economics;
that is how the new American right feels, too, but (for reasons
to be examined) does not talk.

The Populist, anti-Wall Street aspect of the new American
right came into the open during the Republican convention of
1952 at Chicago. At that time, the Republican nationalist
Chicago Tribune, in its drive to prevent the nomination of
Eisenhower, kept emphasizing, often correctly, the huge support he was receiving from big, eastern, internationalist banks

like Chase. From 1952 on, both the uninfluential *Daily Worker* and the influential Republican *Chicago Tribune* have constantly branded Eisenhower as "the Wall Street candidate" (correctly but incompletely: he was that and a lot of other things, including a movement of independent idealism).

A similar Republican nationalist organ, the *National Review*, declared in a Washington newsletter of November, 1955: "Early in 1952 a small band of eastern financiers, international bankers, and industrialists organized the Eisenhower boom and entrusted its inflation to a New York advertising firm. The rest is history." The four key terms of status-resentment in that right-wing Republican quotation—"eastern," "international," "bankers," and "New York"—were also the chief terms of resentment in the speeches of left-wing Populists in the 1890's, Wisconsin Progressives in the 1900's. Note likewise the resemblance in emotional tone: the conspiracy-hunting tone of the phrase "a small band," a band manipulating nothing less than "history."

Since the same impulses and resentments inspire the old Populism and the new nationalist right, let us adopt "neo-Populism" as the proper term for the latter group. Not that the distinct differences between the two groups are here being ignored. The familiar contrast in their economic programs reflected the contrast between poor westerners in a time of depression and rich ones (the same family a generation later) in a time of prosperity. The depression of the Populist era required a capitalist scapegoat. The prosperity of the neo-Populist era does not require one. Instead, the cold war requires a radical-seeming scapegoat, at least on the verbal level.

The Populists were openly egalitarian radicals against America's unwritten hierarchy. The neo-Populists, while emotionally being just as radical against that same hierarchy, are 200% radical-baiters on the verbal level; they even get themselves called "conservative" by the popular press! The open conservatism of the eastern Wall Street Democrat, Grover Cleveland, once counter-produced the open radicalism of the

Populist Democrat, William Jennings Bryan. Today the concealed conservatism with leftist lingo of the New Deal epigones counter-produces the concealed radicalism with rightist lingo of the Republican nationalists.

Partly to blame for this inaccurate reversal of terminology are the New Deal epigones. Self-deceptively they persist in seeing themselves as liberal or radical, persist in using leftist rhetoric. They fail to see that, after twenty years, it is the New Deal that has become the rooted, traditional, conservative institution. It is as if a rich middle-aged heir—with fat paunch, fat wallet—still sees himself as a rebellious lean young man freeing the slaves. So long as the New Deal epigones persist in that self-deception, so long will the Republican opponents of the New Deal be forced to see themselves, with an exactly corresponding self-deception, as conservatives—hence, forced to use rightist rhetoric.

The oratory of smashing Plymouth Rock has today acquired its own cryptography. The cryptography is involuntary; its purpose is to deceive not others but one's self. Let us decode its beloved word "anti-communism" as the artful unconscious code-word for "anti-Wall Street," "anti-England," "anti-gent." But this pseudo-anti-communism has still another self-deceiving purpose. It expresses under a single unifying label—thereby making emotionally possible a unified political movement— what are really two different kinds of Wall-Street-resenters: the rich nationalist thought-controllers and the poor ones. What enraged the excluded McCarthyite millionaires of Texas and Chicago against the Wall Street in-group was not the plutocratic profiteering of Wall Street but its Anglophile internationalism. In contrast, not only the internationalism of Wall Street but equally its capitalism enraged the non-millionaire followers of McCarthy and his successors. They were spiritual descendants both of western Populists and Boston Democrats.

But these descendants could no longer afford, in the anticommunist 1950's, to be openly enraged—as in the days of General Weaver or La Follette—against the capitalist aspect of the in-group. The code-word "anti-communist" was needed in order to conceal, especially from themselves, their motivating rage against the two bogeys of all Populists, old or new: the bogey of Wall Street and the bogey of the English gentle- man. Why must the neo-Populists now conceal that rage? Partly because these underdogs of yesteryear are now driving in Buicks (not yet Cadillacs but no longer Chevrolets) to the topdog side of the railroad tracks. Their consequent worry about social acceptance by their Republican and Episcopalian neighbors forces them to use respectable-sounding words like "anti-communist" and "pro-capitalist" to conceal the radical anti-capitalist resentments they have not yet shed. That explains why their resentments reach fever-pitch against that particular area of the American Social Register where Wall Street and New Deal overlap. The overlapping provides a teasing ambiguity: is the resentment really against the "com- munistic" New Deal half of the overlapping or against—the English-gentleman and mellowed-wealth half?

Why is the fiercest hatred of right-wing neo-Populism not against communism but against those millionaires who support mild social reform (Stevenson, Acheson, Harriman, Chester Bowles, and Eisenhower himself)? Because these enlightened millionaires provide the *necessary* ambiguity of personifying the merger of the otherwise separate scapegoats of Wall Street and New Deal. The same Dwight Eisenhower, who in 1952 was the protégé of the Chase Bank of Wall Street and of the Dewey-Brownell Republicans of the east, was earlier the most favored protégé of Roosevelt, Marshall, Truman. In 1948 none other than the ADA tried to draft Eisenhower for the Demo- cratic nomination.

In an editorial of January, 1955, the rightist *Chicago Tribune* coded the neo-Populist outlook by denouncing the Eisenhower administration as "an extraordinary combination of communism and plutocracy." Simply decode as: "an extraordinary over- lapping of New Deal and Wall Street," both symbols of a hated New York, a hated Roosevelt (patrician squire of Hyde Park), a hated Harvard and Beacon Hill—the exact same hates as those found in the egalitarian Progressive and Populist rhetoric.

The revolts against the old status-hierarchy have sometimes

been outside the two regular parties (forming separate Populist and Greenback parties), sometimes within the two regular parties: Bryan within the Democrats, McCarthy within the Republicans. In foreign policy, Bryan within the Democrats, McCarthy within the Republicans expressed the same mass prejudice against the seaboard élite by being anti-British, pro-German, pro-Irish. We have learned from the poll-analyses of Samuel Lubell that "isolationist" means not neutral but pro-German, pro-Irish, anti-British. Bryan followed this pattern during World War I when—like McCarthy among Republicans —he publicly broke with his own party's President over the issue of pro-British foreign policy: then in Europe, today in China. Bryan's German, Irish, and farmer-Populist votes on the left did not want President Wilson's Marshall Plans for England in 1914–18. Neither do the nationalists and Chicago Tribunites on the right today.

It is not necessary to name a country in order to attack it. If you abstain from naming it and yet do attack it, the abstention may be a clue to the intensity of your hate and to the need of concealing that hate beneath a feigned hate of some less popular country. Today, the less popular country is Red China. And when our Republican nationalists say: the first step in foreign policy is to "cut off American aid to any nation trading with Red China," then the country being hated, and being threatened by the recommended policy, is not the country named but an unnamed England. England unwisely does trade with Red China. But most nationalists who attack such trade in the name of capitalist anti-communism, are really more interested in attacking British capitalist commerce. For example, McCarthy, who is merely one instance among many of this process, has never urged us to sink communist ships but did explicitly urge America to sink British ships trading with communism.

Such attitudes both preceded and followed the McCarthyite interlude. Hence the political death of McCarthyism after 1954 has not at all meant the end of such neo-Populist nationalist attitudes. They still prevail today in the letter columns of the

Chicago *Tribune,* the Hearst press, the Cincinnati *Enquirer,* and the large-circulation tabloids. Here is one such letter, in itself nothing special, cited only because so usual, so symptomatic (Cincinnati *Enquirer,* March 28, 1956):

> Both political parties are committed to the Social Security fraud and both are vying for the privilege of giving away the largest amount of our sustenance to foreign countries. Truman called Communism "witch-hunting," and Ike stopped the one man who was uncovering the rats. . . . We need a new party composed of Americans who wish to see our country's sovereignty preserved instead of being dictated from Downing Street.

This typical letter begins as an attack on things alien, untraditional, leftist, and plebeian, ranging from social security to alleged communism. But in the very last sentence, the letter unfolds itself as unwitting cryptography for a deeper-level attack (what Nietzsche called *ressentiment*) against things Anglo-Saxon, traditional, conservative, and aristocratic, the four adjectives symbolized in Populist shorthand by the trigger-phrase "Downing Street"—four adjectives that are really the direct opposites of alien, untraditional, leftist, and plebeian.

In the above letter, the literal meaning of the phrase "Downing Street" refers merely to a foreign government. Yet that phrase seems chosen precisely because a domestic rather than foreign humiliation is motivating the more emotional of such nation-wide letter outbursts. Foreign policy by itself does not arouse *that* much emotionalism. In a shorthand within a shorthand, the *ressentiment* against "Downing Street" seems directed less against Anglo-Saxon traditions overseas in England than against Anglo-Saxon traditions at home in America: against the good part of our domestic Anglo-Saxon heritage (aristocracy's libertarian individualism: 1215, 1688) as well as against the vicious part (ethnic and cultural snob-nonsense).

To love England is only normal, when within moderation; is it not the country of lyric poetry and likewise of parliamentary liberties? Some Americans, however, love England not with that normal, moderate affection but with a consuming passion. Such was the case, judging by his editorials, with the late publisher of the *Chicago Tribune*. Clues to his passion for everything British were Colonel McCormick's ineradicable trace of British accent; his passion for polo playing and for riding to hounds; his habit, so rare in Chicago, of afternoon tea; his un-midwestern habit of wearing not a pocket watch but wrist watches—two of them, one on each wrist. Add to that his country-squire manorial style of life, worthy of Mark Twain's Duke de Bilgewater. His very nickname, "Bertie," was straight from P. G. Wodehouse. Obviously this Elder Statesman of American nationalism was not an American at all, least of all a midwesterner; he was one of those eccentric British Lords whose jolly lark is to travel incognito among unexplored aborigines, disguising himself by adopting, and even outdoing, their more primitive tribal rituals. This venturesome pukka sahib was trying to "go native" in the wild outer provinces of the Yankee jungle before returning to his London club and his Coldstream Guards.

After the above clues, the reader need not be surprised to learn that this anti-British, anti-New England, and anti-Roosevelt isolationist was educated not in the midwest but at a fastidious grade-school in England, thereafter attending Groton with young FDR. Like Averell Harriman, a second New Deal target of the *Chicago Tribune*, McCormick was both a Grotonian and a Yale clubman.

Familiar enough is the process by which an unreciprocating beloved can force the passionate lover into making himself half-believe that his love for her is hate. So let us merely moderate Anglophiles of the eastern seaboard honor the gallant Chicago colonel as the most passionate England-lover of us all. How explain the violence of his Anglophobe speeches but as love's coyness? Did not his lifetime of sulking isolationist editorials add to his tenderness for England the delightful spice of a lovers' quarrel?

To a genuine midwest isolationist, the British titles of nobility and its House of Lords are too remote, too unimportant to notice unduly. Only somebody in love with British noble titles would take them so seriously as to denounce them day and night. That anti-aristocratic process reached such extremes in the *Chicago Tribune* that finally its polo-playing, riding-to-hounds Colonel banned the mention of all titles from the newspaper, the House of Lords being referred to as the "House of L—ds." Genuine midwest isolationists disliked the Marshall Plan as much as did the Colonel but found other reasons for denouncing it than the issue of snobbery. Only a man for whom British snobbery has a deeply wounding fascination would declare of the Marshall Plan, as Bertie McCormick did, "To hell with [it]. It's really a snob plan."

Needless to say, the mere prestige-appeal of Anglo-Saxon social pretensions in America is disgracefully frivolous (like all social snobbery) in an age overshadowed by the H-bomb. Not on such frivolous grounds must the symbol "England and New England" be defended against our neo-Populists but because it represents rule of law, the ethical self-restraint of parliamentary procedures, a free mind rooted within a still-living traditionalism. None of America's other allies against communism—hardly Germany, Spain, Formosa—has represented these free values so well and so long. But American Anglophobes—Populist left, neo-Populist right—have above all been allied with German nationalism: from 1914 on, through two hot World Wars and one cold one. "Why die for Wall Street and the British Empire?"—under this euphemism our Progressive and Farmer-Labor left concealed its alliance with German nationalism in both World Wars; "America First" was the corresponding euphemism of the Republican right for the same pro-German alliance (so-called isolationism).

II

Beneath the sane economic demands of the Populists of 1880–1900 seethed a mania of xenophobia, Jew-baiting, intellectual-baiting, and thought-controlling lynch-spirit.[2] General James Weaver, the ablest Presidential candidate of the Populist

---

[2] This revaluation of the Populists has already begun in able essays by Oscar Handlin and Leslie Fiedler among others. A whole book on the theme is announced for the future by Richard Hofstadter.

party, was personally no anti-Semite. Yet he never did repudiate—but welcomed—the aid and the votes brought by the Jew-baiting Ignatius Donnelly, Populism's leading orator. Consider Donnelly's violence; contemplate his constant paranoiac unmasking of "conspiracy," the favorite Populist noun long before McCarthyism. Here is the skeleton in the closet of these western progressive orators, whom most liberals still regard as Galahads of liberalism against the bankers and big interests. Ignatius Donnelly and other important figures in his movement were against the bankers and big interests all right, just as their liberal admirers today praise them for being. But by bankers and big interests they frequently meant what Populist pamphlets called "international Jewry," and this a generation before Coughlin and Hitler.

The three sacred slogans of Donnelly—and of most Populists —were "democracy," "the common man," and "free silver." Donnelly's free-silver credo lumped together "gold," Wall Street capitalism, the patrician eastern seaboard, and their alleged secret master, the "international Jewish conspiracy." An egalitarian democrat, Donnelly naturally favored proletarian movements against Wall Street, but with one qualification: only when they were also nationalist—cf. the later "national socialism" of Germany.

Here is the plot of Donnelly's novel of Populist propaganda, *Caesar's Column,* 1891.[3] The novel's two villains are both Jews. The one secretly controls international plutocracy, the other international proletarian revolution. The plutocratic Jew tries to deflower a young maiden directly descended from George Washington. The symbolism of that seduction attempt seems obvious; needless to say, the young lady vindicates her ancestry by successfully defending her virginity. The villainous banker gets killed by a lynch-mob—what are lynchings but the logical final stage of direct democracy? Meanwhile the other villain, the Jewish mastermind of international proletarian revolution, steals the funds of the workers. He escapes to found a secret world empire in—Palestine.

[3] This is to acknowledge gratefully that the proto-Nazi aspects of this democratic left-wing Populist were called to our attention by Professor Daniel Aaron.

Caesar's Column evoked favorable comment in the 1890's from periodicals of the Populist and National Grange movements. The novel was presented as a prophecy; its Jewish-plutocratic destruction of American democracy was dated in the future, not the present. Accordingly, the president of the National Farmers' Alliance (a group supporting the western radical-plebeian revolt against Wall Street) said of the book: "The author has postponed the catastrophe a hundred years. Unless the power of money to oppress is modified or destroyed very soon, the present generation will witness the crash."

Like so many of the finest citizens in our valuable melting-pot, Donnelly was the son of an immigrant from County Tyrone, Ireland. Despite that fact or because of it, he was second to none in disparaging foreigners and alien ways. He served as lieutenant-governor of Minnesota 1859, re-elected in 1861; Congressman 1863, re-elected 1865. As early as 1861, he was nationally famous for the silver-throated eloquence of his oratory against usury. In Congress he fought for laws protecting workers and farmers from the rich.

In those robber-baron days, such social legislation was particularly necessary (Populist proto-fascism and proto-McCarthyism, not Populist humane reform is our legitimate target). It would, therefore, be gratifying if the researcher could conclude that only the humane side of Donnelly represented the Populists and that his paranoiac, racist side was unrepresentative of them. Unfortunately that enticing assumption does not square with the facts. Even aside from Donnelly, the same anti-intellectualism and anti-Semitism occurred in many other Populist pamphlets and demagogues also, not in the majority of them but in a large, important minority. Between 1880 and 1900, a vast crusade of grass-roots radicalism swept out of the west to "smash Plymouth Rock" and Wall Street capitalism. Part of the crusade, certainly not all but a rather important part, attacked the Jew as the mastermind behind capitalism and behind everything reactionary and right-wing.

Weekly caricatures of the Jew appeared in such magazines of Populist sympathies as *Puck* and *Police Gazette*. Cartoons pictured Wall Street as a giant pawnshop with a Rothschild pulling the strings. Rothschild was a favorite target, often cartooned with caricatured features, resembling the later anti-Semitic cartoons of the Nazi war criminal, Julius Streicher. For example, a typical anti-Semitic joke with an anti-Semitic cartoon is found in the February 24, 1892, number of *Puck*. These Populist attitudes reflected those of much of the grain-belt and the Bible-belt. The Germans and Irish were the ethnic good guys of Populist orators, the British and Jews the ethnic bad guys. Nordic farmers (German, Scandinavian) and the exploited Irish toilers were seen as virtuous proletarians, folksy and democratic. Jewry and England, often including New England, were seen as respectively plutocratic and aristocratic. With that background, the pro-Nazi orientation of some Farmer-Laborites and other western radicals and anti-capitalists in 1939 should not have surprised eastern liberals as much as it did. For example, Senator Lundeen.

The Bible-belt of Fundamentalism in religion mostly over-lapped with the farm-belt of the Populist, Greenback, and other free-silver parties in politics. Both belts were anti-intellectual, anti-aristocratic, anti-capitalist. By subjecting teachers to Fundamentalist religious thought-control, they anticipated the modern political thought-controllers.

Such was the background of isolationist or Germanophile America Firsters like Henry Ford, Lindbergh, Wheeler, Nye. In addition to being a practical mechanic and an industrialist of genius, Henry Ford had two irrational hates: the bankers of Wall Street and what he called the Elders of Zion. Many readers may recall the famous lawsuit resulting from the publication of anti-Semitic slanders by Henry Ford.[4] Fewer readers may realize how much Ford was thereby the victim of his western Populist background. In 1878 when he was fifteen, the Central Greenback Club of Detroit (center of Coughlinism fifty years later) was sensationally accusing the Jews and

[4] Keith Sward, *The Legend of Henry Ford*, New York, 1948.

Rothschild of causing the depression and the railroad graft that followed the Civil War.

The missing link between the Populism of 1880-1900 and the neo-Populism of today—the missing link between Ignatius Donnelly and the McCarthy movement—was Father Charles Coughlin. Backed by the armed street-gangs of "the Christian Front" and by his popular newspaper, *Social Justice,* this Detroit radio orator was the most influential western demagogue of the 1930's. During the first depression years, Father Coughlin was not yet a fascist but a western egalitarian democrat. As such, he denounced the gold standard and Wall Street, criticized the New Deal for not being radical enough in helping the workers, and demanded as cure-all—yes, "free silver." The steps of Father Coughlin from pro-worker and anti-Wall-Street to pro-Hitler and anti-Jew were as follows. Wall Street equates with the old Anglo-Saxon ruling class of the east, "Plymouth Rock"; hence, equates with England; hence with lend-lease, anti-Hitlerism, internationalism; hence with "international Jewish bankers." By these successive steps, an egalitarian democrat and patriot ended by supporting an anti-egalitarian alien in Berlin.

La Follette Progressives like Wheeler and Nye never went so far as the open pro-Hitlerism and anti-Semitism of Coughlin. That fact must be firmly stressed to their credit. But what of their cautious hints and murmurs about being driven to war with Germany by "war-mongering international bankers," whom you could identify with any particular minority you pleased? Such hints and murmurs reflected, on a more civilized level, the same transition as Coughlin's: from western egalitarian democracy to a stance helpful only to Hitler. Charles Lindbergh's speech at Des Moines during World War II explicitly named by name as anti-German warmongers the two Populist scapegoats: the British, the Jews. Like Ford before him, the anti-British, anti-Jewish Lindbergh of the Des Moines speech was not Lindbergh the capitalist nor Lindbergh the conservative, as shocked liberals imagined (Mrs. Dwight Morrow's anti-Nazi Anglophilia better reflected both capitalist

and conservative opinion). No, the Lindbergh of Des Moines
was Lindbergh the anti-capitalist and anti-patrician radical
of the west, reflecting the special Farmer-Laborite background of his youth. Must liberals persist in blaming *all* sins
against liberty, all racist bigotry, all pro-fascist speeches on
Wall Street, conservatism, or aristocracy when, in the above
concrete instances, the roots were so clearly leftist, radical,
plebeian, egalitarian, democratic?

Only that Populist background explains Ezra Pound's combination of Nazi anti-Semitism with a democratic hate of Wall
Street bankers ("usurers"). Only Populism explains his otherwise incomprehensible combination of radio speeches for
Mussolini with an equally fervent worship of the liberal Thomas
Jefferson. Although the anti-democratic root of Pound and
other American pro-fascists has often been stressed by American
liberals, they have done relatively little research into the democratic Populist root of the same. A new interpretation of
Pound's politics seems the fitting conclusion for our survey of
smashers of Plymouth Rock, from Donnelly to Coughlin to
McCarthy.

One leader of the National Renaissance party, a small
American fascist fringe, has publicly proclaimed his simultaneous devotion to Pound and McCarthy. But Pound's politics
and economics (entirely aside from his far more important
aesthetics) have more reputable devotees also, including a
number of non-fascist, non-racist Americans of important intellectual standing. Even in England, the "Ezra Pound Society"
has been reverently republishing the anti-usury broadcasts he
delivered for Mussolini's radio while Italy and Germany were
at war with America and England.

In *America, Roosevelt, and the Causes of the Present War*,
Pound explained the war as a plot by Jewish international
bankers. He accused them of plotting against the fascist alliance because of its supposed "Jeffersonian" democracy and its
aid to workers and peasants. He defined World War II as
"part of the secular war between usurers and peasants, between
the usurocracy and whoever does an honest day's work. . . ."

Our point is: thereby Pound—and several veterans of the Progressive and Farmer-Laborite movements—were defending Hitler and Mussolini not for the ordinary Nazi or fascist reasons but for egalitarian Populist reasons. In a pro-fascist article in the *Capitol Daily,* May 9, 1939, Ezra Pound was also talking Populist egalitarianism: "The danger in America is not fascism [but gold-economics]. Who owns the world's gold? . . . The Rothschilds are gold brokers profiting by every deal that the Bank of London, the enemy of God and man, makes in gold, to buy or to sell. This swindle is old. . . . Italy has solved the old blah. . . . I want a thirty-hour week for the workingman."

A leitmotif of many Populist orators of the nineteenth century was to denounce New York City as capitalist, internationalist, British-influenced ("fancy"), and Jewish. Their attitude resembled the democratic Rousseau, contrasting the unspoilt Noble Savage of the western hinterland with the corrupt, overcivilized intellectual of the big city. But in addition their attitude toward New York partly foreshadowed that of Hitler's undemocratic "Director of *Weltanschauung*," Alfred Rosenberg, who defined Nazism as a revolt of pure Nordic blood-instincts against "the very concept of New York." Both the Rousseauistic and the Nazi-racist bias combined in Pound's attitude toward New York. According to the *New York Times* account (April 21, 1939) of his visit to Manhattan, he said that he felt "smothered" by its "undesirable" atmosphere and was rushing for relief to the unspoilt hinterland. Pound was further reflecting his Populist origins when he denounced New York's newspapers as "Jewspapers" in his pamphlet of anti-gold economics, *What Is Money For?*

Though radically egalitarian in economics at home, abroad the Populists (being nationalists) distrusted the internationalist kind of radicalism. Pound, too, attacked not only capitalism but international communism, calling it—in the Ignatius Donnelly tradition—"merely Hebrew" (in *Culture,* New York, New Directions, 1949).

A study of the now-forgotten American pro-fascists of the 1930's, both intellectuals and popular demagogues, confirms that Pound was no unrepresentative eccentric, no irresponsible "madman" whose politics should be compassionately ignored as uncalculated, unrealistic, harmless. His important and already familiar aesthetic contributions are another matter (cf. Chapter 31). But in regard to his fascist politics of the 1930's, he was (like the now equally fashionable Wyndham Lewis)[5] a responsible, representative member of an important world movement, including calculating realists, whose bid for power almost succeeded. The American and British portion of this movement is now forgotten merely because Hitler (at the cost of twenty-two million lives) was finally beaten.

Had Hitler won, some of these exquisite "pure aesthetes," whose former solidarity with genocidal torturers it is so tactless, so vulgar to dare mention today, might be sending to the gas chambers the subtle literary critics now defending Pound against "philistine" charges of fascist treason. In the American contingent of this important might-have-been movement, why did a number of products of the Populist, Progressive, and Farmer-Labor parties—men who once were heroes of our Jeffersonian liberals—end up by favoring, with varying reservations, Nazi tyranny over British liberty? Often because of the following process:

From Tom Paine through Jackson, Weaver, Bryan, La Follette, the American Populist tradition has rested squarely on faith in the natural goodness of man, the infinite perfectibility of the masses. That faith was shared by the otherwise more moderate Jefferson. (In *Brother to Dragons*, Robert Penn Warren has shown that the optimistic repudiation of original sin proved as fatal in Jefferson's private life as it did in the French Revolution's political life.) If you deem evil external, if consequently you deem utopia just around the corner, then you cannot blame human nature or the masses for the failure of utopia to arrive. Instead, you are then tempted to blame

[5] Cf. Geoffrey Wagner's documented analyses (*New Mexico Quarterly*, winter 1954–55; *New Republic*, May 16, 1955) of the Wyndham Lewis cult and of his pro-Nazi and later anti-Nazi writings. The two versions of totalitarianism being ethically inseparable, why the one-sided current concern with only the communist infiltrations of the 1930's? Both or none, no?

some small aristocratic or plutocratic "conspiracy." The next step, while still believing in democracy and "the people," is to set up an undemocratic terrorist dictatorship in order to purge these "unnatural" aristocrats or plutocrats (British snobs, Jewish bankers), sole obstacles to the mass utopia inherent in "nature." These attitudes underlay Robespierre's Committee of Public Safety; they underlie, on a bloodless level, the coercive egalitarianism and anti-traditionalism of the Populists and now of our neo-Populist Committees on Un-American Activities. Robespierre:

We wish a peaceful enjoyment of freedom and equality . . . the rule of reason in the place of the slavery of tradition. . . . At home, all the friends of the tyrants conspire. . . . Therefore . . . the principle of our Republic is this: to influence the people by the use of reason, to influence our enemies by the use of terror. . . . The government of the Revolution is the despotism of liberty against tyranny.[6]

In contrast with Robespierre, Populists, and neo-Populists, philosophical conservatives deem evil inherent in man himself, not in some easily-guillotined external institution or group like aristocracy, the gold standard, capitalists, New Dealers, or racial scapegoats. Victor Ferkiss has ably analysed still another motive leading from democratic monetary reform to authoritarianism:

A despair of ever restoring monetary freedom through constitutional democratic means has meant the addition to the Populist credo . . . of an authoritarian corporate state as the sole suitable means to economic reform. . . . Significantly, most of the old Populist strongholds, and the political leaders bred of them, were bitter-end isolationists and carried their nationalism to the point of receptivity to economic apologias for the fascist powers not unlike those used by Ezra Pound. Much evidence can be adduced to support the contention that, had certain nationalist mass-agitations of the pre-Pearl Harbor years, such as the America First Committee, developed into full-fledged political movements, much of their economic doctrine would have been drawn from the ideas of leaders like

[6] Maximilien Robespierre, *Speeches: Voices of Revolt*, I, New York: International Publishers, 1927; pp. 72–75.

Father Coughlin and Gerald L. K. Smith, just as much of their membership was drawn from among the followers of these men.[7]

A certain sociological interest, and not merely the trivial
personal one, may perhaps justify the recording of the irate
reactions to newspaper accounts of our earlier paper (at the
1954 forum of the American Historical Association) on
the leftist-Populist root of McCarthyism. The irate letters
came from McCarthy nationalists and anti-McCarthy liberals
alike. The majority, but not a large majority, came from
McCarthy nationalists; never before had this writer received
so many epistolatory threats against his livelihood, even life
and limb, and so many reflections upon his personal integrity.
The experience, the kind sometimes called "harrowing," was
interesting first of all for its educational value. The surprisingly
open cult of physical violence in the pro-McCarthy letters was
even more educational than their awkward-to-reprint obscenity.
Their one redeeming feature was their constant endearing
inability to spell. This writer, too, has never been able to spell
very well; at least in that respect, he is a true red-blooded
McCarthyite.

The letters from liberal New Dealers, after that same 1954
forum of the American Historical Association, were more
gently-bred in diction than those of the McCarthyites but just
as indignant. One might have expected liberals to be pleased,
not angered by a document that drew blood from their
McCarthyite foes by disproving the latter's claims of being
anti-communist. But apparently the conformity of liberal
nonconformists is so rigid that you are allowed to draw blood
from freedom's foe only according to the strictest liberal ritual,
in which the toreador must always intone egalitarian clichés
while the snorting McCarthyite bull must always be labeled
as "anti-radical" and "anti-communist," no matter how radical
and how similar in method to the communists he really is. The
epistolatory ire of both sides against the author's analysis of
McCarthyism may perhaps be explained as follows:

[7] *Journal of Politics*, Vol. 17, 1955.

1. The McCarthyites were angry at the denuding of an emotion they dared not face in themselves: the fact that their pathetic desire to "pass" as anti-communists and conservatives concealed an uneasiness about their proud new suburban status, an uneasiness triggered explosively by the élite-symbols "England" and "higher education." Nor did these nationalists seem to welcome with gratitude the documented point that their intolerance of alleged "un-Americanism" was not in the least shared by Americans of older, deeper roots than their own.[3]

2. Inflexible liberals were angry at being discovered in exactly the same camp with Wall Street, the camp of conservative anti-Populist internationalism. (Meanwhile flexible liberals are coming to terms with Wall Street by writing apologies, sometimes reasonable and sometimes fawningly undignified, for robber barons and for economic bigness.) Still other liberals and New Dealers were angry at the kind of attack on McCarthyism that would also prove an abattoir for two of their own sacred cows: egalitarianism and the Populist-Progressive movement. In America you can sometimes attack with impunity the morals and the politics of an intolerant, thought-controlling enemy. But never dare to expose the clichés of a tolerant, civil-libertarian friend.

[3] This point, and similar ones in other chapters about the thought-controlling "Americanism" of status-resenting immigrants, might merely be a tasteless self-congratulation if made by old-stock Anglo-Saxonry. Instead, these necessary, tactless points are being made by a writer descended from immigrants just as obviously un-Mayflowerish as all those xenophobe xenos whose letters boiled him in oil. These pages are meant as a loving tribute; in an informal, unoptimistic way, the author happens to be in love with a third America, more open-hearted, more free-minded than the America of the neo-Populist nationalists or the America of that liberal in-group which provokes the nationalists by its snob-nonsense (not even a candid in-group snob-nonsense but picturing itself as an underdog "persecuted by witch-hunts"—as indeed it sometimes is but less dangerously than it likes to believe). It is no use arguing which of these three Americas is the real one; America is a becoming, not a being. And what it becomes, gets determined every minute of the day by the irrevocable turns now being taken at various crossroads by individual Americans, each with an individual ethical responsibility that may be ignored but not with impunity. It seems undignified that such a merely personal aside is today necessary for points intended to be judged by their objective merits or demerits. Time was when it was not necessary; the nationwide loss in dignity of debate is a measure of the hard-won ground America has lost, owing to the respectability given temporarily (until late 1954) by the Republican party to the nationalist thought-controllers.

No better morally than the animal ferocity of our McCarthy-style nationalists, though no worse either, was the intellectual ferocity of the anti-anti-communist wolf-pack in the 1930's, whenever its book reviewers caught a novelist like James Farrell criticizing the lies of the Moscow trials. Let us, therefore, apply not a double standard but a single standard of ethical decency against both sides throughout. If American opinion-molders had much earlier applied such a single standard of means to all salvationist ends, they would have forestalled both the fellow-traveler episode and the McCarthy episode, two related episodes now virtually closed but with lessons for the future.

Chapter Twenty-one   TRANSTOLER-

ANCE: Monster Rally of the Status-

Resenters

"All social disturbances and upheavals have their roots in crises of individual self-esteem, and the great endeavor in which the masses most readily unite is basically a search for pride."—*Eric Hoffer*, THE PASSIONATE STATE OF MIND, *1955*

> "CALIBAN: 'Ban, 'Ban, Ca-caliban
>   Has a new master. —Get a new man.
>   Freedom, heyday! . . .
> STEPHANO: O brave monster! Lead the way."
>   —*Shakespeare*, THE TEMPEST, Act II, Scene 2

Among many other things, the new nationalist toughness is the revenge of those who felt snubbed in 1928, when bigotry cheated the man with the brown derby of his deserved election as President. They felt snubbed the second time in 1932, when the Democratic nomination went to Al Smith's victorious rival from Groton. The third snub occurred in 1944, when Jim Farley, another nationwide symbol of the Irish Catholic in politics, had his Presidential aspirations vetoed by FDR. How could it go entirely unnoticed that the last two of these wounds, 1932 and 1944, were inflicted by the same Harvard Mayflower millionaire? These old wounds partly paved the way for the partial secession of this sensitive minority from Democrats to Republicans in 1952, a secession aided as much by the Democrat McCarran as the Republican McCarthy.

213

214 The Unadjusted Man

Even so, the secession would have been much smaller, had it not combined with the rise in income and dwelling-area among the secessionists. If more of that unjustly snubbed minority had remained day-laborers, if many had not moved over-assimilatingly into white-collar residential areas and attitudes, they would still have voted Democratic in 1952. Many returned to the Democratic fold, as future elections will prove, after the new calm of 1955 made them edge away from McCarthy-style nationalism as a kind of halitosis: "giving our group a bad name."

The characteristic battle between the various McCarthy-style committees and Protestant clergymen is already familiar. For example, the attempt to slander Bishop Oxnam. Therefore, it becomes necessary to publicize among one's fellow Protestants the equally characteristic but less familiar battle of Catholic leaders against McCarthy. While still at the height of his former power, McCarthy was attacked by the two leading weekly organs of intellectual Catholicism: by the conservative Jesuit weekly, *America*, just as much as by the more liberal *Commonweal*. Despite the historical reasons for isolationist Anglophobia and anti-intellectual Harvard-baiting within Boston Catholicism, even there the Catholic *Pilot* printed editorial warnings against McCarthy. And the *Pilot* not only speaks for thousands of its devoted Irish readers but is the official Catholic newspaper for the archdiocese of Boston. Although both Joseph McCarthy and Paul Blanshard may deny this, the Boston *Pilot* and the McCarthy-denouncing Bishop Sheil of Chicago were more representative of Irish-American Catholicism than was the Wisconsin Senator.

The most important aspect of the McCarthy issue, the moral aspect, cut across ethnic and religious lines, with Catholics, Jews, and Protestants found plentifully on both sides. The moral issue was one of conservers versus subverters; the choice was between conserving our old Constitutional liberties or subverting them. Liberals and philosophical conservatives both stood on the conserving side of this issue, while the right-wing radicals stood on the subverting side (disguised, as usual, under "anti-subversive" slogans, self-deceptions).

Ethnic favoritism and anti-immigrant snobbery are not only silly but wicked. Their wickedness bears much of the blame when their victims are goaded into rightist radicalism in America, leftist radicalism in Europe. History does avenge its wrongs but often upon the innocent, not the guilty. In 1928, bigoted Mayflower fathers put salt in the wounds of an Al Smith. Two decades later, their unbigoted liberal Mayflower sons had to put sugar in those hoarded wounds by crawling, on hands and knees, to the investigating committee of some McCarran or McCarthy.

The abasement of the Holy Roman Emperor at Canossa, barefoot on snow, seemed parodied in pantomime during McCarthy's Senate questioning of James Bryant Conant, Harvard's ex-president and now America's valuable ambassador to Germany. There in the arena stood the former "Emperor" of that ancient educational institution whose scepter of cultural-social prestige had once ruled unchallenged even over South Boston. There he stood, hauled before the McCarthy committee and publicly subjected to bar-room ridicule by McCarthy himself, who addressed the Ambassador as "perfessor." The real clue to that Canossa was the special sarcastic intonation with which McCarthy pronounced that loaded word. The Wisconsin Senator, no fool, showed by the relish of his intonation that he understood the symbolism of the drama better than did the disheartened liberals, who saw the issue in terms of mere politics (reactionary versus liberal) instead of in terms of America's secret castes. In a professed democracy, the battles for social and educational caste can be fiercer, meaner—because unofficial, unmentionable—than in an open oligarchy.

During the Jacobin Revolution of 1793, in those quaint days when the lower classes still thought of themselves as the lower classes, it was for upper-class sympathies and for *not* reading "subversive leftist literature" that aristocrats got into trouble.

Note the reversal in America. Here the lower classes are in two senses also the upper classes: in power, in attitude. Theirs the cars, the curtains, and the votes. So in America it is for alleged lower-class sympathies that the aristocrats are indicted by the lower classes.

Why is it necessary to allege those lower-class "leftist" sympathies—why the pretext in the first place? Because in America the suddenly enthroned lower classes cannot prove to themselves psychologically that they themselves are now upper classes unless they can now indict the old upper class for not being sufficiently upper-class in sympathy; that is, unless they can indict for pro-proletarian subversion those whom they half-know in their hearts to be the real intellectual and social aristocracy, from whom they have hoarded many an unadmitted social bruise.[1]

What we are witnessing in the public square is the guillotining (metaphorically speaking) of Louis XVI and Marie Antoinette. Ostensibly they are charged with signing twenty years ago some pinko petition by that egghead Voltaire (a typical mirror-image reversal of the 1793 charge) and with the crime of saying not "let them eat cake" but "let them read books." But in reality they are being guillotined for having been too exclusive socially and, even "worse," intellectually, at fancy parties in Versailles-sur-Hudson, where aristocratic, pro-proletarian conspirators slink around saying shamelessly "he doesn't" instead of the loyal, red-blooded "he don't." McCarthyism was the revenge of the noses that for years were pressed against the outside windowpane while Marie Antoinette danced. In Populist-Progressive days those noses were pressed against the window with openly radical, openly lower-class resentment. During 1952–54 the same noses snorted triumphantly with right-wing Republicanism. Though McCarthyism in the narrow sense died in late 1954, the guillotine of the new nationalist right will continue its intermittent chopping sprees:

[1] Thus considered, the drama of Alger Hiss may be entitled, with those alternate titles old melodramas used to sport, "Revenge Is Sweet, or: The Tables Turned On FDR's Harvard Club."

decapitating America's intellectual and social upper class in the name of a 200% upper-class ideology.

This ideology-of-overcompensation gets accepted at face value by many American liberal intellectuals. They make the overcompensation a success by denouncing it as a conservative movement, an anti-communist movement, which is exactly what it wants to be denounced as. The reason it wants to be attacked by bourgeois-liberals as being bourgeois-conservative instead of radical, is owing to a uniquely American situation. Namely, a situation where the masses are more bourgeois than the bourgeois and even more desirous of being considered quality-folks. Huey Long's slogan of "Every man a king" has come true for much of America today in terms of economics. But not in terms of mass-respect; *there* every man is a king except the kings. The real kings (the élite of education and of artistic creativity, who would rank royally in any traditional value-hierarchy of the Hellenic-Roman west) are in some circles becoming declassed scapegoats.[2]

America is the country where the masses won't admit they are masses. They pretend to be pillars of respectability even when supporting a revolution of direct democracy against those crypto-aristocratic institutions—courts, Constitution, Bill of Rights—that alone protect, from the majority, the minority élite known as the educated. The nationalist thought-controllers threaten liberty not by representing privilege, capitalism, or Wall Street but by representing (in a distorted way) democratic equality. The spread of democratic equal rights facilitates, as Nietzsche prophesied, the equal violation of rights.

As the Jacobins demonstrated in 1793, any sudden *égalité* may as easily diminish *liberté* as increase it. It was, as the 1930's would say, "no accident that" an American Legion meeting in New York, in August, 1954, passed two resolutions side by side: the first condemned another Legion branch for racial discrimination (the "Forty and Eight" society); the second endorsed McCarthy's demands in the Peress case. This

[2] Cf. the chapter "Kings in Exile," page 306.

juxtaposition is noted not in order to disparage, even by snide implication, such long overdue anti-racism but in order to caution against the oversimplifying optimism of many liberal reformers, who assume that the fight for free speech and the fight for racial tolerance are synonymous.

It is a measure of the difference between New York and the south that neither of the New York resolutions (anti-segregation, pro-McCarthy) was sustained in that form when the Legion met a month later in Washington, D. C. Tardy about new trends, the south had always been more opposed than the rest of America to the good cause of Negro rights, the bad cause of McCarthyism. Sometimes the southern kind of nationalists will denounce as communistic the defenders of Negro civil liberties and will then go on to denounce the north for "not fighting for its civil liberties against that fascist Catholic McCarthy." Conversely, at a mass meeting of northern nationalists, in August, 1954, McCarthyite speakers denounced all racial discrimination as un-American and then went on to denounce as communistic whoever defended civil liberties against McCarthy.

At the same meeting, a Rabbi accused the opposition to Roy Cohn of anti-Semitic intolerance. Next, Cohn was called "the American Dreyfus Case" by a representative of a student McCarthyite organization, "Students for America." This young representative of both McCarthyism and "racial brotherhood" concluded amid loud applause: "Roy Cohn and Joe McCarthy will be redeemed when the people have taken back their government from the criminal alliance of Communists, Socialists, New Dealers, and the Eisenhower-Dewey Republicans."[3] This outburst of direct democracy came straight from the leftist rhetoric of the old Populists and Progressives, a rhetoric forever urging "the plain people" to take back "their" government from the "conspiring" powers-that-be. With the same Progressive party rhetoric, Rabbi Schultz, at another Cohn-McCarthy banquet of 1954, urged "the plain people of America" to "march on Washington" in order to save their tribune

[3] *Time,* August 9, 1954, p. 15.

McCarthy from the big bosses of the Senate censure committee.

Let us not overstate the argument by ignoring the exceptions to the decline of racist violence. The Till case of 1955 was too outrageous an example to permit complacency. Yet these outrageous exceptions, usually not connected with *political* nationalism, sound like the last convulsions of a dying and sectional phase of bigotry. Bigotry's new political line was better evidenced by McCarthy's conspicuous abstention during 1950–55 from anti-Semitic and anti-Negro propaganda. The same new line characterizes the post-McCarthy nationalists like "For America." "For America" is a xenophobic, rightist revival of the old America First Committee. But in contrast with those blunt old days of appeasing an openly Nazi dictatorship, the subtler bigots of "For America" greatly expanded their mass base by deciding in 1954 to "quietly canvass Jewish and Negro prospects."[4]

In the old days, racial and intellectual intolerance went hand in hand. Today racial and religious intolerance often decrease in proportion as intellectual intolerance increases. Since our vocabulary lacks any term for this new relationship, why not coin the word "transtolerance"? Transtolerance gives all racial and religious minorities their glorious democratic equality— provided they accept mob conformity against all intellectual minorities.

Transtolerance is the form that xenophobia takes when practiced by a "xeno." Transtolerance is becoming the Irishman's version of Mick-baiting, the Jewish version of anti-Semitism, and so on. Transtolerance is partly a movement of recent immigrants who present themselves (not so much to the world as to themselves) as a 200% hate-the-foreigner movement. And by extension: hate "alien" ideas. Transtolerance is a strictly kosher anti-Semitism: against "wrong" thinkers, not "wrong" races. It is a sublimated Jim Crow; it can be participated in with clear conscience by the new, nonsegregated, flag-waving Negro, who will be increasingly

[4] Article on "For America" by Walter K. Lewis in *The New Leader*, first week of September, 1954.

emerging from the increased egalitarian laws in housing and
in education. Negro intellectuals have already expressed their
concern over the open support given McCarthy by two leading
Negro editors and by the spread of anti-intellectual, nationalist
intolerance in their communities. The final, surrealist climax
of American transtolerance would be for the Ku Klux Klan to
hold a nonsegregated lynching-bee.

Admittedly not all nationalist bigots have yet caught on to
transtolerance as the most lucrative new gimmick of their own
racket. Many will continue to persecute racial minorities as
viciously as in the past. But surely decreasingly and with
less profit.

Typical of our decade is this significant juxtaposition in a
New York Times headline (September 4, 1954, page 1):
"President Signs Bill To Execute Peacetime Spies / Also
Bolsters Ban On Bias." Thus even a representative, middleroad
Administration was increasing its ideological toughness and its
racial tolerance in the same breath. It is not even necessary
to go to the unrepresentative far right for examples of transtolerance. The change has affected America as a whole. But
the new right will continue to represent a greater nationalist
toughness than Democrats or Eisenhower Republicans.

At the same moment when America is nearer racial equality
than ever before (an exciting gain insufficiently noted by
America-baiters in Europe and India), America is moving
further from liberty of opinion. "Now remember, boys, tolerance and equality," (our very progressive schoolma'am in
highschool used to preach) "come from cooperation in some
common task." If *1984* ever comes to America,[5] "some common
task" will turn out to be a "team" (as they will obviously call
it) of "buddies" from "all three" faiths, all "cooperating" to burn
books on civil liberties and to segregate unadjusted individualists of all faiths, "without restrictions of race, creed, or color."

At the McCarthy rally of November 29, 1954, in Madison
Square Garden, the nationalist mob, presumably including
the racist readers of America's sick and filthy hate-sheets,

[5] Cf the fantasy on page 223.

roared ecstatically: "Roy Cohn for Vice-President!" Here
indeed was transtolerance: the replacement of ethnic lynching
by ideological lynching. At that same rally (to quote James
Rorty's able analysis in *Commentary,* January, 1955): "When
somebody mentioned the New York *Times,* they booed from
their shoes. When Lisa Larsen, *Time's* petite candid-camera
photographer, ventured into the audience, she touched off a
near-riot; as the police escorted her from the hall, a venomous
voice shouted 'Hang the Communist bitch!'" Now, *Time*
magazine and the New York *Times* are the obvious symbols
not of "communism" but of Wall Street, of Anglophile internationalism, and of the Eisenhower administration; that is to
say, of that mellowed eastern big-business which is hated both
by western hick big-business and by Populist mob-egalitari-
anism. These two concrete incidents of November 29, 1954—
the cheering of Cohn as a nationalist, the booing of a representative of big-business Republicanism as "a Communist
bitch"—confirm two of our main hypotheses about the would-
be conservatism of the nationalists: first, its transtolerance;
second, its coding of its Populist Wall-Street-baiting as "anti-
communism."

Thus our hypotheses about the new American right are not
abstract speculations but meet the empiric test of working out
in the actual practice of an actual monster rally.

Many social and ethnic injustices of the past deserve to be
avenged today, but must they be avenged on the lowest
possible level? It is as if the only way to avenge the unjust
persecution of Al Smith, Sacco and Vanzetti, and Dreyfus
respectively were for Father Coughlin, Al Capone, and
Leopold-and-Loeb to enroll together in the "American Nationalist party" of Gerald L. K. Smith, all singing "God Bless
America" together. The range of strange bedfellows at current
rallies of the nationalist right recalls the ad recently posted
by a comic horror-movie featuring Bela Lugosi, Boris Karloff,
and Lon Chaney, Jr.: "All your life you have been forced to
see Count Dracula, Frankenstein's robot, and the Wolf Man
separately. Tonight for your special enjoyment we present all

three monsters in the same show." The unique achievement
of McCarthyism was to "present in the same show" the three
separate movements founded by the Jew-baiting and Catholic-
baiting Reverend Gerald L. K. Smith, the Jew-baiting and
Protestant-baiting Father Coughlin, and a well-known
McCarthyite Rabbi who baited almost everybody. When
these three movements converged to cheer McCarthy at
Madison Square Garden in 1954, here was indeed a monster
rally America had never seen before.

It required Robespierre to teach French intellectuals that
égalité is no synonym of *liberté*. It required McCarthy to
educate American intellectuals out of liberal faith in the masses
and back to conservative faith in the Constitution. The intellectual liberals who twenty years ago wanted to pack the Supreme
Court for frustrating the will of the masses (which is exactly
what it ought to frustrate) and who were quoting Charles
Beard on the Constitution as mere rationalization of economic
loot, those same liberals today are hugging Court and Constitution for dear life.

Our right to civil liberties, our right to unlimited non-
conspiratorial dissent, is as ruggedly conservative and traditional as Senator Flanders and his mountains of Vermont. It
is a right so aristocratic that it enables a single lonely Unadjusted Man, sustained by nine non-elected nobles in black
robes, to think differently from 99% of the nation, even if
a majority of all "races, creeds, and colors," in an honest
democratic election, votes to suppress the thinking of that one
individual. But what will happen to that individual and his
liberties if ever the 99% unite in direct democracy to substitute, as final arbiter of law, the sheeted white robes for the nine
aristocratic black robes?

Chapter Twenty-two MODEST PRO-

POSAL: A Vice-Presidential Speech in a

Surrealist Future[1]

Ladies and Gentlemen:

Cards on the table, and straight to the point! We know who *we* are, and we know who *they* are, and we know why we are here today. Bold, democratic men of the people, lounging behind our lace curtains in suburbs from coast to coast, long ago cleansed of misfits and eavesdroppers, we can talk in manly candor about the Crisis In National Fun. We, the teeming masses—but ever the respectably teeming masses, must act at once. Smiling boyishly, vibrant with health and the disarming sincerity of it all, I herewith proclaim fun and loyalty—loyalty and fun—the twin foundation-stones of the American dream. And, fellows, if I had to name a third foundation-stone of Americanism, it would be hygiene. What is our deep, instinctive revulsion against disloyalty, ideas, and lice but part of our century-old crusade against unwashedness?

I assume no one will challenge the need for compulsory loyalty. But I do owe it to you to explain the need for now making fun compulsory also. Fun is but another word, a straightforward shirt-sleeve word, for adjustedness. From now on, the American campaign against the unadjusted is no longer merely an unwritten law but an explicit part of our criminal

[1] This television address to the nation was ghost-written (for some unknown future Republican Vice-President) by that lovable man of letters, Gaylord Babbitt. Although he called himself a "200% Popular Front liberal" in the 1930's and 1940's, he suddenly changed his label to "200% clean-living nationalist" after the public reaction to the Hiss case, on the idealistic assumption that not only the Supreme Court "follows the election returns."

statutes. Our very existence depends on everybody feeling a Calvinistic duty to have a good time.

The killjoy, the killjoy, smash the windows of the killjoy! In a society whose existence depends on fun and loyalty, not only is it sneaky to snivel; it is the same thing—by objective guilt if not by intention—as spitting on Old Glory. And whatever you do to Old Glory is the same as doing it to your own mother. Will you just stand by and watch all the smirkers and shirkers fiendishly spitting on Mumsy—I mean, objectively spitting—or what are you going to Do About It? Whenever you smoke out long-haired men and short-haired women, dip them in honey—the wholesome, homey honey Ma used to make—and feed them alive to the giant science-fiction ants of the nearest handy Brazilian jungle. Wake up, you throbbing, vital young idealists; and *after* it, *follow* it, follow the gleam.

Hitler, Mussolini, Stalin, Mao, all those old-fashioned re-adjusters of subversives, were unprogressive—even verging on unlibertarian—in their methods. Torturing, shooting, and jailing, they let their enthusiasm for noble ends carry them away to downright overzealous means. But today we have more peaceful and democratic means for removing subversive ideas. The Good Tidings of science today, the new salvation to ensure a fun-loving face, is mass lobotomy: a jolly, neighborly little operation for painlessly removing the frontal lobe of the human brain. Nothing essential gets removed from the cerebrum, nothing any of you would ever want to use, nothing except the tiny, parasitic blob of gray that fools around with sissy stuff like ideas and art. A grin on every face: such is the medically guaranteed result. The grins may be a wee bit on the vacant side; but at least where there's vacancy, there's no disloyalty.

Those old stick-in-the-muds of *1984* were rank amateurs. They wasted time and money, either by expensive propaganda campaigns to argue the subversive out of his ideas or else by breaking his bones, pulling out his fingernails. They committed a serious moral offense—namely unthriftiness—by thus wasting his economic manpower. In contrast, we scientists of fun will neither argue with an idea nor jail it; we will simply—cut it away.

Not the sword but the surgeon's knife is mightier than the pen.

The American goal, as all of us know, is adjustment, the "well-adjusted child," the good sport who never "makes difficulties." Yet no adjustment so far, even in the Kiwanis Club of Zenith City, has ever been one hundred per cent perfect. Why not? Who or what is the treasonable criminal preventing perfect adjustment? The traitor, according to the latest "unevaluated report" of the secret police, is the frontal lobe. This gray agitator for unadjustedness has set up his secret cells— literally "cells"—by infiltrating behind the solid, thick, reliable bone of the forehead. But now at last our adjustment will be no longer ninety-nine per cent but one hundred per cent. For medical journals describe as follows the lucky post-lobotomy patient: *"Tractable, cheerful. Disinclined to argue or debate. Incapable of intellectual or imaginative speculation."*

This sunshine-spreading solution will now be open to everyone, not just to a few privileged aristocrats rich enough to pay for private surgeons. Mr. and Mrs. America, I present to you the ideal of the one and only Totally Adjusted Man: my hero, the Lobotomized Man! Free, state-supported, and compulsory lobotomy will replace free, state-supported, and compulsory education for all future American babies.

Those dreadful bigots—a Hitler, a Mao—used to brainwash only one particular group: enemy class, enemy race, or enemy religion. Thus they were guilty of undemocratic discrimination, of—O dreadful word—INTOLERANCE. Instead, our plan achieves democratic equality by tolerantly lobotomizing every single citizen at birth, regardless of race, creed, or color.

Never again will it be necessary to use force to prevent student-cadets from debating the wrong topics or libraries from stocking the wrong books. Force is undemocratic and against the Rights of Man; mass-lobotomy will create an America where the adjustment is voluntary, unforced, nay eager—where no one *wants* to debate anything whatever or read any book whatever, even if you pay him. Ultimate paradise of total happiness: a lobotomized globe with its nose glued voluntarily and safely to the screen of four-wall television twenty-four hours a day.

Naturally it is always to the experts that we turn whenever we crave know-how. It is our team of buddies in spiritual know-how to whom I now hand over the center of the stage, so that they can bless freedom's new epoch of loyalty-by-surgery. Enter our special four-way monster rally: Father Coughlin, Father Divine, the Very Reverend Gerald L. K. Smith, and that venerable Rabbi Schultz who in his youth had helped organize a now completely forgotten movement called "McCarthyism." These four unworldly men of the cloth are right now pronouncing the spiritual benediction upon non-discriminatory, non-segregated mass-lobotomy. True liberty has arrived at last: liberation from the ancient tyranny of gray matter. For this brief moment, let me humbly serve as merely the commentator, describing to all you millions of onlookers this awesome ceremony:

Arm in arm, the four good shepherds stand before the television cameras, ears tilted expectantly skyward, intoning in chorus: "Heavenly watchman, what of the night? How goes it with Old Glory?" And hark, hark, in reply a voice booms downward, sounding real distinguished—no "he don'ts," lots of "ye" and "thee"—not sentimental but wellbred like in the parlor: "Ye mortals ask: how goes it with yon fabulous thing that is America? Sure and 'tis My own little heart-throb country, the sweetheart of the cosmos, the biggest success-story since Archangel Michael exposed Lucifer for the Committee on Unheavenly Activities."

[*Directive to stage-prop mechanics: At this climax, the transtolerance-quartet fades off the screen to the sound of firecrackers, football cheers, and other reverent church music. The original speaker now moves back to the center of the stage—adjust spotlight accordingly—to deliver a non-partisan inspirational conclusion.*]

Call me, if you will, an impractical dreamer of visions, but there is that which catches in my throat as I now conclude my powwow with my people. I feel proud and yet humble, resolute and yet strangely tender, as if the vast sprawling All of us were sharing the communion of some nationwide clambake-of-the-soul. We entered this rally as desperate men, but we leave it serene and glowing. With bowed heads, let us all glow together. Here is the news your grandchildren will tell your greatgrandchildren proudly: today we have inaugurated for all mankind the Year One of a new era of permanent fun. No smug resting on oars; global lobal liberation from the old gray tyranny shall mean for human achievement not a pause but a redoubling of progress. Here we stand, confidently saying "yes!" to Life and "fiddlesticks!" to Death and "bigger and better!" to the Future.

Part Four THE IMPORTANCE OF

ADLAI STEVENSON

"The strange alchemy of time has somehow converted the Democrats into the truly conservative party of this country—the party dedicated to conserving all that is best, and building solidly and safely on these foundations."—*Adlai Stevenson, 1952*

Chapter Twenty-three A THIRD

VIEW OF THE NEW DEAL

"Men fight and lose the battle, and the thing they fought for comes about in spite of their defeat; and when it comes, turns out to be not what they meant; and other men have to fight for what they meant under another name."—*William Morris*

I

New Deal liberal: "The New Deal was not communist-infiltrated, as the hysterical witch-hunters charged. Instead, it represented a native radicalism that wisely hindered Wall Street, educated the masses to become less conservative than before, and discarded outdated institutions."

Republican: "The New Deal was communist-infiltrated, just as our patriotic businessmen charged at the time. *Therefore,* it helped communism, foolishly hindered Wall Street, made the masses less conservative than before, and discarded our traditional institutions."

Third view (new conservative): "Both wrong: the former in denying the New Deal was communist-infiltrated, the latter in believing it helped communism. It was indeed infiltrated, just as charged by Republican businessmen and documented by the testimonies of Weyl, Wadleigh, Massing, Pressman, Chambers. Because its communist sympathizers were often so *conspicuous, therefore* the New Deal hindered communism, helped Wall Street, made the masses more conservative than before, and preserved our traditional institutions."

In this imaginary trialogue, the word "conspicuous" explains the word "therefore." Entirely aside from its harmful quota of cleverly secret spies like Ware, Silvermaster, Hiss, the New

Deal contained a helpful quota of stupidly conspicuous pro-communists. Helpful: because their presence deluded business-men into deeming the New Deal radical and anti-capitalist. If businessmen had been less naive, more sophisticated, better informed, if they had realized that the New Deal was actually rescuing and stabilizing capitalism (via SEC, guarantee of bank deposits, a larger, richer consumer-market), then they would not have been enraged beyond endurance against the New Deal. Had they not been enraged beyond endurance, they would not have attacked the New Deal with an intemperance so extreme that it performed an otherwise impossible miracle: it converted the then radical masses to the New Deal, as opposed to the more radical alternatives to which they would otherwise have turned in the context of the depression era.

Let us reconstruct that forgotten depression-context of over twenty years ago. Starving, unemployed masses, embittered to the brink of radical revolution. Unemployed apple vendors at every corner. Hooverville shacks and bonus-marchers dispersed by armed force. Farmers burning mortgages. Workers shot down by company guards or in turn lawlessly taking over factories in sit-down strikes. In short, a revolutionary powder-keg, needing only a spark.

In America the spark never came. Why? All over the rest of the world, the same depression was goading the masses into revolutionary extremes: usually of the communist left, as in France's trade-unions and Front Populaire; sometimes of the radical right, as in Germany. Even sober, evolutionary England felt temporarily the violent passions of class war. The American masses proved the solitary exception to the universal radicalism, meekly letting the New Deal canalize their grievances back into the old, middleclass, parliamentary framework. The New Deal reforms may seem drastic from the smug and prosperous viewpoint of today, but they were small potatoes from the viewpoint of the economic and psychological desperation of 1933. The confidential Ickes diary of that period has recently reminded us that the only feasible alternative to the New Deal reforms, the mood of the masses being what it was, was not an abandonment of reform, a restoration of business influence, but still more drastic reform, a still more drastic step against business and toward class war.

Normally that still more drastic step would have been taken. The country would have moved not to the right but to the left of Roosevelt. In that case America would today be paralyzed by some kind of radical class-war party as big as that of the communists in France or Italy, making Russia mistress of the globe. During 1933-36, nothing could save the day for conservatism and the traditional status quo, nothing could cheat the revolution of its almost certain triumph, unless the fighting-mad workers, farmers, share-croppers, bonus-marchers could be persuaded to accept Roosevelt's small potatoes instead. Then the miracle happened; the workers were persuaded; the revolutionary moment passed, and today their prosperous sons move into suburbia and ungratefully vote Republican.

If any deception can ever be salutary, then this one was. For neither the workers nor America would be better off if the New Deal had really undertaken the revolutionary chaos and class war that the workers then thought they wanted. A Marxist sleuth may argue: Roosevelt, a Machiavellian opportunist, purposely planned his pseudo-radical gestures in order to deceive the revolutionary workers and steal socialism's thunder. But such Marxist reasoning attributes to the makers of history, whether Roosevelt or any other, qualities they almost never possess: detailed long-range planning; conscious hypocrisy; consistent awareness of their class interests; a capacity for conspiracy sufficiently complicated and ingenious to delight paranoiacs and detective-story fans. Granted that Roosevelt obviously was often a Machiavellian opportunist (with unconscious humor, his cultists employ the daintier adjective "pragmatic"). Yet not even a Machiavellian President is able on purpose to deceive the masses into deeming him anti-business; not even a diabolically clever businessman is able on purpose to feign resentment of a New Deal if he really does know it is rescuing him; history does not work that patly. Both these deceptions rang true for the then anti-capitalist workingman because they were not planned but absent-minded; they rang true because they were *self*-deceptions.

The conspicuousness (elephantine lightness of foot) of several of the capitalist-baiting pro-communists in the New Deal goaded the business world into a sincere—not planned, not feigned—frenzy against the New Deal. This frenzy converted the workers—deceived the workers—into a New Dealism of which they would otherwise have been suspicious as being too moderate. No insincere shadow-boxing, deliberately planned between Roosevelt and Wall Street, could have converted them, deceived them. Sincerity on both sides: the New Deal sincerely deemed itself anti-business; business sincerely deemed the New Deal its enemy and not, as now is so clear, its stabilizer and rescuer. Saved by ignorance: no deliberate capitalist conspiracy but plain ignorance of their respective historical roles caused business and the New Deal to give the masses the impression that the New Deal was as radical as the millionaire Weirs said it was.

This is not to deny the existence of deliberate capitalist plots. But these usually fool nobody, get laughed off the stage, get taken seriously by nobody except Marxists. For example, the so-called "Liberty League" of anti-Roosevelt millionaires fooled nobody with its grand talk of "liberty"; it helped poor, bewildered Landon lose the 1936 election so overwhelmingly. Similarly the Dixon-Yates contract helped the Republicans lose their southern gains of 1952. Capitalist plots sometimes really do occur—and are the enemies not of the workers but of capitalism. The real strength of American capitalist free enterprise, making it superior to rigid statist regimentation, is not its gauche conspiracies of selfish materialism but its flexibility, its freedom from doctrinaire theories (in practice even from its own Adam Smith theories), its capacity for voluntary self-reform. Thereby it superbly practices the warning of Prince Metternich to his monarchs: "Stability is not immobility."

Thus it came about that the concealed conservatism of a

pseudo-radical New Deal defeated the pseudo-conservatism of the Republican party's concealed radicalism. Roosevelt's thrashing of Old Guard businessmen, before they could provoke the country into class-war, saved them from themselves and doubled their dividends. The world depression of 1929–33 turned the masses of continental Europe toward revolutionary extremes; it would also have done so in America under another Hoover Administration. Instead, the unintentionally conservative New Deal won the worker, the farmer, the share-cropper, the Negro, the unemployed veteran—all who were underprivileged economically or ethnically—away from revolutionary extremes by giving them a real stake in America. For the first time they felt that America was also *their* country. This psychological feeling, not mere economic reform, was the greatest achievement of the New Deal and was, in its consequences, conservative.

The year 1688 killed radicalism and republicanism in England by proving to the Stuart-resenting masses that their aspiration for political liberty could be met—via William III—*within* the traditional monarchic framework; hence, no more need for Cromwellian republican revolution as an alternative to the Stuarts. The year 1933 killed radicalism and communism in America by proving to the plutocrat-resenting masses that their aspiration for economic liberty could be met—via the Squire of Hyde Park—*within* the traditional Constitutional, semi-squirearchical framework; hence, no need for communist or even socialist alternatives to the plutocrats. The day will come when 1933 occupies for American conservatives of the future the same ancient and sacred aura, the same role of basic *starting*-point, that 1688 has occupied for British conservatives like Burke and Churchill and for America's Federalist party. When that day comes, maturer conservatives than many today will hail the Roosevelt inauguration of 1933 with the same phrase with which Burke hailed the bloodless inauguration of King William III: not as a revolution but as "a revolution averted."

II

Important qualification: in reacting against the shared Republican and New Deal view that the New Deal was anti-conservative, let us not carry our third view to the opposite extreme of calling the New Deal conservative as a whole. It was conservative—the new 1688—in its substantive aspect: in the revolution-preventing consequences of its reforms and its anti-plutocracy. But its procedural aspect—direct democracy, trying to pack the Court, by-pass the Constitution—was sometimes just as radical as the business world believed it to be. Today Adlai Stevenson, the consolidator of the substantive achievements of the New Deal, is the purifier, pruner, discarder of its procedural defects. His twofold role is to continue liberally its humane social heritage, yet to restrict it conservatively within a rigorous procedural framework, not to be subverted even by popular majorities and noble goals.

New conservatives refuse to see the New Deal as black or white; so they alternately get accused of slandering it and over-praising it. They defend its humane reforms as a return to the old medieval sense of a personal, organic relationship between fellow humans, instead of the impersonal, mechanical relationship of cash-nexus that followed the middleclass French Revolution and that lives on today in the Jacobins *endimanchés*[1] of Old Guard Republicanism. So considered, the New Deal has deeper traditional roots than its would-be "traditionalist" critics. This basic acceptance of the New Deal does not prevent new conservatives from attacking its three main unconservative qualities, the first two radical, the third liberal: first, its procedural aspect of direct democracy; second, its sometimes excessive statism, depersonalizing and overadjusting the individual; third, its unhistorical liberal faith in human nature and mass progress.

In other words, America needs a government both accepting the New Deal and pruning, purifying it. This dual need would be fulfilled by Stevenson-style Democrats certainly; by Eisen-

[1] See page 80.

hower-style Republicans very likely; by Old Guard Republicans not at all (they would not accept the New Deal); by doctrinaire ADA-style New Dealers hardly (they would not prune it).

From this picky and choosy approach towards the New Deal, the new-conservative position may seem merely a compromise dependent on the pro and con extremes, merely adding them up and dividing by two. But in reality the new-conservative position towards the New Deal is independently evolved, reflecting a perspective older than either of theirs, that of the *Federalist* papers. This third position has been summarized by the new conservative August Heckscher. His essay "Who Are the American Conservatives?"[2] refutes the argument according to which those conservatives who support the revolution-preventing New Deal reforms in *politics* become indistinguishable in *philosophy* from liberals and New Dealers and should, therefore, stop calling themselves conservatives:

The failure to understand the true nature of conservatism has made political campaigns in the United States signally barren of intellectual content. In debate it is difficult at best to admit that you would do the same thing as the opposition, but in a different way. Yet the spirit in which things are done really does make a difference, and can distinguish a sound policy from an unsound one. Social reforms can be undertaken with the effect of draining away local energies, reducing the citizenry to an undifferentiated mass, and binding it to the shackles of the all-powerful state. Or they can be undertaken with the effect of strengthening the free citizen's stake in society. The ends are different. The means will be also, if men have the wit to distinguish between legislation which encourages voluntary participation and legislation which involves reckless spending and enlargement of the federal bureaucracy.

It is easy to say that such distinctions are not important. A conservative intellectual like Peter Viereck is constantly challenged, for example, because in a book like *Shame and Glory of the Intellectuals* he supports a political program not dissimilar in its outlines from that which was achieved during twenty years of social renovation under the Democrats. But *the way* reforms are undertaken is actually crucial. Concern for

[2] In *Confluence* magazine (Harvard University Summer School), September, 1954.

the individual, reluctance to have the central government perform what can be done as well by the state or to have the public perform what can be done as well by private enterprise—these priorities involve values. And *such values,* upheld by writers like Mr. Viereck, are at the heart of modern conservatism. . . . Conservatism at best remains deeper and more pervasive than any party; and a party that does claim it exclusively is likely to deform and exploit it for its own purposes.

As chief editorial writer of the *New York Herald Tribune,* August Heckscher has the greatest editorial influence of any new conservative today. Unlike the present writer, he happens to be a loyal Eisenhower Republican. But he is fair-minded enough to recognize a great conservative statesman when he sees one, even in the opposing camp. Here are Mr. Heckscher's precise reasons for finding none other than Stevenson "the most consistent and philosophically mature conservative . . . in this century":

Conservatism is rarely a program and certainly never a dogma. It is not an ideology. At its best conservatism is a way of thinking and acting in the midst of a social order which is too overlaid with history and too steeped in values, too complex and diverse, to lend itself to simple reforms. It is a way of thought which not only recognizes different classes, orders, and interests in the social order but actually values these differences and is not afraid to cultivate them. . . . So persistent have been the reverberations of this period that many people saw Adlai Stevenson as something close to a radical because he bore the Democratic banner. They failed to discern that he was by all odds the most consistent and philosophically mature conservative to have arisen in this century in either party. Stevenson had to a unique degree a sense of the diversity of which American society is composed. He had a feeling for the way separate groups could be brought into the service of the whole.[3]

[3] *Loc. cit.*

Chapter Twenty-four SQUIRES IN-

COGNITO: The Advantage of Being

Slandered as "Leftist" by Rightists

"Fair is foul, and foul is fair."—*The witches in* MACBETH

Today aristocracy no longer has any inherent connection with Almanachs of Gotha, titles, Social Registers (though its occasional coincidental overlapping with them should not, out of snobbish fear of condoning snobbism, be denied). Today the aristocracy is one of status, unofficial and "unwritten," in the same sense that the real constitution, the real value code of any country is the unwritten constitution, the unarticulated code. By definition, an élite possesses greater power than the rest of the community. That greater power, in the case of the American libertarian, anti-egalitarian Federalist tradition, consists not of European-style titles and not (or not merely) of wealth. The greater power consists of something more intangible and unwritten: greater dignity of status in the community, greater power to influence the more serious and discriminating citizens in the high I.Q. bracket and the more rooted citizens in the low I.Q. bracket.

Aristocracy is justified when its contribution exceeds its privileges. It is unjustified when its *noblesse* fails to *oblige*. In that sense, the great revolutions from below were partly caused by default from above. Radicalism is the penalty history imposes upon an inadequate conservatism. Left-wing radicalism results when the aristocracy degenerates into a mere plutocracy, ignoring the need for humane social reforms.

Right-wing radicalism results when the aristocracy ignores totalitarian traitors in its midst if they happen to be not poor, non-Anglo-Saxon immigrants but sharers of the old-school-tie. Hence, the disgraceful attempts to shield an Alger Hiss in America, a Burgess and Maclean in England (Harvard and Oxford respectively); these attempts were not made by the aristocracy on behalf of the Communist Rosenbergs in America, the Nazi William Joyce in England. Usually the positive slightly outweighs the negative in aristocracy. The social gains of traditional continuity, *noblesse oblige,* and a power made more humane and mellow by time than the insecure brute power of the parvenu are gains usually outweighing the social losses of a leftism-provoking plutocracy, a rightism-provoking coddling of Hisses. Both the latter defects in aristocracy result from the same source: an ethically irresponsible snobbery. Snobbery, then, is the main evil to combat uncompromisingly within aristocracy in order to make it worth conserving.

In 1800 America's conservative and aristocratic Federalist party went down to permanent defeat because too explicitly a squirearchy. The second disaster struck in 1828: Jacksonian mass-democracy.[1] Since those dates, American conservatism, though still performing its indispensable function of protecting minority rights against majority tyranny, has been able to perform it effectively only when tactful and temperate enough to operate under unconservative labels; so great has been the prevalence of mass-democratic terminology among all big voting blocs and parties. Thus it was not his friends but his Republican enemy, John T. Flynn, who coined for Franklin D. Roosevelt the accurate term "the squire of Hyde Park," while his friends, borrowing the anti-aristocratic terms of Henry Wallace, won the mass-vote for Roosevelt by inaccurately calling him the mouthpiece of "the century of the common man." The latter term would more accurately have applied to Huey Long at home, Hitler abroad; the great moments of

[1] Cf. pages 23–26 on why the terms "massman" and "Jacksonian" should not be confused with "workingman" and why "massman" is at least as likely to mean petty bourgeois, as opposed to the sometimes more traditional trade-unionist.

the sometimes noble, sometimes shockingly unscrupulous leadership of Roosevelt were when he was not mouthpiece but re-educator of the common man.

Whether for better or worse and cutting across party-lines, Theodore Roosevelt, Franklin Roosevelt, Adlai Stevenson, Averell Harriman, Governor Christian Herter, and Senators Flanders, Watkins, Saltonstall, and Lodge are squires. For better or worse, Truman, Eisenhower, Nixon, and Kefauver could never be squires. Here is how the millionaire George Backer, a close advisor of Harriman, explained President Roosevelt's friendly reliance on Harriman throughout the New Deal:

They were both squires. A squire is a man with good property and unearned income, who doesn't have to work, who has been financially independent for generations. All of this Roosevelt likes. He did not like industrialists who worked for their money. Besides Harriman went to Groton. And nobody could be too bad if he went to Groton.[2]

Owing to the non-elective institutions of Supreme Court and Constitution, with their undemocratic—and liberty-conserving—restraints on majority dictatorship, the American voter is experienced enough to elect conservative and aristocratic leadership. But only when it humors his Jacksonian conditioning by never, never calling itself conservative and aristocratic. The blend between our underground Federalist tradition and our top-of-the-brain Jacksonian tradition has produced a nation that is most itself when voting for conservative candidates with a strongly anti-conservative terminology. Millionaire products of exclusive schools like Harriman and Stevenson are able to serve so effectively the interests of a

[2] *Time,* November 14, 1955, page 19. "Nobody could be too bad if he went to Groton": this kind of stage-Englishman comedy—the Colonel McCormick line in reverse—gets pretty hard to take as it approaches the nausea-threshold. The toadies of the élite and its *Chicago Tribune* enemies (the independent-minded Mr. Backer is neither) make the same mistake: treating Groton, Harvard, etcetera, as something unique, something qualitatively better or worse than similar schools. Thereby both the toadies and the enemies replace the proper point of focus—namely, a candidate's objective merit—with disproportionate subjective reactions to some isolated datum of his biography.

responsible capitalism only because their services are rewarded
by roars of "anti-capitalist" from the irresponsible far right.
A cessation of these vote-giving roars of rage would be the kiss
of death. If ever the Stevensons and Harrimans were praised
as either conservatives or friends of Wall Street by the unpopular right, then the Jacksonian-conditioned mass-vote would
switch to some dangerous demagogue genuinely on the left.

What if, by some unlikely accident, the gentlemen of the
mass-media of the far-right should be reading, at this very
moment, the above hypothesis that they can injure a Stevenson
or a Harriman by praising him? Even then, their mass-media
mentalities being what they are, no harm will be done. For
fortunately, at this very moment, as they read the hypothesis
that can give them victory, they will inevitably dismiss it as
a contemptible egghead paradox not worth the attention of
busy men of the world. Thus their undoing can be openly
discussed under their very noses without even resorting to the
medieval anti-thought-control protection of Latin, so great is
the split into two different American languages. The two
American languages differ not in denotative vocabulary but in
connotations, in reading media, in entertainment media, in
respective genres of overadjustedness, and consequently in
mutually incomprehensible signal-systems for spotting the
transition between the deadpan and the ironic.

The impossibility of exchanging ideas across this diction-
barrier makes it impossible to prove, even to the more reasonable members of the mass-level nationalist right, the following
five axioms.

First: if these would-be conservatives wish to conserve
capitalism and American interests and prevent global communism, let them begin by objectively realizing that they
themselves are incapable of doing that job. Second: that job
of conserving is more effectively done by the liberal in-group
they hate, a group less liberal than they think it is, a group
lumping together everybody of the liberal-conservative middle
road, whether Eisenhower Republican or Stevenson Democrat.
Third: they hate the liberal in-group more than anything else

in the world; they hate it even more than they hate communism, which indeed benefits from their attacks on foreign aid, U.N., and the middle road. Fourth: while their jargon-reason for hating the liberal in-group is its "leftism" (a leftism sometimes all too real, especially back in the 1930's, but today mostly imaginary), their real reason for hating the liberal in-group is the fact of its being an in-group, aristocratic and "accepted," while they of the nationalist far right are a moneyed but status-resenting out-group. Actually some of the in-group deserves to be in, some deserves to be ousted; but this unsweeping, ethical approach, judging each individual only on his own merits, is rarely found among either the in-group or the out-group. Needed is an unadjusted independent position re-interpreting both groups.

Fifth and finally: in those cases where the nationalist right did become a temporary in-group—occasionally in America, frequently abroad—it unintentionally helped to popularize communism and radicalize the globe by making capitalism inflexible, unviable. Similarly the valid ideal of hereditary monarchy, once indispensable for maintaining historic continuity, was made inflexible, unviable by those Bourbon ultra-royalists of whom Metternich wrote: "The Legitimists are legitimizing the Revolution."

Even if there were some way to suggest these five axioms through the barrier between the two American languages, the message would meet a blank stare of incomprehension: "Why, everybody knows that the followers of the late Colonel McCormick and such patriotic elder statesmen as the gossip-columnists of the tabloid press are the only true anti-communists and saviors of capitalism." This reaction of incomprehension from the right-wing nationalists is a blessing. For their continued attacks on the in-group aristocracy will continue to keep its conserving function safely incognito— just as twenty years ago their attacks on Roosevelt as "revolutionary" persuaded the revolution-minded, mortgage-burning, apple-selling, bonus-marching masses to support (on mistaken revolutionary grounds) the revolution-preventing New Deal instead of turning, like the European unemployed during that same depression, to the real left of revolutionary class-war.

What is the purpose of American elections? Certainly not to "let the people rule," a mere abstract copybook-maxim. In concrete reality, if the direct power to rule were given to "the people," they would in turn hand that power over to the thought-control dictatorship of some plebiscitarian demagogue of status-resentment (whether Populist left or neo-Populist right). Instead, the purpose of American elections is to decide which subgroup of the élite shall dominate the people. Dominate, yes, but never arbitrarily—that, too, would be tyranny—but subject to constant checks: elections, newspaper vigilance, our written Bill of Rights, and equally our unwritten traditions of freedom. Not least among the unwritten traditions is the American sense of humor, a healthy irreverence towards sham, making it psychologically difficult for an élite to freeze its humanity into heartless snobbery, pompous loss of the common touch, and "class lines" (in the frozen or European sense of the term).

To return to the above list of checks against arbitrary domination: elections, though the most effective check when supplemented by the other checks, are the least effective of all when unsupplemented. Elections have become a farce in many non-Anglo-Saxon countries because such countries usually lack those non-exportable, special traditions that characterize only England, America, and a very few other lucky accidents of history. Liberals have fantastically overestimated the effectiveness of conscious, articulate voting as freedom's shield; they have fantastically underestimated the effectiveness of unwritten, semiconscious traditions. If human rights depended mainly on elections, even on fair and free elections, a very popular despot like Peron would still be ruling Argentina, and McCarthy would never have been censured into oblivion by the Senate. What stopped such despots was an unwritten tradition of ethical *noblesse oblige,* whose violations no true élite condones, no matter how popular those violations may be in terms of mass-votes.

Thus that exceptional, unblueprintable accident of history known as a free society combines a traditional, incognito aristocracy with traditional, unwritten checks upon that aristocracy, permitting the pruning and replenishing of The Club peacefully, without barricades. The combination prevents at one stroke the majority-tyranny of pure democracy and the minority-tyranny of an inflexible, unprunable aristocracy. That balanced combination, as best envisaged by John Adams (*Defense of the Constitutions*, 1787–88), was launched in America despite Jefferson, despite Paine, and thanks to the Federalist party. But a combination so complex rests not merely on any particular party, such as the transient Federalists, nor on any individual's written formula. Even in America, the combination rests ultimately on British roots older than 1776 or even 1688, roots unique and unexportable, representing centuries of dark, unplanned, unsymmetrical growth. The fruit of that unplannable, unexportable growth is freedom. Freedom has never yet endured very long without reverence for ancient precedent and without some kind of sublimated aristocracy to protect the individual from the conformist, freedom-hating majority of every society. The function of the squirearchic Tory spirit, said Disraeli in a Parliamentary address of 1862, is "to protect us alike from individual tyranny and popular outrage, equally to resist democracy and oligarchy, and favor that principle of free aristocracy which is the only basis and security for constitutional government."

Were America the mass-democracy she sincerely imagines she is, she would soon become, like Louisiana under Huey Long, an unbenevolent despotism tempered by assassination. Instead, America blithely remains a benevolent squirearchy tempered by character-assassination.

Chapter Twenty-five A SHARED

FRAMEWORK FOR LIBERALS

AND CONSERVATIVES

During the relatively stable era of 1815–1914, liberalism and conservatism seemed at times the only real alternatives in the western world. Hence, their spokesmen stressed their differences: for example, Gladstone versus Disraeli. Since then, the rise of communism and fascism has forced liberals and conservatives to stress their similarities: shared liberties, a shared procedural framework. In culture, philosophy, and personal way of life, they should still continue, uncompromising, to argue their deep differences. But in politics they should work out a cooperative compromise lest their disunity enhance the class-war left, the nationalist right. For example the French elections of January, 1956, enhanced the communist left, the Poujadist right only because the liberal-conservative center was disunified (Mendès-France versus Faure). Also in America, the statesmanship of freedom must uphold against polarization a shared central framework. Adlai Stevenson, ably upholding that framework, calls it "the politics of moderation."

In certain American situations, the only thing conservatives find at hand to conserve is—liberalism. That fact is disconcerting to doctrinaires, conservative or liberal, but is not really paradoxical. For the liberalism thus conserved often turns out to be the *conservative*-tending, law-centered[1] liberalism of

[1] For example, Lincoln: "Let every American, every lover of liberty . . . swear . . . never to violate in the least particular the laws of the country. . . . Let reverence for the laws be breathed by every American mother to the lisping babe . . . taught in schools . . . preached from the pulpit. . . . Let it become the political religion of the nation." (*Perpetuation of Our Political Institutions*, 1838.)

Locke, Lincoln, Wilson, not the radical-tending, mass-centered liberalism of Rousseau, Jackson, Weaver, Donnelly, La Follette (both kinds are too confident of man and progress to be conservative even though the former is conservative-tending). The former respects civil liberties, also property rights; the latter tends toward mass-dictatorship, state-coerced leveling. Only the former kind constitutes the liberal half of Stevenson's centrality. The conservative half, equally important, here receives corrective stress because less familiar. His Republican foes, his liberal friends both have motives of their own (campaign propaganda) for stressing only his liberal half.

Conservative is Stevenson's extremely important insistence on reversing America's centralizing trend, on nurturing local patterns, traditional diversities. Centralization, the bureaucrat's sublimated will to power, was listed on page 236 as one of the three main conservative objections to the New Deal. Stevenson's record as Governor demonstrated his conservative respect for the rich variety of free local traditions.

In foreign policy Stevenson never shared the former illusions of many New Dealers about Yalta, Red China. Nor did he share their former loose use of "fascist" against non-fascist businessmen, comparable to loose Republican use of "Red." For example, Truman, autumn, 1948: "Powerful forces, like those that created European fascists, are working through the Republican party. . . ." By quietly pruning away these unconservative illusions and diatribes of the New and Fair Deal, Stevenson shows his greater maturity, his centrality.

There is no contradiction between calling Stevenson more genuinely conservative than the wild Republican nationalists and saying he particularly merits trade-union support. Whoever misuses "conservative" journalistically to mean anti-labor, overlooks how rooted and conservatized[2] the trade-unions and New Deal labor laws have by now become. They are hated for that very reason by communists and right-wing radicals alike. Definition of "trade-unions" in the *Soviet Dictionary of Foreign Words* (1951): "Primarily opportunists and adherents of class

[2] See the Tannenbaum hypothesis, page 85.

collaboration with the bourgeoisie." Stevenson represented a class-war-preventing framework of humanitarianized but not socialized capitalism. He is entitled to support from that majority of workers and businessmen who are willing to canalize their labor-capital rivalry within that common framework. Businessmen to the right of it, workers to the left of it would produce European conditions of class war.

Liberals and conservatives, sharing the same procedural framework, sound alike when defending its free institutions against totalitarian left and right. Hence, those right-wing periodicals that used to glorify McCarthy, now feature articles unmasking the new conservatism as "really the same thing" as liberalism, just one more conspiracy of civil-libertarians and internationalists. Reciprocally, the more doctrinaire liberal periodicals unmask the new conservatism as a conspiracy of bigots, reactionaries, and, worst of all, conformists. The right-wing nationalist sees only that most new conservatives differ from him about thought-control and hucksterdom; therefore, he correctly notes that in politics they are closer to liberals. The doctrinaire liberal sees only that most new conservatives differ from him about human nature and the source of evil; therefore, he correctly notes that in philosophy they are closer to reactionaries. To cease confusing the new conservatism with either liberalism or the far right, one should see it as a whole, instead of only its short-run politics or only its long-run philosophy.

The above combination—to join political liberals in defending civil liberties and humane reforms, yet to remain a philosophical conservative in evaluating tradition and human nature —seems best represented in public life by Adlai Stevenson. Often a similar combination (except for the right-wing Republicanism of the high-minded but romanticizing Russell Kirk) characterizes the young scholars known as new conservatives: Thomas I. Cook, Raymond English, Francis Wilson their most representative spokesmen in the learned journals; August Heckscher in the press; Chad Walsh, Hyatt Waggoner in literature; John Hallowell, Robert Nisbet in political philosophy; Daniel Boorstin, Clinton Rossiter in revaluating American history; moving on to older, already familiar names, Reinhold Niebuhr, Will Herberg in social theology.

American conservatism is most influential when linked to no economic class nor political party but diffused, unlabeled, among all movements, classes, parties. Two examples of diffusion, both important in the Stevenson movement, are the adoption by some liberals of the conservative view of human nature and their adoption of the conservative view of a central framework. The first example was summed up by Paul Bixler, editor of *Antioch Review*[3]: "No accomplishment of conservatism has been plainer to date than its effect on current liberalism. The effects of conservatism can be seen in Mr. Arthur Schlesinger's own belief in 'moderate pessimism', in his rejection of centralized state planning, in his belief in moderate change tempered by the cooling hand of experience. . . ." Chadwick Hall's forthcoming *Labyrinth of the Conservative Mind* confirms liberalism's unacknowledged trend toward the conservative view of human nature:

The prewar progressive was a happy optimist. He insisted that man was good; he deified change and reason. . . . The shift in outlook which has prepared the way for a more sympathetic reception of the conservative's message is clearly visible in Schlesinger's analysis of the contemporary crisis. . . . Even the idea that man is good jeopardizes freedom, Schlesinger declares. . . . Progressivism is only possible, he argues, if the fact of man's depravity is acknowledged because constructive change can only be achieved in the realm of the possible. . . . This [conservative view of human nature] attracted the Federalists but, since the death of John Adams, had no articulate spokesman. . . . Yet now this . . . new outlook, so conservative in tone, is . . . so pervasive that it has even altered the foundations of progressive thinking.

The second conservative diffusion among liberals is the view that freedom rests on a central traditional framework, excluding radicals of left and right. This concept—aptly called "the vital center" by the contemporary liberal who did most to

[3] Letter of August 11, 1955, to the *Reporter*, rebutting an anti-conservative article of Arthur Schlesinger, Jr.

popularize it—originated in such key conservative thinkers as John Adams, Burke, Donoso Cortés, Metternich, Tocqueville. They and other conservatives were among the first to point out how closely right and left extremists resembled each other in threatening the traditional center. Such right and left extremists were the Carlists and republicans in Spain, whom Donoso Cortés attacked simultaneously in his famous essay of 1832; the ultra-royalists and Jacobins in Metternich's day; the reactionaries and radicals in Tocqueville's sarcastic memoirs of the revolution of 1848.

In 1825 the Austrian chancellor Metternich wrote from Paris: "The red and white doctrinaires shun me like the plague." Misunderstood and diabolized by nineteenth-century liberal historians, who still hoped for an impossible liberal version of nationalism and who would not admit that liberty could also gradually develop within the Hapsburg monarchic framework, Austria's great internationalist conservative was being a "premature" vital-centrist when he declared: "From the school of radicalism, I fell into that of the émigrés and learned to value the mean between the extremes." For the extremist ultra-royalists of Charles X, who served their white Bourbon flag with the violent or "red" methods of the Jacobins, Metternich coined the witty label "white Jacobins." And what but "white Bolsheviks" are the violent would-be anti-communists of America's nationalist right?

Nationalism, too, was correctly diagnosed by Metternich as an anti-conservative subverter of the moral order. He called the intolerant German nationalists of his day "national Jacobins," despite their claim of being the only alternative to the international radical Jacobinism of France. Comparable, in America since 1929, have been the anti-centrist claims of fellow-traveler leftists and nationalist rightists to be each the only alternative to the other.[4] Whoever doubts that the

[4] Additional documentation of Metternich's centrism, beyond the sources cited for all his above quotations in *Conservatism Revisited* (New York, Scribners, 1949), occurs in P. Viereck, "New Views on Metternich," a monograph read at the 1950 session of the American Historical Association and published in *The Review of Politics*, Notre Dame, April, 1951.

American right strengthened communism during 1949–54 by weakening international centrism, should reread the history of not November but September, 1917: Kornilov as Russia's MacArthur. The communists, concentrating their main energy against the moderate Weimar Republic, brought Hitler to power in the same way that General Ludendorff's train (carrying Lenin back to Russia) and General Kornilov's anti-Kerensky campaign were the two rightist adventures of 1917 bringing Lenin to power.

John Adams and Edmund Burke defended the centrist heritage of 1688 against King George and the ultra-Tories in 1776 and against the French Revolution and Tom Paine in the 1790's. Thereby Adams and Burke, two Protestant conservatives, permanently established the vital-centrist tradition in the English-speaking world. Similarly, Catholic conservatism in many countries calls itself simply "the center" or "the Center party." Long before American liberals became sufficiently chastened to settle for the sane moderation of Mr. Schlesinger's vital-center concept, it had been a typically centrist remark of the conservative Irving Babbitt that nothing so much resembles a bump as a hollow.

This centrist view of fascism and communism was a leitmotif of the present author's *Metapolitics: From the Romantics to Hitler,* 1941, whose title-page epigraph was, accordingly, Yeats's

> Things fall apart; the centre cannot hold . . .
> The best lack all conviction, while the worst
> Are full of passionate intensity.

Conservatism Revisited, 1949, concluded with the same appeal for conservative and liberal unity against left and right. It would, however, be absurdly unjust to attach any significance to the coincidence that these two books of 1941 and 1949 appeared prior to Mr. Schlesinger's *Vital Center,* 1949 (a truly valuable book, stressing both the centrist viewpoint and the relevance of that same wellknown Yeats quotation). The coincidence lacks significance because it is a matter of record that Arthur Schlesinger, Jr. reached his centrist conclusions entirely *independent* of these two earlier books. Therefore, the point is not one of originality nor of priority (priority belongs to Adams, Burke, Tocqueville in any case). The point is that centrism was so much in the air in the 1940's that different writers reached the same concept independently, even though not always simultaneously.

The reason centrism was in the air was that the simultaneous rise of rightist and leftist totalitarian threats in the Hitler-Stalin pact had forced liberals to adopt the centrist hypothesis they had earlier rejected in Adams, Burke, Tocqueville. In view of this welcome liberal-conservative alliance against the rightist-leftist totalitarian alliance, it is ironic that the coiner of the conservative phrase "vital center" has become the official liberal polemicist against the new conservatism, a non-party philosophy close to that of Adlai Stevenson among Democrats, Clifford Case among Republicans. Mr. Schlesinger's defenses of direct democracy (in the *Reporter*, February 10, 1955) and of the Jacksonian egalitarian massman, root of modern coercive conformity, were leftward-facing relapses from his own wise centrism.

But worse were the rightward-facing relapses of that minority of new conservatives who had failed to stand up and be counted on the McCarthy issue. Both relapses were inconsistent with the centrist alliance that alone can block leftist-rightist totalitarianism. Needed as cure is not some abstract intellectual consistency but moral consistency in concrete dilemmas. Needed equally today among liberal and conservative writers is a moral and emotional capacity for generosity. Such gauche, generous commitment, in an age of noncommittal urbanity among writers, would take the form of more civic courage, taking stands without first cannily calculating the risk. It would take the form of passionately defending the free mind wherever threatened, even where the threatener uses one's own pet intellectual pretexts and ideological jargon.

Then let us not bog down in abstract arguments with fellow centrists when today the concrete, unabstract reality is the felicitous centrality of the Stevenson movement. Its centrality

is made all the more effective by the fact that its enemies call
Stevenson "radical" or "dangerously liberal," owing to the outdated attachment of these adjectives (a cultural lag) to the
New Deal's revival of capitalism. The same lag blinds older,
more doctrinaire liberals to Stevenson's conservative function:
having reached political maturity in the depression era, they
are still unconsciously "waiting for Lefty."

Stevenson represents the point where the New Deal
became conservatized, rooted; and this without sacrificing the
valuable aspects of the American liberal tradition, which
Stevenson continues to represent also. Therefore, the Stevenson
Democrats best represent the shared central framework within
which our liberal tradition of Jefferson and our conservative
Federalist one of John Adams—both loyal to their British 1688
origins—can coalesce against right and left today. The spirit
of Burke—the Burke who defined gradual social change as
essential to viable conservatism—was best expressed in contemporary conservatism by these words of Adlai Stevenson:

> The strange alchemy of time has somehow converted the Democrats
> into the truly conservative party of this country—the party dedicated to
> conserving all that is best, and building solidly and safely on these
> foundations. The Republicans, by contrast, are behaving like the radical
> party—the party of the reckless and the embittered, bent on dismantling
> institutions which have been built solidly into our social fabric. . . .
> Our social-security system and our Democratic Party's sponsorship of the
> social reforms and advances of the past two decades [are] conservatism
> at its best. Certainly there could be nothing more conservative than to
> change when change is due, to reduce tensions and wants by wise
> changes, rather than to stand pat stubbornly, until, like King Canute,
> we are engulfed by relentless forces that will always go too far.

Middleroad politics may result from two different motives,
only one of them creditable: complacency and ethics. Complacency chooses the middle road as something easy, un-
demanding, safe. But ethics chooses it only because such a
liberal-conservative alliance against extremes causes less tyranny, less suffering, less disillusionment than the right and left

extremes. At the moment it may be safe and conformist to support the middle road. But again and again in history the time comes when societies are polarized between fascist-style and communist-style extremes. At such times, advocacy of a middle road becomes dangerous, courageous, unadjusted. The centrism of Stevenson Democrats (and of the similar Eisenhower Republicans) will prove harmfully overadjusting to America whenever motivated by complacency; helpfully unadjusting whenever motivated by ethics.

Chapter Twenty-six ARTICULATOR,

NOT YET INCARNATOR

Stevenson articulates the highest standards of statesman-ship currently available. Yet it is Eisenhower, so far, who better incarnates the aspirations of ordinary men of good will. He does so in the inarticulate manner wrongly derided by liberal intellectuals (cf. page 297 on the liberal preference for quick articulateness). Dangerous in other contexts, in the case of Eisenhower the incarnating mystique is safely remote from the romantic-ecstatic "general will" of Rousseau and from the dynamic, masses-on-the-march mystique of totalitarian dema-gogues.[1] Instead, the Ike mystique is a fourth dimension of the prosaic, a radiance of drabness, an excitement of relaxation. It is as mystical as the absurd and wise appeal of heavy American apple-pie. The triumphant plainness of both appeals embodies not merely the dullnesses but the reassuring decencies of American life. Eisenhower's incarnating function is one of America's greatest assets of stability in any crisis. This kindly figure, this *good* man, performs that function best when he is his own attractively homely self. He performs it worst when he lets his "team" sell his smile with methods more appropriate to dental cream. Judging by those stage-managings, you are supposed to vote for him not because he knows what is really going on in the government but because he will make your teeth shine. "No grit or abrasives" seems to be the motto of this smoothest public-relations job in American history.

As noted earlier in examining Lord Plushbottom in *Moon Mullins* and Maggie in *Bringing Up Father*, comic strips pre-

[1] McCarthy, for example, also used to incarnate. But whereas Eisenhower incarnates *people* (asleep or golfing or burning leaves on lawns), McCarthy incarnated *masses* (wide-awake and hotfooting to Western Union, telegraph-ing "their" Congressman to "investigate" good and hard everybody who is different).

sage American political trends more frankly than do the articulated credos of our actual politics because less inhibited, less self-conscious. The hero-worshipped image of "Ike" is not merely (that goes without saying) paternal; it is also wealth-centered. It is the image not merely of a trusted marriage-counselor, glossing-over incompatibilities with reassuring platitudes; it is also the image of a very benign millionaire. Against the frivolity-disapproval of one's shocked better judgment, another comic-strip parallel insists irresistibly on obtruding itself: Daddy Warbucks in *Little Orphan Annie*.

Stevenson's over-articulateness is the one main point on which he is still an abstract liberal instead of his usual happy blend of conservative and liberal patterns. In a public opinion poll[2] just before the 1952 elections, half those polled chose "really high intelligence" as the phrase best describing Stevenson (significantly the only category where Eisenhower had not much of a lead). A mere fifth chose Stevenson for "inspiring confidence," whereas half chose Eisenhower for that synonym of the incarnating ability. Here, then, is one explanation of why the otherwise better-qualified statesman lost the election of 1952. In none of the other main categories—labor, problems of subversion, the Korean war—did the polls reveal so large a gap between Eisenhower and Stevenson as in this indefinable, almost intuitive category of emanating "confidence." In Stevenson's defence it should be noted that he entered national politics as an unknown Illinois governor; Eisenhower entered as America's best-known war hero, with the voters prepared in advance for his confidence-emanations.

Perhaps the ideal government would be a small Ruritanian parliamentary monarchy in which both these men could rule together: the incarnator as the king, ritual-symbol, Court of Appeal; the articulator as the chancelor, the actual policy-maker. In America only a major crisis could create such a pooling of talents.

The illogical but real magic of Eisenhower's monarchic function was shown by the calming public effect emanating

2 Louis Harris, *Is There a Republican Majority?*, New York, 1954.

from his personal calm. That public effect has reduced American bad nerves at home as well as international war tensions. The world calm that his relaxed personal appearance created at Geneva in 1955 was not necessarily a gain; if it makes America relax her alertness against Soviet expansion, the calm may prove ominous.[3] The present point, however, is not to assess prematurely the gains or losses of Eisenhower's monarchic-magnetic function but to stress its remarkable effectiveness. Until Stevenson acquires at least a touch of this kind of effectiveness, he will remain vulnerable to the charge of being, by cerebrality of temperament, better suited for the role of enlightened advisor than for the role of supreme head of state.

If, on the other hand, Stevenson ever does grow into the incarnating function, then it will be a function founded on the legitimate magic of his contagious ethical integrity, not the suspect magic of B.B.D.&O.

[3] Though the original "Geneva spirit" of summer, 1955 is no longer taken seriously in America as evidence of Soviet conversion to pacifism, similar pseudo-peace drives will recur frequently enough to justify our recalling the following official Communist speech made in 1930 by the then secretary of the Communist International, Dmitri Manuilsky: "In 20 or 30 years, we shall spring a surprise, and since the surprise is an essential element for our victory, the bourgeoisie must be put to sleep. We will start by launching the most spectacular pacifist move of all time. We will make electrifying and unheard of concessions. The stupid and decadent capitalist countries will then complacently cooperate in their own destruction. They will greet with open arms a new opportunity to resume friendly relations with us and as soon as they let down their vigilance we will knock them out." [Quoted in *Political and Social Information*, Rome, October 15, 1955.]

Chapter Twenty-seven   RESTORER OF

THE INTELLECTUALS

"When an American says that he loves his own country, he means not only that he loves the New England hills, the prairies . . . the great mountains and the sea. He means that he loves an inner air, an inner light in which freedom lives and in which a man can draw the breath of self-respect."—*Adlai Stevenson*

American conservatism, notably the intellectual tradition today of Henry Adams, Melville, Faulkner, has a role primarily cultural and ethical. Are new conservatives who support Adlai Stevenson betraying that non-party, non-political role? Not in the light of Stevenson's recently published speeches: so high, so brave a cultural and ethical level, approached by no rival, deserves the grateful support of all. It deserves the enthusiastic support even of those of us who have joined no party, have no interest in politics—except as politics affects, by ricochet from outside, the ethical and aesthetic scope of the creative imagination, that inward bedrock of any really free society.

Stevenson is the first Presidential candidate in American history to recognize fully the danger of the American Over-adjusted Man. His speeches deserve the gratitude of future generations for educating his audiences to that danger. For example, his speech of June, 1955, at Smith College urged students "to frustrate the crushing and corrupting effects of specialization, to integrate means and ends, to develop that balanced tension of mind and spirit which can be properly called integrity. . . . not just better groupers and conformers (to casually coin a couple of fine words) but more idiosyncratic, unpredictable characters." His defence of the concept of the Unadjusted Man (even though not using that particular term) ended with words all Americans ought to heed:

While I am not in favor of maladjustment, I view this cultivation of neutrality, this breeding of mental neuters, this hostility to eccentricity and controversy, with grave misgiving. One looks back with dismay at the possibility of a Shakespeare perfectly adjusted to bourgeois life in Stratford, a Wesley contentedly administering a county parish, George Washington going to London to receive a barony from George III, or Abraham Lincoln prospering in Springfield with nary a concern for the preservation of the crumbling union.

In the opening chapter of this book, the Unadjusted Man was defined as a necessary hero because he defends the *inwardness* of the individual against the busybody bustling of external mass progress. By that definition, Stevenson was speaking more unadjustedly and more heroically than any other statesman of our time when he gave his version of American patriotism: "When an American says that he loves his country . . . he loves an inner air, an inner light in which freedom lives and in which a man can draw the breath of self-respect."

May we not call Adlai Stevenson the restorer of the intellectuals? His national impact is partly restoring them to their proper leadership in ethics and wisdom and helping them outgrow their bad and silly aspects of the 1930's and 1940's. Why bad, why silly? Bad: insofar as they sacrificed ethical means to a progress achieved by Machiavellian social engineering. (Defined metaphysically, the ethical double-standard of many toward Russia was a logical consequence of the initial false step of seeking a short-cut to material progress outside the moral framework.) Silly: insofar as they alternated this expediency with the opposite extreme, that of idealistic *a priori* blueprints and abstractions (these always lack the concrete context of any mature, organically evolved idealism). An oscillation between these extremes was likewise characteristic of the eighteenth-century liberal intellectuals, oscillating between impractical utopian yearnings and an all-too-practical softness (double-standard) toward Jacobin social engineering.

Here is a small but revealing example of the more ethical guidance that Stevenson has been giving to American liberal intellectuals: he declined to let his name appear on lists endorsing the *Nation* magazine (that Last Mohican from the Popular Front illusions of the 1930's). What made his refusal significant was the fact that such routine endorsements had heretofore come automatically from the highest liberal intellectuals and from leading New Dealers, including President Truman and several important Democratic Senators. Liberal intellectuals have closed some of the gap separating them three years ago from conservative intellectuals by having learnt to distinguish more clearly than some of them did between the double-standard "liberalism" of certain *Nation* experts on Russia and the valid liberalism of the *New Republic*, the *Progressive*, the *Reporter*. Three years ago, when the much-denounced chapter about the double-standard of the *Nation* appeared in *Shame and Glory of the Intellectuals*, that ethical distinction was still unclear to many liberal intellectuals and was still rejected as if it were mere "Red-baiting."

How much saner America would be today if those nationalists who would like to be "conservatives" had a Republican version of Stevenson to teach them, by a comparable refusal to endorse the right-wing equivalents of the *Nation*, the comparable distinction between endorsing valid anti-communism and endorsing the "anti-communism" of the demagogues. The intellectual and the anti-intellectual each has his characteristic version of one bad error, one silly one. The intellectual is outgrowing both of his (as discussed above); the anti-intellectual is not yet outgrowing his particular bad one (thought-control) and silly one (hucksterdom).

No personal hero-worship, no "great-man" theory of history is in order; the name Stevenson is here being used as the replaceable symbol for a broader, impersonal change for the better. That change consists of a maturer America, outgrowing the false alternative of Babbitt Senior Republicans, Babbitt

Junior liberals. Ahead potentially, though not yet more than potentially, lies an American reconciliation of Jefferson with John Adams, of liberal free dissent with conservative roots in historical continuity.

Our analysis is concerned with social psychology, not political utility; with candidly exchanging impractical, deeply-felt views in a modest-sized literary and scholarly periphery, not with drumming up trade in the marketplace for any particular candidate or party. Indeed a deliberate attempt is made to write *without* an eye on any noisy, ephemeral political campaign and its pat party-formulations. Admittedly this attempt is not consistently possible: what is that funny noise going on outside the window? Still, it seems no ivory-tower affectation but the discipline of one's craft to stick to one's subject matter.

That subject matter, among other things, is the problem of whether Americans can partly return from mass culture to unadjustedness, from stereotype to archetype, and whether the restoration of intellectuals to part of their traditional status can be made to serve this return. That subject matter, that problem is concerned not with the candidate but with the symptom; not with the political success of this particular candidate but with the psychological trend of this particular symptom. The trend in question is the impact on America of Adlai Stevenson's thoughtful and ethical leadership. That impact marks the beginning of a new cycle in the interplay between America and her intellectuals. Outcomes of new cycles are unpredictable. Just possibly the cycle may this time record not the shame of the intellectuals but their glory: as America's catalysts of unadjustedness.

Chapter Twenty-eight THE IMPIETIES

OF PROGRESS

"One must always be ready to change sides with justice, that fugitive from the winning camp."—*Simone Weil*

A half-dozen years spanned the interval from the opening of the Hiss case to the new relaxation (decline of McCarthyism) of 1955. During that tense interval, some of America experienced a state of psychological civil war. Many an American community became a veritable arena, in which an eagle-scout named "Anti-Communism" was battling a village Hampden or mute inglorious Milton named "Civil Liberties." What a spectacle!—each side deeming itself a hero against overwhelming odds, yet corroded by self-deception and by dishonest atrocity-stories about its respective martyrdom. Self-deception: for the rival battle-cries of anti-spy and anti-witch-hunt were too often pretexts for rival wills to power.

In the lavish America of today, will to power no longer means economic profit; there is enough of *that* lying around to keep both sides glutted, despite Marx and Adam Smith. The real objective, giving such emotional intensity to the rival wills, was neither economic materialism nor a sane solution of the security problem but the ego-satisfaction and status-bolstering of determining America's future value-pattern. The eagle-scouts fought to impose the new value-pattern of the Republican nationalists (neo-Populists plus western finance); the village Hampdens fought to preserve the old value-pattern of America's educational and social élite (the civil libertarians of the exclusive "traditional" colleges plus the mellowed eastern-seaboard finance). The former camp was a revolution against an élite and, therefore, *needed* to tell itself it was pro-élite and anti-revolutionary. The latter camp was a traditional élite and, therefore, could *afford* to tell itself it was anti-élite and daringly liberal.

So much for the alignment of the recent past. The question for the future is this: which of the two unattractive alternatives can be sufficiently improved and matured to become not merely a lesser evil but a positive good? Since the noble pretexts of both sides ring so hollow, why do these pages favor (while retaining an independent third position) a victory by the second of these two sides?

Not for its *beaux yeux*—not, that is, for its comic snobbism, its mutually contradictory brands of "progressive" political chic, avant-garde cultural chic, and eastern-college, country-club social chic. Its trump card, during our recent psychological war, was, of course, the ethical superiority to McCarthyism of its educated, upper-class liberals; but even that trump had been badly compromised in advance by their silence about highbrow McCarthyism back in the 1930's (Moscow Trials abroad, witch-hunt methods of anti-business investigating committees at home). Still, despite everything, the uncompromised portion of the élite continues to be the preferable alternative; its justification is its function of transmitting the heritage known as "New England." The New England heritage (a moral, not sectional term, a spirit diffused through all sections) inspiringly combines America's two bedrock archetypes: respect for the free mind, respect for the moral law.

This combination of moral duty and liberty is having a new birth of nationwide appeal, owing to the leadership of Adlai Stevenson, a blender of New England and Middle West. He is, first of all and in his primary role, an eastern-style, Ivy-League-educated intellectual who yet is uncompromised by Popular Frontist and Yalta illusions. But at the same time he is a patriotic Illinois anti-communist who yet is uncompromised by the slander methods and thought-control methods associated with much of the headlined anti-communism of Illinois and points west. Thus he has avoided both the characteristic forms of contemporary self-corruption; he has thereby earned legitimately the appellation "man of integrity."

In the psychological civil war discussed above, the value-pattern of the eagle-scout nationalist was resisted alike by Wall Street plutocrats, New Deal anti-plutocrats. What still divides these fellow-resisters is the important issue of the rights of business; what unites them is internationalism, Anglophilia, an eastern schooling. Is there really much basic difference between a plutocratic Wall Street spokesman like Thomas Dewey (or Willkie), namely a Republican who also favors New Deal social reforms, and an anti-plutocratic New Deal spokesman like Averell Harriman (or Acheson), namely a Democrat who is also a Wall Street millionaire? These two groups will continue to vote for opposite parties. But they will become ever more closely allied by their common opposition to the neo-Populist nationalists, whose isolationism they resisted by supporting World War II and whose *Chicago Tribune*-style Republicanism they resist today by backing the Eisenhower Republicans and the Democrats respectively.

Most of the Roosevelt humanizings of capitalism (SEC, insurance of bank deposits) have become a rooted essential of big business itself. The latter's feud with the New Deal became an anachronism when both sides became more moderate and also more traditional. Symptoms of their unofficial rapprochement are the recent defenses by veteran New Dealers of "bigness" in business. Three examples are the recent books of Lilienthal, Galbraith, Berle.[1] These three extremely valuable New Deal theorists are profoundly right on the most important other issues. But let us disagree emphatically with their present complacency by raising this question: despite the never-to-be-condoned social injustices of medieval feudal society, was there not a very sound moral foundation to its "reactionary" distrust of the cash-nexus bourgeois?

Stevenson has abandoned Truman's often-slanderous baiting of Wall Street. But a salutary abandonment of demagogy must

[1] David Lilienthal, *Big Business: A New Era,* New York, 1953. J. K. Galbraith, *American Capitalism,* Boston, 1952. A. A. Berle, *The Twentieth Century Capitalist Revolution,* New York, 1954.

not be allowed to become an over-expedient abandonment of alertness against economic bigness. Such an abandonment would be a surrender of the Unadjusted Man to the mechanized man. And such a surrender in the field of politics by the Stevenson Democrats would mean a parallel surrender in the field of culture by American intellectuals, on whom Stevenson's example is so influential. Part of the special role of writers, artists, intellectuals has always been to defend the concrete human individual against an impersonal, dehumanizing industrialism. If that defense should now be abandoned, then the Stevenson movement and the accompanying restoration of the intellectual in America would fail morally and culturally even while triumphing materially and politically.

Or else are liberal intellectuals, in a Right Bank version of their former Left Bank stance, now suddenly to become joiners, good sports, success worshippers, members of the team? Was it a triumph of their adaptability when they mostly suffered in silence, without the old holy indignation, the spectacle of a Republican auto-dealer patronizing a great scientist as if this were his clerk? But in that case who, if *not* the intellectuals, will resist the periodic stampedes to entrust American culture to the manipulators of gadgets? And this resistance to stampedes ought to express not the conformity of nonconformity but a finer grain of sensitivity, an ear conforming not to bandwagon-tunes but to the finer, older, deeper rhythms of American culture.

A few years ago, liberal intellectuals were reproaching the present writer for refusing to bait big business; today some reproach him for refusing to equate it with Santa Claus. Why do either? Business-baiting was and is a cheap bohemian flourish, a wearing of one's soulfulness on one's sleeve, and no substitute for seriously analyzing the real problem of modern technics. The real problem is the compulsion of technics, whether of capitalist or socialist bigness, to put know-how before know-why.

When the alternative is the neo-Populist and isolationist barn-burners from Wisconsin and Texas, then naturally the big businessmen of Wall Street are preferable, with their internationalism and their sincere acceptance of many New Deal reforms like SEC. Another reason for that preference is that the vanity (desire to seem sophisticated) of big business on the eastern seaboard makes a point of allowing a lot more elbow-room to the free mind. But what a choice! How impious, Melville might ask, can "progress" get when there is no third alternative?

Insofar as they refute the old communist lie about America's imaginary oppression of the worker and Russia's imaginary social justice, let us welcome the belated conversion of liberals to "stop-baiting-business." But what when they go to the other extreme of whitewashing almost everything, from the old robber barons to the new "bigness"? What when the paeans to economic prosperity ignore the psychological starvation, the cultural starvation, the mechanized mediocrity of too-efficient bigness? At that point, the value-conserver must protest: judge our American elephantiasis of know-how not solely in contrast with the low Soviet values but also in contrast with our own high anti-commercial traditions of Hawthorne, Melville, Thoreau, all of whom knew well enough that the railroad rides upon us, not we on the railroad.

Where the Soviet police-state is the alternative, let us continue to emphasize that American big business is an incomparably lesser evil. But beyond that special situation no further concessions, least of all the entirely unnecessary ones being made by "realist" liberals today. Being no ascetics of economic chastity, let us frankly embrace as enjoyable conveniences the leisure and services resulting from IBM efficiency. But must the embrace be corybantic? Shall intellectuals positively wallow in abdicating before a bigness which admittedly gives Americans economic prosperity but which robotizes them into a tractable, pap-fed, and manipulated mass-culture?

Too utilitarian for a sense of tragic reverence or a sense of humor, and prone (behind "daring" progressive clichés) to an almost infinite smugness, one kind of bourgeois liberal is forever making quite unnecessary sacrifices of principle to expediency. First to the fellow-traveler Popular Front line in the 1930's; now to the opposite love-that-capitalism line in the 1950's. But there comes a time when values are conserved not by matey back-slapping but by wayward walks in the drizzle, not by seemingly practical adjustments but by the ornery Unadjusted Man.

Part Five THE FREE IMAGINATION,

ETHICAL AND LYRICAL

"If I had my life to live over again, I would have made a rule to read some poetry and listen to some music. . . . For perhaps the parts of my brain now atrophied would thus have kept active through use. The loss of these tastes is a loss of happiness, and may possibly be injurious to the intellect, and more probably the moral character."—*Charles Darwin in his old age*

Chapter Twenty-nine THE THIRD

FRONTIER

America has had three main frontiers; the first two material, the third cultural; the first horizontal, the second vertical, the third inner:

1. Our first frontier, the horizontal one, was the west. Symbolized by Daniel Boone. Destroyed when the material limits of geography ended our expansion at the Pacific.

2. Our second frontier, the vertical one, was the onward and upward of stock markets, skyscrapers, careers. Symbolized in the nineteenth century by Horatio Alger, in the pre-crash 1920's by George Babbitt. Destroyed by Sinclair Lewis plus 1929.

3. Our third frontier is the inner frontier, the exploration by our new Columbuses in the newly discovered continents behind the forehead. The symbols and the spokesmen of the third frontier are found in poetry, art, psychology, religion.

Today Americans have no really major geographic frontier left to conquer. This development is now pushing us, instead, to increasingly inward conquests. The heroic legends of Daniel Boone and Horatio Alger, frontiersmen respectively of the horizontal and the vertical expansion, have had their day; served their purpose. Davy Crockett is beginning to annoy; his detractors will be heard more loudly, even though sentimental Americanism condemns them. The real "trail-blazer" of today is the frontiersman-behind-the-forehead, rediscovering and conserving liberty in a new area of inner exploration.

But the third frontier means not only greater opportunity in America for unadjusted art. It also means greater opportunity

for stereotyped artiness: introverted professional wincers
replacing extroverted professional boosters. When that happens
long enough, American intellectuals will learn to admit there
are worse cultural alternatives than back-slapping philistinism;
better a real huckster than a fake sensitive-plant. The motto
of the urbaner graduates from the English departments of
Harvard, Yale, Princeton is no longer "go west, young man"
but "go to the Little Magazines." For worse, therefore, as well
as better, the third frontier is already partly bringing a new,
different, more introverted America (though Europeans still
picture America in her old boisterous, extroverted persona).
It was an unrecognized turning-point for many American
intellectuals—the mass invasion of their private shrine ("Mind
if we picnic in your backyard?")—when a popular-level weekly,
entering the third frontier, suddenly put T. S. Eliot on its cover
instead of Marilyn Monroe. Or when ads to mass-audiences
began quoting lines like "April is the cruelest month" to market
their household wares.

So much for the debit side of the third frontier: banality's
New Look of introverted sensitivity. The credit side is the
elbow-room the unadjusted imagination has—in pluralistic,
easy-going America—for producing also a more genuine version
of religious, artistic, or intellectual inwardness. The area of
free will, indeterminacy, and personal responsibility is large
enough in our open society—overadjusted, yes, but never
wholly adjusted—to leave it to the future to decide (to "you
and you and you") whether the credit of America's new
frontier outweighs the debit.

Properly cultivated, the resources of inward exploration have
two very different functions, both needed: the restraining
function of ethics, the unleashing function of lyricism. The
dignity of ethics degenerates into a merely destructive veto
on life (the Puritan extreme) unless supplemented exhilarat-
ingly by the dignity of lyricism. Every abstract, explicit,
formulated code becomes stultifying and sterile unless refreshed
by the concrete, the implicit, the unformulated, the passionate,

the lyrical. Conversely, the lyric impulse degenerates into the vaguely-exalted hogwash of romanticism unless refreshed by the discipline of ethics. Our turning first to the ethical, second to the lyrical function, in the two chapters that follow, does not imply any priority between two functions equally needing each other.

Chapter Thirty   THE DIGNITY OF

ETHICS: Enough of Toughmindedness!

"I have found power where people do not look for it, in simple, gentle, and obliging men without the least desire to domineer—and conversely the inclination to domineer has often appeared to me an inner sign of weakness: they fear their slavish soul and cast a king's mantle about it. . . . Thoughts which come with doves' feet govern the world."—*Nietzsche*

In 1864 the French anti-Marxist socialist Proudhon wrote the following definition of how Marx's kind of socialism would work out in practice:

A compact democracy having the appearance of being founded on the dictatorship of the masses, but in which the masses have no more power than is necessary to ensure a general serfdom in accordance with the following precepts and principles borrowed from the old absolutism: indivisibility of public power, all-consuming centralization, systematic destruction of all individual, corporative, and regional thought (regarded as disruptive), inquisitorial police.

Note Proudhon's correct forecast that a toughminded Marxist state would degenerate into a serfdom "borrowed from the old absolutism." Will America, too, borrow from the newer "old" absolutism (this time that of communism) something partly approaching some of the same "indivisibility of public power, all-consuming centralization, inquisitorial police"? Will we too, like the original socialist idealists of tsarist Russia, let our own liberation movement against a Russian dictatorship sacrifice ideals to victories? The danger is not that we will

ever be too tough for our tough, standardless Soviet enemies—
no illusions about *them*—but that we will be too tough for our
own high standards, our own survival as a free people. To
avoid the "destruction of individual . . . thought, regarded
as disruptive" (which the Proudhon quotation forecast for
Marxism), America needs what "realists" mockingly call
"softmindedness."

Softminded is an epithet not to be ashamed of, never to
apologize for. Toughmindedness made the original socialist
idealism—the Christian brotherhood needed for transcending
an inhuman cash-nexus—degenerate into a still more inhuman
Marxist statism. Toughmindedness would make our anti-
Marxist idealism degenerate into a state-coerced overadjustedness likewise.[1] After enduring both world wars, Alfred North
Whitehead concluded: "The future of civilization depends on
a moral approach to all problems."[2] "All" includes politics and
economics. Our most creative anti-communist political thinkers
are increasingly in accord with Whitehead's conclusion.
They are also in accord with George Orwell's conclusion—it
sounds so obvious now but took so long to learn—that you
cannot defeat totalitarianism by becoming totalitarian yourself.

Disillusionment with the Munich-Yalta era has made the
best Anglo-American social thought more receptive than
ever before to a salutary softmindedness. In view of the
aftermaths of both Munich and Yalta, expediency turns out
to be less expedient—realism less realistic—than the old-
fashioned Victorian decency of being so "bigoted" that you
feel prejudiced against murderers. As an extreme example
of the toughminded 1930's, let us quote not some medieval
Tartar terrorist, fawning for bakshish and hashish at the feet
of his Great Khan, but a personally decent and kindly philosopher, thoroughly educated in the western values in which he

---

[1] A word about terminology. "Toughminded" is here used in the sense of
expediency-minded; so is "realistic." Neither term is used in the technical
philosophical sense of William James's "toughminded versus tenderminded"
nor the still different "realism" (versus nominalism) of the medieval scholastics.
[2] A. H. Johnson, *Whitehead and the Modern World*, Boston, Beacon Press,
1950.

tragically lost faith. Here was Professor Corliss Lamont's comment on the devilish frame-ups of the Moscow purge "trials":

I do not like any sort of bloodshed. But I can hardly blame the Soviet government for dealing sternly with the plotters and wreckers. . . . The utopian liberals . . . overflowing with sweetness and light, believe that vast social changes can be brought about with the same politeness and restraint that characterizes an afternoon tea-party.[3]

In other words: to resist some of the foulest mass-murders in history is defined as "utopian." Behold the *reductio ad absurdum* of Marx's attack on the French utopian socialists. Every Lumpen-intellectual's prostration before brute despotism may call itself both toughminded and strong by scorning ethics as a "tea-party." But true strength champions the weak, over-throws the bully in the name of the softminded decencies that communists and militant nationalists deride. Knightly chivalry is another of the Victorian virtues that the "emancipated" can more easily satirize than live without; in its contemporary form, chivalry prefers death in the underground movement to the dishonor of party-line sycophancy. In the words of Nietzsche (usually misinterpreted as a prophet of brute militarism), "I have found power . . . in simple, gentle, and obliging men . . . the inclination to domineer has often appeared to me an inner sign of weakness. . . . Thoughts which come with doves' feet govern the world."

The 1930's equally witnessed left-wing callousness about communist atrocities, right-wing callousness about Nazi ones. Thereby the toughmindedness of that decade has one quality in common with the new conserving of ethics: both cut across the old distinctions of right and left in politics, economics.

---

[3] In the magazine *Soviet Russia Today*, August, 1937. Granted that this was an openly pro-communist magazine. But the less open evasions of many anti-communist liberal magazines about Stalin's murders were morally no better at the time. A classic perfection was reached in Owen Lattimore's comment in *Pacific Affairs* on these Moscow frame-up "trials": they "sound like democracy to me."

Whether to serve evil or to serve God, in either case man lives ultimately not by politics or economics but by nonmaterial, ethical choices. Therefore, means must never be sacrificed to ends, whether selfish opportunistic ends or noble doctrinaire ones. To enable our own decade to begin to rediscover this ancient truth, it took the heartbreaking price of the tortured millions sacrificed to toughmindedness in the Stalin-Hitler era.

Yet even today, good causes are still being defended with the bad arguments of the old toughmindedness. For example, the anti-segregation decision of the Supreme Court is defended for its expediency in the cold war. That such good deeds win friends in Africa and India is true enough. But an apologetic crawling before toughness is the least dignified way to justify ethics. The dignity of ethics requires us to speak out unapologetically for good deeds simply because they are—good.

The task of the new conserving of ethics is to remove freedom from the realm of collective and outer economic determinism and restore it to the realm of individual and inner moral responsibility. That responsibility is not to be shifted evasively to the big, brotherly shoulders of impersonal forces.

If economics is no longer the savior, it is no longer the villain either, whether capitalist or socialist. The villain is the anti-ethics of totalitarianism, regardless of its economics. The bad means of a "capitalist" fascism and a "socialist" Soviet melts both together into a single photomontage, equally aptly labeled monopoly-capitalism or state-socialism, with the bosses equally aptly labeled "Fuehrers" or "commissars."

In the global duel today between freedom and slavery, ethical parliamentary capitalism (when tempered by social humaneness) and ethical parliamentary socialism (when tempered by anti-statist safeguards) stand on the same free side. That side is the fragile, irreplaceable product of three thousand years of ethical aspirations; it required three thousand years of the most complex historical concreteness, starting from Palestine and Greece and including the preservation of

Athens from Persia in 490 B. C. and of the Greek manuscripts from tottering Constantinople in 1453. In contrast, the side of anti-ethics required nothing more than the first caveman's first axe. The only thing standing between that axe and liberty today is conservation: conserving unbroken the historical continuity of that unnatural, that superbly artificial tradition, the dignity of ethics.

Chapter Thirty-one THE DIGNITY OF

LYRICISM: Form Yes, Formalism No

"Not without celestial observations can even terrestrial charts be accurately constructed."—*Coleridge, 1830*

As ethics is the restraining function of the inward frontier, so lyricism is the unleashing function. Both functions poach jealously on each other's territory, impede each other, yet without each other become self-destructively narrow, arid, inhuman. When they overlap explicitly (in morally didactic art), both are the losers. Yet both gain by overlapping implicitly in round-about, subterranean, invisible ways that no writer will ever analyze with objective detachment because, were he detached from the problem, he would no longer be a writer. Groping, tentative impressions are all that can here be attempted: about the relationship of lyricism to pure formalism on the one hand, to ethics on the other.

The dignity of lyricism requires, in the context of the present American situation, an assertion of unadjusted spontaneity against a New Academy spirit. It is a spirit whose urbane blandness and "rehearsed response" recalls the excellences, the dead excellences of ancient Alexandria. The form that Alexandrianism takes in American poetry today is what we have elsewhere called (in 1947) "the critic's poet." As the "poet's poet" of yesteryear wrote mainly for fellow poets, so the critic's poet of today writes mainly for critics. The critic's poet and his periodicals and mentors concentrate mainly on technique, not even all technique but certain specialized subtopics of the technique of technique. That they neglect content goes without saying. Still worse, they neglect the quality of song most needed in lyricism: full-throatedness.

The overadjusted style of the critic's poet performs like a chewing-gum slot-machine. It responds to each counterfeit slug of critical jargon by emitting a jaw-breaking wad of allusion; if you listen carefully, you can hear the satisfied metallic click. Such a poet is activated not by inner lyric impulse but by outer fashions of criticism. He repeats mechanically (a Kimon Friar, to take a typical minor example, or a John Berryman) what the originators of the New Critic technique (for example, John Crowe Ransom) did creatively and spontaneously. Robots can do everything better than human beings. Except love and sing.

These conveyor-belt dons, and their quarterlies like *Hudson Review*, diffuse a miasma of anti-lyricism over the scene:

> Instead of the professional man of letters we have the professional critic, the young don writing in the first place for other dons, and only incidentally for that supremely necessary fiction, the common reader. . . . The pedant is as common as he ever was. And now that willy-nilly so much writing about literature is in academic hands, his activities are more dangerous than ever. . . . The pedant is a very adaptable creature, and can be as comfortable with Mr. Eliot's "objective correlative," Mr. Empson's "ambiguities" and Dr. Leavis' "complexities" as in the older suit of critical clothes that he has now, for the most part, abandoned.[1]

The aim here is not one of those indiscriminate attacks on criticism that characterize romanticism's incorrect faith in instinct. The aim is to honor, as indispensable in its proper station, the high calling of criticism, "New" or old, and to attack only the idolatry of criticism-for-its-own-sake. In its proper station, criticism is not independent of poetry nor dictatorial over it nor antecedent to it but dependent on the prior creative act. When this dependency is denied, content gets onesidedly sacrificed to form, full-throatedness to minor details of technique, fire to tact:

[1] Donald Davie in the periodical the *Twentieth Century*, London.

A poet may, with the use of a little tact, get off comparatively lightly with his contemporaries. They accept his work as "poetry," and as such it can remain an unacknowledged, and with luck an ineffectual, legislator. But when anyone brings the fires of art, of genius, too close to life itself, there is a far greater hostility, the hostility met by Carlyle, by Ruskin, by Newman, by Nietzsche. . . . Such writers, of course, do not play the academic game; they *speak out too boldly*, and this is, if not exactly dangerous, certainly bad form. But it may be worth remembering that, if they had always played the academic game, there would be no academic game for any of us. Scholarship and criticism alike are parasitic on genius; and when someone, whilst making no great claims for himself, devotes his life to the cause of such genius, he is fighting, if only we could see it, in the same cause of scholarship and criticism *too*. . . . If only those writers who are approved by contemporary criticism were to be read and taught, criticism itself would quickly wither.[2]

Almost all good modern poets have gratefully learnt from T. S. Eliot—and thereafter, if truly unadjusted, revolted against the Eliot cult. His dictatorial cult differs from Eliot himself as Marxism differs from Marx. It is, therefore, unfair to blame Eliot for the humorless, sanctimonious exaggerations of his cultists. His vulnerability as an artist is on another score: despite his extraordinary merits of rhythmic and metaphoric precision (merits rightly—though indoctrinatingly—appreciated in the key English departments), T. S. Eliot almost[3] always lacks the final grace of poetry: sensuous texture. This grace you will find not only in two poets greater than Eliot, Keats and Yeats, but also in a poet otherwise often lesser than Eliot: Beddoes. So it does not of itself suffice to create major poetry. What it does do is make ideas dance, make cogitative verse musical, and make that music full-throated in the old, magic, unashamed fashion.

Wastefulness is the second essential lack in the poet of *The Waste Land*. Missing is that sense of generous overflowing of so much talent that the talent can dare to squander itself

---

[2] G. Wilson Knight in the exciting new Oxford periodical, *Essays in Criticism.*
[3] Exceptions: the almost Keatsian sensuous texture in "La Figlia Che Piange" and the "brown hair" passage of "Ash Wednesday."

even on nonsense and the fun of luxuriant affectations, on all kinds of egomanias and obsessive caprices; can dare, can afford all this because secure in the knowledge that it has enough left over—after these self-indulgences—to produce vital creations *anyway*. Important, and insufficiently reckoned with, is the "anyway" quality, the "*quand-même*-ness" of inspired art. (Like "love" and "death," "inspired" is a word in bad taste; the *salonfähig* critical taste of today is better equipped to cope with irony, ambiguity, allusion.) No stingy hoarding of talent, getting the most out of every clutched grain of it, but exuberant profligacy seems to characterize the great, full-toned voices of world literature.

Without wastefulness, no generosity. Without generosity, no love, no Christian charity, ultimately no Christianity. When a poet lacks the vice of wasting himself casually, lavishly, then he also lacks the virtue of the full range, the universal human note, the rich careless vibrancy of authentic genius. This joyous, full-toned authenticity of the lyric experience is not often conveyed to poetry students today by the Eliot-Pound-New-Critic school. Absurdly denounced as a conspiracy and absurdly praised as a revelation, that school was a liberating force in its unpopular days (after 1912), a stifling force in its faddish days (after the 1940's).

This appeal for spontaneity should not be confused with neo-romantic appeals for a bohemianism of would-be "geniuses" or for a romantic revolt of song and emotion *against* restraint and form. No, only *within* strict restraint and classic form can song and emotion be compressed into lyric intensity, instead of sprawling forth sloppy, formless, diffuse. The more restraint the better, Eliotic and New Critical; but meanwhile let our critic's poets not completely forget Roy Campbell's "bloody horse":

> You praise the firm restraint with which they write—
>   I'm with you there, of course.
> They use the snaffle and the curb all right;
>   But where's the bloody horse?

Nobody can predict how the new poets of today can ever achieve the vitality of the early Pound-Eliot movement that followed 1912. But one can easily predict how they will never achieve it: namely, by continuing to imitate Eliot and Pound, both of whom had the great virtue of not imitating but defying the literary dictators of *their* day. Because of that earlier necessary act of unadjustedness of 1912, Eliot himself was once accused of "impertinence" toward "older poets." Today it is critics of Eliot's who suffer the same accusation, now that the toreador of 1912 has changed into the sacred cow of today. Our Mandarins Junior Grade make official uniforms of Eliot's discarded garments but lack the originality with which Eliot so imperially filled those garments. It is not that the emperor has no clothes—he has too many—but that in most cases the clothes have no emperor.

Because lyricism requires unadjustedness, a maturity of technique in the very young is no longer the virtue it used to be till only yesterday. Even now, it does remain a virtue whenever its possessor remains sturdily independent. But many more young poets, lacking such independence, are frozen permanently into conventionality (a conventionally "unconventional" modernism) by their own technical skill. Because the trail-blazers of the 1920's have become the elder statesmen of the 1950's, their imitators write from the start in these mature styles of their masters, styles originally hard-won but now an unearned inheritance. Such young poets, Glossarists of the New Criticism *ab ovo*, seem to be wearing an urbane, ironic smile already from birth. Their disease is premature maturity.

But other younger poets, teachers, and students are outgrowing this stereotyped modernism and resisting its dominance of much of the college-anthology field. Many of that younger group believe the best of all the pocketbook anthologies of verse to be *100 Modern Poems* and *100 American Poems,* both edited for New American Library by Selden Rodman. His two anthologies, when taken together with his art manifesto *The Eye of Man,* 1955, are a rallying-point for unadjusted taste and the restoration of content, a rallying-point against the current fashion of a trivial formalist veneer in both poetry and painting. What Rodman rightly urges is not less form but equal respect for content also, defined as "a projection through tangible symbols of the artist's attachment to values outside art itself." This most pioneering of editors—Rodman was among the very first to discover and print Theodore Roethke and Robert Lowell—has long been a universal catalyst in poetry, painting, criticism. The important part of his anthology *100 Modern Poems* is the foreign verse, showing the French influence on our symbolism, the Celtic influence (Yeats, Dylan Thomas) on our lyricism. The trans-Atlanticity of these two indispensable influences refutes the chauvinism of our literary isolationists.

Formalism at its ablest today, and its most influential, is represented by the New Critic method of explicating a text. When New Critics discard *irrelevant* historical, psychological, and "moralizing" encrustations (the schoolma'am stress on biography), they splendidly teach us to read the text itself. When they discard the *relevant* historical, psychological, and moral aspects, they misread the text itself. A reader's response to a poem is a total response, a Gestalt in which aesthetic as well as ethical, psychological, and historical factors are inseparably fused together. It is a self-deception to try to separate them with neat demarcations; no alchemist of formalism will ever isolate some quintessence of "pure" aesthetics, to be judged only by certified "pure" mandarins of criticism. This inextricability of form and content may be illogical, undesirable; there it is just the same.

The greatest psychological change in America between the 1930's and 1950's has been the revolt against revolt. In politics this change has been sometimes salutary, sometimes dangerous. Salutary by discrediting the lure of communism and fellow-traveling; dangerous by often lending itself to temporary misuse by nationalist thought-controllers, thereby necessitating in those particular cases a revolt against the revolt against revolt. But if the change has been only a mixed blessing in politics, it has been almost entirely salutary in philosophy, art, poetry. Who today, even among the few remaining Marxists, would want to return to the wooden proletarian verse, proletarian novels, and "songs of social significance" that the *New Masses* used to feature in the 1930's?

As a result of this revolt against revolt, American and British poetry—and often philosophy—have moved from their storming of every possible Bastille (including the decapitation of all those royalist capital letters) to a Bourbon restoration in both credo and technique. In credo, American and British poetry has often evolved from a semi-Marxist radicalism of the 1930's to a Christian liberal-conservatism of the 1950's. In technique, the same poetry has often evolved from free verse to rigorous strictness of form. For example, the representative evolution, in both credo and technique, of W. H. Auden.

In 1912 and 1913, the free-verse technique of Amy Lowell's Imagists seemed the last word in progress. It seemed so again in the proletarian verse of the 1930's, when social conscience added to free verse that defiant panache which that technique had lacked in the ivory-tower days of Imagism. But among the younger contemporary poets, free verse is dead and forgotten. The reason for its death is clear, unanswerable; you cannot, to use a metaphor of Frost's, play tennis without a net. The net of strict form, the more traditional the better, is the challenge that best evokes, provokes, irritates forth the response of beauty. On the need for rigor of form, there is no quarrel here with New Critic formalists. The quarrel begins only at the point where the rigor becomes mortis: the point where their ignoring of content (the importance of content and also the importance of communicating it) makes them as one-sided as the social poets of the 1930's, who overestimated content and sloppily ignored the need for form.

If we may be permitted to use the word "form" in the broader, more classical sense instead of their narrow sense of technique, then it would indeed become possible to say: form is art, form is all. In the broad, classic sense, form means not only technique but the pattern of the human spirit. This broader meaning of form—a pattern as inextricably aesthetic, ethical, spiritual as the soul itself—is no alternative to content but includes it too.

Both life and literature depend on a formal framework: the first on ethical form, the second on aesthetic form. A reader of poetry would not be a real human being unless he belonged simultaneously to life and literature. Therefore, his human response to a poem is simultaneously ethical and aesthetic. The great conservative revolt against the formless, radical, materialist thirties is incomplete if it has no profounder form to conserve than the rhyme scheme of *terza rima*. What a mockery! As if Dante's *terza rima* pattern were something in a vacuum!—instead of the mere shadow thrown by a vaster spiritual pattern. Formalism is a narrowly technical and unimaginatively literal application to verse of the conservative truth that liberty and beauty are sustained by the formal patterns of our traditional spiritual heritage. Form, yes. Formalism, no.

The behavior of some American formalist poets and artists resembles a dapper parasitic insect named "podurans," as described in one learned text:

Podurans . . . these tiny active sprites live as indifferently tolerated ant-guests, flitting about the nest apparently undetected by their hosts and picking up debris or stray bits of food. . . . These guests are harmless enough to their social benefactors and are but little modified to live among them save as they are apparently gifted with a neutral odor and with sprightly ways whereby they slip unobserved through the densest throngs.

Certainly we may admire (knowing that verse butters no parsnips) the charming ability of this sprightly parasite to pick up "stray bits of food." Those of us who were born in New York may also applaud their "slipping unobserved through the densest throngs." But is a "neutral odor" the highest role of the poet when the issue is not some ephemeral party-squabble but the recording of good and evil? On this score,

Dante and Milton—and it seems we are again permitted to mention Milton—don't smell neutral.

Here, then, is the real issue that divided Parnassus into two camps during the most important literary controversy of the decade. Namely, the controversy over whether Ezra Pound's *Pisan Cantos* are, as leading Poundians claim, one of "the greatest masterpieces" of modern man, or whether they are excluded from such greatness not only stylistically but on grounds of moral insensitivity (for example, to Belsen crematories). The last public statement ever made by George Orwell was the comment of that admirable Unadjusted Man upon the 1949 Bollingen Prize, awarded via the Library of Congress to Ezra Pound. In May, 1949, Orwell wrote in *Partisan Review:*

> Some time ago I saw it stated in an American periodical that Pound only broadcast on the Rome radio when "the balance of his mind was upset." . . . This is plain falsehood. Pound was an ardent follower of Mussolini as far back as the 1920's and never concealed it. He was a contributor to Mosley's review, the *British Union Quarterly.* . . . His broadcasts were disgusting. I remember at least one in which he approved the massacre of the East European Jews and "warned" the American Jews that their turn was coming presently. . . . He *may* be a good writer (I must admit that I personally have always regarded him as an entirely spurious writer), but the opinions he has tried to disseminate *in* his works are evil. . . .

When Orwell objects to the poet's gloating over the Nazi massacres, is the objection valid only politically or also aesthetically? Poetry must be judged by poetic criteria, never by political ones. But even when we restrict ourselves to judging Pound's *Pisan Cantos* by poetic criteria alone, it can be demonstrated, line for line, that his gloating callousness toward the victims of Nazi gas-chambers has correspondingly diminished his purely poetic effectiveness. It has done so by diminishing his capacity for human sympathies, his sensitivity, his receptivity. This diminution narrows all aspects of the creative imagination together, equally including poetic and spiritual ones. To give specific examples from Pound's actual text: would even the proverbial observer from Mars, some pure aesthete free from the "aesthetically irrelevant prejudices" of anti-fascism and of human compassion, find beauty in lines like the following? "Pétain defended Verdun while Blum was defending a bidet." Or: "Geneva the usurers' dunghill / Frogs, brits, with a few dutch pimps." Or the book's message that, by resisting fascism, "the goyim go to saleable slaughter" for "the yidd. . . . David rex the prime s.o.b."

The same sterilizing of the creative imagination took place in the once-promising novelist Ilya Ehrenburg. When the imagination gets overadjusted into serving totalitarian Agitprop, whether communism in Ehrenburg's case or fascism (via American Populism) in Pound's case, the same aesthetic aridity results. A mechanized pogrom-spirit dehumanizes not the victims but the victors: its practitioners, its apologists. What dehumanizes, de-lyricizes: in terms of pure *l'art pour l'art*, entirely aside from politics and from ethics. This conclusion, in calm retrospect toward a distant controversy, seems the most important single lesson emerging from that same controversy.[4]

The emergence of that lesson was hindered at the time by irrelevant and unjust accusations from both sides, thereby temporarily reducing a serious aesthetic controversy to political demagogy. Irrelevant to the above real issues and irrelevant to the above aesthetic case against the *Pisan Cantos* were the now-forgotten articles accusing the Bollingen committee of sharing Pound's fascist sympathies. Thus to slander one's non-fascist opponents as fascists, instead of meeting their arguments on their own serious level, is as out-of-bounds as that other recent demagogy of slandering one's non-communist opponents as communists.

Such unjust exaggerations disfigured not only the anti-Pound side but also the side of defenders of the award. Even today, the majority of such defenders still picture even the aesthetically-serious critics of the award as thick-skinned

[4] Cf. the chapters on Pound and Stefan George in P. Viereck, *Dream and Responsibility*, University Press of Washington, D. C., 1953.

philistines, incapable of judging poetry on its own aesthetic terms. No aesthetically-serious critic of the award was denying the positive contributions of Pound to American literature, contributions already familiar and well-publicized in the leading literary circles. Only a critic vindictive toward a figure whose present plight merits compassion, only a critic more concerned with winning a debate than with justice, would deny the occasional (though uncharacteristic) presence of beauty in Pound's later cantos also; the "pull down thy vanity" passage is the particular instance that comes to mind.

Technical virtuosity, a *l'art-pour-l'art* formalism, is preferable to a soap-box poetry that prostitutes art to political propaganda by talking only about the poet's "social responsibility," not about his responsibility to the standards of his craft. Virtuosity is not virtue; but unlike soap-box poetry, virtuosity at least does respect the standards of its craft and is, therefore, the lesser evil. But why confine poetry to this false choice between Agitprop and furniture polish? We have a third alternative: not the moral preachiness of didacticism, but the moral insight of lyrical humanity. Moral insight is as much a part of the human condition as love and fallibility. Moral insight can no more be omitted in a poetry of the whole, three-dimensional human being than can love and fallibility. Beauty, not social utility is the highest goal; on this first postulate of art and life the author and the formalists agree. But the formalist has yet to learn the second postulate: you will capture beauty only by seeking more than beauty.

A catalyst needed only rarely, objectionable in other situations, is not objectionable in the present one, as a way out from aridity, a way out from the anti-lyricism of the Eliot empire and the mandarin critics. That needed catalyst will be a rube voice or else a voice from Toidy Toid Street, a voice grating and ear-splitting, tactless and uneducated, too auto-didact to be spoilt by current fashions of good taste, a voice shrill with embarrassing excitement, no Noble Savage (to be dandled by dandies) but the Ignoble Savage, gauche with the integrity of vulgarity, redeemingly vulgarian because restoring content to formalism, communication to hermeticism, spontaneity to an art decadent with elegance. Via an anger so risky but alive, lyricism may or may not return to America. But it will never return via the present Alexandrian museums: ask the bees—they know when a flower is glass.

The coming return to communication between poets and readers will communicate, among other things, an ethical content. But never, never by explicit sermonizing; rhymed editorials, even on the side of the angels, kill lyricism. And lyricism is the one great function left to the poet, now that the inroads of science and of prose have deprived him of his earlier, non-lyrical roles of law-giver, philosopher, prophet, seer. This depriving is *just as well*. Lyricism is enough; one metaphor, one lyrical gesture of the joy and bitterness of the human heart, can still give us implicitly more moral insight—not didacticism but insight—than "all the sages can." For that matter it gives a more human insight than any romantic "impulse from the vernal wood." And certainly more than the statistics of positivist science.

Statistics and test tubes have their place; so have editorials and ideologies; but it is not they that will move the sun and the other stars. Lyricism and love—the two are synonymous— lyricism and love are the only flame that fuses form and content, aesthetics and ethics, without sacrificing either. When young Mozart was a very young child, an older friend, Gottfried von Jacquin, wrote down these words in Mozart's album to guide his great art: "True genius without heart cannot exist—for neither high intelligence, nor imagination, nor both together make genius. Love! love! love! that is the soul of genius."

Chapter Thirty-two FOUR NOTES

ON VALUES

"If men cannot live on bread alone, still less can they do so on disinfectant."—*Alfred North Whitehead*

1 Why? How?

Our entire society, emphatically including its anti-materialists, enjoys the fruits of American material progress and ought to admit that fact gratefully. Even the artist, the intellectual who derides the fruits as sordid, uses a typewriter, a telephone, an electric light—by-products of these fruits—in order to record his deriding of them for his publisher. To avoid hypocrisy and hollow rhetoric, the case against America's overemphasis on material progress must begin by granting it that major concession. The material gains resulting from the measurable facts of pragmatic science will indeed take us far. As far as the boundary to which any material measurements can take us.

But the total human being moves beyond this boundary; he hungers not only for measurable facts but for unmeasurable truths. He needs the intangible—the spiritual and aesthetic—beyond the gadget world of tangible things. In exploring that "beyond," the complete man turns for guidance to the classic humanities and to religion. These may be flickering and fitful lamps. Yet they are the only lamps we have, once we move past the boundary of measurable facts, the boundary where the top-of-the-brain man prudently stops. Prudently he stops but meanly; unimaginatively; with every hunger satiated except the ultimate hunger that separates us from the beasts, making us often lower than the beasts, occasionally higher, but never the same. Without the understanding of man's inner nature that the classics and humanities offer, and without the inner ethical restraint that religion offers, our outer social progress and mechanical progress will necessarily go beserk.

Sometimes high standards of living and of economic production coincide with high standards of culture and personal freedom. This coinciding raises the question: which of these two desirables comes first, which causes which? Many capitalist as well as Marxist materialists assume: culture and freedom depend on progress in economics—or, more broadly, on material social progress in general. But in reality the causal connection more often works in reverse order: a society with enough aesthetic and ethical genius to create high cultural standards would also have the genius to create an at least passable economy, even when its economic resources are as wretched as those that accompanied the cultural flowerings of ancient Greece, ancient Palestine. Conversely, societies with vaster economic resources than these two poor and arid countries have starved to death because they lacked the aesthetic and ethical inner genius to face outer material problems honestly and perceptively. Man's "why" is more important than his "how."

Conservatives are often mocked for supposedly urging "higher things" on some poor proletarian who needs bread. "Let 'em eat culture" is considered as sinful a conservative evasion of social conscience as Marie Antoinette's "Let 'em eat cake." But what happens after the admittedly primary need for bread is satisfied? Thereafter the humanistic conservative can no longer be accused of fleecing the toilers if he insists: American material progress should from now on make increasing concessions to cultural inwardness. The leisure-giving machines of America have replaced the leisure-giving slaves of Athens. For the first time in history a relatively large proportion of the population is free to concentrate (in case it wants to) on cultural inwardness, without being distracted outwards by stomach-pangs if poor, by either conscience-pangs or fear of revolt if rich.

Liberal materialists and socialist idealists often argue: even after the basic economic needs are satisfied, social progress ought still to continue full speed ahead because it releases tremendous mass energies; supposedly these can be harnessed to cultural creativity as readily as electric power can be switched from one dynamo to another. What falsifies that analogy is the fact that culture requires not only energy but sensibility. Sensibility is released by inner spiritual freedom but is often inhibited or coarsened by outer social progress. Thereby social progress, if continued past the indispensable point where basic needs are satisfied, often becomes the enemy of cultural freedom. Social progress concentrates on collective satisfaction for the masses. Cultural freedom concentrates on personal integrity for the individual.

The Athens of Pericles, a mere sixty thousand free voters, ill-housed, ill-clad, economically dependent on slavery and imperialist war, created a greater cultural flowering than all the prosperous free democracy of a thousand-times-more-numerous America. The social democracy of Sweden does not have the world's highest cultural flowering; it does have the world's highest social progress, highest economic security, and highest suicide rate. Let us imagine a society whose ideal is not social progress but an ever-increasing poverty, with the poorhouse bed as the final, sweetly desired goal. Such a society would lack all social progress; it need not lack—consider the religious and literary achievements of Saint Francis—religious progress and cultural freedom.

Nowadays the experts of social progress are stressing "know-how," a coinage thought up by something very basic in the American psyche. Since ivory towers are not bomb-proof, we obviously need our technical know-how to shield us. But since it can blow us up as well as shield us unless controlled by the moral imagination, why did the American psyche not simultaneously think up a companion coinage: "know-why"?

II Commitment of the Personality

Values are not explicit formulas, black on white, neatly filed. The top of the brain can articulate something limited about values, and what it can it should; up to that limit, rationalism is necessary, justified. But we can never entirely say or know explicitly the values we live implicitly. Every attempt to bridge that gap, including this one, loses part of their essence; loses more of it if our attempt is unsuccessful, less of it if successful, but even then some gap always remains. Schiller: When the soul *speaks,* it is, alas, no longer the *soul* that speaks.

Let us define values as those loving identifications with persons, families, places, institutions, traditions, or rituals that unite the individual and the group, the present and the past, the expressible and the inexpressible. Values make up most of our selfhood, our true personal life, as opposed to the surface life of conscious formulas. Explicit abstractions can represent no man's inner life except the pedant's; he thereby loses touch with the lives of most human beings, lives shaped by affectionate identifications with concrete landmarks. Such values are no timeless, spaceless ghosts floating in the absolute. They can be daily experienced.

Again and again our key word is "concrete": values are the thousand little linkages—ethereal as gossamer, sturdy as steel —linking us into larger concretions. They pull each monad out of his loneliness into some shared community of rooted, living archetypes (the unity neither of rootless, mechanical stereotypes on the one hand nor of anarchic, loveless individualism on the other). Unlike credos, formulas, slogans committing the intellect alone, unlike sensuous moods committing the emotions alone, values commit both in interaction: the entire personality. Anti-rationalists (romantics) omit the intellect, rationalists the emotions. The latter danger threatens Herr Professor, the literary critic, the political theorizer, the sociologist; he often underestimates the part the imagination and the emotions play in value-commitments of the total man, commitments determining the way we live, not just the way we talk. Every commitment of the total personality is an act of affection, in response to something living, lovable, and close.

To love local roots is not isolationism but the foundation for a more effectively anchored progression to internationalism. To love what is close is not an alternative but a foundation to love of humanity. In the beautiful words of 1954 of J. Robert Oppenheimer:

> This is a world in which each of us, knowing his limitations, knowing the evils of superficiality and the terrors of fatigue, will have to cling to what is close to him, to what he knows, to what he can do, to his friends and his tradition and his love, lest he be dissolved in a universal confusion and know nothing and love nothing.

The alternative to what Mr. Oppenheimer calls "universal confusion" is a reverence for landmarks, a continuity with ancient precedent. Whether in defence of his freedom, his country, or his creed, a human being lovingly commits his total personality only "to what is close to him," whether physically close or (in the case of religion) spiritually close. He commits himself wholly to this or that concrete historic right or ritual, not to some abstract "rights of man" improvised by pure reason. In that sense, the conservatives, even the worst bigoted conservatives, have a better sense of the concreteness of values than the most enlightened rationalist progressives. Thus men like Burke, Coleridge, Cardinal Newman, and Barrett Wendell have more feeling than Bentham or John Dewey for the transition where values transcend articulated formulas and become loving identifications. Values are described more perceptively by the intuition of poets and by the reverence of historians than by the pat symmetries of many a political scientist and statistical sociologist.

And since values, as the foundation of actual living, always deal with the relationship of concrete to concrete, of particular to particular, the conservative realizes values can never be captured by general formulations. Even the most logical formula, even or especially the most brilliant, distorts some essential of the original concrete situation. That is why conservatives like Burke, Coleridge, Tocqueville are always impatient with what they call ideologues, who lose the substance of something precious in order to ideologize its shadow.

In ideological debates, the immediate winner will be the progressive, the man with *a priori* formulas for bettering society. The loser will be the conservative, the man who flounders confusedly, like some village idiot, amid concrete history-evolved *conditions* which he is unable to verbalize and which stand in the way—there they are, like them or not! —of his opponent's well-reasoned theory for social betterment. Indeed, the definition of a good conservative is that he always loses the theoretical debates with liberals and radicals. When he begins winning debates, it is a symptom of senility or ill health—unless he can prove he won for the wrong reasons. If he argues the conservative case too well, he has become a mere liberal of conservatism. (The reference is to verbal arguments, not to rival displays of actual local practice.) Our fuddy-duddy good conservative, when asked to refute the progressive argument, will first stand in awkward silence, like some gnarled stump-root, and then mumble to his fellow villagers, "Well, I don't really know, I can't exactly—well, it somehow doesn't seem to be the way we old-timers have been doing things around here."

But after the irrefutable, mechanical reasoning of the brilliant progressive has won the debate, what happens next? The applauding villagers must now translate the winner's blueprint into action. Jubilating, they scrap old landmarks and foundation-stones to set up his brave new world. At that point they often discover—and discover too late—a collision between their benefactor's abstraction and their concrete human flesh. Sometimes that collision means a local village drought, sometimes a nationwide reign of terror, a worldwide civil war.

So far, we have seemed to assume that concreteness means material solidity; and so, in political discussion, it normally does. But in religion and in the arts, concreteness need not mean material solidity. It need only mean experience, and what philosopher can define to what extent experience is material? Concreteness is a personally-felt experience of a shared or shareable nature (the qualification about its nature is added to exclude private hallucinations). Provided it is not solely subjective but also has objective roots in the historically-linked community, an inner dream of the imagination is concrete. It is even more "real," one is almost tempted to add, than the mere prosaic reality of the heap of separate atoms known as a "table" or a "chair." For no law of physics can hold those separate particles together so intimately, so unifyingly as the welding-power of the imagination of man, bringing together vision and beauty out of the separate dust and trash of every-day life.

III The Inarticulate Roots of Free Values

"The trouble with conservative literature," remarked Henry Seidel Canby, "has been that one had to be a liberal in order to write it!" His remark is often quoted to score a point against conservatives. Let us applaud his remark insofar as it gives a healthy jolt to their frequent smug stupor; Mill called conservatives "the stupid party," and conservatives are the first to agree, their stupid inability to theorize in a vacuum being the source both of their weakness and of their strength. But let us partly qualify Mr. Canby's remark insofar as it attacks conservatives not merely for being stupid but for being inarticulate. The pride of conservatives, from Coleridge on, has been that their philosophy is inarticulate, inexpressible,[1] an organic history-rooted growth, not an ideology nor a conscious economic or political program.

It is only fitting that nimble-minded, logical liberals should be the ones who (in Canby's words) "write conservative literature." So doing, they and they alone give conservatism a

[1] Sometimes it takes conservatives, from Coleridge on, a thousand articulate pages to express how inarticulate, how inexpressible they are.

program, a clearcut ideology. The ideology they give to conservatism has only one little fault: it is incorrect. For it has nothing to do with the real spirit of conservatism. Except for this imperceptible drawback, their clearcut ideologizing of conservatism has all the major "literary virtues": it is what editors call well-organized; it lends itself to being classified in some neat pigeon-hole; it provides the comfortable feeling of presenting to you, black on white, everything Marjorie Jane needs to know about conservatism on her fourteenth birthday, complete with diagrams and glossary. Examples of such articulate conservatives—that is, such liberals of conservatism— are those who advocate conservatism as a program or party. Most of those current tomes will tell you less about the conservative spirit, its strength and its weakness, than these thirteen casual words recently retorted by a Conservative M. P. when chided for imprecision: "If I could define my views with precision, I wouldn't be a Conservative."

Self-respect resists being pigeon-holed. The mania for categories (what is your civil service rank? are you a sadist or a masochist?) does as little to explain the seamless unity of reality as does that "precise defining of your terms" so dear to semanticists. On the contrary: imprecise necessities—like the words "conservatism," "freedom," "religion"—ought to be used imprecisely. Reality itself is unsymmetrical, ungeometrical, imprecise.

It may be generalized that the conservative mind does not like to generalize. Conservative theory is anti-theoretical. Cardinal Newman defined Toryism as "loyalty to persons," liberalism as loyalty to abstract slogans. Liberalism argues, conservatism simply is. When conservatism becomes argued, systematized, self-conscious, then—like some French conservatives but no British ones—it resembles the liberalist rationalists it opposes. It then becomes a mere liberalism of conservatism —meaning: a mere doctrinaire theorizing of conservatism. The mentality of liberal rationalism consciously articulates abstract programs; the mentality of conservatism unconsciously embodies concrete traditions. Hence, the wise stupidity, stupor, stolidity of the inarticulate conservative temperament. It is a temperament so stupid that it never invented brilliant, irrefutable utopias sending millions to the guillotine; so stupid that it never joined the most advanced reasoners of its age in donning French "Liberty Caps" in the 1790's or signing pro-Soviet manifestos of the misnamed League Against War and Fascism in the 1930's.[2]

Because conservativism embodies rather than argues, its most valuable insights are not sustained theoretical works nor well-organized, clearly presented, and geometrically consistent treatises, as in the case of liberal rationalism. Rather, its most valuable insights are the quick thrust of epigrams, as in the writings of Metternich, Disraeli, Tocqueville, Burckhardt, Churchill, or the nuggets concealed within the disorganized, wonderfully helter-skelter jottings of Coleridge, most imaginative, most incoherent conservative of them all. To support the above position against that majority of readers who want a "message" organized, consistent, and edifying, let us recall one warning from Yeats, one from Emerson.

Yeats: "Man can embody truth, but he cannot know it." Poetry tends to embody truth, prose to know it. Conservatism tends to embody truth, liberalism to know it. Hence, conservatism more often occurs among minds of artistic imagination, liberalism more often among analytic scientific minds. Because conservatism stresses concrete emotional loyalties more than allegiance to abstract syllogisms, it overlaps more frequently with poetry (that crystallization of the emotional and the concrete) than do any other political isms. The most important conservative minds of nineteenth-century England were also leading poets—Coleridge, Wordsworth, Newman, Arnold—or else at least literary figures of a primarily poetic

---

[2] Apropos conservatives being too stupid to appreciate the brilliant abstract blueprints of communism, the statistics of the Roper and Gallup polls of 1945 and 1946 about Russia are worth recalling. In both polls, the educated American tended to trust Russia's peaceful intentions; the uneducated, the ill-informed, the very poor were far more skeptical about Russia. The latter groups, to quote Roper's analysis, "inclined to charge Russia with dark and sinister intentions," while the educated classes and "those who knew something about Russia" leaned, on balance, "strongly toward friendly understanding." Whereupon a more sarcastic editor commented in 1952: "to predict accurately in 1945 that Russia would act as Russia has acted, you had to be as dumb and poorly informed as an ox."

imagination: Carlyle, Disraeli. A comment similar to Yeats's occurred in Emerson's journal of 1838 (because himself no conservative, note that the liberal Emerson first considered as "a defect" what the conservative Yeats considered a strength): "Once I thought it a defect peculiar to me, that I was confounded by interrogatories and when put on my wits for a definition was unable to reply without injuring my own truth; but now, I believe it proper to man to be unable to answer in terms the great problems put by his fellows: it is enough if he can live his own definitions."

The liberal and prosaic rationalist defines his life; the conservative and poetic intuitionist "lives" (in Emerson's phrase) his definition. Both seem necessary; the fact that the liberal rationalist wins any logical, verbalized debate does not make him the more necessary of the two. Leading the right life is not the same as being right in a debate. Defending a free society is not the same as defending syllogisms about freedom.

According to a Burkean definition by the contemporary Chicago scholar, Stanley Pargellis: "The rationalist or the liberal frames his political decisions in accordance with some theory derived from an abstract notion of universal truth; the conservative takes into consideration an extremely wide variety of [concrete] acts. . . ." In the light of this distinction, let us contrast a typical British approach with a typical French approach and then contrast their possible consequences on the battlefields of 1940.

The traditionalism of the British expresses both the dreadful inefficiency and the wonderful deep-rootedness of their old winding roads, their old non-decimal weights, measures, coins. These seemingly silly old relics the rationalist is itching to straighten out by introducing the admittedly more efficient French metric system of decimal weights, measures, coins. If the latter could be taken by themselves alone, they would be improvements. But you cannot adopt these quintessences of French rationalism without also adopting the mentality of abstract blueprints that produced them and accompanies them. The metric system, in place of the awkward local traditional systems of measure, was adopted in every country conquered physically or spiritually by the invading armies of the French Revolution; it was not adopted by those awkward, traditionalist islanders who alone held out uncompromisingly from start to finish against revolution. They thereby saved the liberty of Europe, in the 1790's as in 1940.

The word "metric system" is being used here as a shorthand symbolizing all the other rational but deracinating changes that tend to accompany it, such as reorganizing the old, loyalty-encrusted provinces into impersonal, geometric-shaped departments. This latter sacrifice of biology to mathematics, of history to abstraction was likewise rejected in England, adopted in France. Every culture must choose between a conservative inefficiency that has historic continuity and an efficient rationality that lacks historic continuity. England pays a high price for its choice: the lack of a modern coherent system of weights, measures, coins, departments, roads. But that loss is compensated for many times over by the following gain: in time of crisis, a concrete-minded country stands deep-rooted and firm for its ancient concrete liberties at some glorious Battle of Britain, while an abstract-minded country, blest with efficient metric systems and with new universal Rights of Man, falls rootless in some Battle of France. Who the devil wants to die fighting for a geometric-shaped province?

Such considerations make G. K. Chesterton's "The English Road" not only a delightful poem in its own right but a perfect crystallization of the conservative nature of liberty:

> Before the Roman came to Rye or out to Severn strode
> The rolling English drunkard made the rolling English road,
> A reeling road, a rolling road, that rambles round the shire;
> And after him the parson ran, the sexton and the squire. . . .
> I know no harm of Buonaparte and plenty of the Squire,
> And for to fight the Frenchman I did not much desire:
> But I did bash their baggonets because they came arrayed
> To straighten out the crooked road an English drunkard made.

Among Slavs, this distinction between traditionalist England and rationalist France repeats itself. Scorned by liberals for their backwardness, but thereby being able to maintain their historic continuity, the inefficient, religious, superstitious, big-oted peasants of Poland battled against Hitler's tyranny more heroically and also more effectively than the efficient, rational, unbigoted, modern-minded tradesmen of Czechoslovakia. You cannot revel too joyfully in the superior logic of your scientific roads and your inorganic geometric institutions without giving up your organic historic continuity; and who gives that up, gives up the first foundation of free values. Bigoted old prejudices, stubborn hereditary ignorances may seem the loath-some dung of history to the enlightened progressive, but from that dung the tree of liberty draws its tempest-resisting forti-tude. Again and again in history, it is not abstract liberals, with fine sentiments and irrefutable syllogisms, but the stub-born bigoted traditionalists who risk their necks to stop the Hitlers, the Stalins, and our own little Huey Longs and McCarthys.

"A virtue to be serviceable," said Samuel Butler, "must, like gold, be allied with some commoner but more durable metal." For "virtue" substitute "civil liberties"; the durable metal, without which the gold of liberty is unserviceable, is the con-creteness of irrational ancient custom.

IV   Indefensible and Uninhabitable

"How can a mere political innovation ever suffice to change men once and for all into happy inhabitants of the earth?"—*Nietzsche, 1874*

So long as people believe in the perfectibility of man, they will continue to use those freedom-destroying "bad means" (totalitarianism) that promise the quickest shortcut to this "good end." According to the perceptive Polish poet and anti-communist, Czeslaw Milosz, "A gradual disappearance of the faith in the earthly paradise which justifies all crimes, is an essential preliminary to the destruction of totalitarianism." By rejecting the possibility of an earthly paradise, conservatism rejects all brands of Rousseauistic perfectibility of man, rejecting the *a priori* utopias not only of Jacobinism and of socialism but also of doctrinaire *laissez faire* capitalism.

The most blood-curdling crimes are done not by criminals but by perfectionists. Criminals normally stop killing when they attain their modest goal: loot. Perfectionists never stop killing because their goal is never attainable: the ideal society.

The guillotine of a Robespierre comes from ideals too abstractly perfect for man, not from the imperfect, the organically evolved. The guillotine occurs in an enlightened geometric France, not in a ramshackle unsymmetric Hapsburg Empire. Tom Paine proved the French Revolution simply had to be good, peaceful, free. Deductively, his proof was irrefutable. Concretely, the French Revolution became the terror Burke had predicted and for the reason he had predicted: namely, that the well-built, infallible bed of Procrustes did not fit the fallible, concrete flesh. When Paine was jailed by the same French Revolution he had defended, that ingratitude was profoundly just. The man who sacrificed concrete flesh to Procrustes's abstract bed became fittingly, like later the Old Bolsheviks, its own victim.

Earth is one of the uninhabitable planets. Unlike the habitable ones, earth is a planet with a built-in cellar of error, death, decay. If frail children scrawl blueprints of progress on the ceiling, how will that conjure away the reality of the cellar? —does not everything in the house, including the ceiling itself, rest on the foundation of that cellar of error, death, decay? Just as our planet is uninhabitable, so our society is indefensible. Every conceivable society of man will always be indefensible, innately unjust, world without end. Yet somehow we must live within the unbearable but inescapable framework of this uninhabitable planet, this indefensible social order. To act as if there were no such things as error, death, decay, will not abolish but redouble their unbearableness.

Then is any human betterment possible at all? Sustained

betterment never; fluctuating betterment often. Gradual, limited reform can indeed be accomplished, always working within a rooted framework, moving always from particular to particular. Such humane reforms can be achieved and urgently ought to be, despite the resistance of reactionaries (a resistance as doctrinaire as progressivism). We must build what society we can out of what clay we have: the clay of decay, the clay of frailty and constant unpredictable blunder. But the good builder builds with the clay at hand; never does he pile up utopias from some ideal airy clay that does not exist on his particular planet.

It is not a question of being inhumanely blind to the monstrous faults of the old order, of all old orders. It is simply a matter of learning inductively the impossibility of any new program too sweeping, any progress long sustained. Only dead chemicals can be sweepingly reorganized, sustainedly perfected; everything alive is indefensible because infinitely precarious. Humanity is wilful, wanton, unpredictable. It is not there to be organized for its own good by coercive righteous busybodies. Man is a ceaseless anti-managerial revolution.

Whenever enlightened reformers expect the crowd to choose Christ, it cheers for Barabbas. Whenever some Weimar Republic gets rid of some old monarchy, the liberated crowd turns its republic over to some Hitler. Then what consolation remains for the brute fact that sustained progress is impossible? Sheer self-deception is the hope of overcoming man's doom by founding a more exact social science. How can there ever be an exact science dealing with man? Science is exact when dealing with predictable chemicals; only art can deal with flesh. There are indeed consolations for man's precariousness, but they consist not of trying to end it but of learning to find in it not only the lowest but the highest reaches of the spirit, not only cruel social wrongs but the holy welding-flame of the lyric imagination, transfiguring frailty into beauty. This is the Baudelairean truth that the best roses grow from manure.

During a recent discussion of these points, an able social scientist rejoined: "Yes, you are partly right. But only about the past. A truly scientific planner has nothing but contempt for communists and Jacobins; they planned things wrong. Men did not know enough in those backward days. But next time we shall have learnt so much more about improving human nature. *Next time we shall plan everything better.*"

When that day comes, when human reactions can be predicted like test tubes and adjusted into bliss, this writer will take to the hills. Meanwhile, whether you blame it on original sin or on the id, the clay remains refractory; and this fact is not only bitter but exalting. The ultimate unadjustedness of the putty of humanity is the source of all the beauty as well as misery of life on earth.

Chapter Thirty-three   FOUR

DEVALUATIONS

I   Kings in Exile

"If a poet asked the state for permission to keep a few bourgeois in his stable, everybody would be amazed. But if a bourgeois asked for some roast poet, it would be considered perfectly natural."—*Baudelaire*

In cases when not even intellectuals and artists, trained savorers of the creative imagination, can resist the overadjustedness of the industrial west, then who else can be expected to? In cases when they do resist it, the risk will simply have to be taken that their resistance will not necessarily be on the free side, the unadjusted side. Often it will partly be on the side of nihilistic coercions making our overadjustedness still more extreme: fascism in the Germany of the 1930's, communist fellow-traveling in the America of the 1930's and in the France of Sartre today.

The status-resentments of massman and intellectual run in opposite directions, require opposite masks. The massman expresses, through nationalist thought-control and through the demagogic kind of anti-intellectualism, the resentment of the plebeian against a social and educational élite. He masks his inadmissible radical motive from himself by calling himself "anti-radical," "anti-subversive" and by salvaging his pride with an exaggerated topdog stance (the two-fisted American patrioteer or, today somewhat less frequently, the anti-Semite and the pusher-around of Negroes). In contrast, the intel-

306

lectual expresses the resentment of an unfrocked élite against being demoted from cleric to clerk, two terms once synonymous. He masks his inadmissible aristocratic motive from himself by calling himself "radical," "progressive" and by the exaggerated underdog stance of trying desperately to merge with the masses. His would-be merger, a particularly pitiful self-deception among the deracinated, is with the proletariat when his protest is communist, with "the folk" of shared blood when his protest is Nazi-style.

"In almost every civilization we know of," writes the perceptive Eric Hoffer, "and in Europe, too, up to the end of the Middle Ages, the equivalent of the intellectual was either a member of a ruling élite or closely allied with it. . . . In the Roman Empire, there was an intimate alliance between the Greek intellectuals and the Roman men of action. . . . In Europe during the Middle Ages, most of the educated people were of the clergy and hence members of an élite." But today, "the homelessness of the intellectual is more or less evident in all western and westernized societies"—and "nowhere so pronounced as in our own business civilization. . . . One cannot escape the impression that there is a natural antagonism between these 'men of words' and twentieth-century America."

The above point—that of the intellectual as the outstanding rebel of our time—is being made ever more frequently in America today. But, owing to the indiscriminately anti-intellectual interpretation often given to the Hiss case (see page 173), the point is often made in order to Red-bait intellectuals on a demagogic level and with immoral (that is, thought-controlling) intentions. Even the excellent Hoffer analysis, though on the highest level and free from anti-intellectual bias, sometimes takes too much at face value the left-wing radicalism seemingly motivating the intellectual. Most Americans making this point overlook the extent to which his radical protest, in countries other than America, may also be right-wing fascist. They also often overlook his true, unaware motive: not at all his professed anti-aristocratic radicalism (proletarian left or folkic right) but the will to neo-aristocracy of the spurned aristocrat. On the stepping-stone of proletariat or folk, the spurned aristocrat hopes to recapture the élite-dignity from which a too materialistic middleclass industrialism has ousted him.

The "subversive" pose of the clerk-cleric, unfrocking the society that has unfrocked him, is the intellectual's version of the discharged foreman shouting: "I'm not fired, I quit!" But more interesting than such obvious face-saving stances is the melodramatic final act: ousted at the front door from a top-dog dignity, the same foreman climbs back to prestige and to self-respect via the rear door, through which he leads a raid of proletarian or folkic underdogs against his own society.

It is already well documented that most of the members of the Bolshevik party were not workers but middleclass intellectuals when it seized power in 1917. Less familiar is the fact that even by 1921–22, according to its historian E. H. Carr,[1] a majority of its members were still intellectuals, not workers, despite the adherence by then of millions of the propagandized masses. Nor was this condition merely a local, untypical Russian one. In a dispatch of 1952 from Teheran, the *New York Times* correspondent Albion Ross characterized the outlawed communist leaders of Iran: "Most of them from the fairly well-to-do middle class with a tendency toward the intellectual side. . . . Somewhat bookish. . . . They feel that their talents are not appreciated, a common disease of the intellectual. . . ."[2]

The chapter "Transtolerance" suggested that America makes "every man a king" except the king. The older, truer king-concept includes not only throne and altar but lawgivers and singers of throne and altar: intellectuals, artists. Occasionally society does grant them, even in America, their original status; but even then they must safeguard from society the unadjusted loneliness indispensable for creativity. They must not evade their calling—public and alone, king and clown—by becoming

---

[1] *The Bolshevik Revolution,* New York, 1951, p. 207.
[2] *New York Times,* August 17, 1952, Sunday editorial section.

merely useful, mere social engineers. This point was partly implied in Nietzsche's noblest tribute to the intellectuals: "My learned friend, I bless you . . . for this, that . . . you do not commercialize the spirit, that your opinions have no cash value. . . ."

In contrast with the creative calling of kings in exile, the plebeian calling connotes applied knowledge, practical functions, especially economic functions. Thus the millionaire, the burgher, the proletarian are in the same category, all three equally plebeian. Naturally "plebeian" is being used not in the silly, the snobbish sense but in an objective, non-derogatory sense: for a function respected as indispensably valuable, no matter how plodding, uncreative.

When a king is dethroned, the fault may be partly his own, partly society's. The blame must certainly be divided between both in the case of the dethroned intellectual or artist; his function oscillates between being very, very good and horrid. When in his glory, he achieves Plato's ideal, the philosopher king. When in his shame, he is either the bloody-minded professor or the bloody-emotioned Wagnerite, the former predisposed toward communism, the latter toward fascism. Woman hath no fury like an intellectual scorned; *cherchez la femme* does less to explain communism (which Orwell called the patriotism of the deracinated) than *cherchez le clerc* and less to explain Hitlerism than *cherchez l'artiste manqué.* John Maynard Keynes:

The power of vested interests is usually exaggerated when compared with the gradual encroachment of ideas. . . . Indeed the world is ruled by little else. . . . Madmen in authority, who hear voices in the air, are distilling their frenzy from some academic scribbler of a few years back.

Yes. And yet the Keynes quotation notes only half the balance-sheet of the oscillating contributions of the exiled kings. Let us, therefore, supplement his quotation: The power of vested interests is usually exaggerated; good men in authority, who hear voices in the air, are distilling their wisdom from some academic scribbler.

II Drive-in Churches: The So-Called Return to Values

The displacement of the relativist materialism of the 1930's by the household pieties of the 1950's is not really a gain, from any earnestly conservative viewpoint, if these household pieties are not the marble but the plaster ones. Writers hitherto known less for the hair-shirt than the main-chance are falling all over themselves to generalize vapidly about conserving America's Christian value-heritage. Those of us who cherish this heritage not vapidly but with commitment should not be deceived by our surface agreement with these new lip-service saints. The internal threat to America's value-heritage no longer comes merely from the discredited old materialism of the Marxists, "hard-boiled" semanticists, and relativistic anthropologists-of-religion but from the new, mealy-mouthed lip-service to religion, tradition, the Constitution, and kindness to dumb animals. (Not to mention opportunistic kindness to a safely Bowdlerized and Republicanized "conservatism," a kindness particularly amusing when coming from liberal magazines that imagine themselves "fearless" detectors of sham.)

Then what of the much-heralded "return to values" on the campuses? "Youth," we are told with stage trumpets, "again believes." The churches and the middlebrow magazines preen themselves on the increased figures for college chapel attendance, campus religious discussion. Statistically the increased figures are valid enough. But they raise a different question: do people believe more than before, or do they only believe they believe? Or believe they ought to believe? Or finally: how many of the new unctious-voiced ones mean that life would be convenient for their ambitions—less world crises, less pushing around—if everybody *else* believed in God and practiced Sunday School manners?

Recently a movie actress chose to inform her fans of her "acceptance of God." She did so with all the self-conscious mandarin solemnity of a T. S. Eliot informing a hushed world that he had become "Anglo-Catholic in religion, royalist in politics, and classicist in literature." Confidentially under kleig lights, she explained that, when you really get to know Him, God is "a living doll." Not an inner change of heart but an outer Act of Congress, namely the new public law 140 of 1955, requires on all American coins: "In God we trust." It provides a reassuring glow to find Him also added to the pledge of allegiance and the latest postage stamps. In fact, Congress has now officially dedicated to God a "meditation room" in the Capitol, furnished as plushly as the rooms allotted to all the other lobbyists; long a shady internationalist of no fixed abode, God has now been made a 100% American by majority vote. Besides being approved by movie actresses and Acts of Congress, the sanctimonious stampede to the womb has received that ultimate imprimatur, a commercial "market-research analysis" by "promotion executives":

Greenwich, Conn., April 27—The National Council of the Protestant Episcopal Church learned here today about a new counter-attack on the menace of paganism in American cities. . . . The question is one of salesmanship. . . . "Plans are under way," said the Bishop, "for a market research analysis, religion potential surveys and similar emphasis, led by competent sales and promotion executives."[3]

Churches are hawking more of their wares than before by installing more neon lights and loudspeakers than before. Religion is made more "convenient" for the car-owner-in-a-hurry by a new institution proudly advertised as "drive-in churches." That phrase seems the ultimate comment on the entire "great revival of religion." What is still lacking is any money-back guarantee to car-owners-in-a-hurry that their new sanctity has brought them any closer to a drive-in heaven.

Something or other is certainly being revived in America today, judging by all these countless examples, but is it religion or religiosity? Religion is demanding, unglib; it com-

[3] The *New York Times*, April 28, 1955.

bines the hardest spiritual discipline with the most shattering emotional experience. Therefore, the Overadjusted Man prefers religiosity; it is easy, painless, provides a warm, comfortable feeling. Such is ever the fate of values when made bourgeois. Here "bourgeois" is being used not in the economic sense employed by Marx (nor in the political sense in which practically everybody in America, ours being a non-feudal, non-proletarian country, starts off as a mild Lockean-liberal bourgeois) but in the spiritual and also aesthetic sense employed by Baudelaire. In that sense, the bourgeois subverts traditional spiritual values—and also subverts serious aesthetic commitments—not by rebelling against them but by giving them the two wrong kinds of support: hypocrisy, dowdiness.

Hypocrisy—"he talks God and means cotton"—is the less important of the two subversions; few bourgeois are deliberate knaves. Dowdiness, in contrast, is not hypocritical but all too sincere: "At our bridge table we think religion and culture are just too grand for words." How many rebels have been goaded into radicalism by hearing traditional values praised too stuffily, too meanly?

Conservatism (in the sense of Coleridge, John Adams, Adlai Stevenson) is no such painless bourgeois complacency but a painful soul-searching critique of our capitalist-materialist progress. Therefore the present Eisenhower-era complacency, currently denounced as "America's creeping conservatism," is not conservative at all. It is a liberalism, a nineteenth-century, *laissez faire* liberalism, grown too successful, too stodgy, too fat. The best Biblical comment on this overadjusted conformity of the Eisenhower-era prosperity is to quote the Proverbs of Solomon, "The liberal soul shall be made fat" (*Proverbs*, xi, 25). What passes for left and right in America is usually merely a family quarrel between lean and fat versions of the same liberalism, the same (in Baudelaire's sense) bourgeoisie, the same optimistic, top-of-the-brain faith in the blessings of industrialism and the inevitability of progress. Hence, the philosophical conservative in America (in the Melville-Hawthorne tradition) has nothing in common with so-called "right-wing politics" (nationalist isolationism), which is really not so much right of center as midwest of center.

How, then, are traditional cultural and religious values conserved if the hypocrisy and dowdiness of their present would-be conservers are really subverting them? Universal values are conserved by inner personal experience—thereby the universal and the particular meet—and not by wholesome social adjustedness. Even the most social and shared of values will not remain alive unless first conserved anti-socially: namely in that "morbid" lonely isolation where all impersonal truths and social blessings have their intimate personal roots. Thus, in terms of conserving cultural and religious values, even a utilitarian cannot deny the social utility of being anti-social, the collective healthfulness of lonely "morbidness."

The spirit of an age is sometimes better captured impressionistically than statistically. Note the clue that Norman Vincent Peale's *Power of Positive Thinking* was America's most popular nonfiction best-seller during the same years that Eisenhower was America's most popular personality. High-minded evasion of problems, affable relaxation of critical alertness, comfortable religiosity and harmless platitudes, a genuine kindliness blended with pap—there you have the *impression* the decade makes, whatever its *statistics* say about a "return to serious spiritual values."

Normally one would expect the universities to be a gadfly-corrective against this folksy-wholesome spirit. Why, instead, are professors and students more averse to serious personal commitments than ever before? Because the thought-controlling demagogues invade the campus, say many liberals. But the campus of the 1920's and 1930's, facing even worse thought-controllers, responded by commitment, not apathy. Therefore, the explanation for campus apathy lies not merely in an external threat but in an inner mood independent of that threat. The external threat to academic freedom is being successfully repelled in the better universities; not so that inner mood. What that mood fears is not merely the anti-intellectual demagogues but the ridicule of fellow pro-intellectuals. You suffer ridicule if you commit your personality passionately, generously; if you create novels, poems, paintings of vitality and moral challenge; if you respond with spontaneous excitement to ideas, whether dangerous or safe ones, political or nonpolitical.

The preference is for ideas, poems, creeds made impregnable against ridicule by an elegant knowingness. Why not debate ideas and write literary criticism with gusto, instead of with a bland savoring of technique? Think ye because ye are virtuosos there shall be no more cakes and ale?

The campus politics of the 1930's, with its radical illusions, was wrong-headed, the art crude. Were these important disadvantages outweighed by the important advantages of a more exciting, creative atmosphere than today's? Each alternative has its costs, its compensations. In one sense, the radical, materialistic commitments of the 1930's sometimes contained a more religious spirit than the elegant savorings of religion—even the many sincere ones—in the academic drawing-rooms today. For religion requires the willingness to be embarrassing, inelegant. Because it is an act of love, every true religious commitment is and ought to be a gaffe.

And yet, at the risk of seeming endlessly to multiply distinctions, let us add: an act of love, while enthusiastic, must not consist of enthusiasm alone. Enthusiasm alone is a mere romanticism of undisciplined instinct, running amok into pantheism, sentimental nature worship. Absence of enthusiasm is a merely partial, merely cerebral, merely syllogistic commitment to God. Christian love is simultaneously enthusiastic and disciplined.

III   The Burrow of Ironic Conformity

Frequently the Unadjusted Man finds the mechanization, the mass pressure too overwhelming for his limited energies to resist on all fronts simultaneously. He then confines his open resistance to whatever sector has the first, the most concrete moral claim on him. But even on the less urgent sectors, unconditional surrender to the break-throughs of the Over-adjusted Man is not the only alternative to open resistance. A third alternative is the strategic retreat—the Scythian tactic—of ironic conformity. Henri Bergson: "Allow me to furnish the interior of my head as I please, and I shall put up with a hat like everybody else's."

No conceivable mitigating circumstance can condone self-deception, insincerity toward one's self. But circumstances sometimes condone conforming toward others, with an ironic "eppui si muove." Such conformity can be justified ethically when used not for personal advancement but to shield temporarily—no longer than needed for mob passions to subside—the partly disinterested prowl for truth or of beauty.

The moral and intellectual case on behalf of writing on two levels of meaning, one for the marketplace and one for the Stendhalian happy few, will be found in Leo Strauss's *Persecution and the Art of Writing*, 1952. That book must be read in its entirety by anyone who writes about ideas in an age of mass literacy and mass pressure and who lacks the old medieval cryptography known as Latin. The theoretical analysis of that book has been confirmed empirically and independently by Czeslaw Milosz's *The Captive Mind*, 1953. Milosz analyzes the successful use against totalitarianism of an ironic conformity long known to the Moslem world as "Ketman." His analysis of Ketman will prove valuable reading to all contemporary writers, despite the important qualification that our western conformity is incomparably more free and easy than the eastern kind from which this Polish poet fled.

Ironic conformity degenerates into opportunistic concessions when directed only against one of the two levels of overadjust-ment. It must be directed against both at the same time. In that case it disposes of Babbitt Junior, the show-off non-conformist, by flabbergasting him with an unexpected outburst of conservatism ("bigotry") just when he sidles up for the chummy in-group agreement expected from a "fellow intellec-tual." At the same time and with the selfsame double-valued "liberal-baiting" gesture, ironic conformity disposes of the stodgy Babbitt Senior conformist by agreeing with his cultural or political pap to such an exaggerated extent that he discovers much too late—already over the brink of the precipice—that he is being monstrously parodied into his own destruction. With him your conversations would begin by remarking that you don't know much about art but know what you like or that the trouble with these here social reformers is that they never had to meet a pay-roll, concluding profoundly that, when you come right down to it, it is the worthwhile things of life that count.

In a society like ours, where free discussion is relatively feasible, ironic conformity is merely a temporary device; it bides its time for the proper moment for speaking out on lesser things in order meanwhile to gain time for thinking through in privacy the more important things. Privacy, seclusion are crucial prior to an important decision; obtrusive outer influences, by forcing you to react to them, make an honest free decision less likely, no matter in which direction you react to them. To take stands merely by reacting is equally over-adjusted whether reacting positively ("sensible," "practical") or negatively ("bold," "shocking"). Beyond conforming and nonconforming: that theme of our opening definition remains ever the central one for the Unadjusted Man, unself-conscious of whether fashions (the mass kind or the coterie kind) sometimes agree with him, sometimes disagree.

Bohemian nonconformity long served effectively (but now no longer) as the defence-mechanism against conformity; ironic conformity, coming one step later, is a defence-mechanism *against* the defence-mechanism against conformity. Ironic conformity criticizes liberalism so liberally, is so negative even toward negation, that it enters temporarily the darkness of total alienation from everything. "From everything"?—but thereby it finally becomes alienated even from alienation and emerges on the other side of the darkness with a new affirmation, a new organic belongingness, a new conservatism: at the point where the double negative equals the positive. The old, "straight" traditionalism differs from this new, ironic kind in the same way that an ordinary plus in mathematics differs from the plus produced by two minuses: the same, yet not the same.

This new emergence, via darkness, into conservatism lacks the innocence of the original, uncomplex conservatism of the days prior to darkness. What the new affirmer of tradition loses in naturalness, he gains in subtlety; what he loses in vigor, he gains in empathy and compassion: less depth of roots, more range of insight. But nothing can ever make up, among self-conscious new conservers, for the lost casual faith of the old unself-consciousness. Let conservers face it: a Garden of Eden revisited is never the same. Traditionalism left its Eden in 1789 and left it forever. Or was it in 1865? Or 1917? Or 1929?

IV Squire Cabot Babbitt: New Conservative

When the burrow of ironic conformity, temporarily necessary for thinking things through in seclusion, becomes the plushy, suspiciously comfortable burrow of sophisticated servility, unnecessary and lasting, then the strong word "sell-out" seems called for. Sell-out of the twofold code of the Unadjusted Man: independence from stereotypes, loyalty to organic roots.

Hence, when conservatism becomes not merely a valuable means to freedom but an inflated end in itself, its resultant stereotypes parallel, in their own equally bad way, the commercialist ones of Sinclair Lewis' George Babbitt and the progressive ones of his imaginary son Babbitt Junior (presented in *Shame and Glory of the Intellectuals*) who changes his first name to Gaylord in order to sound more *civilisé*. Today in America the justified reaction against Gaylord's liberal and avant-garde banalities is losing its refreshing initial integrity, is becoming an opportunistic banality of its own. Therefore, the time has come to invent a third generation. Enter Gaylord's son

Cabot Babbitt, epigone of the new conservatism, improvising his first name to sound not *civilisé* but *distingué*. He is conservative not in the valid sense of that outlook but in the fad-parroting sense.

If you want to make Babbitt the Third purr with pleasure at a dinner party, introduce him not as "Mister" but "Squire" Cabot Babbitt. Not a mad but unmad squire, self-appointed. This overnight traditionalist is a pillar of (front for) every "patriotic" racket devoted to proving that moderate conservatives are really liberals and that liberals are really Reds. He constantly cites Burke and God as his authorities, Burke without having read him, God without having felt him. But then, Gaylord had never read a line of Marx, whom he used to cite until it became inopportune. Nor had George really read the NAM bulletins he displayed in his real estate office.

Every successful fraud spawns a counter-fraud to outfox it (Hegel's thesis, antithesis). As George Babbitt's Rotary Club was trumped by Gaylord's Café Chic on 56th Street, so the latter now gets trumped by Squire Cabot's Hunting-Lodge Salon for Cultivating Choice Old Values. The Unadjusted Man continues to prefer Irving Babbitt to all three of his overadjusted namesakes. The botanists of ferns have a phrase for it: "alternation of generations." In America the alternations of overadjustment have been between the stereotyped artiness of Gaylord, the stereotyped anti-art of George-plus-Cabot. Since 1952, Grandfather George's tastes and prejudices have been having a brief, doomed, but gaudy Indian summer. And this time, via Cabot's would-be conservatism, their rationalization is different, more sophisticated, more "spiritual."

II

In this section our concern is the cultural, not the political retrogression of Babbitt the Third; but it may be regarded as a parable of retrogression in all fields: political, philosophical, religious. His right-wing politics has already been analyzed in the chapter "The Rootless Nostalgia For Roots: Defects in the New Conservatism," page 97; need not be repeated here. Suffice it to say: his political dream-world is as rootless, apriorist, abstract as that of any radical. It is a dream of what would have happened if Sir Walter Scott had ever written a novel combining Europe's Middle Ages with America's pre-1865 south. This never-never-land is a picturesque pageant, ideal for color TV but not for the ethical and political dilemmas of twentieth-century America. Like Robinson's Miniver Chevvy, Cabot B. was "born too late":

> Cabot loved the Adamses
> Albeit he had never seen one;
> He would have conserved incessantly,
> Could he have been one.

This third American Babbittry, opportunistically riding the bandwagon of a periodic return to orthodoxy, makes retrogression a deliberate principle. The result is an unconscious mirror-image (if we may keep reverting to this leitmotif metaphor) of the liberal cult of progress. How far will the retrogression go in returning to ever more valueless "old values"? At what point will it reach its inevitable *reductio ad absurdum?* Let us fancifully picture what will happen when it finally heralds a return to, say, Edgar Guest in literature, and some McKinley Republican equivalent thereof in politics, as the newest *dernier cri* in traditional folk-wisdom. Definition of newest: whatever has been so long, so totally discredited among the thoughtful that it can now be rediscovered as quaint. Once the laureate of the lowbrows, today Edgar Guest should become the laureate also of the highbrow intellectuals, now that they are rediscovering God, country, motherhood at the most synthetic level ("drive-in churches").

It may even prove diverting to watch the debate over, say, Guest between Cabot and Gaylord, each trying to out-snub the other's snobbery, out-avant the other's garde. Cabot will win the day and convert all Gaylords to his camp when, by skilfully evoking the conditioned reflexes of preciosity, he preaches the daring paradoxes of Mandarin Guest, his rich allusiveness, his urbane irony of achieving poetry by sounding prosaic, unity by sounding fragmentary. What more is needed to convert every Summer Writers Conference for Yearners? Those whose conditioned reflex consists not of new-critical but sociological jargon will be converted also. To them Babbitt the Third need only point out the Higher Synthesis of Thomas Aquinas and the *Federalist* papers implied by Pastor Guest's deepest line of verse: "It takes a heap o' livin' to make a place a home."

Thereupon universities will begin explicating Miglior Fabbro Guest in their "workshop" seminars in soulfulness-by-the-book and mass-produced individual craftsmanship. Why, before he knows it, Guest the Exquisite will be receiving Propositions from some funny little literary gangster, shooting his way into prestige-status, who will offer to anthologize Guest in the latest "Petite Treasury," provided Guest the Influential reciprocates by signing unread a letter of recommendation (for a creative-writing fellowship) calling the anthologist a genius. At that point the cup of fame—or at least of nice blurbs—floweth over. Or, to misquote e. e. cummings, "Beauty hurts, Mr. Success."

What the rationalizations of the new retrogression can thus do to standards in literature, they can do in "statesmanship" also: for characters so diverse as, say, Senator Dirksen and General Franco. Why not?—the game has merely one rule: to condone, in lofty diction about vague eternal verities, the uncondonable. Yet such speculations take too seriously something that is more nuisance than menace. More likely the new conservatism (meaning throughout: not the real thing but the adulteration) will end merely as a vaudeville version of the Oxford Movement. The new conservatives, too, are producing their owlish yet urbane representatives—chins challenging yet fingernails well groomed—dazzling the dowagers at the campus tea, the church bazaar.

No longer functional but decorative: no longer to prevent malaria but to diffuse a pukka glamor, the fad of gin-and-tonic came to Levittown from the far porches of Poona, accompanied by station wagons once functional for colonial Africa. In the same way the fad of a doctrinaire, apriorist, counter-revolutionary conservatism will finally dribble down to the women's-club circuit from France's far-off Royalist underground of the 1790's.

The same ear-to-the-ground literati who quoted Henry Wallace in the 1930's and 1940's, are now often sloganizing neo-conservatively about original sin, the need for a tragic sense, the need for roots. The truth behind these phrases remains as indispensable as ever (for reasons suggested in the chapters preceding). But that truth sounds hollow when it reflects no personal concern with the human predicament but an in-the-swim glibness. Squire Cabot Babbitt's pleas for a "tragic sense" sound as complacently untragic as his unoriginal pleas for "original sin."

Chapter Thirty-four   FOUR NOTES

ON IMAGINATION

I The Amateur Hour

"Police officials believe that the methodical *efficiency* of bankers and businessmen . . . often are the biggest assets to hold-up men. Police recommend that bankers mix up their time schedules."—*Boston, I.N.S. dispatch,* SPRINGFIELD DAILY NEWS, *October 1, 1951*

"Poole said the post office money was locked in a vault. The burglar, apparently an *amateur*, got into the post office through a large post office box, Poole said."—TIMES-PICAYUNE, *New Orleans, 1954*

To remain individual in an overadjusted society, start out, first of all, by being an amateur at everything, never a professional. This is true whether you are a poet, scholar, or political leader, whether you are an artist of life, love, or billiards. According to Mark Twain, to play billiards moderately well is the sign of a gentleman; to play it too well is the sign of a mis-spent life. In an age of boorish, narrow specialists and of efficient experts who do everything "too well" in unimaginative, slavish stereotypes, in such an age only the amateur stays inwardly free.

An amateurish life is a life of harmonious proportion because it alone finds time to cultivate the complete human being, public and private, cerebral and emotional. A free society requires not only free ideals, free institutions, but free personalities. The free personality is an "amateur" in both senses·

1. he who does things for love, not utility;
2. the non-technician, not yet deprived of creative imagination by expertise.

Clemenceau remarked against professional soldiers: "War is too important a matter to leave to generals." We may add: atom bombs are too important to leave to scientists; freedom too important to leave to political theorizers; literature too important to leave to English departments.

Even humor is too important to leave to its specialists. The learned Professor Albert Rapp, a professional scholar in the field of humor, in the Letter Column of the *New York Times* Book Section of February 4, 1951, accused the cartoonist Al Capp, creator of *L'il Abner,* of making "amateur statements" about humor and lacking "professional status." Capp's reply: "Professor Rapp haughtily dismisses my review as an 'amateur statement.' I—gulp!—guess I am an amateur. I have been so busy for the last eighteen years creating humor (effective enough at least to hold the daily attention of forty million people) that I just ain't had time to study up on how to do it." It is good to hear specialists being talked back to. The point is more than mere banter; ultimately freedom's advantage over totalitarianism lies in the greater imaginative resourcefulness of the non-specializing free individual. His imagination overcomes the advantage in discipline that totalitarianism has over freedom, whether in war or peace.

Only by *not* knowing how to write or think "too well" or how to fight a war of professional strategy, can the imagination get the insights needed for the highest literary, philosophical, or military trumphs. Revealing is the remark made by the baffled police after a recent bank robbery. They rightly pointed out that they had been prepared to stop all the latest, most scientific methods used by "professional" criminals. One policeman exclaimed in exasperation: "It's not our fault; why, these *unfair,* unscientific burglars were rank amateurs!"

II   Half-Pint of Soul

"A little learning is a dangerous thing;
Drink deep, or taste not the Pierian spring:
There shallow draughts intoxicate the brain,
And drinking largely sobers us again."
                                    —*Alexander Pope*

Suppose that the American arts do return to the dignity of lyricism (the unleashing half of the imagination). Suppose that the mainstream of American intellectuals, after too long appeasing leftist materialism in the 1930's and big-business materialism in the 1950's, returns to the dignity of ethics (the restraining half of the imagination). Suppose, finally, that these increased imaginative achievements of the artist and the intellectual are reciprocated by increased efforts at understanding them on the part of the lazy modern reader. After these three "supposes," it would at last become possible to create *a new community of imaginative understanding* between the creator and his public, a new community reducing some of the mutual distrust and misunderstanding between modern poets and their readers, modern writers of experimental prose and their readers, modern intellectuals and their public. Since both sides are partly to blame for the schism between them, the above "supposes" make demands upon both sides.

Let us consider some alternative "supposes." Suppose mutual communication is not restored. Suppose the new community of imaginative understanding is made impossible by the taste of the Overadjusted Man for the glib and painless. In that case there will still be plenty of communication going on, but it will not be by the good writers; it will continue to be left to the bad writers, the demagogues of literature. The default of the good poets in communicating their spiritual values to their readers, creates a moral vacuum filled by pseudo-spiritual best-sellers like Kahlil Gibran.

The success of such books—and of astrology, Rosicrucianism, and the rest—owes its hard-boiled commercial triumph to its noncommercial idealistic opposite: an unsatisfied nonmaterial thirst in the modern reader. For our unread and uncommunicating serious artists, it is a danger signal that millions are reading such worthless but communicative pseudo-poetry as Gibran's *Prophet*. Men not only need moral refreshment but will shop around till they get it. If they cannot get it from their legitimate dealer in intellect, the serious artist, then they will get it adulterated in some bootleg half-pint of soul. Either the true Pierian spring or Southern California.

III The Dream-Nexus

The stars of the universe, the cells of the brain are said to be approximately equal in number. A felicitous metaphor in this: the giant scales of reality, forever weighing cosmos against soul, are balanced evenly at the fulcrum of the forehead. Star matter against gray matter: imagine them balancing with a one-to-one correspondence between the units without and within the skull; between the stars and the no less radiant brain-cells. This balance is upset by any philosophy (too materialistic or too idealistic-solipsistic) that deems either half of the scales "more real."

In the past America has placed too much weight on the outward side. It is still too early to predict whether the third frontier will create a better balance at the forehead's fulcrum. But whatever the future, the American complacency of pre-1929 did sacrifice the imaginative to the external. America's greatest domestic cataclysm of the century—the economic crash of October 28, 1929—was, among several other things, the protest of Things As They Are against a gruntingly prosperous pig-ethics. Things As They Are: the pre-industrial pattern of man, psychological, cultural, religious. This pattern has been driven underground; its secret empire lives on below the verbalized level of our official, public lives.

Causality is complex, pluralistic. The economic causes for 1929 were obviously important, perhaps primary. But no such crash of material pride can occur without at least some psychological causes also. These psychological causes, for want of a more reasonable-sounding metaphor, we may call "magic." They involve the seemingly arbitrary, inexplicable, hence seemingly magical causality that is exercised by the claims of inwardness, the claims of imagination, creativity, religion. These claims are difficult to understand consciously, inconvenient to formulate abstractly. Hence, society often ignores them. But at its peril.

Psychologically America in any case was riding for a fall— almost willing a fall—in the shallow material pride of the 1920's. All that was needed was an occasion—almost a pretext—for falling. If the important economic causality of 1929 had not come along to provide that occasion, something else would have done so. The result in either case would have been some sort of nervous breakdown for a deracinated business world.

One of the laws of magic dooms the sorcerer's apprentice who cannot control the powers he summons. No medieval alchemist, trying to hocus-pocus baser metals into gold, was so gaga as that sorcerer's apprentice known as "sober high-finance." In the end his spells and numerals could not control the revolt of his tickertape djinn and fairy gold, the lurking bearishness of his phantom bulls. For imagination is not merely pleasure-giver and servant but weapon, whether as white magic or black. Hence Coleridge's warning to whoever denies imagination its due:

O gentle critic! be advised. Do not trust too much to your professional dexterity in the use of the scalping knife and tomahawk. Weapons of diviner mold are wielded by your adversary; and you are meeting him here on his own peculiar ground, the ground of idea, of thought, and of inspiration.

The disaster of 1929 was, among other things, such a Coleridgean weapon, wielded by a spurned inwardness. The creative imagination had been spurned too long, or else had been degraded into a fashionable social accomplishment. Religion had been degraded into a wholesome social convention, God into a scoutmaster awarding merit-badges for hygiene. Whenever man's life becomes superficialized into a downright gymnastics of adjustment, then a deeper self erupts —cataclysmically, exaltingly—to remind him of a wider-ranging gamut: heartbreak, radiant happiness. The infinities of heartbreak are too unbearable for the optimistic good sport to "grin and bear"; the infinities of radiant happiness are too useless for the unhappy pleasure-seeker to know how to use.

It violates the love that moves the sun and the other stars whenever society denies to the creative imagination either its spiritual or its sensuous claims. The archetypal pattern of Things As They Are is elastic. Push it too far, it snaps back. It snapped back once in 1929. Amid the present new grunts and wallows, it will snap back again—unless enough Americans conjure up a magic dream-nexus of creative aspirations to sweeten and transfigure the cash-nexus of economic aspirations.

The imagination as sorcery: this concept explains society's economic need for anti-economics. The impact of economic aspirations on society is disruptive, atomistic. The impact of lyrical and ethical aspirations (imagination's unleashing and restraining functions) is cohesive, organic. Therefore, even on its own materialist terms, economic materialism depends on a spiritual, anti-economic base. In practice, glue for glue, dream-nexus is a more effective social cement than cash-nexus. The practical world of all our economic materialists is held together by the unintended, subsurface poet in their own souls. That "unacknowledged legislator" within them, never entirely stifled, saves them despite themselves. But he saves them only up to a point, only when his "weapons of diviner mold" are not exasperated too far by "the scalping knife and tomahawk" of poor, feeble practicality.

Consider how increasingly unconvincing is our outer reality, how unsolid its respectable solidity, how lifeless its hectic liveliness. Consider how *implausible* is this outer world of juxtapositions: social security next to atomic insecurity; stock-markets next to marching drum-majorettes; clambakes next to "mortician-parlors" (latest neon sign: "Frozen Caskets To Spare Your Loved Ones Inhuman Embalming"); drive-in churches next to the movie-palaces whose "dignity" (bigness) they enviously imitate. What a combination of the unbelievably banal and the unbelievably strange, in either case not really real. Without the imagination's dream-nexus to hold *that* sort of an outer world together, its atoms would crack and scatter in an instant like blown sand.

IV Secret America:
The Liberating Gesture

"Change *not the mass* but change the fabric of your own soul and your own visions, and you change all."—*Vachel Lindsay*

What keeps earth air breathable? Not oxygen alone. The earth is a freer place to breathe in, every time you love without calculating a return—every time you make your drudgeries and routines still more inefficient by stopping to experience the shock of beauty wherever it unpredictably flickers.

To enrich the inner sensibility with love and with beauty is not only a sensuous but also a moral act—and thereby, indirectly, even a political act. It is a liberating gesture in politics precisely because not intended politically. The Soviets recognized this significance in reverse. They officially condemned the lyric poetry of Akhmatova and Pasternak for the crime of expressing emotions of private love and loneliness. These emotions are always feared as grit in the cogwheels of a collectivist machine. From their viewpoint, the Soviets are right in fearing such a gesture. Its spontaneity, its unpredicta-bility reassert human flesh and blood against the metallic totalitarian goal. That goal is the disincarnation of man:

> Not that they starve, but starve so dreamlessly;
> Not that they sow, but that they seldom reap;
> Not that they serve, but have no gods to serve;
> Not that they die, but that they die like sheep.

Though naturally far less than Soviet Russia, the free world also suffers from the depersonalizing trend. For example, research has documented[1] the appalling unprivateness of the private family life of American corporation officials. But western Europe and India are no more immune than America to that trend. They cannot exorcize it by projecting the world-wide characteristics of industrialism onto the particular scapegoat of American capitalism. We are all in the same boat.

In furthering the worldwide trend away from the sponta-neous and private, literary intellectuals are for once united with businessmen. Among intellectuals: no more Dylan Thomases, ever more Ph.D. theses about Thomas. Among businessmen: clerk-mentalities instead of unadjusted scientific geniuses like Charles P. Steinmetz, a Mad Squire of the business world; without his personal imagination, the now impersonal corpora-tions like General Electric could never have been built in the first place. This change means short-run gain, long-run loss; the cooked goose tastes delicious but lays no more golden eggs.

Modern industrial societies tend to oscillate between two extremes: an anarchic perversion of individualism, a tyrannic perversion of unity. The anarchic individualism of the com-mercialized kind of democracy is atomistic, based on cash-nexus rivalry, not on inner independence. At the other extreme, the tyrannic unity of statism (by going far beyond the humane needs of what we have called the new legitimacy) is mechan-ical, without traditional organic roots; to hold together, it ultimately requires the coercion of the police-state.

There remains a third alternative (to tie together briefly, in conclusion, the themes of the book's first two chapters and of

[1] *Fortune* magazine, New York, October and November, 1951.

the "Four Notes on Values"). The third alternative is a unity not mechanical and political but organic and psychological: the shared personal commitments of free individuals, the affectionate value-commitments of the private imagination. Deeper than our public surface-life of politics and economics, such unity, such commitments fulfil rather than standardize the personal life, the private imagination. "Fulfil" is the key word; it excludes the false (hysterical) kind of organic collectivity— the "folk" cult of continental Europe—that swallows rather than fulfils individual freedom. But in the case of America, the danger is not the false or excessive organic unity but the uprooting of the organic by the mechanistic.

Happily America still has countless flowerings of the true organic unity, the kind that fulfils freedom by voluntary personal commitments. Such flowerings are unlabeled, unideologized. They grew up by spontaneous muddling, branching forth vigorously without geometry, without symmetry, originally cultivated more by love—local, concrete, personal, amateurish—than by efficient social horticulture.

The result of such free growing is a refreshing pluralism of diverse personal unities all over America: the absentmindedly conservative, almost medieval movement known as trade-unionism; the unacknowledged, subsurface Federalist-party heritage of squires-incognito, with their shared sense of higher self-imposed standards; the business community with its shared rules of the game, its research foundations, its altruistic community-chests; a close-knit family management in stores;[2] a communal religious worship; the living traditionalism of parochial religious schools; the living traditionalism of our small private colleges, each very individual in personality

---

[2] In non-Latin countries nepotism is officially abhorred for its inefficiency and its graft. But American industry is already efficient enough to afford the first of these defects, prosperous enough to afford the second. Moreover, both serve as useful counter-irritants against a too Calvinistic sense of duty in economics. In any case, nepotism does provide relationhips more loyal, more personal than those of cold financial exploitation. According to a morally-aghast survey by the American Institute of Management, "fully half of 23,000 corporations in America suffer from concealed nepotism." This blithe fact is another example of how the true, secret America is based on concrete, organic relationships in practice; on abstract, atomistic relationships in theory.

yet with its own kind of unifying *esprit de corps;* the geographic diversity of our regionalism, with the shared cultural or historical experiences that enrich many a decentralized, idiosyncratic locality; in short, wherever cooperation is not state-imposed but voluntary; wherever motivated humanly, not merely financially. Smaller concrete examples (small but they add up) include: local public-libraries; town-hall forums; city music-festivals, museums, playgrounds; voluntary fire-brigades, blood donors, the voluntary service of great surgeons in public clinics.

America contains more of the spirit of these examples than Americans themselves realize. Are these examples private competition, or are they centrally-blueprinted by the government at Washington? Usually neither. Yet they come closer to our concrete, flesh-and-blood America than our various official abstractions, whether the ideology of *laissez faire* capitalism and unlimited competition or the rival ideology of a centralizing bigness (big government, big labor, or big business).

The true and secret America is one of voluntary cooperation. It is a cooperation based on the spiritual qualities of trust, shared goals, shared traditions. It is also based on a very individual responsibility toward this social trust. In America this organic unity of personal relationships has never been theorized; if ever it is, it will by then have become too self-conscious, too contrived. Yet it sustains freedom and the creative imagination more effectively than do the two alternatives: the dehumanizing impersonality of capitalist competition and the standardizing unity of statism.

A voluntary cooperation between unstandarized personalities avoids the anti-individual unity of socialism and the anti-social individualism of capitalism. Of that unmodified, cash-nexus kind of capitalism, Americans have always had far less than they officially believe. Unofficially, they have always had far more of the voluntary cooperation that transcends both Marx and Adam Smith. This third alternative, this dream-nexus, this secret America is the unfamiliar, non-materialist base for many

of our familiar material achievements. It is the unspoken
spiritual base for whatever is sound in the vast productivity,
power, prosperity that the official surface-America attributes
to mere utility, profit, pragmatism. (Whatever is unsound
therein, the reckless materialist pride, was the subject of the
preceding pages on 1929.)

No solutions are more than provisional, partial. This third
alternative provisionally reconciles the interdependence of
social unity with the independence of free individualism.
This partial solution is too rooted in centuries of cultural and
religious traditions, in centuries of archetypal patterns of psychology and humanity, to be lost to us or far away, no matter
how lost or far it may sometimes seem. Near, substantial, it
reappears daily wherever there is the liberating "magic" gesture
of the unadjusted personality to evoke it. It re-roots the
intellectual, re-humanizes the man of commerce.

In order to be liberated from the mechanizing stereotypes
of the Overadjusted Man, years of professional philosophical
or political articulations about liberty would not be enough.
Yet a second's gesture of humanity—warm, amateur, personal
—may suffice. The universals of beauty and of liberty are
given flesh and blood only when some private gesture of love
or loneliness reincarnates these remote grandeurs in concrete,
individual experiences. Thereby, within the complete personality, the universal and the particular meet without sacrificing
either: without chaotic romantic subjectivism on the one hand,
without mechanical rationalist abstractions on the other.
Fusing the universal and the particular into the single creative
act, the unadjusted imagination concretizes the spiritual,
spiritualizes the concrete. So doing, it moves beyond the
propagandistic, the temporary, the overadjusted—beyond
the corrupting successes of even the best of isms—and gropes
toward the lasting aspect of things.

Postscript 2004   VACHEL LINDSAY,

DANTE OF THE FUNDAMENTALISTS:

The Suicide of America's Faith in Technology

I

The end of an outer material frontier to explore in the west and midwest has helped cause the increasing inner explorations of the spirit. Vachel Lindsay represents a transition: apparently still an outer explorer, an evoker of picturesque place-names and loud American noises in the fashion of an older school; yet in reality an inward voyager of the religious imagination and the aesthetic imagination. Lindsay remains the finest religious poet produced by America's most local native roots. He is the Dante of the Fundamentalists. A Yankee Doodle Dante.

The comparison of Lindsay with Dante is intended not in terms of greatness, whether of poetry or thought, but in terms of voicing one's roots. In their respective religious communities, each was the poet who best voiced his particular heritage. The sharply contrasting views of man in those two heritages will broaden the second part of this discussion from Lindsay to American culture as a whole, our split between Burkean and "progressive" views. (Page numbers after quotations refer to the excellent Macmillan edition of Lindsay's *Collected Poems*.)

By itself, to call Lindsay the Fundamentalist bard is nothing new.[1] What is indeed new, perhaps initiating a neo-Burkean "unadjusted" aesthetics applicable to poetry criticism in general, is my try at analyzing the threefold interaction between Lindsay's human crack-up, his Ruskin-aesthete mission, and his self-destructive devotion (despite increasing qualms) to his Rousseau-

333

Bryan utopianism: that is, to his faith in Fundamentalist religion and in Populist politics. What will last, despite his self-imposed straitjacket, is a few dozen lines (to be cited presently) of truly lyric art.

The patronizing condescension with which Lindsay is read today is his penalty for having had the courage to be generous, enthusiastic, inelegant. The resultant full-throated song is particularly needed to counteract the fear of being ridiculed, ultimately a fear of being lyrical. His best poetry, admittedly infrequent, is just the right corrective to our unlyrical elegant wincers; his worst poetry, though more frequent, can no longer do harm, being too remote from fashionable fastidiousness to make the wrong sort— the faddish sort—of converts.

Lindsay is the Dante of America's only indigenous church: Fundamentalist Bible-belt revivalism. For that church he wrote major poetry of mystical vision, as well as the jingly junk (boom-lay-boom) for which he is better known. Carrying further, church for church and relic for relic, the analogy with the Florentine poet of Catholicism, we may summarize: Lindsay's Rome was Springfield, Illinois; his Holy Roman Emperor was the specter of Abe Lincoln; his Virgil-guide was Johnny Appleseed. His Beatrice was "A Golden-Haired Girl in a Louisiana Town" : "You are my love / If your heart is as kind / As your eyes are now." His martyred Saint Sebastian was Governor Altgeld (persecuted for saving the Haymarket anarchists from lynching). His angel hosts were the Anti-Saloon League and the Salvation Army, lovingly washing in "the blood of the lamb" the stenos and garage mechanics of Chicago.

To continue the analogy: Lindsay's version of the Deadly Sins, as a middle-class Fundamentalist schoolma'am might see them, were the beguiling depravities of "matching pennies and shooting craps," "playing poker and taking naps ." These two lines are from "Simon Legree," a combination of a Negro spiritual with a Calvinistic morality, the result of that combination can only be called: intoxicated with sobriety. Dante's medieval heretics partly corresponded to what Lindsay called "the renegade Campbellites," a Fundamentalist splinter-group secession:

O prodigal son, O recreant daughter
When broken by the death of a child,
You called for the graybeard Campbellite elder,
Who spoke as of old in the wild...
An American Millennium...
When Campbell arose,
A pillar of fire,
The great high priest of the spring...

But then, in the same poem, comes the sudden self-mockery of:

And millennial trumpets poised, half-lifted,
Millennial trumpets that wait. (p. 354)

Here the verb "wait," mocking the ever-unfulfilled prophecies of Fundamentalist revivalism, is the kind of slip that occurs accidentally-on-purpose. Such frequent semi-conscious slips represent Lindsay's protest against his self-imposed, self-deceiving role of trying to be more Fundamentalist than any Fundamentalist and more folkish than the real folk.

That self-imposed role, which ultimately became his shirt-of-Nessus, may have resulted from two tacit postulates. First, that poetry readers have no more right to laugh at the homespun Fundamentalist theology of the old American west than at the subtler but perhaps no more pious-hearted theology of Dante's day. Second, that the American small-town carnival deserved as much respect as Dante's medieval pageants; it was as fitting a literary theme; it was no less capable of combining the divine with the humdrum.

Once you concede these two postulates to Lindsay, all the rest seems to follow, including such lofty Lindsay invocations as. "Love-town, Troy-town Kalamazoo" and "Hail, all hail the pop-corn stand.." It follows that the Fundamentalist prophet, Alexander Campbell, should debate with the devil upon none other than "a picnic ground." It follows that real, tangible angels jostle Lindsay's circus-barkers and salesman of soda pop. And certainly Lindsay has as much aesthetic right to stage a modern Trojan war, over love, between Osh Kosh and Kalamazoo as Homer between Greeks and Trojans. So far so good. But Lindsay often absurdly overstrains this aesthetic right, these old-world analogies. For example, he hails not an easily hailed American *objet* like, say, Washington's monument but the popcorn stand.

Lindsay's motive for choosing the popcorn stand is not unconscious crudeness but conscious provocation. In effect, he is saying: "By broadening the boundaries of aestheticism to include such hitherto-unacceptable Americana, my poetry is deliberately provoking, and thereby re-educating, all you supercilious eastern-seaboard-conditioned readers or Europe-conditioned readers."

But at the same time there is a suppressed saboteur within Lindsay, as within every exaggerated nationalist. That underground saboteur infiltrates Lindsay's poems via the most awkward-looking, absurdity-connoting letter in our alphabet, the letter "K.". For whatever psychological reasons many Americans go into convulsions of laughter over the names of foreign towns like Omsk, Tomsk, Minsk, Pinsk, and nearer home, Hoboken, Yonkers, Keokuk, Sauk Center, not to mention. those two Lindsay favorites, Osh Kosh and Kalamazoo. The core of each of those place-names is a throaty, explosive "K." Try to picture each of that same list, from Omsk through Kalamazoo, being spelt with a modest initial "C" or a chic final "que" in place of the "K"; in that case the names would lose half their comic effect on the ordinary American. The letter "K" even looks lopsided, about to topple helplessly forward, an off-balance rube with metaphoric haywisps in its hair. More than any other letter, it connotes the awkward yokel. The words "awkward" and "yokel" themselves would not connote half so much awkwardness, were they not so conspicuously spelt with a "K."

Aside from above place-names and as further evidence for the hitherto unanalyzed role of "K" in American English, here are still other types of "K" usage with contemptuous connotations:

1. Awkward-looking alien animals: auk, aardvaark, kangaroo. In each instance, the animal's ridiculousness seems diminished if "c" or "que" are substituted for "K," no awkward or comic connotation is attached to the Italian word for kangaroo, namely "canguro." An awkward-thinking as well as awkward-looking person, a crackpot extremist, is called a "Kook" in American slang.

2. Epithets for allegedly crude aliens: yank (from southerners), kike, gook, chink, mick, kraut, bohunk (for Bohemian or Czech), hunky (for Hungarian), spik (for Puerto Rican) smoke and spook (for Negro), snorky (for Swede), dink (for Viet), canook (for French Canadian). These are too many examples to be coincidental, despite the non-K terms of racial contempt that also occur. Since, except for sauerkraut, "K" is lacking in the source-words for these epithets (e.g., Chinese into chink), it seems as if "K" were deliberately added —perhaps as an imitation of throat-clearing —to make a nickname more insulting.

3. Compare, the old comic-strip spelling of "Krazy Kat" with the sarcastic spelling of "Kommunist Khrushchev" in a 1960 press release by the New York State Secretary, Caroline K. Simon (self-hatred of her own middle initial?), and with the 1960 appeal by Admiral Arleigh Burke, Chief of Naval Operations, asking us to spell "Communists" as "Kommunists" in order to make clear their "foreignism" and their "Kremlin bosses."[2] These absurdities (would "Cremlin Communists" evoke a more trustful response?) reflect a very American linguistic bias.

4. Unlike the plain "K," the combination "ck" fails to connote "foreignism" or awkwardness. But it does still connote contempt. Indeed, "ck" has become the standard termination—explosively coughed out —of a surprisingly large number of the unprintable "four-letter words" (in some instances five letters), both nouns and verbs, as well as the longer compounds of noun plus verb. Curiously enough, this added connotation of obscenity enters only when a "c" gets prefixed to the "k."

5. Without "c," countless "k" words of four letters are derogatory slang: fink, junk, bunk, wonk, muck, guck, jerk, suck, yuck, wank off, jack off, knock up, etc.

Of course, no such deliberate linguistic analysis determined Lindsay's obsessive use of awkward town-names with "K." Rather, his use was determined by a blind instinct—a shrewdly blind instinct—for catching the very soul of spoken Americana. No one has ever equaled Lindsay's genius for manipulating the unconscious connotations of the colloquial, even though he perversely misused those connotations for the self-torturing purpose of provoking and then staring-down the ridicule of sophisticated audiences.

That willingness to provoke ridicule may produce his worst poems. Yet it is also the root of the moral courage producing his best poems, such as his elegy for Governor Altgeld of Illinois. Altgeld had defied a nineteenth-century kind of "McCarthyism" by his idealistic defense of slandered minorities. Political poetry, even courageous political poetry, is by itself merely a rhymed editorial, better written in prose, unless universalized beyond journalism and arid ideologies into the non-political realm of artistic beauty. Lindsay's Altgeld poem remains one of the great American elegies because it does achieve this humanizing process, transfiguring courage into lyric tenderness:

> Sleep softly...eagle forgotten...under the stone..
> The mocked and the scorned and the wounded, the lame and the poor
> That should have remembered forever...remember no more...
> Sleep softly...eagle forgotten...under the stone,
> Time has its way with you there, and the clay has its own...
> To live in mankind is far more than to live in a name,
> To live in mankind, far, far more...than to live in a name.

However, more frequently the heroes Lindsay's poetry presents as the American equivalent of old-world Galahads are not exactly Altgelds. For example, the subtitle of his actual poem "Galahad" reads: "Dedicated to all Crusaders against the International and Interstate Traffic in Young Girls." The subtitle of his poem "King Arthur's Men Have Come Again" was equally earnest and uplifting, namely: "Written while a field-worker in the Anti-Saloon League of Illinois." Of course, the moral heritage of rural Fundamentalism particularly objects to alcohol, along with "playing poker and taking naps."

These twin odes to the Anti-Vice Squad and the Anti-Saloon League are bad poems not because the evil they denounce is unserious but because their treatment of that evil sounds like a mock-heroic parody. To explain such bad writing in so good a poet, let us suggest the hypothesis that Lindsay's mentality included a demon of self-destruction, forever turning the preacher into the clown. This compulsion forced Lindsay, again and again in his verse, to strip himself in public of every shred of what he most prized: human dignity. Perhaps this inner demon was related to the compulsion that finally made Lindsay choose not just any method of suicide but the most horribly painful method imaginable: swallowing a bottle of searing acid.

When a poet consistently exalts whatever heroes, place-names, and occupations sound most ludicrous to his modern poetry audience (for example Lindsay was an avid exalter of college cheerleaders), it may be either because he has no ear for poetry or because he has an excellent ear knowingly misused. The first explanation is easily ruled out by the beauty of the above Altgeld elegy. Aside from the self-destructive aspect, there is an important messianic-pedagogic aspect making the second explanation the more plausible one. For example, by inserting the pedantic adjective "interstate" in front of "traffic in young girls" and thereby incongruously juxtaposing the prosaic Mann Act law with the poetic word "Galahad," Lindsay says in effect:: "If you accept my hick-fundamentalist approach to morality, which I happen to consider the only true and autochthonous American religion, then you must also accept the further implications of that approach. You must accept its humorless terminology, its ridicule-provoking bigotries. What is more, you must accept them with a religious spirit exactly as earnest as that with which Homer and Dante accepted their own autochthonous religious traditions."

Thus considered, Lindsay's poetry is not mere clowning, whether intentional or unintentional, but—in his own revealing phrase—"the higher vaudeville." The adjective "higher" makes all the difference; it means a medieval vaudeville, a messianic circus, a homespun Midwest equivalent of the medieval fool-in-Christ.

II

In refusing to be apologetic toward the Old World about America's own kind of creativity, Lindsay does have a valid point. In refusing to allow European legends, heroes, place-names a greater claim on glamour than American ones, he again does have a valid point. Likewise when he establishes the American gift for finding loveliness in the exaggerated, the grotesque. But the self-sabotaging demon within him tends to push these valid points to extremes that strain even the most willing "suspension of disbelief."

When Lindsay fails to make us suspend our disbelief, the reason often is this: he is trying to link not two compatibles, such as prosaic object with prosaic rhetoric or fabulous object with fabulous rhetoric, but prosaic object with fabulous rhetoric. Modern university-trained readers of poetry react unsolemnly to: "Hail, all hail the popcorn stand." Why? Because of a gap I would define as: the Lindsay disproportion. The Lindsay disproportion is the gap between the heroic tone of the invocation and the smallness of the invoked object. But Lindsay's aim, rarely understood by modern readers, was to overcome that disproportion between tone and object by conjuring up a mystic grandeur to sanctify the smallness of American trivia. That mystic grandeur derived from his dream of America as a new world free from Old World frailty, free from original sin. His dream-America was infinitely perfectible, whatever its present faults. Even its most trivial objects were sacred because incarnating the old Rousseauistic dream of natural goodness of man and eternal progress.

Lindsay believed, or felt he ought to believe, in the impossible America invented by the French poet Chateaubriand and other European romantics. Later, much later (nature imitating art) that invented America was sung by Americans themselves, by Emerson and Whitman. In poetry this utopian American myth culminated in Lindsay's "Golden Book of Springfield" and Hart Crane's "The Bridge"; in politics it culminated in the Populist and Progressive movements of the west.

But the laws of history and human nature permit no "new world" to be really new: Americans contain the same very human mixture of aspiration and fallibility as the old world. Europe's romantic expectation of superhuman achievements in democracy or in culture from America, an expectation that duped the Lindsays and the Hart Cranes as well as the European romantic school that invented it, has helped cause the current European disillusionment with America (even entirely aside from the lies of communist propaganda). Had Europeans not been so exaggeratedly pro-American in their hopes, they would not be so exaggeratedly anti-American in their despair but would see us as ordinary human beings like themselves.

The paradox behind European expectations of the New World appears in a supposed anecdote of the 1800's about Chateaubriand. He had arrived in America to flee Old World artificiality and to search for the unspoilt noble savage. And sure enough, as Chateaubriand was creeping through the wild jungle then filling northern New York State around Niagara Falls, he glimpsed a tribe of wild Indians between the trees. They were moving in a circle, as if in some primordial folk-ceremony. Bravely defying the dangers primitive America holds for older civilizations, he crept closer and closer through the thicket, to record for his friends in Paris an eyewitness account of unspoilt Americana in the midst of nature's wilderness. Suddenly he recognized what the redskins were dancing. Led by a little mincing French dancing-master, whom they had imported at great expense from Paris for that purpose, the Indians were pirouetting daintily through the latest steps of a formal Parisian ballroom number.

This anecdote is an allegory for European-American literary relations ever since. European critics are forever visiting our American literature to find a mystical, non-existent Noble Primitive. Instead they find some blasé professor, with a tweedy Oxford jacket and Boston accent, dancing with dreadful nimbleness through some complicated *explication de texte* of Proust...

Instead of pouncing with shoddy glee on the absurd aspects of the Lindsay disproportion between tone and object, let us re-examine more rigorously the Chateaubriand-style dream of

America behind those absurd aspects. That American myth is part of a romantic, optimistic philosophy seriously maintained, whatever one may think of it, by great or almost-great minds like Rousseau and Emerson. Therefore, it is unjust to dismiss that same philosophy contemptuously in Lindsay merely because his name has less prestige than theirs. What is wrong-headed in him, is wrong-headed in his preceptors also. He and they dreamed of a new world miraculously reborn without the burden of past history. That unhistorical myth of America distinguishes Whitman and Lindsay from Hawthorne and Faulkner in literature. It distinguishes Jefferson from John Adams in political philosophy. It distinguishes Fundamentalist revivalism, with its millennium just around the corner, and the hope of quick redemption that Lindsay's poetry hailed in the Salvation Army, from Niebuhrian pessimism within the American Protestant religion. While Lindsay is the Dante of the Fundamentalists, he differs from the Old World Catholic Dante by substituting a romantic, optimistic view of man for the tragic view held by traditional Christianity as well as by Greek classicism.

On this issue American literature has two conflicting traditions, the first romantic and progressive, the second classical and conservative. The first heartily affirms American folklore, American democratic and material progress. That Whitman-Emerson literary tradition cracked up in Vachel Lindsay and Hart Crane.[3] It cracked up not merely in their personal breakdowns and final suicides—let us not overstress mere biography—but in the aesthetic breakdown of the myth-making part of their poetry. The non-mythic part of their poetry, its pure lyricism, never did break down and in part remains lastingly beautiful.

A second American tradition is that of the literary pessimists, a New World continuation of the great Christian pessimists of the old world, from Saint Augustine to Kierkegaard and Cardinal Newman. In America the second literary tradition is just as authentically American as the first one but has never received the same popular recognition, being less comforting. The most influential literary voices of our second tradition are Melville, Hawthorne, Henry Adams, William Faulkner. Its greatest political heritage comes from the Federalist papers and from the actual anti-Jeffersonian party of the Federalists, with their partly European source not in Rousseau but in Burke. Its most influential theological voices in America are Paul Tillich and Reinhold Niebuhr. Note that all these literary, political, and theological voices are characterized by skepticism about man and mass and by awareness of the deep sadness of history. Therefore, their bulwark against man and mass and against the precariousness of progress is some relatively conservative framework of traditional continuity, whether in culture, literature, politics, or religion.

The necessity of tragedy, the necessity of recognizing human frailty, human limitation, the perpetualness of evil, a chastened skepticism about human nature and progress: such are the tenets of the primarily philosophical and aesthetic, primarily non-political view of my 1949 *Conservatism Revisited* (2004 reprint, Transaction) (not to be confused with vulgarized current political "conservatisms" of the Reagan Republican kind). These tenets of tragedy seem partly confirmed by the failure of Lindsay's and Hart Crane's attempts to create a new, untragic kind of myth for America. As if original sin stopped west of the Alleghenies! As if the democratic American, like the noble savage of Rousseau, were immune from human frailty and immune from the spiritual price paid for industrial progress.

To be sure, the attitudes of Emerson and of Whitman (often more tragic and ambivalent than realized) were never so naive or unqualified as the above. But such was the over-simplified form their liberal American creed often took in their main literary heirs, including Lindsay and Crane. Note which two are the only American poets Lindsay names in his long "Litany of the Heroes":

> Then let us seek out shining Emerson,
> Teacher of Whitman, and better priest of man,
> The self-reliant granite American.

Emerson, it will be remembered, appealed to what he called "the great optimism self-affirmed in all bosoms." The germ of

Lindsay's and Crane's attempts to force themselves to affirm industrial Americana lies in the following optimistic affirmation of material progress that Emerson noted in his journal for 1871: "In my life-time have been wrought five miracles—I. the steamboat; 2. the railroad; 3. the electric telegraph; 4. the application of the spectroscope to astronomy; 5. the photograph—five miracles which have altered the relations of nations to each other." The best rebuttal to this attempt to affirm "miracles" like the railroad, before having made sure whether they were man's master or slave, came from Emerson's friend Thoreau: "We do not ride on the railroad; it rides on us."

Anticipating the attempts of the Emersonian Lindsay to make a "Troytown" out of every Kalamazoo and to find a Helen in every Osh Kosh, Emerson wrote: "Banks and tariffs, the newspaper and caucus" were "dull to dull people but rest on the same foundations of wonder as the town of Troy and the temple of Delphos." There in one sentence stands the whole Lindsay crusade to rebaptize Americana with wonder, a crusade in itself justifiable but lacking, in both Emerson and Lindsay, the criteria for discriminating between which industrial Americana were wonder-worthy and which ones, being tied to mean goals, were wonder-destroying. Apropos the mean goals of so much mechanical progress, it was, once again, the profounder Thoreau who punctured in advance the Emerson-Whitman-Lindsay-Crane optimism by warning: "We are now in great haste to construct a magnetic telegraph from Maine to Texas; but Maine and Texas, it may be, have nothing important to communicate."

The optimistic progress-affirming and folklore-affirming voices of Emerson and Whitman cracked up in their disciples Lindsay and Crane when the crushing of the individual in modern mechanization became simply too unbearable to affirm. The modern poet of progress may try to keep up his optimistic grin for his readers while the custard pie of "higher vaudeville" drips down his face. But past a certain point, he can no longer keep up the grin, whether psychologically in his private life or aesthetically in his public poetry. Our overadjusted standardization becomes just one custard pie too many for the unadjusted poet to affirm, no matter how desperately he tries to outshout his inner tragic insight by shouting (in Lindsay's case) "hail, all hail the popcorn stand" and by hailing (in Crane's case) the Brooklyn Bridge as "the myth whereof I sing." Lindsay and Crane committed suicide in 1931 and 1932 respectively, in both cases in that depression era which (by coincidence) seemed temporarily to end the boundless optimism of American material progress.Whatever the other motives for his suicide, Lindsay by 1931 had lost his popularity, the once insatiable demands for his readings, and was no longer taught in English departments. In this sense, Eliot killed Lindsay. Once the taste makers were converted to the more brilliant, urbane, cosmopolitan Eliot, Lindsay came across as a hick (another "k" word). Gone forever were the days when Yeats personally applauded Lindsay readings. Preparing this monograph, I studied the Lindsay house and archives in Illinois. The curator blamed his suicide on his complaining wife and money problems, obviously an oversimplification. His son Nicholas told me my monograph was by the one person who "understood" the psychology behind his father's poems.

On a far lower slope of Parnassus than Yeats are the two midwesterners Hart Crane and Lindsay. The former sophisticated, New Yorkized; the latter deliberately unsophisticated, defiantly provincial. To redeem American materialism, they spiritualized American machine culture in the music of their meters and frequent rhymes, Crane with his cult of the Brooklyn Bridge, Lindsay with his Springfield, Illinois. Crane's line about the Brooklyn steel "choir"—"How could mere toil alone align thy choiring strings"—could also have been written by Lindsay.

Both mostly stuck to good old iambic pentameter, sometimes truncated or irregular; a form so flexible and at such exciting tension, both with and against speech rhythm, has outworn all those who call it "outworn." It even underlies the so-called "free" verse of Whitman; his magnificent long lines are iambic pentameter stretched on the bed of Procrustes.

Poetry's turning point: after the fatwahs of Eliot-Pound. In contrast, imagine the road not taken: a mixed, independent road of,

say, Hardy (his inspired, moving awkwardness), Edwin Arling-
ton Robinson (once too popular, then sidelined), Frost (first popular with the wrong people for the wrong reasons, then by the
exquisites too late for the road not taken), poignant Charlotte
Mew, Edward Thomas, late Yeats, early Karl Shapiro ("The Cut
Flower"), Hart Crane ("Voyages"), Lindsay (just a few), Roethke
("Shape of the Fire"). Ponder the gains, the losses of road two.
Losses: the rich ambiguities, the fecund ironies, (even though
schoolmarmed to death by the "New Criticism"). Gains: full-throated
song, the alchemy of "it don't mean a thing if it ain't got that swing,"
freed from the strictures against metric strictness and freed for the
resonance of rhyme. The art of these other-roaders was made possible by their refusal to adjust. Define overadjustment? Cosmetic
surgery on the brain.

Lindsay's "Golden Book of Springfield" and Crane's "The
Bridge" though so different in other respects, are the two outstanding examples of trying to contrive an untragic myth of affirmation out of our modern industrial progress. Lindsay and Crane
celebrated the American myth more enthusiastically than would
the philistine kind of booster because, unlike the philistine, they
were boosters not by temperament but by a self-coercion which
their temperament was constantly sabotaging. The genuine
booster will affirm not all but most Americana; Lindsay and Crane
sometimes seemed to try to affirm all. Lindsay's idealizing of
the Hollywood cinema and Hart Crane's romanticizing of what
he called the oil-rinsed ecstasy of even such gadgets as ball-
bearings were acts of desperation; they were forcing themselves to affirm even those crass aspects of American mechanization that they themselves suffered from most. In both cases
the self-coercion proved literally unbearable; neither of our greatest
literary optimists could *bear* staying alive on his own yes-saying
terms.

Perhaps there is a profound lesson in the fact that both these
poets of affirmation led miserable and so-called unsuccessful. lives,
ending in suicide, while T. S. Eliot, the fastidious no-sayer, who
wrote the pessimism of *The Waste Land* instead of glorifying

Springfield or the Brooklyn Bridge, has been thriving most successfully. Perhaps the lesson is that our modern industrial age is
so unbearable that it drives its own boosters to insanity and self-
destruction while acclaiming its knockers with Nobel prizes.

But even aside from our own particular age and the madness
that strikes down the muse that would embrace its machines, it is
a conservative fact of life that unqualified optimism about human nature results in disaster. Robert Penn Warren showed this
in his long poem about Jefferson, *Brother to Dragons.* When
events do finally force the excessive optimist to allow for human
frailty, he ends up more disillusioned, more inclined to either
self-destruction or terrorism than the conservative who was pessimistic from the start.

Lindsay's poems celebrate by specific references every single
one of the main voices of American optimism: the Rousseau-
Jefferson view of human psychology, the political utopianism of
Jacksonian democracy, the economic utopianism of the Populists, the religious utopianism of Fundamentalist chiliasm, and the
Emerson-Whitman literary tradition. All five of these often separate voices converge to produce one of Lindsay's most revealing
couplets:

> God has great estates just past the line,
> Green farms for all, and meat and corn and wine.

The key line preceding that couplet is "Turn the bolt—how
soon we would be free!" That line recalls the radical, anti-traditionalist slogan of that Bible of the French Revolution, Rousseau's
Social Contract of 1762: "Man is born free and is everywhere in
chains." Actually what makes man free is precisely those so-called
"chains" of tradition, of established religion, of unbroken historical continuity; they free him from the *hubris* of his own
nature, which becomes self-destructive if without traditional
"chains." To vary the metaphor, freedom, in the older Christian and Burkean view, depends on a reverent conserving of traffic lights, not on a Rousseauist—optimist—radical smashing of
them.

Despite coercing himself painfully into enjoying progress, Lindsay also had his bitter side about the relationship between the muse and the machine age. Our decade, like his 1920s, suffers from the pressure of overadjusted public life against the privacy or the free imagination. Resuming the analogy with Dante's *Divine Comedy,* we note that Lindsay's poetry had not only its Paradiso, in his dream of his future Springfield, but its Inferno in the Springfield of his own day. His Inferno was the same as ours: the standardizing side of the America he secretly hated when he affirmed her, secretly loved when he rejected her. "Inferno" is not too strong a word for the soul-destroying commercialism whose symbols, in his poetry, were broken factory windows. This occasional bitterness about commercialism reflected the same kind of unadjusted poetic imagination as Baudelaire's bitterness about *l'esprit beige.* In Lindsay that anti-cash-nexus reaction produced two of the strongest, leanest lines ever written on the subject:

> Factory windows are always broken…,
> *End of the factory-window song.*

Lindsay hoped a rooted, American Fundamentalist religion from the midwest would soon, in his own words, be "Building against our blatant, restless time / An unseen, skilful, medieval wall." This neo-medieval wall would overcome, he hoped, the secular materialism he attributed to the midwest of his day. He hoped to regenerate industrialism not by rejecting it pessimistically but by sanctifying it optimistically through a new religious era:

> Think not that incense-smoke has had its day.
> My friends, the incense-time has but begun…
> And on our old, old plains some muddy stream,
> Dark as the Ganges, shall, like that strange tide—
> (Whispering mystery to half the earth)—
> Gather the praying millions to its side. (p. 52)

Being also an amateur painter, Lindsay distributed on street corners his pictures of censers in the sky, swinging their "incense-time" redeemingly above Springfield, Illinois. To the open-mouthed, dumbfounded burghers of Springfield he distributed, as free messianic tracts, a poem called "The Soul of the City Receiving the Gift of the Holy Ghost":

> Censers are swinging
> Over the town…
> Censers are swinging,
> Heaven comes down.
> City, dead city,
> Awake from the dead! (p. 207)

Whenever Lindsay came to believe something, he believed it strongly enough to want to make all his neighbors believe it also. Risking mockery and rebuff, he had the courageous idealism of giving unsolicited home-printed copies of his message to those who least wanted to receive it: "I flooded Springfield with free pamphlets incessantly." For such crusades he might be called either a crank or a genuine American saint. Instead of either of these alternatives, he pictured himself as following the footsteps of his religious and folk hero Johnny Appleseed. Thus in his prose piece, *Adventures Preaching Hieroglyphic Sermons*, Lindsay wrote: "Johnny Appleseed, whom I recommend to all men who love visions, was a man of lonely walking, a literal Swedenborgian all his days, distributing tracts when occasionally he met a settler…I am for Johnny Appleseed's United States"(p. xxii).

The more the forces of cash-nexus made Springfield secular, materialistic, overadjusted, the more did Lindsay (in his own words) "hand out to anyone who would take it in the street" the counterforce of his poem "Springfield Magical":

> In this, the City of my Discontent,
> Sometimes there comes a whisper from the grass,
> « Romance, Romance —is here. No Hindu town
> Is quite so strange. No Citadel of Brass
> By Sinbad found, held half such love and hate »…
> In this, the City of my Discontent! (p. 62)

How did his good neighbors respond to all this distribution of rhymed broadsides, this revivalist saving of their souls at street corners? Lindsay comments wistfully: "It was at this point that I was dropped from such YMCA work and Anti-Saloon League work as I was doing in the Springfield region" (p. xxxv).

Such was America's negative response to Lindsay's often-valid gospel of beauty. Yet his faith in the American myth prevented him from becoming the type of the irreconcilable martyr-crank. If anything, he was reconciled all too easily to the commercialist society that rejected him. For example, he tried symbolically to beautify and thereby redeem the industrial revolution by his poem in praise of the electric-light ads on Broadway:

> The signs in the street and the signs in the skies
> Shall make a new Zodiac, guiding the wise,
> And Broadway make one with that marvellous stair
> That is climbed by the rainbow-clad spirits of prayer. (p. 39)

These flashing ad-signs of Times Square would indeed be, as Lindsay pretended, the most beautiful thing in the world if only (as Chesterton said) we did not know how to read.

Lindsay could not have continued writing, or even staying alive, in any society to which he could not be reconciled more easily than reality ever permits; he was too steeped in the boundless expectations of the Fundamentalist millennial spirit, the spirit he called "the Resurrection parade." Thus Lindsay quoted with approval Alexander Campbell's appropriately named magazine *The Millenial Harbinger,* in which that Fundamentalist prophet wrote in 1865, "the present material universe... will be wholly regenerated" (p. 352). Himself a learned man and by no means "crude" in the more popular meaning of Fundamentalist revivalism, Campbell nevertheless fitted into the optimist-Rousseauist tradition by rejecting Original Sin and by rejecting baptism at birth as unnecessary and reactionary, evil allegedly not being present in human nature that early but added by corrupt society later.

What is shoddy in the American myth is not affirmation itself; classic tragedy affirms ("Gaiety transfiguring all that dread"). What is shoddy is not the hard-won affirmation that follows tragic insight but the facile unearned optimism that leads only to disillusionment. Here is a prose example of how Lindsay's valid crusade against the adjective « standardized » collapses suddenly into a too-easy optimism:

I have been looking out of standardized windows of "The Flat-Wheeled Pullman Car." I have been living in standardized hotels, have been eating jazzed meals as impersonal as patent breakfast-food...The unstandardized thing is the overwhelming flame of youth...an audience of one thousand different dazzling hieroglyphics of flame...My mystic Springfield is here, also, in its fashion.., a Springfield torn down and rebuilt from the very foundations, according to visions that might appear to an Egyptian...or any one else whose secret movie-soul was a part of the great spiritual movie. (pp. xxv-xxvi)

Note the typical Lindsay disproportion by which this moving passage ends with an appalling anticlimax, equating Hollywood's facile commercialized "visions" with the tragically earned classic ones. Yet his best and worst writing are so intertwined that this "movie soul" gush is immediately followed by one of his finest prose passages about American democracy at its noblest:

I believe that civic ecstasy can be so splendid, so unutterably afire, continuing and increasing with such apocalyptic zeal, that the whole visible fabric of the world can be changed...And I say: change not the mass, but change the fabric of your own soul and your own visions, and you change all. (p. xxvi)

In Lindsay's Springfield Paradiso of tomorrow: "civic ecstasy." But in his Springfield Inferno of today: « Factory windows are always broken ». Hence his outburst: "I went through the usual Middle West crucifixion of the artist. " That outburst, so typical of the midwest artist of the 1920s and so rarely heard in the culture-vulture midwest of today, was valid enough for his time. It should not be snubbed as sentimental by later and sleeker artists, battening on fellowships and snob appeal and producing art more elegant, less anguished than Lindsay's. But let us of the post-Sinclair Lewis generation note also the converse of Lindsay's outburst: namely, the usual verbal crucifixion of the Middle West by the artist.

When Lindsay was a child, an old duck-pond diviner pronounced this Delphic utterance about America's future laureate of Fundamentalism: "A child of destiny and also fond of sweets." This comment, in which the word "also" is particularly important, proved prophetic of Lindsay's combination of a messianic religious message with a lyrical aestheticism. In his messianic aspect of propagating the untragic American myth, he called himself a "cartooning preacher," a half-mocking phrase reminiscent of his phrase "the higher vaudeville." In his aesthetic aspect, preaching what one of his poems called "A Gospel of Beauty," he sometimes saw himself as a log-cabin Pater; it is often overlooked that, in such poems as "The King of Yellow Butterflies," Lindsay was more of a "pure aesthete" than most of the French Parnassians at their most ethereal. But Lindsay's aesthetic aspect was more frequently modeled on Ruskin's semi-moralized kind of aestheticism: "One of my crimes was a course of lectures at the YMCA on Ruskin's famous chapters on the nature of Gothic" (pp. 19-20). No wonder "there were days in my home town when the Babbitts...were about ready to send me to jail or burn me at the stake for some sort of witchcraft, dimly apprehended, but impossible for them to define"; that quotation reveals Lindsay's admirable courageous honesty about making no concessions to the anti-poetic clichés of his burgher audiences. But the darker undertone of the quotation also reveals his self-destructive compulsion to state his beliefs, in this case perfectly reasonable beliefs, in the terms most calculated to provoke incomprehension and ridicule.

Lindsay's authentic western Americana were never presented for their own sake, never merely as quaint antiques for the tourist trade. Rather, they were presented for the more serious purposes of either his Whitman-messianic aspect or his Ruskin-aesthetic aspect, depending on whether the given poem happened to be fond of destiny or of sweets. The obsessiveness these two aspects had for him was best summed up in his own words: "Incense and splendor haunt me as I go." In the end, the psychological and social meaning of his poems remains secondary to their lyricism, and indeed his poems achieve their occasional social effectiveness only via their lyricism, rather than apart from it. At his best, Lindsay incarnates for America the importance and dignity of spontaneous song: its ennobling and re-humanizing role in a standardized machine age.

Part of Lindsay's aesthetic compulsion, giving him the uniqueness only possessed by major poets, lies in his juxtaposition of the delicate and the grotesque: for example, in his phrase "the flower-fed buffaloes of the spring" subject of one of his purest lyrics. Running through his diversities of titles and subject matter, note also the delicate and the grotesque color-juxtapositions of "the king of yellow butterflies" with "the golden whales of California" and the semantic juxtaposition of "harps in heaven" with "the sins of Kalamazoo." Such gargoyle tenderness is a genre of sensibility explored by few other poets beside Beddoes, Rimbaud, Dylan Thomas, the poets with whom Lindsay's *unfulfilled* genius, beneath its tough loud disguises, properly belongs. In a situation Beddoes would have cherished, here is a typical example of gargoyle tenderness in Lindsay; "The Song of the Garden-Toad" expresses the agony and hate of worms when the gardener crushes their soil, with unconscious cruelty, in order to plant airy flowers:

> Down, down beneath the daisy beds,
> O hear the cries of pain!....
> I wonder if that gardener hears
> Who made the mold all fine
> And packed each gentle seedling down
> So carefully in line?
> I watched the red rose reaching up
> To ask him if he heard
> Those cries that stung the evening earth
> Till all the rose-roots stirred.
> She asked him if he felt the hate
> That burned beneath them there.
> She asked him if he heard the curse
> Of worms in black despair. (p. 265)

Delicacy is not a noun most modern readers associate with Lindsay. Yet his sense of cadence was so very delicate that it disguised itself defensively, his time and place being what they were, beneath ear-splitting auditory signposts. His signposts deliberately pointed in the wrong direction, the loud indelicate direction. Living where he did and believing the myth he believed, he needed to conceal his bitter, introverted sensitivity beneath the extroverted optimism of American folklore. That is, beneath a tone deliberately coarse, chummy, whooping, the whiz-bang claptrap of poems like "The Kallyope Yell." In such curiosities of. our literature, no poet was ever more perversely skilful at sounding embarrassingly unskilful. No poet was ever more dexterous at sounding gauche. What in Whitman was merely a would-be "barbaric yawp" does yawp with an unbearably successful barbarism in Lindsay:

> I am the Gutter Dream,
> Tune-maker born of steam…
> Music of the mob am I,
> Circus-day's tremendous cry:
> Hoot toot, hoot toot, hoot toot, hoot toot,
> Willy willy willy wah HOO!

Followed, as if that were not enough, with the dying fall, the final fading yawp of: "Sizz, fizz."

Consequently Lindsay's poetry is often defined as mere oratory, to be shouted aloud by a mob chorus. Part of him wanted this view to be held. Another part of him lamented: "I have paid too great a penalty for having a few rhymed orations. All I write is assumed to be loose oratory or even jazz, though I have never used the word 'jazz' except in irony." His best work, often his least known work, was produced by the part of him that once confessed: "All my poetry marked to be read aloud should be whispered…for the inner ear,.. whispering in solitude.".

Admittedly Lindsay is to blame (via the pseudo-tough defense mechanism of his sensitivity) for the fact that his work is generally associated with an extroverted booming voice: for example, with his University of Kansas football cheers, his Salvation Army trumpets. Yet the truest voice of his poetry is its quietness. That quietness produced line after line of imaginative evocation. Line after line of it comes tumbling again and again—at random from a dozen unconnected poems —over that "inner ear" in all of us to which he "whispered." To which his lyricism still whispers today, quietly beautiful, in line after line like this:

> "The little lacquered boxes in his hands."

> "They shiver by the shallow pools."

> "I am a trout in this river of light."

> "Stealer of vases of most precious ointment."

> "Her ears became the tiniest humorous calf's-ears."
> [this of the Egyptian bovine deity of love, Hathor].

> "You will go back as men turn to Kentucky,
> Land of their fathers, dark and bloody ground."

> "Abraham Lincoln Walks At Midnight."

> "Sleep softly...eagle forgotten...under the stone."

> "O empty boats, we all refuse, that by our windows wait."

And even when an actual loud "cry" is described, what a dreamy inner cry: "We will sow secret herbs and plant old roses" while "Green monkeys cry in Sanskrit to their souls." Many poets have written of the "sounding sea"; none has made it sound so hushed, so inward as this:

> Useful are you. There stands the useless one
> Who builds the Haunted Palace in the sun.
> Good tailors, can you dress a doll for me
> With silks that whisper of the sounding sea?

Here is an entire poem of delicate quietness:

> *Euclid*
> Old Euclid drew a circle
> On a sand-beach long ago.
> He bounded and enclosed it

> With angles thus and so.
> His set of solemn graybeards
> Nodded and argued much
> Of arc and of circumference,
> Diameter and such
> A silent child stood by them
> Prom morning until noon
> Because they drew such charming
> Round pictures of the moon. (p. 231)

This Lindsay parable of the two meanings of circles purges the modern reader of arid, abstract rationalism and re-humanizes, re-lyricizes, de-mechanizes him. The poem avoids coyness and cuteness, even if only by a triumphant hair's breadth, and thereby achieves not the facile but the difficult kind of simplicity.

Like Yeats, Lindsay transforms sentimentality into true art by means of the accompanying anti-sentimentality of nervously sinewy rhythms. Note, for example, the craftsmanship with which the lean rhythmic rightness of these two Lindsay quatrains redeems their otherwise sentimental rhetoric:

> Why do I faint with love
> Till the prairies dip and reel?
> My heart is a kicking horse
> Shod with Kentucky steel.
> No drop of my blood from north
> Of Mason and Dixon's line.
> And this racer in my breast
> Tears my ribs for a sign. (pp. 352–3)

Such poetry is a pure art for art's sake. Yet the same author could also be a poet of urgent social polemic. Here is Lindsay's higher-vaudeville imitation of how a sixteen-year-old Bryanite Populist Democrat in 1896 would have viewed the revolt of western mass egalitarianism against the traditionalism and aristocracy attributed to America's eastern seaboard:

> Defeat of western silver.
> Defeat of the wheat.
> Victory of letterfiles
> And plutocrats in miles
> With dollar signs upon their coats
> And spats on their feet.
> Victory of custodians,
> Plymouth Rock,
> And all that inbred landlord stock,
> Victory of the neat...
> Defeat of the Pacific and the long Mississippi...
> And all these in their helpless days
> By the dour East oppressed...
> Crucifying half the West,
> Till the whole Atlantic coast
> Seemed a giant spiders' nest...
> And all the way to frightened Maine the old East
> heard them call...
> Prairie avenger, mountain lion,
> Bryan, Bryan, Bryant Bryan,
> Smashing Plymouth Rock with his boulders from the West.
> (p.6)

Let us consider that extraordinary. Bryan poem first aesthetically, then politically: Note the sensuous concreteness of imagery. Instead of characterizing Bryan's enemies with the abstract, unlyrical word "the rich," Lindsay says concretely: "Victory of letter files / And plutocrats in miles / With dollar signs upon their coats." His self-mocking sense of humor, the subtlety of his pseudo-crudity, explains the surrealist fantasy of pretending, with wonderful preposterousness, that plutocrats literally wear dollar signs on their coats.

Taken in its political symbolism, Lindsay's aesthetic image of the Populists "smashing Plymouth Rock"[4] tells more than many prose volumes about the psychology of this recurrent American form of social protest. The invocation "avenger, mountain lion," brings out the motivating importance of revenge in Populism, revenge for having been humiliated and patronized by "that inbred landlord stock" of Plymouth Rock. The same emotion of revenge-for-humiliation is often shared by recent immigrants in Boston and the east as well as by the older American stock in the west, including Wisconsin. Therefore, the emotion portrayed in Lindsay's Bryan poem helps, explain the neo-Populist nationalist demagogy of the early 1950s, some times known as McCarthyism. No wonder McCarthyism was, in part, a demagogy of social inferiority complex that resented primarily not the Communists, whom it denounced, but the social elite (Ivy League colleges, State Department of Groton-Harvard Acheson), whom it implicated.

In Lindsay's day, the midwest dream of messianic "civic ecstasy" in politics (really, Fundamentalist revivalism secularized) still had a touching youthful innocence; his Bryan poem, despite its doctrinaire social message, could still succeed in being movingly lyrical; American optimism was cracking but not yet cracked up. In contrast, the neo-Populist nationalism of our own day can find no voice, whether poetic or social-reformist, of Lindsay's cultural or moral stature. For meanwhile American standardization plus Ortega's "revolt of the masses" have transformed salvation-via-mob from innocent dream to sordid nightmare. And from genuine economic needs (such as Populist farmers exploited by railroads) to economic hypochondria.

Even the early Lindsay had not been able to celebrate without tragic qualms (disguised as comic hamming with K's and popcorn stands) this utopian faith in the mass-instinct. After his death, this pure young optimism of the west degenerated into a frustrated and scapegoat-hunting optimism, a soured and hence lynch-mob-minded faith in the avenging People. On the biographical plane Lindsay himself partly succumbed to this process in the final paranoid[5] fantasies accompanying his suicide. On the plane of social psychology: it is the process whereby soured left-wing radicals, the Populists and La Follette Progressives of yesteryear, have become right-wing radicals (would-be conservatives) while significantly still retaining their basic Populist-folksy-isolationist resentment against eastern-Anglophile élites.[6] Ponder, for example, the isolationist-Anglophobe career of a Senator Nye or a Senator

Wheeler (both Progressive Party), forever "smashing Plymouth Rock"—first from left, then from right —"with his boulders from the West."

Here are two examples far more extreme. Father Coughlin, starting out as a western free-silver radical of the old Populist left, became a pro-Nazi, Anglophobe, anti-Semitic radical of the "right" without ever having to change his (and his mass-movement's) true emotional bias, the bias against fancy eastern city slickers and international bankers. Likewise Ezra Pound's wartime broadcasts for Mussolini, against Jewish and British international bankers, have their true psychological and social origin in the midwestern free-silver Populist background of Pound's earlier tracts on economics and on the "conspiracies" of the Wall Street gold standard.

From this salvation-via-mob dilemma, with its false choice between leftist and rightist mob-hatreds, Lindsay himself pointed the way out. The way out was love; not that philistine-humanitarian love of progress (so aptly refuted by Edmund Burke and Irving Babbitt) whose hug squashes individuals into an impersonal mass, but the creative lyric love that flows healingly from the integrity—the imagination—of great art. In short, when Lindsay did voice deeply enough the roots of the human condition, he became a fundamental poet, rather than merely the poet of the Fundamentalists. His poem "The Leaden-Eyed" describes perfectly the human price paid for unimaginative standardization and at the same time, through the very act of being lyrical, demands the re-humanizing of the machine age:

> Not that they starve, but starve so dreamlessly,
> Not that they sow, but that they seldom reap,
> Not that they serve, but have no gods to serve,
> Not that they die but that they die like sheep.
> (pp. 69–70)

Such a re-humanizing-through-creativity as Lindsay achieved at his best, seems the only way out from our age of the three impersonal M's: masses, machines, and mediocrity. And at his worst? It takes genius to write so unbelievably badly as Lindsay at his corniest. (Self-tortured: donning by choice his poisoned shirt of Nessus.) Remembered by few, this holy fool merits the adjective "God-intoxicated" because he found the redeeming religious imagination everywhere, everywhere—in the absurd as well as in the high:

> Once, in the city of Kalamazoo,
> The gods went walking, two and two.

And finally (after noisy boomlay-booms are forgotten) there remains his noble seven-word line that expresses the exhausting yet creative tension between the outer ethical demands of society and the aesthetic demands of inwardness; let us conclude, then, with Vachel Lindsay's quietest line:

> Courage and sleep are the principal things.

Notes

1.   Already in 1932, L. Lewisohn wrote in *The Story of American Literature* (N.Y., Harpers, p. 573): "American Fundamentalism has produced its mystic poet…in Lindsay." After my lecture at the Brandeis Arts Festival, Mr. Lewisohn had urged me to publish my own Lindsay re-interpretation. I herewith have done so.

2.   Burke-Simon quotes are from the *New York Times*, March 20, 1960, p. 43, and *Paris Herald-Tribune*, ed. p., April 2, 1960.

3.   For a parallel analysis of Crane's machine symbolism see P. Viereck, "The Poet in the Machine Age," essay in the *Journal of the History of Ideas*, N. Y., January 1949; also reprinted as appendix of Viereck, *Strike through the Mask* (New York: Charles Scribner's Sons, 1950, reprinted 1972 by Greenwood Press, Westport, CT).

4.   In 1964, when the Western plebeian-rightist Goldwater defeated the *eastern* aristocratic-liberal Rockefeller for the Republican nomination, this pseudo-conservative neo-populism was a case of smashing Plymouth Rockefeller.

5.   Lindsay's reputed dying words, after swallowing a bottle of searing Lysol: "They tried to get me; I got them first," cf. Hart Crane's comparable *cri de coeur*: "I could not pick the arrows from my side"—with his similar frustrated optimism (so much more tragic than Eliotine pessimism) about the mechanized American dream.

6.   For full documentation of this admittedly debatable hypothesis, see the section "Direct Democracy: From Populist Left to Nationalist Right," above, pp. 129–223.

SELECTED BIBLIOGRAPHY OF BOOKS BY PETER VIERECK

PROSE BOOKS

MetaPolitics: From the Romantics to Hitler. (New York: Alfred A. Knopf, 1941), out of print.

MetaPolitics: The Roots of the Nazi Mind. (New York: G. P. Putnam Sons/ Capricorn paperback, 1965), out of print.

Metapolitics: From Wagner and the German Romantics to Hitler, Expanded Edition (New Brunswick, NJ: Transaction Publishers, 2004).

Conservatism Revisited: The Revolt against Revolt, British hardcover edition, preface by Sir Duff Cooper (London, 1950), out of print.

Conservatism Revisited and the New Conservatism: What Went Wrong? (New York: Macmillan Free Press Paperback, 1956), out of print, reprinted in hardcover by Greenwood Press.

Conservatism Revisited: The Revolt Against Ideology (New Brunswick, NJ: Transaction Publishers, 2004).

Dream and Responsibility: Test Cases of the Tension between Poetry and Society (Washington: University Press of Washington, DC, 1953), hardcover and paperback, out of print.

Shame and Glory of the Intellectuals: Babbitt Jr. Versus the Rediscovery of Values (Boston: Beacon Press, 1952, out of print; New York: G. P. Putnam Sons/Capricorn paperback, 1965), out of print; reprinted by Greenwood Press, 1978, with supplement "The Radical Right From McCarthy to Goldwater."

Conservatism from John Adams to Churchill: A History and Anthology (Westport, CT: Greenwood Press, 1978), hardcover reprint of the out of print 1956 Van Nostrand edition.

The Unadjusted Man: Reflections on the Distinction between Conserving and Conforming (Westport, CT: Greenwood Press, 1973), hardcover reprint of 1956 Beacon Press edition.

Unadjusted Man in the Age of Overadjustment: Where History and Literature Intersect (New Brunswick, NJ: Transaction Publishers, 2004).

"Conservatism." A long historical monograph in the 15th edition (1979-1986) of the *Encyclopedia Britannica*.

Strict Wildness: Discoveries in Poetry and History (New Brunswick, NJ: Transaction Publishers, forthcoming).

POETRY BOOKS

Terror and Decorum (Westport, CT: Greenwood Press, 1972), reprint of out of print 1948 Scribner's edition. Awarded Pulitzer Prize for poetry in
Strike through the Mask: New Lyrical Poems (Westport, CT: Greenwood Press, 1972), hardcover reprint of out of print 1950 Scribner's edition.
The First Morning. (Westport, CT: Greenwood Press, 1972), hardcover reprint of out of print 1952 Scribner's edition.
The Persimmon Tree: New Lyrics and Pastorals (Ann Arbor, MI: University Microfilms), hardcover reprint of out of print 1956 Scribner's edition.
New and Selected Poems, 1932-1967, selections from five books with frontispiece by the Spanish painter Fernando Zobel (New York: Bobbs-Merrill, 1967), out of print, 1980 reprint available from University Microfilms, 300 North Zeeb Road, Ann Arbor, Michigan 48106 or 30 Mortimer Street, London, England WIN 7RA.
Archer in the Marrow: The Applewood Cycles of 1967- 1987 (New York: W.W. Norton Company, 1987). Out of print.
Tide and Continuities: Last and First Poems, 1995-1938, with a preface in verse by Joseph Brodsky (Fayetteville: University of Arkansas Press, 1995).
Transplantings: Stefan George and Georg Heyrn, Englished and Analyzed. With Reflections on Modern Germany, on Poetry, and on the Craft of Translation. Work in progress.

VERSE DRAMA

The Tree Witch (Westport, CT: Greenwood Press, 1973) hardcover reprint of out of print 1961 Scribner's edition. Staged 1961 by the Poets Theater at Harvard University's Loeb Theater.
OpComp. A modern medieval miracle play, work in progress.

BOOK ABOUT PETER VIERECK

Marie Henault, *Peter Viereck, Historian and Poet* (New York: Twayne Press, 1969), hardcover; (New Haven, CT: College and University Press, 1971) paperback. Both out of print.

INDEX

Aaron, Daniel, 97, 202n
Acheson, Dean, 44, 116, 166, 168, 197, 246
Acton, Lord, 50
ADA, 49, 50, 51, 106, 196, 237
Adams, Henry, 26, 40, 90, 124, 258
Adams, John, 17, 27, 35–36, 44, 50, 99, 104, 108, 113, 120, 122, 130–131, 140, 144–145, 147–149, 179, 186, 245, 250–253, 261, 312
Adams, John Quincy, 39, 44, 99, 138–141, 144, 149
Adams, Sam, 44
Adenauer, Chancellor, 98, 111
Adler, Alfred, 56
Aiken, Senator, 123
Aldrich, Bailey, 146
Alger, Horatio, 114, 271
America, 214
American Daily, 116
"America First," 156, 201
America First Committee, 209q, 219
American Historical Association, 210, 250n
American Legion, 217, 218
American Scholar, 163n
Americans for Democratic Action. *See* ADA
Antioch Review, 249
Aquinas, Thomas, 320
Arnold, Benedict, 116
Arnold, Matthew, 32, 90, 91, 299
Arvey, Jake, 113
Atlantic Monthly, 97
Atlantic Pact, 71–72
Auden, W. H., 106, 285

Babbitt, Cabot, 318, 321
Babbitt, Gaylord, 14, 24, 68, 223n
Babbitt, George, 14, 68, 117, 271, 317–318
Babbitt, Irving, 26, 32, 34, 36, 53, 62, 99, 103, 108, 138, 140–141, 251,

318; *Democracy and Leadership*, 99
Backer, George, 241
Bagehot, Walter, 30, 32
Baldwin, James, 9
Baltimore Sun, 156n
Balzac, Honoré, 40
Barère, Bertrand, 149
Barzini, Luigi, Jr., 33n
Baudelaire, Charles, 10, 40, 48, 52, 90, 306, 312
Beard, Charles A., 154–157, 185, 190, 222
Bell, Daniel, 44n; *The New American Right*, 162n
Bemis, S. F., 39n
Bendiner, Robert, 98
Bendix, R., 167n
Bentham, Jeremy, 295
Berle, A. A., 264; *The Twentieth Century Capitalist Revolution*, 264n
Bernanos, Georges, 53
Bevan, Aneurin, 70
Bismarck, Otto von, 56, 58
Bixler, Paul, 249
Black, Hugo, 152, 190; Black Committee, 155
Blanshard, Paul, 214
Blease, Cole, 47
Blum, John, 125
Bohlen, Ambassador, 120, 169
Bohn, William, 123
Bolshevik Party, 308
Boorstin, Daniel, 249
Bowles, Chester, 197
Bricker, Senator, 119, 171
Brownell, Attorney General, 121, 197
Bryan, William Jennings, 45, 46, 194, 196, 198, 208
Bukharin, 158
Burke, Edmund, 18, 27, 28, 36, 50, 51, 78–81, 89, 98, 99, 100, 104, 105, 122, 128, 131, 136, 139, 140,

363

150, 235, 240, 250–253, 295, 296, 303, 318
Burckhardt, Jakob, 23, 26, 53, 55, 56, 90, 129, 299
Bush, Douglas, 20n
Butler Samuel, 302
Byron, Lord, 34

Calhoun, John, 24, 36, 98, 99, 108, 131, 138, 140, 144
Campbell, Roy, 282
Canby, Henry Seidel, 297
Capone, Al, 221
Capp, Al, 323
Cain, Harry, 157
Carlyle, Thomas, 91, 281, 300
Carr, E. H., 308; *The Bolshevik Revolution*, 308n
Carafa, Ettore, 33
Case, Clifford, 82, 122, 123, 125, 157, 174, 252
Castlereagh, Lord, 81
Cecil, Lord Hugh, 89
CGT, 75
Céline, 32
Chamberlain, Neville, 111
Chamberlin, W. H., 110
Chambers, Whittaker, 231
Charles X, 250
Chekhov, Anton, 66n
Chesterton, G. K., 301
Chicago Tribune, 110, 171, 194, 195, 197, 199, 200, 201, 241n
Churchill, Winston, 29, 34, 80, 87, 98, 109, 111, 136, 235, 299
Clemenceau, Georges, 323
Cleveland, Grover, 195
Cohn, Roy, 156, 218, 221
Coleridge, Samuel, 22, 26, 36, 53, 87n, 90, 91, 93, 98, 117, 129, 279, 295–297, 299, 312, 326
Commentary, 151n, 221
Commonweal, 214
Communist International, 257n
Communist Party, 156q
Conant, James Bryant, 120, 215
Confluence, 11, 155n, 237n
Congressional Record, 64n
Conservative party, 84. *See also* Tory party

Cook, Thomas I., 12, 95, 102, 248
Cooper, John Sherman, 123, 125
Corneille, 28
Cortés, Donoso, 26, 56, 90, 98, 250
Coughlin, Rev. Charles, 24, 45, 47, 133, 166, 201, 205, 206, 210q, 221, 222, 226
Crane, Hart, 15, 26
Culture, 207

Daily Worker, 163, 195
Damian, Saint Peter, 78
Dante, 65, 69, 286, 287
Darwin, Charles, 269
Daugherty, Harry, 154
Davie, Donald, 280n
Debs, Eugene, 191
Del Vayo, Alvarez, 71
Democratic party, 122
Devine, Father, 226
Dewey, John, 20, 295
Dewey, Thomas, 123, 177, 197, 264
Dickinson, Emily, 67
Dirksen, Senator, 114, 171, 320
Disraeli, Benjamin, 17, 36, 79, 83, 84, 90, 122, 245, 246, 299, 300
Dixon-Yates contract, 234
Donnelly, Ignatius, 202, 203, 205–207, 247
Dostoyevsky, Feodor, 26, 42, 90
Dreyfus, Alfred, 150, 151, 176, 221
Drucker, Peter, 48n
Dulles, John Foster, 125

Economist, 70
Ede, Chester, 145
Eden, Anthony, 111
Ehrenburg, Ilya, 288
Einsiedel, Heinrich von, 67
Eisenhower, Dwight D., 73, 74, 78, 82, 119–126, 139, 174, 177, 195, 197, 255–257, 313
Eliot, T. S., 272, 280q, 283, 311; *The Waste Land*, 281
Emergency Civil Liberties Committee, 158
Emerson, Ralph Waldo, 12, 13, 88, 299, 300
Encounter, 33n
Engelbrecht. H. C., 156

English, Raymond, 102, 248
Ervin, Senator, 152q, 153q, 157

Farley, Jim, 213
Farrell, James, 212
Faulkner, William, 5, 26, 40, 67, 90, 258
Faure, Edgar, 246
Federalist papers, 44, 104, 123, 131, 140, 237, 320
Federalist party, 27, 44, 93, 104, 124, 134, 147, 148, 168, 209, 235, 240, 245, 330
Fichte, Johann, 58
Fiedler, Leslie, 163n, 201n
Flanders, Ralph, 123, 125, 157, 174, 222, 241
Flynn, John T., 155, 240
"For America," 219
Ford, Henry, 204, 205
Fort Monmouth, 122, 126, 164
Fortune, 156, 329n
Franco, Francisco, 320
Frankfurter, Felix, 157
French Revolution, 80, 89, 105, 130, 132, 150, 186, 208, 251, 303
Freud, Sigmund, 56
Frost, Robert, 285
Fulbright, Senator, 64n

Gaitskell, Hugh, 70
Galbraith, J. K., 264
George III, 81, 116, 251, 259q
Gentz, Friedrich von, 53
Gibran, Kahlil, 324; *The Prophet,* 325
Gladstone, William, 83, 246
Glazer, Andrew, 163n
Goebbels, Joseph, 110
Goethe, Johann Wolfgang von, 17, 26, 31, 65
Goldman, Eric, 156n, 188
Goldwater, Senator, 169
Görres, Joseph, 22
Gregg, Hugh, 133
Greenback party, 180, 194, 198, 204
Gress, Elsa, 11
Grossman, James, 151n
Guest, Edgar, 14, 319
Guttman, Robert, 186

Hall, Chadwick, 249
Haller, K. L. von, 22
Hallowell, John, 248
Hamilton, Alexander, 44, 98, 147, 148
Handlin, Oscar, 201n
Harlan, John M., 119, 187
Harper's, 152
Harriman, Averell, 126, 178, 197, 200, 241, 264
Harrington, Alan, 9n
Harris, Louis, 256n
Hart, A. B., 186
Harvard University, 115, 120, 166, 167, 168, 171, 197, 213, 215, 240, 241n, 272; Harvard Law School, 168, 173
Hawthorne, Nathaniel, 26, 40, 53, 90, 266
Heckscher, August, 102, 237, 238, 248
Hegel, G. W. F., 112
Hemingway, Ernest, 16
Henry, Patrick, 44
Herberg, Will, 50, 102, 160, 163n, 249
Herter, Christian, 44, 82, 123, 125, 241
Hitler, Adolf, 7, 37, 57, 69, 107, 109–112, 132, 136, 138, 142, 143n, 157, 163, 189, 190, 201, 205, 207, 208, 224, 225, 240, 251, 302; *Mein Kampf,* 137
Hitler-Stalin pact, 38, 111, 252
Hoffer, Eric, 213, 307
Hofstadter, Richard, 162n, 163n, 201n
Hoover, Herbert, 181, 235
Hopkins, Harry, 115
Higgins, Marguerite, 64
Hiss, Alger, 114, 156, 164, 172–174, 216n, 231, 240; case of, 223n, 262, 307
Hudson Review, 280
Hubbard, Elbert, 29
Hughes, Charles Evans, 44, 108, 126

Ickes, Harold, 232
Institute of Pacific Relations, 70
Ives, Irving, 123

Jackson, Andrew, 39, 45, 108, 130, 131, 208, 247
Jackson, Robert, 158
Jacquin, Gottfried von, 290
Jacobins, 43, 80, 132, 149, 217, 250, 305
James, William, 275n
Jay, John, 98, 147
Jefferson, Thomas, 35, 44, 65, 104, 108, 131, 141q, 142q, 148, 184, 186, 206, 245, 253, 261
Journal of Politics, 210n
James, Henry, 40
Jenner, Senator, 45, 182
Johnson, A. H., 275n
Jordan, G. R., 187
Joyce, William, 4, 9, 13, 240

Kafka, Franz, 6, 52
Kaufmann, W., 57n, 60n
Keats, John, 281
Kefauver, Estes, 45
Kempton, Murray, 152
Kerensky, Alexander, 251
Keynes, John Maynard, 309
Kierkegaard, Soren, 48, 50, 52, 53, 102, 103
Kirk, Russell, 248
Knight, G. Wilson, 281n
Knowland, Senator, 171
Korean war, 256
Kornilov, Lavr, 251
Kubizek, August, 57
Kuehnelt-Leddihn, Erik von, 137, 145
Ku Klux Klan, 220

Labor party, 82, 84, 111
La Follette, Robert Marion, 108, 124n, 134, 156, 167, 179, 181, 184–192, 196, 205, 208, 247
La Follette, Robert Marion, Jr., 180
La Follette law, 182–184
La Follette's Magazine, 183, 185–187
Lamont, Corliss, 276
Landon, Alfred, 234
Lattimore, Owen, 276n
League of Nations, 189
Le Bon, Gustave, 162
Lee, R. H., 44

Lemke, William, 38, 47
Lenin, Vladimir, 43, 132, 137, 190, 251
Leopold and Loeb, 221
Lewis, Sinclair, 15, 68, 271, 317
Lewis, Walter K., 219n
Lewis, Wyndham, 208
Liberal party, 84. *See also* Whig party
Liberty League, 234
Lilienthal, David, 264, 264n
Lincoln, Abraham, 90, 246n, 247, 259q
Lindbergh, Charles, 204–206
Lindsay, Vachel, 26, 193, 328
Lippmann, Walter, 157
Lipset, S. M., 163n
Locke, John, 100, 247
Lodge, John Cabot, Jr., 44, 123, 125, 241
Long, Huey, 24, 45, 47, 133, 138, 144, 166, 217, 240, 245
Louis XVI, 134, 216
Longfellow, Henry Wadsworth, 29
Lowell, Amy, 285
Lowell, Robert, 284
Lubell, Samuel, 198
Ludendorff, General, 251
Lukacs, J. A., 102

MacArthur, General Charles, 174, 251
Madison, James, 98, 104, 105, 131, 138, 140, 144, 147
Maine, Sir Henry, 36, 129, 138; *Popular Government*, 91
Maistre, Joseph de, 36, 56
Man, Henri de, 110
Mansfield, Katherine, 9
Manuilsky, Dmitri, 257n
Mao, 43, 75, 224, 225
Marshall, George, 116, 120, 174, 189, 197
Marshall plan, 71, 72, 166, 201
Martin, Kingsley, 71
Marx, Karl, 50, 87n, 90, 108, 138, 262, 274, 276, 281, 312, 318, 331
Mavrinac, Albert A., 155n
McCarran, Pat, 47, 177, 213, 215
McCarthy-Army hearings, 182
McClaughlin, A. C., 186

McCormick, Robert, 200, 201, 241n, 243
McKinley, William, 82, 90, 124n
Melville, Herman, 26, 40, 41, 53, 67, 90, 91, 258, 266
Mencken, H. L., 186
Mendès-France, Pierre, 246
Metternich, Prince, 25, 26, 79, 82–85, 87n, 90, 98, 134, 234, 243, 250, 299
Mill, John Stuart, 130, 297
Miller, Charles G., 186, 187
Milosz, Czeslaw, 302, 315
Milton, John, 287
More, Paul Elmer, 32, 62, 108
More, Sir Thomas, 6, 7
Morgan, J. P., 154, 155
Morris, Gouverneur, 44
Morris, Robert, 44n
Morris, William, 231
Morse, Wayne, 163n, 179n
Mortimer, Lee, 167n
Moscow trials, 38, 158, 212, 263, 276
Müller, Adam, 22
Munich, 110, 111, 275
Mussolini, Benito, 111, 132, 137, 206, 207, 224

Napoleon I, 43, 132, 133
Napoleon III, 132, 137–138
Nation, 76, 105, 106, 110, 155, 260
National Farmers' Alliance, 203
National Review, 195
Nenni, Pietro, 71
Neutrality Act, 189
New Leader, 12n, 44n, 106, 123, 160, 163n, 219n
Newman, Cardinal, 90, 91, 101q, 102n, 281, 295, 298, 299
New Mexico Quarterly, 15, 208n
New Republic, 50, 153, 154, 157n, 208n, 260
New Statesman, 70, 71
New Yorker, 9
New York Post, 108, 152, 191n
New York Herald Tribune, 111, 238
New York Times, 20n, 44n, 185n, 207, 220, 221, 308, 311n, 323
Niebuhr, Reinhold, 16, 48–52, 102, 104, 105, 136, 249

Nietzsche, Friedrich, 11, 23, 26, 53–60, 62, 63, 90, 93, 101, 128, 162, 166, 170, 175, 199, 217, 274, 276, 281, 302, 309
Nisbet, Robert, 248
Nixon, Richard, 114, 125, 139, 176, 177
Nye, Gerald P., 38, 155–157, 181, 188, 190, 204, 205; Nye Committee, 154, 156, 157

Oppenheimer, J. Robert, 122, 126, 295
Ortega y Gasset, 23, 26
Orwell, George, 53, 95, 105, 275, 287, 309
Oxnam, Bishop, 214

Pacific Affairs, 276n
Paine, Tom, 43, 44, 51, 80, 93, 108, 131, 139, 143, 147, 148, 208, 245, 251, 303
Pareto, Vilfredo, 170
Pargellis, Stanley, 300
Parsons, Talcott, 163n
Partisan Review, 287
Peale, Norman Vincent, 313
Pearl Harbor, 109, 184
Peress, Major, 174; case of, 217
Peron, Juan, 24, 133, 136, 138, 142, 143n, 244
Peron, Eva, 115
Philbrick, Herbert, 164
Pilot, 214
Pitt, William, 28
Podach, E., 58n
Poe, Edgar Allan, 26, 40, 90
Police Gazette, 204
Political and Social Information, 257n
Pope, Alexander, 324
Popular Front, 38, 39, 191, 232, 267
Populist party, 131, 180, 194, 198, 204
Poujade, 132
Pound, Ezra, 32, 206–209, 283, 287–289; *Pisan Cantos,* 287, 289
Princeton University, 167, 272
Progressive, 260
Progressive party, 38, 131, 179–181, 191, 218

Proudhon, Pierre Joseph, 274, 275
Proust, Marcel, 9
Puck, 204
Pusey, Nathan, 120

Rapp, Alfred, 323
Rath, R. J., 83n
Reader's Digest, 68
Reed, Senator, 154
Reporter, 139, 163n, 249n, 252, 260
Republican party, 78, 119, 120, 122–125, 181, 235
Review of Politics, 250n
Riesman, David, 16, 17, 163n
Rimbaud, Arthur, 4
Robespierre, Maximilien, 132, 135, 209, 209n, 222
Rodman, Selden, 283, 284
Roethke, Theodore, 284
Rohde, Erwin, 63
Roosevelt, Eleanor, 116, 174
Roosevelt, Franklin Delano, 44, 106, 110, 119, 139, 158, 173, 177, 190, 197, 200, 213, 233, 234, 240, 241, 243, 264
Roosevelt, Theodore, 118, 124, 125, 241
Root, Elihu, 44, 126
Rorty, James, 175, 221
Rosenberg, Alfred and Ethel, 70, 207, 240
Ross, Albion, 308
Rossiter, Clinton, 102, 249
Rothschild, 204, 205
Rousseau, Jean Jacques, 55, 108, 130, 139, 149q, 185, 189, 207, 247, 255; *Social Contract*, 132
Ruark, Robert, 16
Ruskin, John, 91, 281
Russell, Bertrand, 29

Sacco and Vanzetti, 221
St. Louis Post-Dispatch, 44n
Saltonstall, Leverett, 241
Santayana, George, 136
Sartre, Jean Paul, 71, 72, 306
Schine, G. David, 174
Schlesinger, Arthur, Jr., 39, 139, 249n, 251, 252
Schultz, Rabbi, 218, 226

Scott, Sir Walter, 319
SEC, 47, 232, 264, 266
Sewanee Review, 48n
Shaftesbury, seventh Earl of, 83, 84
Shakespeare, William, 62q, 65, 213, 259q
Sheil, Bishop, 214
Sheridan, Richard, 28
Silvermaster, Gregory, 231
Smith, Adam, 50, 80, 108, 124, 234, 263, 331
Smith, Al, 213, 215, 221
Smith, Gerald L. K., 210q, 221, 223, 226
Smith, Margaret Chase, 123, 125, 174
Smith Act, 158
Social Justice, 205
Southwest Review, 15
Soviet Dictionary of Foreign Words, 247
Soviet Russia Today, 276n
Spencer, Herbert, 124
Spillane, Mickey, 16, 67
Stalin, Joseph, 7, 72, 107, 137, 224
Steffens, Lincoln, 43
Steinmetz, Charles P., 329
Stendhal, 33
Stephenson, Nathaniel, 190
Stevenson, Adlai, 44, 50, 74, 82, 126, 173, 197, 230, 236, 238, 241, 246–249, 252, 253, 255–265, 312
Stimson, Henry, 44, 126
Stone, I. F., 110
Stouffer, S. A., 136
Stowe, Harriet Beecher, 149
Strauss, Leo, 315
Streicher, Julius, 204
"Students for America," 218
Sumner, W. G., 124
Supreme Court (U.S.), 118, 119, 136, 146, 147, 149, 150, 153, 158, 159, 181, 184, 187, 222, 223n, 241, 277
Sward, Keith, 204n
Sykes, Gerald, 39
Synge, J. M., 18

Table Talk, 22n
Taft, Robert, 45, 81, 82, 117, 123, 124
Taine, Hippolyte, 36, 53, 130
Talleyrand, 81

Tannenbaum, Frank, 85, 86
Taylor, Telford, 174
Tempo, 137
Thomas, Dylan, 284, 329
Thomas, Norman, 74, 95
Thoreau, Henry David, 2, 30, 53, 67, 266
Till, Eustace, 219
Time, 218n, 221, 241n
Tocqueville, Alexis de, 4, 26, 36, 37n, 53, 56, 74, 98, 118, 162, 170, 193, 250, 252, 296, 299
Tory party, 104. *See also* Conservative party
Truman, Harry, 119–121, 197, 247, 260, 264
Truman Doctrine, 71
Twain, Mark, 115, 200, 322
Tweed, Boss, 135
Twentieth Century, 280n

United Nations, 116, 243
U.S.I.A., 126

Veblen, Thorstein, 46
Virgil, 79
Visconti, Count Luchino, 33
Vishensky, Andrei, 158
Vittorio, 137
Vogelsang, Karl von, 22
Voice of America, 122, 126, 164
Voltaire, 216

Wadleigh, Julian, 231
Waggoner, Hyatt, 41, 248
Wagner, Geoffrey, 208n
Wagner, Richard, 22, 32, 57, 58
Wagner Act, 47
Wallace, Henry, 191, 240, 321
Walsh, Chad, 102, 248
Ware, 231
Warren, Chief Justice, 119, 123
Warren, Robert Penn, 208

Washington, George, 44, 81, 98, 108, 120, 147, 150, 184, 186, 202, 259q
Washington Post, 44n
Watkins, Senator, 133, 146–148, 152q, 153q, 241
Watkins committee, 157
Watson, Tom, 47
Weaver, General, 196, 201, 208, 247
Wechsler, James, 187
Weil, Simone, 53, 262
Weimar Republic, 251
Welker, Herman, 133, 182
Wendell, Barrett, 32, 108, 295
Wesley, Charles, 259q
Weyl, Nathan, 231
Wheeler, Burton K., 38, 154, 156, 157, 181, 188, 190, 204, 205
Wherry, Senator, 122–124
Whig party, 44, 104. *See also* Liberal party
Whitehead, Alfred North, 275, 291
William III, 99, 235
Willkie, Wendell, 123, 264
Wilson, Francis, 248
Wilson, Woodrow, 108, 198, 247
Wolfe, Bertram, 137
Wodehouse, P. G., 200
Woolf, Virginia, 9
Wordsworth, William, 299
World War I, 156, 182, 186
World War II, 67, 71, 109, 110, 111, 112, 158, 177, 189, 198, 205, 206, 264

Yale University, 115, 166–168, 171, 272
Yalta, 74, 105, 110, 164, 180, 247, 263, 275
Yeats, William Butler, 251, 281, 284, 299, 300
Youngdahl, Judge, 184

Zwicker, General, 174